Making the Invisible Woman Visible

Making
the
Invisible
Woman
Visible

ANNE FIROR SCOTT

University of Illinois Press
Urbana and Chicago

Library of Congress Cataloging in Publication Data
Scott, Anne Firor.
Making the invisible woman visible.

Includes index.
1. Women—United States—Biography. 2. Women—
United States—History. 3. Women—Southern States—
History. 4. Women—United States—Societies and clubs—
History. 5. Women—United States—Addresses, essays,
lectures. I. Title.
HQ1412.S36 1984   305.4′0973   83-17962
ISBN 0-252-01110-4 (cloth)
ISBN 0-252-01123-6 (paper)

For
JOHN WILLIAM SCOTT-RAILTON
b. February 19, 1983
and
in memory of
JOHN WILLIAM FIROR
1887-1956

Acknowledgments

It is impossible, of course, to acknowledge all the generosity and help one has had over thirty years, but in the actual creation of this volume I have drawn on the support and advice of several people. As always, Andrew Scott has been a part of the enterprise from the beginning. Rebecca Scott and Peter Railton, David Scott and Anne Geer, William Chafe, Barbara Cleaveland, John Demos, Jack Hexter, and Marjolene Kars all read and commented on the introduction and headnotes. Bobbi Handwerger, Grace Guyer, and Vivian Jackson were indispensable technical assistants. Richard Wentworth was present at the creation. I hope none of them will be embarrassed by the final product.

Contents

A *Historian's* Odyssey

Reading one's own words, some of them written more than thirty years ago, stirs up memories, reflections, anxieties, questions. How did I get here from there? History, and historians, have changed remarkably over those years. Some of my early mentors and models were social and economic historians, and some of them were laying the groundwork for the explosive development of the discipline which was soon to take place, but none apologized for writing narrative history. Only a few felt the need to use an "explicit conceptual framework," to start from a "clear theoretical position." Methodology meant close attention to the precepts of Langlois and Seignobos; or it was something that scientists, and possibly economists, had to worry about. Though some of these historians wrote about blacks, women, or ordinary people, they did not yet have names for their work. There was sophisticated thinking about the nature of the historical enterprise on the part of a few philosophers and a handful of reflective historians, but an eager graduate student might be years finding out about it. The changes I see in my work reflect change and ferment in the discipline, as well as the gradual development of confidence in my own insights.

But for me there is a prior question: How did I come to choose this difficult discipline in the first place—one which it has taken me thirty years to begin to understand? Why did I fix upon history rather than zoology or literature? Why, indeed, did I choose scholarship rather than business or politics? Was it chance, or some half-understood personal predilection, which guided my choices? Historians are taught to be wary of autobiography, for who, after all, can tell the truth about oneself? Yet no one else is likely to try, and no other method (except perhaps psychoanalysis) suggests itself as a means of answering these questions.

Fortunately I do not have to rely entirely upon treacherous memory.

Since 1937 I have kept a journal, which now approaches twenty volumes. Some of it tells me more than I really want to know, but the existence of a record made on the spot inhibits the inevitable human tendency to rewrite the past and make it nicer. I have no recollection, for example, of what was apparently a moment of some despair in 1954:

I have been on a long jag of reading and doing little or nothing on my thesis. It almost amounts to a complete failure of will—over and over I resolve to sit down and write that damn chapter—but nothing happens. Nursery school had a holiday, but that is really no excuse. Probably the fact of the thing is that I have no business trying to *be* a historian, and only an undue consideration for what people will say if I give up now keeps me even theoretically at it.

Was I really on the verge of giving up? Was it really "what people will say" that drove me on? I have no idea; but in due course the "damn chapter" and its successors were written, and a few pages later certain journal entries foreshadow ideas which would evolve into a project not then even envisioned. The mind, as well as the Lord, works in mysterious ways. . . .

Perhaps one should begin at the beginning.

It makes a good bit of difference when you happen to be born. I arrived in the world nine months after the suffrage amendment was added to the Constitution, so I never have to count on my fingers to find out how long women have had the right to vote. It was the year the number of women in state universities first equaled the number of men. It was also the first time women in other occupations outnumbered domestic servants among female wage earners. It was a year of sudden depression: my parents lost their savings in a bank failure and had some difficulty paying the doctor who had delivered me, at home.

My father, who had married late because he was helping to support a widowed mother and a younger sister, took to child-raising with enthusiasm. My brothers and I have been told that he began when we were babies reading to us, not from children's books—which he found boring—but from his own favorites. He also told us long historical tales, dealing with the Indian tribes which, he said, had lived on the hill by the Oconee River in Athens where the Georgia State College of Agriculture stood.

A rough analysis of the biographies of women historians in *Notable American Women* shows that three-fourths were either eldest children, only children, or only girls. I was both the eldest child and the only girl, with three brothers. As far as any of us can remember there were no intellectual distinctions on the basis of sex in our upbringing, and, if anything, more was expected of the firstborn. When I read now that "society" convinces all girls of their own inferiority, I am struck by the fact that parents who did not share the common view countered these supposedly overwhelming social messages so effectively that I was twenty-one before it crossed my mind (thanks to a rude comment from a favorite philosophy professor) that being female would in any way limit what I did in the world. (I should make it plain, of course, that the assumption that their male and female children were equally intelligent did not prevent my parents from bringing me up to be a proper southern lady in behavior, speech, manner—but that is another story, perhaps not relevant here.)

As far as I can tell, I began to do history by chance. A stimulating freshman course on the English constitution at the University of Georgia led me to take other history courses until, without planning it, I had a major. But I found chemistry, literature, even math, equally interesting, and dreamed impartially about becoming a medical doctor or the mother of six. In a vague way I thought I would have a career, but I had no notion what that involved, how it would affect marriage (which was also on my agenda), or what its substance would be. Indeed, I can think of no one of my female classmates who had the sophistication and sense of direction about future possibilities which are now commonplace among women students.

If my journal is to be believed, I went out into the world in 1940 in search of fame, fortune, and a husband, in no particular order. As to *how* that search was to be conducted the journal is significantly silent. It was very much a matter of what might turn up.

Neither a job at IBM nor a brief turn in a graduate program for personnel managers seemed quite the thing (though my IBM boss promised the fortune would come in due course if I would only be patient). The first opportunity which struck me as leading in the right direction came in the form of an internship in Washington, where, along with thirty or so other recent college graduates, I was inducted into the mysteries of the federal government. After a California Congressman named Jerry Voorhis made a compelling talk to our group, I attached myself to him as an intern. Happily for me, he was a man who believed in encouraging the young. Senator Paul Douglas said, years later, that he had only known three saints in politics and Voorhis was one. Saint or not, he was a most unusual man, a Yale graduate of socialist inclination who had run a school for orphan boys before he came to Congress as one of the young radicals of the early New Deal. "When I came here," he said, "I planned to vote right on every issue; now after seven years I am only absolutely sure about one vote." Writing speeches for him and listening to his reflections made me so painfully aware of my ignorance that I went back to school.

An M.A. in political science made me a bit more employable; whether it made me any wiser is debatable. Still, it was 1944 and the war was opening new doors to women. The president of the National League of Women Voters, having watched much of her senior staff depart for higher wartime salaries in the government, took a chance on three very young women of whom I was one. The league, child of the National American Woman Suffrage Association, was still inhabited by, and to a degree run by, ancient suffragists: women of such force and power that I do not remember having for them any of the usual scorn of youth for age. While my work dealt with public affairs, economic issues, international problems, I was also learning—though I was not much conscious of it—a great deal about a certain kind of American woman and about the inner workings of a women's voluntary association.

I shared a house with three other women who had come to Washington as I had. The war gave a peculiar intensity to life—the men we had known in college came to visit on their way to countries we hardly knew existed and sent back letters from which all mention of place and time had been censored. In our various jobs, all of which dealt in some way with international relations, we believed ourselves to be helping shape the future of the country, even of the world.

Then came Hiroshima. In my mind's eye I can still see our household along with several friends, on that hot August night in 1945 gathered on an upstairs porch hearing the celebration in the streets but not feeling celebratory at all. We constituted ourselves a Ten Years To Live Club— it would take about that long, we said, for the atomic bomb to do us all in. The postwar world for which we had thought we were preparing would, clearly, be somewhat different from our hopes. Within three months two of us were married; and a third had enrolled in Columbia's Russian Institute; I was left to find new roommates and ponder the future, mine and the world's, while the league put me to work writing pamphlets about the control of atomic energy. That task made me again uneasily aware of how little I knew and how much there was to know, but if the world was doomed to self-destruction, did it matter?

Such musings were interrupted by an interesting and ebullient young man who invited me to marry him and go to Harvard—an offer I couldn't refuse. Once we were in Cambridge the question was not whether to study but what. The program in American Civilization seemed to have few requirements and plenty of scope. But two people could not live and pay tuition on the munificence of the G.I. Bill, so I went round to Radcliffe and asked for a fellowship. Bernice Cronkhite, then dean of the Graduate School, fixed me with a stern eye: "Do you expect to complete the Ph.D.?" Until that moment the thought had not occurred to me, but it was fellowship or job-hunting, so I said, "Yes." Ten years later, having just successfully defended my dissertation, I stopped by to thank the dean for all her help. "Well," she said, "I always knew you would finish." It flashed through my mind that she had known exactly what she was doing that first day. . . .

Cambridge was an exhilarating place in 1947, especially for a young person whose educational experience had hitherto been mostly in the South or Middle West. For a while I almost took Harvard at its own assessment, which was not altogether a bad thing, since it made me work very hard. Being married to a strong-minded maverick who took nothing at face value and wanted to argue about most things—the more distinguished the faculty member, the more he wanted to argue—made this venture into higher learning different from earlier ones, and more productive. Once I got over being embarrassed by his temerity, Andrew Scott taught me how to tangle with authority and to stand up for my own ideas. In the crowded returning-G.I. period it was hard to get the attention of most of the faculty, but there were notable and important exceptions; I remember especially Benjamin Wright, Kenneth Murdock, and F. O. Matthissen.

Though the American Civilization program had requirements in history and literature, it was remarkably flexible and I continued to think of myself as a political scientist planning to write a dissertation in American political thought. Then, two days after the preliminary examination, my middle-aged mentor was made a college president, and I turned to Oscar Handlin who, in addition to being scarcely older than I was, had been my most challenging teacher. Together we decided that I would tackle the southern progressives, a term hitherto thought by most American historians to be a contradiction in terms. Thus for the second time, through a turn of chance, I found myself specializing in history—although still political history.

The dissertation was not destined to be written quickly. My husband, a notable workaholic, had taken his degree, and we headed back to Washington where he planned to gain some direct experience in international affairs.

All our planning was for his career; it did not occur to me to think this odd. Once we were settled, I took myself to the Library of Congress in search of those elusive southern progressives. The Manuscript Division in those days was a small and friendly place in which I was made to feel entirely welcome and soon viewed as one of the regulars. Reading manuscripts fascinated me, though I was not entirely sure what I was looking for, or how it would all someday come together; at that stage I hardly knew the questions, much less the answers. Nothing amazed me more than the sight of various weighty scholars who would appear for a few days, go to one collection or another, find precisely what they were looking for, and depart. I longed for the day when I would have that kind of assurance: to know what I was looking for, find it, and incorporate it at once into a developing book.

All this insecurity was temporarily laid aside in the summer of 1950 when our first child was born. Sudden immersion in parenthood is a traumatic experience: I could not imagine how one could combine scholarship with this voracious small being who never stopped demanding love, food, and care. With a very un-historical sense of time, I looked ahead and saw nothing but diapers and baby food for years to come. At that moment the president of the League of Women Voters came for lunch and offered me a job. I could work part-time, I could work at home, I could do whatever I wanted if *only* I would agree to become editor of *The National Voter.*

The baby, it turned out, managed quite well with a part-time nursemaid; and I found one could, after all, sustain attention and stretch one's mind on more substantial fare than Dr. Spock. In the 1960s when the need for part-time work for young mothers became a feminist issue I often thought of Percy Lee, that league president who with no fanfare at all recognized the problem and solved it and in the process kept me on track at one of those moments when it would have been easy to slip off completely.

What *was* off track, for the time being, was the dissertation. The league was over its ears in debates about the cold war, the Point Four program, international trade, and a wide range of domestic issues. In preparation for the 1952 presidential election we embarked upon a series of twelve articles on women's part in the political process for a mass circulation magazine. With so much going on in the present, it was hard to think about the past. By the time Rebecca was three, the idea that I might someday become a historian had receded into the distance.

But just then my husband decided he had finished his practical apprenticeship and was ready to join the academy. The snow-enclosed and male-dominated environment of Dartmouth College made it easier to write, and two chapters took shape before the next baby arrived. Then came another change of scene: we moved to Haverford College and had a third child. Once again my scholarly plans were in abeyance; once again a woman's voluntary association came to the rescue. Since the 1890s the American Association of University Women had been sustaining women scholars, generally by sending them to Europe to study. Mine may have been the first fellowship the AAUW knowingly provided to pay for a nursemaid. It made all the difference. At last—seven years and three children beyond the preliminary examination—the dissertation was finished.

The manuscript was safely in Cambridge; the degree was all but in hand. For the first time in years I could wonder what next? without having a ready-made answer. Coming out of the library on a beautiful spring day, I met one of Haverford's two historians who said that he was about to take a leave and wondered if I could suggest some young man who might like a one-year appointment in American history. I agreed to think about the question and started home. As I walked across the campus it suddenly came to me: here was a Job. I turned back and intercepted my friend: "Tom, why not me?" He looked surprised, but thoughtful: after all he was a committed Quaker and Quakers have long been given to treating men and women equally. He agreed to consult the acting-president (who was, fortunately, a sailing companion of my husband's) and that is how I became a lecturer in history. My career as a historian had begun.

If I came to history by indirection, my decision to study the history of women was not, in retrospect, accidental.

Two images mark the earliest moments when I was conscious of women as part of history. Both are associated with a grandmother I barely remember, since she died when I was five. One is of her worn, leather-bound diary, with a rose pressed in its pages and a poem by Father Ryan copied inside the front cover. I saw this volume only once, in a disorderly storeroom supposed to be off-limits for children. The ink was faded, the handwriting difficult: I still remember my intense curiosity and frustration when I could not read the words. Years later, by then experienced in deciphering nineteenth-century handwriting, I searched in vain for that tantalizing volume.

The other memory is of a letter, found in the same storeroom (I was an inquisitive and disobedient child) in which my grandfather wrote to one of his sons in the year 1921 saying something like this: "Your mother is travelling around the state organizing for the League of Women Voters. They give her a Ford car and her expenses, but of course *I* wish she were doing this for the church." That letter, too, disappeared, and it was twenty years before I fully understood how much it told me.

My grandmother, according to family legend (which is about the only surviving record of her life) had longed to go to college, but found her very proper Virginia family adamant. She went instead to a teacher-training school in Nashville and married a friend of her Georgia roommate. She was beautiful, talented, and much constrained by a patriarchal father-in-law who forbade her, among other things, to sign the articles she wrote for the local paper. She seized every chance to carry on her education while raising five children. She was a mild supporter of suffrage, a leader in voluntary associations in her town and state, and died young. She was one of the few people her son-in-law, my father, admired without reservation. For that reason, and because of elements of the legend which, even as a small child, appealed to me, she has always been a presence in my life. One of my childhood fantasies was that she had not died but had lived to be my guide and friend.

My journal reveals other small foreshadowing events. In 1944, after I had seen Greer Garson's *Madam Curie*, I recorded a resolution to write a history of women, beginning with Eve. It was one of those passing thoughts, never referred to again. Yet when I left the league for the second time in 1953 my friends on the staff who knew me well chose as farewell presents Mary Beard's *Woman as a Force in History* and Simone de Beauvoir's *Second Sex*. And in a file of old letters I find one to my father in June 1954 saying that I was sharing a room in the obstetrical ward with a woman who had just given birth to her fifth girl. "All her friends are commiserating with her," I wrote, "and since I am a moderately militant feminist this upsets me." This at a period characterized, we are told, by the domination of the feminine mystique.

As I searched the record for southern progressives I kept stumbling over women: well-dressed, well-spoken southern ladies taking a strong hand in social and political issues. At first I was puzzled since none of the people who had written on this subject (luminaries such as C. Vann Woodward and Arthur Link) had prepared me to find women there at all. But women *were* there, and they made a difference. So timid I was about this finding, arguably the only original part of the study, that it took up three or four pages at most.

But one thing led to another. Reading Congressional hearings I had been astounded to find members of Congress listening respectfully to a woman: Jane Addams. Who could this person be, I wondered, who could command the attention of old-fashioned southern gentlemen not noted for their sympathy for women in political life? A passing comment by my friend Louise Young who called her "America's greatest woman" caught my interest. Someone told me that the Addams papers were not twenty miles away, and when summer came after my Haverford year I began spending four days a week in the Swarthmore Library trying to answer that question. The journal throws no light on my broader purpose (if there was one) unless it was to balance the responsibilities of child-raising with something less demanding, but before long I began to envision a biography of this woman whose papers steadily increased my interest in her and in the multiple currents through which she was navigating in the 1890s.

Just then my husband took a new job, this time in North Carolina. Jane Addams's papers were left 500 miles behind. With three young children and very little money it seemed unlikely that I could travel about looking for the other widely scattered manuscripts that would be needed for a serious biography. With naive optimism I sent off grant applications right and left, all of which yielded somewhat chilly form letters saying, in a word, No. Only later did I discover that at that time grants were for established scholars, rarely for the ambitious beginner.

I did find a precarious part-time job in the history department of the University of North Carolina. A young colleague, perhaps intent upon astonishing his elders, asked me, the first and only woman in the department, to give a paper at a departmental seminar. I had four months to prepare: what to do? I remembered those women in the progressive movements and now, after a summer in the Addams papers, I knew they had not been a figment of my imagination. I took myself to the Southern Historical Collection, intent at first only on constructing a respectable paper for that all-male and highly traditional history faculty. In the end the work thus begun would occupy much of the next decade.

Before I settled down in earnest to pursue my southern women, two or three things happened which may have a bearing on this story. In 1960 Andrew was appointed Fulbright lecturer at the University of Bologna in Italy. A year abroad, with three children, in a city where English was rarely spoken; vacation camping trips to Greece and Spain and then to nearly all of western Europe and England; all this was worth ten years of ordinary life for stretching the mind and stirring up questions. While we were there, a letter from a member of the Duke history department for whom in our youth we had served as babysitters asked if I would consider coming to teach for a year as a part-time instructor . . . a young man had left late in the year . . . they needed more time to find a suitable replacement. I replied by return mail, asking only (with considerable deference) whether a Ph.D. and three years teaching experience might qualify me to be a part-time assistant professor. That point settled, I went to Duke in the fall of 1961. Presumably the department never found a "suitable replacement" for the departed colleague, since I am there yet.

While we were in Italy, too, George Tindall had written asking whether I could be ready to give a paper on southern women at the fall meeting of the Southern Historical Association. As with the job offer, I did not lose any time saying yes, so that by the time I met my first class at Duke I was hurrying to finish what would become "The 'New Woman' in the New South." The Southern met in Chattanooga; at the end of the session, and after a three-hour lunch with Oscar Handlin, I had committed myself to a monograph about southern white women.

In retrospect the whole enterprise seems a little unlikely. I had always seen my work as something to be picked up and laid down as the family needs and Andrew's career dictated. In 1961 he was busy at work on what would become *The Revolution in Statecraft*; faculty wives were then still expected to bear a hand with entertaining colleagues and students, with typing and proofreading; nor did I question the expectation. The Duke job, whatever the department thought, seemed to me to offer a possibility for a permanent attachment, especially if one were quick to publish. Yet here I was embarking upon a study for which there was almost no historiographical tradition and no network of established scholars. My temerity rested not on courage but on ignorance: if I had known what was involved I might never have begun.

I look back at my journal to recapture the flavor of that busy life. One sign of it are the long gaps in the record—occasionally months go by without a word. On October 30, 1961, I noted: "Time must be measured with different calipers here. It goes by all too fast. Thirty-nine days ago I began teaching and have hardly drawn a deep breath since. We are having a long beautiful fall . . . Andy is once again trying to grow a lawn . . . the children are doing well."

Nothing more for another twenty-seven days when I noted the trip to Chattanooga, a visit from my brother for Thanksgiving, and the need to get on with Christmas presents lest we "wake up Christmas morning with nothing done at all." By February the notations are staccato and telegraphic: "Up at 6:30, to Durham by 8:10 [first class]. Visit to Woman's College Library, sentimental journal through a picture book *Europe*. Picked up some intriguing items on women. Two other classes. Number of students dropping course etc., time a bit broken up. Worked on article on southern progressives in Congress—why did I not do this last year? Atmosphere has so much to do with what work gets done. Home. Walk around the circle with Mary Helen discussing School Board. Many children and dogs out enjoying the spring weather. Visit with Tan. Dinner. *Chapel Hill Weekly*. Phone calls. But a pleasant, interesting and demanding life. Rising to the demands is the only satisfaction. . . . Where has the Berlin crisis gone?"

And so the days went: teaching, neighboring, parenting; an occasional glance at public affairs—and trying to write a book.

Looking back I see that I was held to the course by several kinds of support. Andrew Scott was constantly encouraging, and since he was a born parent (perhaps the best I have ever seen in action) the children never seemed to mind when I disappeared to the library on weekends. Then colleagues at the University of North Carolina and Duke and Oscar Handlin, off in Cambridge, kept offering encouragement, even enthusiasm. Then, there were the survivors: the southern women in their eighties who had never doubted that they and their comrades were part of history, but who had long ago ceased expecting anybody to say so. How could I let them down? And there was Julia Spruill, who had meant, once, to write the book I was undertaking but finding that the groundwork did not exist had instead spent thirteen years creating her classic *Women's Life and Work in the Southern Colonies*. She was like a retired athlete urging a younger runner on around the track. From Washington my friend Louise Young, like Spruill a pioneer scholar in the history of women, wrote bracing letters and offered a roof when I could get to the Library of Congress. It is hard to overestimate the importance of encouragement to anyone embarking uncertainly upon a new terrain.

Though the history of southern women became my principal work, Jane Addams did not disappear entirely. The news that three young men were embarking on biographies took care of my ambition to do that, but when first Edward James and then Bernard Bailyn gave me a chance to write about her, I did—and with enthusiasm—and learned a great deal about what have become the major themes of my work in women's history.

Then came another kind of learning experience. In 1963 Terry Sanford, the governor of North Carolina, like many young Democratic governors in that year, had taken John F. Kennedy for a model and had decided to appoint a Commission on the Status of Women. How he hit upon me as a possible chairman I do not know. I had not the faintest idea about what such a commission could, or should, be, but some latent fantasy about being in political life led me to accept the job and thereafter to learn fast. I left my library study with its notes about nineteenth-century women activists and plunged into intense association with contemporary ones. It was a cold bath that cured me of many romantic images and taught me something of the complexity of human motivation—particularly the mixture of motives which lead anyone, male or female, into public life.

The commission functioned the way such things do in this bureaucratic age. Most of the work was done by committees or staff people, and the final report was a joint production. My task was to put it all together, wield a firm editorial pencil, and meet a deadline. The historian in public affairs is often, unconsciously, a participant-observer. While I worked hard on the problems we had set ourselves, part of my mind wondered, "How would anyone who has not been part of this process ever write an accurate account of this Commission's work?" I realized all over again how partial even the best history must be. To be sure we left behind us a vast file of documents, safely deposited in the North Carolina Department of Archives, but the tough battles, the shaping arguments, took place face to face or over the phone and were never recorded. Nor were the complex motives of any of us, from the chair to the least active committee member, ever put into words.

The other great learning experience of the 1960s, for me as for so many people, was the Civil Rights Movement. As I watched my students, my children, myself caught up in different ways I began at last to gain a faint glimmer of what it must have been like to have been part of the progressive excitement in the first two decades of the century or how it might have felt to be an ardent suffragist. I realized, too, that much of what I had thought I knew about southern black women needed re-thinking; that *their* history had not yet begun to be written.

With all this experience to ponder and its implications to incorporate in the manuscript I was struggling to write, I went back to the library. In 1970, in the midst of teaching, child-raising, and all the rest there appeared at last a book—*The Southern Lady*—as well as two readers in women's history, one for high school and one for college students.

The timing, through no forethought of mine, was excellent. Resurgent feminism was sweeping the country and bringing a demand for women's history; a considerable number of young scholars were enthusiastically creating a new field of study. I remembered Jane Addams, only six years after the founding of Hull-House, writing her sister: "I am considered the grandmother of social settlements" (she was thirty-five at the time). The handful of established historians of women who existed in 1970—most of us well beyond thirty-five—had much the same feeling. We were grandmothers, with a rapidly proliferating group of interesting grandchildren.[1]

Someday a student of the sociology of knowledge will write an illuminating article on the early development of the new women's history. Sparked about equally by feminism and the burgeoning interest in social history, a group of historians, mostly young, mostly women, began to appear on the scene in the mid-1960s. Dismissed as political or ignored completely by many colleagues, we responded by forming a community of scholars that cut across generations, ideologies, race, and class. Sharing ideas, sources, and material, instinctively seeking safety in numbers, we did the one thing that could develop a new field quickly. We learned from each other with an élan which is rarely seen in academic life. All in all 1970 was an exhilarating year; feminism rampant, women's history developing in all directions, and—in our family—the children growing up—Rebecca, indeed, was busy writing a college paper on "Women in

[1] To the best of my knowledge, when "The 'New Woman' in the New South" appeared in 1962, Eleanor Flexner, Alma Lutz, Janet Wilson James, Louise M. Young, Eugenie Leonard, and A. Elizabeth Taylor were actively engaged in scholarly work in women's history. Gerda Lerner was finishing a Senior Honors Thesis on the Grimké sisters at the New School for Social Research and teaching a course in women's history there. Julia Spruill, Elizabeth Anthony Dexter, and Mary Benson were no longer publishing. It is startling to realize that ten years later more than 1,000 people turned up for the first Berkshire Conference in Women's History held at Douglass College.

Stuart England." But at the end of a nine-year endeavor the actual publication of the book raised again the question, What next?

In the summer of 1971 I taught my first formal college course in the social history of American women, to an enthusiastic group of students at the University of Washington. It had long been clear to me that history itself grew and developed when one brought women's experience to bear; now I began to see that pedagogy likewise benefited enormously from the introduction of this subject. I have taught many kinds of courses in twenty-five years, some good, but none has elicited the kind of hard work and commitment that this one did, and still does.

Developing the course and composing a number of public lectures complicated the question of what research to do next. There had been, briefly, some pressure from colleagues to do some "real history" (that is, with nothing to do with women) so that I might be viewed as a "real" historian. Happily this pressure diminished when two men with impeccable credentials wrote favorable reviews of *The Southern Lady*. The more serious problem was that so little had been done, the possibilities were so vast, and new ones turned up every time I prepared for a class or wrote a lecture. At first I wanted to do it all. There are an embarrassing number of false starts in the file.

The discipline I was having trouble imposing on myself came from outside in the form of an invitation to my husband and me to write an interpretive history of the suffrage movement. *One Half the People* was our first joint enterprise to be labeled as such, though we had worked together for years, first on *Political Thought in America* (published under Andrew M. Scott's name) and then on *The Southern Lady*, of which I appeared to be sole author. Now we made our collaboration public. Our irreverent eldest child remarked that she could see, as she read the manuscript, where the historian left off and the political scientist began, but in fact the whole essay was the result of a constant exchange of ideas and drafts.

The publication of *Notable American Women* had stirred me to think about the potential for a collective biography of the 1,359 women contained therein, and I experimented a bit with that idea. Gradually, partly as a consequence of writing the essay which gives title to this volume, I began to realize that my principal interest in these elite women focused on two things: first, the effect of education on women's lives and the effect of a growing body of educated women on American society;

second, on the way women used voluntary associations to pursue objectives otherwise difficult for them to attain.

The serendipitous discovery of the Emma Willard materials, described in a headnote on page 34, and the composition of three articles based on them, helped clarify these concerns. I began to realize that at least since 1800 there had been an on-going interaction between women and education at many levels with far-reaching consequences for our social structures. In 1980-81 the hospitality of the National Humanities Center allowed me to begin to write a book which will attempt to trace this interaction and show some of what it means. The early stages of that effort are included here.

Somewhere along the line I had begun to define myself as a social historian. I found the intense discussions of social history in the 1970s giving me a way to define what I had been trying to do for a decade or more. In the spring of 1983 I was startled to hear a young professor, who had been in several of my undergraduate courses in the early 1960s, tell a group of his graduate students that I had introduced him to social history. Was it true? In the 1960s? As he and I talked, I realized that in the process of trying to reconstruct women's historical experience I had found my way to new kinds of sources and had looked to psychology, anthropology, and sociology for ideas to help me make sense of what I was finding. Without making a conscious shift from my earlier interest in political history I had begun, so he reminded me, assigning to students research projects which were similar to the work I was doing myself. For example, he had written an undergraduate paper that was essentially a community study; the process of studying women had pushed me to ask questions about social structures and social change, and I in turn had pushed him. In *The Southern Lady* (then in its early stages) I was feeling my way. Orest Ranum, after reading a draft of that book, wrote an admonitory letter suggesting that while I had been isolated in manuscript rooms many American historians, taking a cue from French and English colleagues, were using demography to study family history and that I seemed unaware of that fact. He was right. It embarrasses me a little now to read the section of the book in which I used manuscript census data in a random and intuitive way with no effort at scientific sampling (indeed, I hardly knew there was such a thing, outside of public opinion polls). From Professor Ranum and other colleagues I have learned a great deal and hope it shows in the later essays.

Life, as well as other historians, has taught me a good deal. I have lived through a good part of the twentieth century and been a participant, as well as a recorder, of the history of American women. I have confronted many of the perennial issues: the interaction of personality and environment, of class and sex, of economic condition, race, education, war, marriage, children, and dual careers. In retrospect, I realize that all kinds of seemingly irrelevant experience feeds into historical scholarship. "It is not in vain," Elizabeth Cady Stanton wrote to Susan B. Anthony in June 1856, "that I myself have experienced all the wearisome cares to which woman in her best estate is subject." She was thinking of their effort to bring about what she called a moral revolution, but a scholar seeking to understand the lives and experience of women long dead might say the same.

Probably few of us, looking backward, fail to find things that could have been done better had they been done differently. Reading the record I am appalled at the amount of time I have put into university business with no visible consequence whatever. But perhaps even in those seemingly endless hours I was learning some things about human interaction that help me understand all the failed endeavors which are as much a part of the past as the successes. In any case, in coming to terms with my own life I have been much helped by the women I have studied and have come to agree with Jane Mecom (whom the reader will meet a few pages hence): "When I look round me on all my Aquaintance I do not see won I have reason to think happier than I am and would not change my neighbour with my Self where will you find one in a more comfortable State as I see Every won has ther Trobles and I sopose them to be much as fitts them best and shakeing off them might be only changing for the wors."

The world of the 1980s has many talented young historians and occasionally one empathizes with John Updike's Rabbit: "The kids keep coming. They keep crowding you up." But most of the time the crowding is challenging and keeps one alert. The history of women is now a flourishing field producing such a large quantity of good work that it will require considerable skill to make use of it in our teaching and our textbooks. This book represents a small contribution to that growing corpus.

The essays below are grouped according to subject. My first thought had been to put them in order of publication—and my able young graduate assistant argued forcefully for the value of illustrating my evolution as a historian—but when all was said it seems to work best to keep like topics together, with dates of publication clear for all to see. I have resisted the constant temptation to rewrite, to eliminate infelicity of language and other failings. To do so would falsify the historical record, and so I have confined myself to correcting outright errors, eliminating some repetition, and bringing references up to date. Even so, some material is repeated (with different emphasis) when I could find no way of removing the repetition without destroying the structure of the essay in question; I hope the readers will understand.

In the end this project, which began as a chore, turned into a stimulating experience; I hope it may be one for readers as well.

Chapel Hill, North Carolina   ANNE FIROR SCOTT
July 1983

PART I

The Biographical Mode

The perennial question—is biography a part of history? —will doubtless continue to be argued, but no one doubts that life histories contribute to that imaginative feel for the past without which even the most careful accumulation of data is sometimes lifeless.

I would not claim, however, that I read biography, and write it, solely to gain insight into historical processes. I have always been intrigued by other people's lives, other people's ways of dealing with the comedies and tragedies and challenges of life. If the fairies round my cradle had given me a choice, I would have been endowed with George Eliot's talent and would have written a nineteenth-century southern version of *Middlemarch*. Since they didn't ask me, I have had to settle for writing about real people. (It is a fine line which divides the good novel from first-rate biography.) Telling stories about people seems to come naturally to many southerners; it certainly has to me.

The biographical sketches presented here range from the eighteenth to the twentieth centuries and were composed for a number of different purposes. They have in common the fact that all the subjects are women. I have put them in order of the birthdates of their subjects, so that the reader may gain some sense of the way women's lives have changed over the generations.

Self-Portraits: Three Women

This essay went through several metamorphoses before it came to rest in the festschrift for Oscar Handlin published in 1979. A year at Johns Hopkins University provided access to a fine collection of colonial materials; an invitation to give three lectures covering the history of American women provided the initial impetus for going into the eighteenth century.

My models were provided by a novelist-critic and an economist. Over the years I have gone back again and again to John Maynard Keynes's Essays in Biography, especially the essay on Mary Marshall. Virginia Woolf's Common Reader was an even greater influence. During the summer of 1975 my normal day began with an hour rereading one of her biographical sketches, after which I worked on the recreation of one of these colonial women. That I was writing in a Nova Scotia fishing village, from which the eighteenth century has never entirely disappeared, may also have contributed something. Doubtless it is hubris, but I believe—could I be miraculously transported back to their time—I would recognize each of these women on first encounter.

> [Collections of letters] heap up in mounds of insignificant and often dismal dust the innumerable trivialities of daily life, as it grinds itself out, year after year, and then suddenly they blaze up; the day shines out, complete, alive, before our eyes.
> —Virginia Woolf, "The Pastons and Chaucer"

The eighteenth century, to borrow Bernard Bailyn's phrase, was not incidentally but essentially different from the present, and many of the elements of that essential difference can be most clearly seen in the lives

Reprinted from Richard L. Bushman et al., eds., *Uprooted Americans: Essays to Honor Oscar Handlin* (Boston: Little, Brown & Co., 1979), pp. 43-76.

of women. Colonial history has so long been written in terms of high achievement, of political theory, of Founding Fathers, of economic development, of David-and-Goliath conflict that it is easy to forget how small a part such things played in most individual lives. Seen from the standpoint of ordinary people, the essential theme of the eighteenth-century experience was not so much achievement as the fragility and chanciness of life. Death was an omnipresent reality. Three children in one family die on a single day from epidemic disease; fathers are lost at sea; adolescents mysteriously waste away; mothers die in childbirth; yet life goes on to a constant underlying murmur of "God's sacred will be done." In these circumstances, how is the meaning of life perceived? What social structures do people build to sustain the spirit? What, in this context, become the central values? What is the texture of daily life?

The life histories of three colonial women give some clues.

The three women are Jane Franklin Mecom of Boston, Elizabeth Sandwith Drinker of Philadelphia, and Eliza Lucas Pinckney of Charleston. Taken together their lives cover nearly a century, from 1712 when the first was born to 1807 when the youngest died. Their experience encompassed three cultures—Puritan, Quaker, and plantation—and covered a broad spectrum of colonial social classes. The life of each is illuminating, each in a different way. All three loved to write, and each created a self-portrait—two in letters, one in a journal she kept from the time she was twenty-four until a few days before her death. Various depredations have washed out important parts of their life histories; and many things went unrecorded. Yet the documents which have survived bring us into the midst of daily experience and reveal, from time to time, their most deeply held cultural values.

Jane Franklin Mecom

Jane, youngest of Josiah Franklin's seventeen children, was born in 1712, six years after Benjamin. Because in later life she would become her brother's favorite correspondent, we know more about her than about any other woman of her social class in eighteenth-century Boston.

She was eleven when Benjamin made his famous getaway, breaking his apprenticeship and embarking upon the legendary career which would make him the archetypal self-made American. In old age both looked back with favor upon their early childhood: "It was indeed a Lowly Dwelling we were brought up in but we were fed Plentifully, made comfortable with fire and cloathing, had sildom any contention among us, but all was Harmony: Especially betwen the Heads—and they were Universally Respected, & the most of the famely in good Reputation, this is still happier liveing than multituds Injoy."[1]

Even allowing for the rosy glow the passage of time creates, the recollections of both brother and sister suggest that the parents were remarkable people, and that such education as children get at home, both had gotten. The things Jane Mecom singled out for recollection were central values all her life: a good reputation and the respect of the community. She always tried to "live respectable," and her fondest hope was that her children should do so.

At the age when her brother had run away to begin his climb to fame, Jane Franklin married a neighbor who was a saddler. Her brother sent a spinning wheel, an appropriate gift for a seventeenth child who could expect no dowry. The best efforts of both spouses would be required to keep up with a growing family, as—for a quarter of a century—every second year brought a new baby. Three died in infancy, but nine survived to be fed, clothed, and trained for self-support.

By the time we catch another glimpse of Jane Mecom she was already thirty, living in a house owned by her father, taking in lodgers, and caring for her aging parents. Her twelve-year-old son was learning the saddler's trade, and she was searching for appropriate apprenticeships for the younger ones. Between caring for parents, children, lodgers, and her husband's shop it is no wonder that the only written word of hers which survives from this period is a postscript to a letter her mother wrote to Benjamin. His letters to her began a pattern which would last a lifetime, as he spoke of sending "a few Things that may be of some Use perhaps in your Family."[2]

His help was more than financial. Busy making his own way in Philadelphia, he took time to find an apprenticeship for his namesake, Benny Mecom, who gave some promise of talents similar to his own. There were problems "such as are commonly incident to boys of his years," although, Franklin added, "he has many good qualities, for which I love him."[3] Diligence was not one of those qualities, and Jane Mecom was deeply concerned lest Benny never learn to work. He never did, at least not steadily, and would continue to cause his mother anxiety as long as he lived.

We get our next clear glimpse of Jane Mecom when she was fifty-one and entertaining her brother in her own house. While he was there, she enjoyed what would ever after be her measure of "suitable Conversation," and shone, however briefly, in the reflected glory of Dr. Franklin as Boston admirers paid court to him at her house. The fact that he chose to domicile himself with the Mecoms, rather than with the far more affluent and equally welcoming "cousen Williams," says something about the quality of her conversation, or, perhaps, about his sensitivity to her feelings.

That interval of pleasure was brief. Four of the twelve Mecom children were already dead; now Sarah, at twenty-seven a "Dear and Worthy child," died, leaving a husband and four children who promptly moved into Jane Mecom's house. Within six months two of the four grandchildren were dead. She was still grieving for them when Edward Mecom, her husband of thirty-eight years, also died. She wrote one of the two comments about him to be found in any of her letters: "It pleased God to call my Husband out of this Troblesom world where he had Injoyed Little and suffered much by Sin & Sorrow."[4] Two years later she lost her youngest and favorite, Polly, at eighteen: "Sorrows roll upon me like the waves of the sea. I am hardly allowed time to fetch my breath. I am broken with breach upon breach, and I have now, in the first flow of my grief, been almost ready to say 'What have I more?' But God forbid, that I should indulge that thought. . . . God is sovereign and I submit."[5]

In 1766 she was fifty-five. Of five surviving children the oldest was thirty-four and the youngest twenty-one, but none was in a position to support a widowed mother. Two sons had been bred to the saddler's trade; one had died and the other gone to sea. Peter, a soap-boiler like his grandfather, showed signs of the mental illness which would eventually incapacitate him, and the feckless Benjamin was not earning enough to support his own wife and children. Her son-in-law Flagg was an unskilled workman, hard put to take care of his two children. The one daughter who still lived with her was a melancholy and sickly young woman.

Jane Mecom's thoughts turned, therefore, to self-support. She continued to take in lodgers, and her brother sent from England a small stock of trading goods which arrived just as Bostonians decided to boycott

English goods in protest of the Stamp Act. Poverty, she concluded, "is Intailed on my famely."[6]

She was acutely aware of her dependence on her brother's help. She tried to repay him with reports of life in Boston. "The whol conversation of this Place turns upon Polities and Riligous contryverces," she wrote, adding that her own sentiments were for peace. With his reply he sent her a set of his philosophical papers, which she proudly read.[7]

Somehow in 1769 she contrived a trip to Philadelphia, where Franklin's wife and daughter found her "verey a greabel"—so much so that he was moved to suggest, from London, that she consider staying on permanently.[8] But Boston was home, and back she went into the midst of the rising conflict with Great Britain.

Her brother, though thoroughly engrossed in the same conflict in London, took time to write Jane Mecom asking for detailed instructions as to the making of "crown soap," a family secret which he feared might be lost if it were not preserved for the next generation. Here at last was something she could do in return for all his help; her instructions were given in minute detail.

At about this time her letters began to grow longer and more revealing. Perhaps her visit to Deborah Franklin had reduced her awe of her famous brother; perhaps confidence in her own capacities was growing. Whatever the reason, she began to speak more freely, range more widely, and fill out—for us—the scanty self-portrait belatedly begun.

An admirer of Thomas Hutchinson and a lover of peace, Jane Mecom was no early patriot. By 1774, however, "Proflegate soulders," making trouble and harassing citizens on the streets of Boston, pushed her closer to the rebel position. The battle of Lexington finished what the soldiers had begun, as she locked her house, packed such goods as she could carry, and took refuge in Rhode Island.

In some ways the war changed her life for the better. Catherine Ray Greene, with whom she stayed at first, became her good friend. Her granddaughter, Jenny Flagg, married Elihu Greene, brother of General Nathanael Greene, a solid farmer, merchant, and entrepreneur. A man of his standing could well have demanded a dowry, but his willingness to marry Jenny for love marked a change in the hitherto unbroken stream of Mecom bad luck.

In the fall of 1774 Franklin came home after a decade in England, and not long after took his sister for a prolonged stay in Philadelphia. His wife, Deborah, had died, and Jane was able to be helpful to him until he went off to France. In two years General William Howe's decision to occupy Philadelphia sent her back to Rhode Island to her granddaughter's house, where she was "much Exposed & . . . under constant Apprehensions" that the British would invade.[9]

Yet the British were not as troublesome to her as a personal crisis brought on by wartime inflation. The country woman who cared for her son Peter suddenly demanded more money for that service than Jane Mecom had or could see any way to get. Dependence on her brother was galling enough when he anticipated her needs; now she had to ask for help. Her spirits felt "so deprest" that she could scarcely write, but what else could she do?

The war had disrupted communication, and her letter was a long time reaching him. Meanwhile, relief came in a painful guise: Peter died. Accustomed as she was to accepting God's will, Jane Mecom reflected that Peter had been "no comfort to any won nor capable of injoying any Himself for many years."[10] His death was a blessing.

But at the same time she had heard nothing for five months from her daughter Jane Collas in Boston and began to worry lest this last remaining child might be going the way of her brothers into insanity. Apologizing for burdening a busy and important man, she wrote her fears to Franklin: "It gives some Relief to unbousom wons self to a dear friend as you have been & are to me."[11]

Her daughter was, it turned out, physically rather than mentally ill, but sick or well she was never able to live up to her mother's standards of energy and enterprise. "You say you will endeavour to correct all your faults," Jane Mecom wrote in 1778 when Jane Collas was already in her thirties, and proceeded to outline in some detail what those faults were: a tendency to look on the dark side of "God's Providence," an inclination to despair and to extravagance, laziness, and a lack of ingenuity in working to meet her material needs, an unseemly fondness for a great deal of company. She also tended to lie abed late, which her mother found "a trouble to me on many accounts." To top it off, she aspired to gentility without the means to support her aspiration—a tendency Jane Mecom scorned whenever she encountered it.[12]

Nine children had survived infancy, and none had fulfilled their mother's hopes. Most had died in early adulthood. Benjamin simply disappeared during the battle of Trenton, and no trace of him was ever found. Peter's tragic end has already been noted. The fate of her children pushed Jane Mecom to a rare moment of questioning God's will: "I think there was hardly Ever so unfourtunate a Famely. I am not willing to think it is all owing to misconduct. I have had some children that seemed to be doing well till they were taken off by Death."[13] But there was nothing to be done. One must accept these things or go mad.

In the late 1770s the long train of bereavement, displacement, and struggle abated for a while. Her granddaughter Jenny Greene, with whom she was living, was a most satisfactory young person whose conversation and attention to her comfort she much appreciated, and whose husband she respected. Though there was no neighbor for two miles, many visitors dropped in. She herself never left home unless someone sent a carriage (the Greenes owning none) since "I hant courage to ride a hors."[14] She made and sent to Franklin several batches of crown soap, which he wanted for his friends in France, took care of Jenny Greene in her successive lyings-in, helped with the babies, supervised the household, and, from time to time, sold "some little matter" from the small store of goods she had brought from Boston in 1775. "My time seems to be filld up as the Famely I am in Increases fast," she wrote. She was sixty-eight and very energetic, though "as I grow older I wish for more Quiet and our Famely is more Incumbered as we have three children Born since I came & tho they give grat Pleasure . . . yet the Noise of them is sometimes troblesom."[15] She knew "but little how the world goes Except seeing a Newspaper some times which contains Enough to give Pain but little satisfaction while we are in Armes against each other."[16] In spite of the inflation and the losses the Greenes were suffering as many of their ships were captured, her life was pleasanter than it had been since childhood. "I contineu very Easey and happy hear," she wrote in 1781, "have no more to trroble me than what is Incident to human Nature & cant be avoided in any Place, I write now in my own litle chamber the window opening on won of the Pleasantest prospects in the country the Birds singing about me and nobod up in the house near me to Desturb me."[17]

Life had taught Jane Mecom to be wary when things were going well. Ten months after that happy note her granddaughter died, giving birth to the fourth child in four years, and at seventy Jane Mecom was suddenly again the female head of a household of young children who needed, she thought, "some person more lively and Patient to watch over them continualy"; but since there was no one else, she did it anyway.[18] Fortunately she found them a comfort as she grieved for her beloved grandchild, a sacrifice to the age's custom of unbroken childbearing. She was too busy to pine, though the war had cut off her communication with Franklin for three years.

His first postwar letter included a "grat, very grat, Present," for which she thanked him extravagantly, adding that his generosity would enable her to live "at Ease in my old Age (after a life of Care Labour & Anxiety)."[19]

By 1784 she was back in Boston, in a house long owned by her brother, where she was able to "live all ways Cleen and Look Decent."[20] It was a great comfort. She had leisure to read and write, a minister she respected with whom to discuss theology and other things, the care and companionship of her granddaughter Jenny Mecom, the regular attention of her nephew-in-law Jonathan Williams. Her grandchildren and great-grandchildren were often a source of pride and pleasure.

One grandchild, Josiah Flagg, turned up in Philadelphia and, as she saw it, presumed upon his relationship to persuade Franklin to take him on as a secretary. He beseeched his grandmother to conceal the fact that he, Josiah, had once been a shoemaker, thus bringing down upon himself the scorn she reserved for false pride. She lectured him severely, betraying trepidation lest her demanding relatives threaten her warm relationship with her brother. Fortunately Josiah turned out to be an excellent penman and behaved well in the Franklin family.

With her brother back in Philadelphia, correspondence quickened. He was still concerned that someone in the family be trained to carry on the tradition of the crown soap. Might she teach the younger Jonathan Williams, or even Josiah Flagg, how to make it? She would think about it. She had thought earlier of teaching her son-in-law Peter Collas, whose difficulties in earning a living had become almost ludicrous. Whenever he took berth on a ship, it was promptly captured. But she had decided that the soap required a man of "Peculiar Genius" and that Collas was not.[21] Meanwhile she continued to make the soap herself, sending batch after batch to Franklin.

He felt the urge for some "cods cheeks and sounds," a favorite New England delicacy. She managed to acquire a keg to send him. She wished him well in the enterprise of the federal convention, and when the Constitution arrived in Boston she reported that while some quarrelsome spirits opposed it, those of "Superior Judgement" were going to support it.

She assured him that she followed his advice about taking exercise and walked even when a chaise was available, "but I am so weak I make but a Poor Figure in the Street."[22] She had her chamber painted and papered against the day she might be confined to it.

A ship captain friend took a favorable report of her to Philadelphia, for which she was grateful: "The Gratest Part of my time when I am sitting at home I am apt to Imagine as Samson did when He lost his Hare, that I can Arise & Shake my Self & Go forth as at other times but on Tryal Like him I am wofully disapointed & find my Feet cripling & my Breath short, but I am still chearful for that is my Natural Temper."[23]

In January 1788, replying to his request for a "very peticular" account of how she lived, she provided a detailed description:

I have a good clean House to Live in my Grandaughter constantly to atend me to do whatever I desier in my own way & in my own time, I go to bed Early lye warm & comfortable Rise Early to a good Fire have my Brakfast directly and Eate it with a good Apetite and then Read or Work or what Els I Pleas, we live frugaly Bake all our own Bread, brew small bear, lay in a little cyder, Pork, Buter, &c. & suply our selves with Plenty of other nesesary Provision Dayly at the Dore we make no Entertainments, but some Times an Intimate Acquaintance will come in and Pertake with us the Diner we have Provided for our selves & a Dish of Tea in the After Noon, & if a Friend sitts and chats a litle in the Evening we Eate our Hasty Puding (our comon super) after they are gone; It is trew I have some Trobles but my Dear Brother Does all in His Power to Aleviat them by Praventing Even a wish, that when I Look Round me on all my Acquaintance I do not see won I have reason to think Happier than I am and would not change my neighbour with my Self where will you Find one in a more comfortable State as I see Every won has ther Trobles and I sopose them to be such as fitts them best & shakeing off them might be only changing for the wors.[24]

Six more years of life remained to her. The new Constitution was inaugurated, George Washington took office, merchants and politicans concerned themselves with their own and the nation's prosperity, foreign conflicts flamed and threatened. Jane Mecom, for her part, worried about Benjamin Franklin's illness with "the stone" and prayed for his tranquillity in the face of pain. Their correspondence ranged around topics mostly personal and family, and upon reflections on life as they had lived it. "I do not Pretend to writ about Politics," she said, "tho I Love to hear them."[25]

Franklin's death in 1790 was a blow, but she was now seventy-eight herself and prepared to be philosophical about this, as she saw it, temporary separation from her best friend. In his will he provided for her, and when she died four years later this woman who had lived so frugally was able to leave an estate of a thousand pounds to Jane Collas (in trust — she still worried about her daughter's extravagance!) and to her fifteen grandchildren and great-grandchildren.

When the historians came to treat the years covered by her life, they dwelt on wars and politics, on the opening of land and trade and manufacture, on the economic development of a fertile wilderness, the rapid growth in population, the experiment in representative government.

That all these things shaped Jane Mecom's life experience there can be no doubt. Yet life as she perceived it was mostly made up of the small events of which great events are composed: of twenty-one years of pregnancy and childbirth which, multiplied by millions of women, created the rapid population growth; of the hard struggle to "git a living" and to make sure her children were prepared to earn theirs; of the constant procession of death which was the hallmark of her time; of the belated prosperity and happiness which came to her in old age. What added up to a wilderness conquered, a new nation created, was often experienced by individuals as a very hard life somehow survived. It is only in retrospect that all the separate experiences together create something we call "economic development," or "manifest destiny," or — simply — "history."

The events of Jane Mecom's life might have destroyed a weaker person, but some combination of natural resilience, good health, belief in the virtues of diligence, industry, and ingeniousness, and firm faith that God had good reasons for all the pain and sorrow which befell her carried her through. Perhaps her final judgment on the whole experience was summed up in that sentence: "Every won has ther Trobles and I sopose them to be such as fitts them best & shakeing off them might be only changing for the wors."

In chapter three of Virginia Woolf's *Room of One's Own* there is a clever and moving fantasy: what if Shakespeare had had a sister as gifted as himself? The end of the fantasy is tragic, for Shakespeare's imaginary sister, born with a great gift, was so thwarted and hindered by the confines of "woman's place" that she killed herself. In Jane Mecom we have a real-life case, for of the sixteen siblings of Benjamin Franklin, she alone showed signs of talent and force of character similar to his. At the age of fifteen one ran off to Philadelphia and by a combination of wit, luck, and carefully cultivated ability to get ahead began his rise to the pinnacle among the Anglo-American intelligentsia. At the same age the other married a neighbor and in a month was pregnant. From that time forward her life was shaped almost entirely by the needs of other people. Like her brother she had a great capacity for growth, though the opportunity came to her late and was restricted by her constant burden of family responsibilities. The Revolution broadened her experience as it did his, yet she was almost never without children to care for, even in her seventies. Her letters showed a steady improvement in vigor of style and even in spelling. Her lively intelligence kept Franklin writing her even when he was very busy. Perhaps she had herself half in mind when she wrote in 1786: "Dr. Price thinks Thousands of Boyles Clarks and Newtons have Probably been lost to the world, and lived and died in Ignorance and meanness, mearly for want of being Placed in favourable Situations, and Injoying Proper Advantages, very few we know is able to beat thro all Impediments and Arive to any Grat Degre of superiority in Understanding."[26]

The "impediments" in her own life had been many, some might have thought insuperable, yet clearly by the age of eighty she had arrived at the "superiority in Understanding" which makes her letters a powerful chronicle of an eighteenth-century life.

Elizabeth Sandwith Drinker

Jane Mecom's life emerges full of interest from the most fragmentary records. Elizabeth Drinker, by contrast, left the most detailed record of any eighteenth-century American woman, one which provides an intimate view of daily life among the tight little community of Philadelphia Quakers of which she was a part.

Born Elizabeth Sandwith, of Irish inheritance, she was orphaned in her teens and lived with her sister in another Quaker family. In 1759 when she was twenty-four she began a laconic record of how she spent her time ("Went thrice to meeting; drank tea at Neighbor Callender's") which gradually grew into a regular journal wherein she recorded the details of her life and speculated a little upon them. The last entry was made a few days before her death in 1807.

As a child she had had the great good fortune to go to Anthony Benezet's school, and she knew French as well as English. To a solid basic education she brought an inquiring mind—science and medicine were particularly fascinating to her—and a touch of intellectual (though not religious) skepticism.

At twenty-six after a long courtship she married Henry Drinker, a widower her own age, who after an apprenticeship to a merchant firm, and the requisite trading voyage, had been taken into the company.

For thirteen months the journal lay untouched but for one minor entry, and by the time she began to keep it regularly again "my dear little Sal" had already joined the family. For the ensuing nineteen years pregnancies, miscarriages, births, deaths of four infants, and the weaning and raising of the other five formed the principal focus of her life. Henry, for his part, was on the way to becoming one of the busiest men in Philadelphia, constantly "from home" on business or on Quaker affairs, for his progress in business was paralleled by his gradual accumulation of responsibility in the world of the Friends.

As child after child was born and lived or died, the journal became in part a medical record. Capable of serving as midwife for her friends, Elizabeth Drinker could do little to ease her own very difficult childbirths, "lingering and tedious," as she called them. She liked to nurse her babies, but was often forced for reasons of health to put them out to nurse. Though the family could afford the best doctors in Philadelphia, she was an independent-minded practitioner herself who often went contrary to their advice. When one of her sons fell out of a tree and broke a collarbone, she was pleased to find herself able to help the doctor set it. When newly acquired indentured servants (often under the age of ten) arrived with the itch and with lice and without smallpox inoculation, she undertook to deal with all these problems. Her husband and children fell ill with astonishing frequency. Along the way she read weighty medical books and speculated, sometimes in conversation with her good friend Benjamin Rush, about the cause and cure of various diseases.

The conflict with Great Britain marked a turning point in Elizabeth Drinker's development. Quakers tried to remain aloof, both for religious reasons and because those who were merchants had much to lose. One consequence was that in 1777 Henry Drinker and a number of others were arrested and taken off to prison in Winchester, Virginia. At forty-two Elizabeth Drinker was suddenly head of a household composed of her sister Mary, five children, and five indentured servants, and the British army was about to occupy Philadelphia. While she dutifully trusted that "it will please the Almighty to order all for the best," it was clear that she would have to lend Him a hand, and she prayed for resolution and fortitude.[27]

There were daily challenges. Barrels of flour disappeared, and rumors of widespread looting sped through the town: "Tis hardly safe to leave the door open," she noted; "I often feel afraid to go to bed." Henry's business affairs had to be attended to. One of her servants was first "very impertinent and saucy" and then ran away altogether with an audacious British soldier. Meeting the soldier on the street, Elizabeth Drinker confronted him, demanding that he pay for the servant's time. The British began commandeering blankets and other things. Horses were stolen; wood was scarce; other servants disappeared, to the point that "we have but 9 persons in our Family this winter; we have not had less than 13 or 14 for many years past."[28]

As if they had overheard her, the British authorities arranged to enlarge the family again by quartering a certain Major Crammond, his two horses, two cows, and a Hessian stableboy in the Drinker household. The major kept the family awake with late dinner parties.

In the midst of the effort to keep the household fed, warmed, and healthy, she joined with other wives of incarcerated Friends to visit George Washington on behalf of their absent spouses. By some means which the journal does not make clear, release was arranged and she could thankfully turn back the headship of the household to H.D., as she always called him.

His return was quickly followed by the British evacuation. People who had been too friendly with the enemy were now turned out of their houses, their goods were confiscated, and a few, including some Quakers, were hanged. The Drinkers were understandably nervous, but only one member of the family, Henry Drinker's brother, ran directly afoul the American government. Still, the Americans were worse than the British in expropriating what they wanted (calling it taxation), and good furniture, pewter, blankets, and provisions were hauled off under their eyes. Servants continued to disappear, and they found themselves with only one. When news of Cornwallis's defeat arrived, Quakers who refused to illuminate their houses in celebration were subjected to a mob. Seventy panes of glass were broken in the Drinkers' house.

By the time the treaty of peace was signed, she, like the new nation of which she was somewhat reluctantly a part, had reached a new stage of life. "I have often thought," she wrote in later years, ". . . that women who live to get over the time of Childbareing if other things are favourable to them, experience more comfort and satisfaction than at any other period of their lives."[29] When that was written in 1797 she was certainly commenting upon her own life, which by our standards would not seem to have been precisely one of comfort, whatever it might have enjoyed of satisfaction. Though her last child had been born when she was forty-six, illness continued to be a major theme of the Drinker experience through the rest of her life.

Eleven pregnancies had left her own health uncertain at best; her son William had tuberculosis; H.D. was a constant victim of intestinal disorders and even more of the heroic treatment he received for them; one child had yellow fever and the whole family lived through three yellow fever epidemics; everyone sooner or later had malaria; in the household someone—husband, children, grandchildren, and servants—was always ill. Yet this seemed to interfere very little with the daily routine. Sick people entertained visitors along with the rest of the family, and people down with chills and fever one day were riding their horses off to the country the next. To the twentieth-century mind the whole situation is quite baffling.

Though she regularly worried about the ill health of her daughters, all three married and began at once to have children of their own. One daughter, the youngest, caused a family crisis by running away and marrying "out of meeting" a perfectly respectable young Friend whose only disability, apparently, was that he did not wear the plain dress. Henry Drinker took a hard line: no one was to visit the miscreant daughter. Elizabeth Drinker, after a few months, defied him, noting without contrition: "I feel best pleased I went."[30] Henry finally relented, and Molly and her husband became part of the growing clan of sons and daughters and in-laws.

Elizabeth Drinker attended each of her daughters in childbirth, assisting the midwife and the doctor. After a hard time with Sally's fourth, she recorded that she had slept only two of the preceding fifty hours and noted that she was "much fatigued, bones ache, flesh sore, Head giddy, etc. but have at the same time much to be thankful for."[31] Mother and child had both survived.

Two years later Molly and Sally were in labor at the same time. Sally's delivery was a very hard one; Molly's baby was stillborn. "The loss gives me great concern, not only being deprived of a sweet little grandson, but ye suffering of my poor Child, who lost, what may be called the reward of her labour . . . [and who] may pass through, if she lives, the same excruciating trouble a year the sooner for this loss."[32] In 1799 Sally was in labor with her sixth child and very depressed. Elizabeth Drinker tried to cheer her, reminding her that she was now thirty-nine and this "might possibly be the last trial of this sort, if she could suckle her baby for 2 years to come, as she had several times done heretofore."[33] It is odd that Elizabeth Drinker should have offered this particular argument, since she herself had twice become pregnant while nursing a baby, but it was standard advice from mothers to daughters in the eighteenth century. Neither she nor her daughters made any bones about their dislike of pregnancy and childbirth, though it seems in no way to have diminished their affection for the children themselves. Indeed, rather the contrary, since the burgeoning family was the center of Elizabeth Drinker's life. Children, in-laws, grandchildren moved in and out of the house daily and formed the subject for much of what she wrote. All her children lived nearby and visited each other as well as their parents constantly, sharing carriages, lending servants, sharing summer houses, exchanging children. In 1799 Eliza Downing, a granddaughter, came to spend the winter with Elizabeth and Henry Drinker. "I trust it will be for the child's good," her grandmother wrote, "[I] having no other little ones to attend to."[34] She was much concerned to teach the young people "wisdom and prudence."

The Drinkers included servants in their conception of family — bound boys and girls or indentured adults. Often they came as children of seven or eight. Once there were three black boys under ten at the same time. Elizabeth Drinker gave them careful attention, mending their clothes and trying to teach them. "I have much to do for the little black boys; these small folk ought to be of service when they grow bigger, for they are very troublesome when young."[35] Pretty bound girls were likely to flirt or, worse, to get pregnant. One who had lived with them since she was ten gave birth to a mulatto baby, at the Drinkers' expense. There followed much soul-searching as to what the child's future should be, but it died before they could decide. Elizabeth Drinker, who had raised the mother, thought she was as good a servant as she ever had, but for this "vile propensity" for getting pregnant. She was hard put to understand how all her training in moral values had gone for naught.

There was no doubt in her mind that the "poorer sort" were different from herself, yet some of her former servants were close friends who came back often to visit. When one favorite servant came down with yellow fever, the family reluctantly decided to send her to the yellow fever hospital where, of course, she died. The matter weighed on Elizabeth Drinker's conscience.

She recognized that much of the comfort and satisfaction of her later life was because of Mary Sandwith, who never married, and who chose to care for household things, leaving her sister free to "amuse myself in reading and doing such work as I like best."[36]

The natural world interested her greatly: insects, butterflies, turtles were brought for her inspection by children and grandchildren who knew of her curiosity about such things. Eclipses fascinated her. She speculated as to the causes of all sorts of natural events, and she loved to read about science.

Her reading, indeed, was prodigious. She felt constrained to note in her journal that it was not her sole occupation; but it was certainly an increasingly important part of her life as she grew older. She kept lists of books read, and they encompass most of what eighteenth-century Philadelphia had to offer. She read Mary Wollstonecraft's *Vindication of the Rights of Women* and noted that "in very many of her sentiments, she, as some of our friends say, *speaks my mind.*"[37] Then she read William Godwin's memoir of Mary Wollstonecraft and modified her opinion: "I think her a prodigious fine writer, and should be charmed by some of her pieces if I had never heard of her character."[38]

She read Tom Paine and abhorred what she took to be his dangerous principles. She took *Gargantua and Pantagruel* from the library and, after one quick look, hastily sent it back. She was equally shocked by Rousseau's *Confessions*. She read Swift, seven volumes of Sterne, tracts by Madame Roland, dozens of religious books, Plutarch's *Lives, The Letters of Lady Russell*, medical books, *The Whole Duty of Woman* ("a pretty little book which I have read several times within forty years"),[39] a book on logic, Mungo Park's *Travels in the Interior of Africa*, Edmund Burke, Maria Edgeworth, Wordsworth's *Lyrical Ballads*, Francis Bacon's *New Atlantis*, Paley's *Principles of Moral Philosophy*, and on and on.

While she read and wrote, children and grandchildren (by 1804 there were seventeen) moved steadily in and out; often twenty people came to dinner. Friends from other towns arrived for the Yearly Meeting and lodged with the Drinkers. Henry continued to be the busiest man in Philadelphia, and she remarked that if good works would take a person to heaven he would certainly get there. William, so careful of his health, was her companion for walks and talks. She was not in the best of health herself but was "seldom Idle." She took snuff and taught her grandchildren. Nancy's husband had an urge to move to "ye back woods," and she dreaded the thought. Every year she took stock on the first of January and was surprised to find herself still alive. More and more she enjoyed solitude, which had been disagreeable to her when she was young.

Her son Henry went off to India on one of the Drinker ships and wrote home about seeing a widow burned on her husband's funeral pyre. An old black woman came to call who had been her slave fifty years before, when she and her sister were orphaned, and whom they had sold. Not long after they had been conscience-stricken and tried to buy the child back, but the new owner refused. He had freed black Judey in his will, and now here she sat in the kitchen telling her life story. Elizabeth Drinker observed and reflected on the life around her.

As she grew older, her interest in politics quickened. When John Adams came to town as president, her feelings were at war with her Quaker principles. "He went by our door attended by the Light-horse and a few others. Tho' I am not for parade of any sort, in ye general way, yet on this occasion, everything considered, I should have been pleased to see a little more of it."[40] In 1800 she took note of the disputed election and of Thomas Jefferson's popularity in Philadelphia. She read Fenno's paper and quoted it.

When the new century arrived, she tried to make her own determination of the vexed question: did it begin on the first day of 1800 or the first day of 1801? She decided the latter.

Friend after friend died. The last pages of the journal recorded an endless succession of deaths and funerals, accompanied by the small sense of triumph that oneself was still alive. Sally's death at forty-six bore heavily on her spirit. I have had nine children, she mused, and now my first, third, fifth, seventh, and ninth are all dead.

She fell and bruised herself, and the doctors wanted to bleed her, "which I would not comply with."[41] Old age had brought the courage to resist their violent treatments, of which she had long been rightly skeptical. On the eighteenth of November in 1807 she noted in her journal that the weather was clear and cold, and the moon out. One grandson dropped in; she sent William to make the rounds of all the family dwellings. He came back to report that, but for one toothache, all were in good health. With her world thus in as good order as it could be, Elizabeth Drinker died.

The newspaper spoke of her remarkable personal beauty, her superior education, her journal, and her goodness. Perhaps it was, as she was fond of saying of obituaries of her friends, a "just character." She had lived seventy-two years. Born in a prosperous colony when no more than three-quarters of a million people lived in all British North America, she died a citizen of a nation of nearly seven million. Her own town had grown remarkably in those years, had been the scene of the Declaration of Independence, the Constitutional Convention, and the early years of the new government. James and Drinker, her husband's firm, had exemplified in microcosm much of the mercantile history of the colony and the new nation. Her son who sailed off to India and her son-in-law with a yen for the backwoods were both part of much larger movements.

Yet for Elizabeth Drinker, observant, thoughtful, well-read person that she was, life almost began and ended with family, work, and religion. From the day Sally was born until the day she herself died, she was deeply concerned with the welfare, first of children, then of grandchildren. They were part of her daily experience, even when they were grown and settled in their own houses. She was never without a child in her house and never ceased trying to teach them the ways of righteousness as she saw them. She abhorred idleness and made sure that her journal noted this fact lest some future reader think she spent all her time reading books! And, like Jane Mecom, she believed the Almighty knew what He was about.

One of her descendants, who used her journal to write a medical history of the eighteenth century, confidently asserted that she was an invalid from the age of forty-nine.[42] It is a strange definition of an invalid. Her household and medical responsibilities could each have counted for a full-time job, and while she used her uncertain health as the excuse to provide a certain amount of solitude, she never shirked work. In contrast to certain nineteenth-century women who used ill health as a way of avoiding the challenges of life, Elizabeth Drinker and her children seemed to take it as simply a part of life, a nuisance, perhaps, but not disabling.

Her descendants continued to flourish in Philadelphia, and it is pleasant fantasy to imagine the shock (but secret pleasure, too) with which Elizabeth Drinker might read part of their story in Catherine Drinker Bowen's *Family Affair*.

Eliza Lucas Pinckney

Born almost midway between Jane Mecom and Elizabeth Drinker, in the West Indies, daughter of an army officer whose family had owned land in South Carolina (or just "Carolina," as the family invariably referred to it) and Antigua for three generations, Eliza Lucas came from more favored circumstances than either of the others. The contrast between Jane Mecom's rough-hewn prose and phonetic spelling, and her equally rough-hewn handwriting, and the elegant language, copperplate penmanship, and ritual formality of Eliza Lucas's early letters is remarkable. While Jane Mecom's friends and relatives included people in almost the whole range of the social scale, and Elizabeth Drinker belonged to the solid middle class, with Eliza Lucas we move at once to the top of the scale and stay there.

There had been money to send her "home" to England for a careful education, and, when she was seventeen, her father had settled her, along with her mother and her younger sister, on one of his plantations in Carolina while he carried on his duties as governor of Antigua.

In contrast to the other two, we can see Eliza Lucas clearly in her youth, and an astonishing young person she was. As vigorous and enterprising as the young Franklin or the young Jefferson, she began at once to administer the work of three plantations. For five years she taught the three R's to her sister and the slave children, experimented with new plants, dealt daily with overseers and factors, wrote long letters on business matters to her father and to his business associates, taught herself law and used her knowledge to help her neighbors who could not afford a proper lawyer, and read so much in Locke, Boyle, Plutarch, Virgil, and Malebranche that an old lady in the neighborhood prophesied that she would damage her brain.

A touch of humor and of self-deprecation was all that saved her from being unbearably didactic when she wrote to her younger brothers or younger friends. With older people—especially her much admired father—she was witty and straightforward.

Given her talents and wide-ranging interests, it was no wonder that she found the run of young men dull. "As to the other sex," she wrote, "I don't trouble my head about them. I take all they say to be words ... or to show their own bright parts in the art of speechmaking."[43] Her father proposed two possible candidates for her hand. She thanked him but declined both suggestions, saying of one "that the riches of Peru and Chili if he had them put together could not purchase a sufficient esteem for him to make him my husband." She hoped her father would agree that she should remain single for a few years.[44]

So she continued happily as his agent, writing dozens of letters, dealing with the factor and with the agent in England, supervising planting, instructing overseers, paying debts, and contracting new ones. "By rising early," said this female Poor Richard, "I get through a great deal of business."[45] It was an understatement.

The social life of Charleston appealed to her less than the work of the plantation. "I own," she wrote, "that I love the vigitable world extremely."[46] Loving it meant study, experiment, and constant attention. The most visible consequence of her love affair with vegetables was the development of indigo as a major export crop for South Carolina. At her father's suggestion she began to plant indigo seeds, and when, after several failures, a crop was achieved, she worked with servants he had sent from Antigua to refine the process by which it was prepared as a dye.

A true exemplar of the Enlightenment, she believed religion and right reason could coexist and said that "the soports of the Xtian religion" enabled her to view life's hazards with equanimity. She endeavored to resign herself to events as they came, since "there is an all Wise Being that orders Events, who knows what is best for us," and she believed in subduing the passions to reason.[47]

Migraine headaches hardly slowed her down. It occurred to her to plant oak trees against the day when South Carolina might run out of hardwood. In a careful letter she compared the agriculture of England and South Carolina, somewhat to the advantage of the latter, and observed that "the poorer sort [here] are the most indolent people in the world or they could never be so wretched in so plentiful a country as this." Indolence was, in her view, pretty close to a deadly sin.[48]

This precocious young woman who found men her own age a little boring was intrigued by the intelligent conversation of a man in his forties, Carolina's first native-born lawyer, Charles Pinckney. She had met Pinckney and his wife soon after her arrival, liked them both, and carried on a lively correspondence across the ten miles that separated the plantation from Charleston. He lent her books, encouraged her to report to him on her reading, and enjoyed the discipleship of so eager a pupil. Once, in 1741, she absentmindedly signed a letter to him "Eliza Pinckney."[49]

Three years later in December 1744 Mrs. Pinckney died. On May 2, 1745, Eliza wrote her father thanking him for permission to marry Charles Pinckney and "for the fortune you are pleased to promise me." She also thanked him for the pains and money laid out for her education, which "I esteem a more valuable fortune than any you have now given me." She assured him that Mr. Pinckney was fully satisfied with her dowry.[50]

To a cousin who had warned that she was so particular she was bound to "dye an old maid," she wrote: "But you are mistaken. I am married and the gentleman I have made choice of comes up to my plan in every tittle . . . I do him barely justice when I say his good Sence and Judgement, his extraordinary good nature and eveness of temper joynd to a most agreeable conversation and many valuable qualifications gives me the most agreeable prospect in the world."[51]

She bore with equanimity the talk of the town about their somewhat precipitate marriage, but was righteously indignant when gossip told it that the late Mrs. Pinckney had been neglected in her last illness. Writing to that lady's sister, she said firmly that she would never have married a man who had been guilty of such a thing.[52] As she had earlier striven to please her father, so now she made every effort to please her husband. "When I write you," she told him, "I . . . desire . . . to equal even a Cicero or Demosthenes that I might gain your applause."[53]

Her father seems to have worried lest the strong-minded independence in which he had reared her might not sit well with a husband, and she reassured him that "acting out of my proper province and invading his, would be inexcusable."[54] She and Pinckney apparently agreed that her proper province was a spacious one, since she continued to supervise her father's plantations, assumed some responsibility for Pinckney's as well, and carried forward the experiments with indigo which were in midstream at the time of her marriage.

Her self-improving urge was as strong as ever. She wrote a long list of resolutions and planned to reread them daily. With God's help she hoped not to be "anxious or doubtful, not to be fearful of any accident or misfortune that may happen to me or mine, not to regard the frowns of the world." She planned to govern her passions, improve her virtues, avoid all the deadly sins, be a frugal manager while extending hospitality and charity generously, make a good wife, daughter, and mother, and a good mistress of servants. At the end of this long list of injunctions to herself for ideal behavior she made a typical note: "Before I leave my Chamber recolect in General the business to be done that day." Good advice for any administrator.[55] Once she noted that "nobody eats the bread of idleness while I am here."[56] It might well have been her lifetime motto.

Her married life was as busy as her single life had been. In ten months Charles Cotesworth Pinckney was born. Perhaps the childlessness of Pinckney's first marriage explains the extraordinary eagerness of both parents to cherish "as promising a child as ever parents were blessed with." Eliza could see "all his papa's virtues already dawning" in the infant. A friend in England was asked to find a set of educational toys described by John Locke, while his father set about designing toys to teach the infant his letters. "You perceive we begin bytimes," Eliza added, "for he is not yet four months old."[57]

A second son was born and died. Then came Thomas and Harriott. Though Eliza Pinckney had slave nurses to suckle her infants, she was intensely preoccupied with the training, education, and shaping of her children.

In 1752 political maneuvering deprived Charles Pinckney of his seat as chief justice of the colony, and he left for England to serve as South Carolina's agent there. The family took a house in Surrey and lived much like their neighbors. Eliza Pinckney was appalled at the amount of time the English gentry wasted, especially in playing cards. On the other hand, she loved the theater and never missed a new performance if she could help it. She called on the widowed princess of Wales and found her informality and her interest in South Carolina and in "little domestick questions" very engaging. The boys were sent to school, and Harriott was taught at home. It was a good life, and she was in no hurry to return to South Carolina.

Increasingly concerned by developments in the Seven Years' War, fearful that France might take over a large part of North America, the Pinckneys decided to liquidate their Carolina estate and move to England. To this end they sailed the war-infested sea in 1758, taking Harriott and leaving their sons in school. Three weeks after they landed Charles Pinckney was dead. Eliza Pinckney at thirty-five was once again in charge of a large and complex plantation enterprise. It was just as well, she thought, to have so great a responsibility; otherwise the loss of this most perfect of husbands would have undone her.

I find it requires great care, attention and activity to attend properly to a Carolina estate, tho but a moderate one, to do ones duty and make it turn to account, . . . I find I have as much business as I can go through of one sort or other. Perhaps 'tis better for me. . . . Had there not been a necessity for it, I might have sunk to the grave by this time in that Lethargy of stupidity which seized me after my mind had been violently agitated by the greatest shock it ever felt. But a variety of imployment gives my thoughts a relief from melloncholy subjects, . . . and gives me air and exercise."[58]

In letter after letter she recited Pinckney's virtues, the same ones she had praised when she married him. His religious dedication, "free from sourness and superstition," his integrity, charm, and good temper, "his fine address"—she thought she would never find his like again.[59]

Fortunately she still loved books, agriculture, and her children. It was for the children she told herself (and them) that she worked so hard, overseeing the planting, buying, and selling, writing ceaselessly to England (in several copies since no ship was secure), nursing slaves through smallpox, supervising the education of Harriott. She expected reciprocal effort from her sons. She wrote Charles Cotesworth: "though you are very young, you must know the welfair of a whole family depends in a great measure on the progress you make in moral Virtue, Religion, and learning. . . . To be patient, humble, and resigned is to be happy. It is also to have a noble soul, a mind out of the reach of Envy, malice and every Calamity. And the earlier, my dear boy, you learn this lesson, the longer will you be wise and happy."[60]

She was convinced that happiness for all her children depended in great measure on a "right Education," and she encouraged Harriott; she was "fond of learning and I indulge her in it. It shall not be my fault if she roams abroad for amusement, as I believe 'tis want of knowing how to imploy themselves agreeably that makes many women too fond of going abroad."[61]

She thought highly of female talent. Once a letter from a friend in England came with the seal broken. Perhaps someone had read the letter? No matter; "it may teach them the art of writing prettily . . . and show how capable women are of both friendship and business."[62]

She fell ill, lay four months in her chamber, but was too busy to die. A friend in England wanted seeds of all the trees in Carolina, and she was happy to oblige. The planting at Belmont, her plantation, was following an old-fashioned pattern; she decided to modernize, working harder, she said, than any slave. She revived silk-making experiments begun when Pinckney was alive and endeavored to teach the skill to other women. Harriott's education continued to be one of her chief joys: "For pleasure it certainly is to cultivate the tender mind, to teach the young Idea how to shoot, &c. especially to a mind so tractable and a temper so sweet as hers."[63]

Though she still talked of going back to England, of taking her sons to Geneva for their final polishing, any observer could have foretold that it would never happen. She was busy and, therefore, happy, and the boys were doing well. Both, despite their long absence, were ardent in the American cause, and Thomas had astonished his schoolmates by his articulate opposition to the Stamp Act.

In 1768 Harriott at nineteen married a thirty-five-year-old planter, Daniel Horry, and set about replicating her mother's career. "I am glad your little Wife looks well to the ways of her household," Eliza wrote her new son-in-law; "the management of a Dairy is an amusement she has always been fond of, and 'tis a very useful one."[64] Harriott was soon running much more than the dairy.

While Harriott was busy in the country, her mother set about planting a garden at the Horrys' town house. In her own well-organized household five slaves had each their appointed tasks; none was idle and none, she said, overworked. She herself was constantly industrious.

In such good order, then, were the family affairs in 1769 when Charles Cotesworth Pinckney at last came home from his sixteen-year sojourn in England, already an American patriot. He was at once admitted to the bar and in a month had been elected to the South Carolina Assembly. A year or so later Thomas arrived to join him. The children for whom she had seen herself as working so hard were all launched.

Perhaps, though it would have been out of character, other circumstances would have permitted Eliza Pinckney to slow down at forty-five. But public affairs were in turmoil, and in 1775 both her sons were commissioned in the first regiment of South Carolina troops. Their business and financial affairs remained in the hands of their mother and sister, who were quite prepared to carry on while the men went to war.

It was 1778 before the full force of hostilities reached the Pinckneys. They had chosen Ashepoo, the family plantation belonging to Thomas Pinckney, as the safest place for all their valuables. It was a bad guess. Augustine Prevost's forces burned it to the ground on their way to Charleston, leaving Thomas — as he thought — wiped out and his mother's interest severely damaged. Charles Cotesworth wrote from his military post that of course whatever he had left when the war ended would be divided with them. Eliza wrote to Thomas: "Don't grieve for me my child as I assure you I do not for myself. While I have such children dare I think my lot hard? God forbid! I pray the Almighty disposer of events to preserve them and my grandchildren to me, and for all the rest I hope I shall be able to say not only contentedly, but cheerfully, God's Sacred Will be done!"[65]

The loss of Ashepoo was only the beginning. British troops impressed horses, took provisions, commandeered houses. Eliza Pinckney had to take refuge in the country, leaving her town property to who could know what depredations. In the midst of all this stress Thomas was wounded, Charles Cotesworth, already suffering from malaria, was imprisoned, and two grandchildren were born. In 1780 the British captured Charleston, and by that time plenty had given way to pinched poverty. She owed sixty pounds to a creditor in England and could find no way at all to pay it. For a while it seemed that the fruit of thirty years' hard work was all lost.

Even before the war ended, however, it was clear that Eliza Pinckney's labors had accomplished much more than the building of a prosperous planting interest. She had created an enormously effective family. Planting and business, important as they were, had always taken second place to the upbringing and education of her children. Now, as adults, the three saw themselves, with her, as almost a single entity. The men, at war, often wrote their mother once, sometimes twice, a day. Harriott, who had been Tom's close friend and confidante before he was married, and whom he had always treated as an intellectual equal, continued after his marriage as his business agent and political adviser. For both brothers she managed plantations (as well as her own, after Daniel Horry died), handled money, and looked after their wives and children. They, in turn, took time from their pressing military duties to oversee the education of her son.

After the war, the pattern continued. Both Pinckney men moved into public service. Charles Cotesworth was a member of the Constitutional Convention; Thomas was elected governor of South Carolina by an overwhelming majority and was in office when the state ratified the Constitution. Both were part of the developing Federalist party. Each was to be a foreign envoy and to give his name to important treaties. These careers were made possible by the labors of their mother and sister.

In 1792 Eliza Pinckney developed cancer, and almost the entire family proposed to accompany her to Philadelphia, where a physician with considerable reputation in that field was to be found. She refused to go if they all came along: she could not risk the whole family on one ship. So, while Charles Cotesworth and his children reluctantly remained in Charleston, Harriott took her to Philadelphia. It was too late. She died and was buried there, George Washington at his own request serving as one of her pallbearers.

Building notable families was one of the things American colonials had to do for themselves when they came away from England. Franklin and Drinker were to become well-known family names because of the work and the public service of their men. Pinckney, too, became famous as a consequence of the public service of Thomas, Charles Cotesworth, and their cousin, also Charles. But the family was created, sustained, and developed a strong sense of itself as a consequence of the work, the vision, the exhortation, the constant attention of Eliza Pinckney. Her children carried on the vision to the end of their very long lives, and it is a measure of their success that a modern historian, dealing with eighteenth- and early nineteenth-century Charleston, chose to call his book *Charleston in the Age of the Pinckneys*.[66]

Reflections on the Microcosm

"As familes are such at last the Church and Commonwealth must be," James Fitch remarked in Boston in 1683. More than a century later Chief Justice John Marshall was moved to comment that he had "always believed that the national character as well as happiness depended more on the female part of society than is generally imagined."[67]

It is with similar assumptions that I have tried to learn from the records left by these three women what it was like to be an eighteenth-century person. They take us to the heart of daily life: to scenes of childbearing and nerve-racking struggle to keep babies alive, to scenes of mysterious illness and sudden death, of wartime stringencies and dislocations, to the struggle to "git a living" or—at another level—to get rich. Through their eyes we see the chanciness of life and begin to understand the central role of kinship in providing such security as was possible in a world so filled with uncertainty.

Different as these women were, each put family at the center of life. Eliza Pinckney and her three children viewed the world, not as individuals, but *as a family*. A threat to one was a threat to all; fame and fortune were also shared. They took care of each other's interests, of each other's children, as a matter of course. Tom's rice crop failed and Charles Cotesworth's wife put 500 pounds at his disposal, "cheerfully," his brother noted. The family wanted Tom to stay in London. Earlier, when the British burned most of the family's movable assets, Charles Cotesworth announced at once that all he had left was to be divided among the rest of them. When the brothers went abroad, Harriott had their power of attorney; she made sure their plantations were cared for, their debts paid.

Together they took responsibility for the younger generation. Young Daniel Horry was a spendthrift and showed signs of becoming a monarchist. His grandmother and his uncles tried to set him right, and his debts were settled as a family responsibility. Meanwhile the young women in the family were trained by their aunt and grandmother so that they, too, could run plantations. By the time Eliza Pinckney died the family had a full-fledged "tradition" for many of its activities, and doubtless no one remembered that it had all been created in two generations.

The Drinkers were equally knit together by kinship. The sons-in-law were brought into the family business and encouraged to help each other. When one had business reverses, the whole family helped out. The cousins were grouped around the grandparents and encouraged to see the family as their most basic commitment.

Jane Mecom's life was shaped by her relationship to Benjamin Franklin, but beyond the two of them lay a wide network of Franklin kin, in-laws, cousins in various degrees. Late in life Benjamin asked his sister to send him a detailed and complete list of all their kinfolk in Boston which he could use for reference. He was constantly being asked for help of one kind or another, and he wanted to be sure that he gave the proper priority to blood relations. In-laws were addressed as "sister" and "brother" and were entitled to at least formal statements of affection. They clearly recognized some members of the clan as more "valuable" than others, but blood created a responsibility even for ne'er-do-wells. While historical demographers argue about nuclear and extended families, we must pay close attention to the actual experience of families, and beware of false dichotomies.

Deism may have flourished in certain circles in the eighteenth century, but women's lives were too close to tragedy for such cool beliefs to be very satisfying. A deep need to believe that all the deaths, particularly of children, had meaning encouraged them to believe in a personal God and in life beyond the grave.

No one who reads these pages will doubt that women's lives were different from those of men. In a day when contraception was all but unknown there is no mystery about a sexual division of labor which allotted men tasks in the public sphere and women those which could be carried out at home. Each of these women was pregnant within a month of marriage, and two continued to bear children into their late forties. Eliza Pinckney's family was unusually small for the time, but she was widowed at thirty-five. Shortly before his death Charles Pinckney had discussed with the princess of Wales his plans for his next son.

Nor was it only their own children who kept women close to home. All three of these women were as much involved in raising the second generation as they had been with the first, and Jane Mecom, for a time, was responsible for four great-grandchildren. Grandmothering was an important part of their lifework.

All three believed in work as a moral value. They reserved their strongest criticisms for indolence in any form, and none of them saw old age as justification for idleness. For Jane Mecom and Elizabeth Drinker, "work" was largely domestic, though both dealt also in some mercantile ventures. Jane Mecom ran her own little shop for a while, and Elizabeth Drinker kept accounts for her husband's firm. Eliza Pinckney's work encompassed the larger world of plantation trade. Through most of her life she was busy with shipments, payments, factors, and the like, while she also planned and supervised the actual production of rice, indigo, silk, and the hundred other products of the relatively self-sufficient plantation. Though nominally working, first for her father, then for her husband, and finally for her children, she seems not to have felt any inhibition about acting in her own name, making her own decisions. The fact that legal ownership belonged to father or husband was of no great operational significance.

Woman's life in the eighteenth century was fundamentally influenced by marriage. In a day when conventional wisdom had it that for both men and women it was wise to marry close to home, all three did so. But the luck of the draw varied widely. There is little record of Edward Mecom's life, but circumstantial evidence suggests that Jane Mecom might have done better on her own. Elizabeth Drinker admired Henry, and his success in business provided her with a life of material comfort. Gradually as she grew older, he was replaced at the center of her emotional ties by her son William, and her other children and grandchildren occupied her mind.

Eliza Pinckney was convinced that Charles Pinckney was incomparable, and despite various offers she never married again. During her marriage she had played the role of the properly subservient wife; her father had written to her husband the directions he had once sent to her; and her time had been much engaged in childbearing and child care. Widowed, she assumed the role of head of the family and continued to make vital decisions, even when her sons were grown and had families of their own. With their help she created the "Pinckney Family."

These were only three of millions of women who lived and worked and died in colonial America. In this age of statistical sophistication, it is a bold historian who builds any case upon three examples, yet in these lives we see exemplified cultural values which were those of many of their contemporaries. In their experience we see much of the common life of eighteenth-century woman, no matter what her social class. In another sense, of course, all three were uncommon women, whose achievements tell us something about the possibilities as well as the probabilities for women in their day and generation.

NOTES

1. Jane Mecom to Benjamin Franklin, Aug. 16, 1787, in Carl Van Doren, ed., *The Letters of Benjamin Franklin and Jane Mecom* (Princeton, 1950), p. 296.

2. *Ibid.*, p. 52.

3. *Ibid.*, p. 43.

4. *Ibid.*, p. 84.

5. The original of this letter is lost. It is here reprinted from Jared Sparks, ed., *The Papers of Benjamin Franklin*, 7 (New Haven, 1965), p. 515n. Sparks corrected spelling and punctuation.

6. Van Doren, ed., *Letters*, p. 114.

7. *Ibid.*, pp. 106-7.

8. *Ibid.*, p. 111.

9. *Ibid.*, p. 183.

10. *Ibid.*, p. 189.

11. *Ibid.*

12. *Ibid.*, p. 174.

13. *Ibid.*, p. 171.

14. *Ibid.*, p. 197.

15. *Ibid.*, p. 208.

16. *Ibid.*, p. 210.

17. *Ibid.*

18. *Ibid.*, p. 214.

19. *Ibid.*, p. 221.

20. *Ibid.*, p. 245.

21. *Ibid.*, p. 206.

22. *Ibid.*, p. 230.

23. *Ibid.*, p. 263.

24. *Ibid.*, p. 306.

25. *Ibid.*, p. 322.

26. *Ibid.*, p. 275.

27. H. D. Biddle, *Extracts from the Journal of Elizabeth Drinker* (Philadelphia, 1889), p. 49.

28. Typescript of manuscript journal, Dec. 7, 11, 14, 1777, Historical Society of Pennsylvania, Philadelphia; hereafter cited as Ms. Journal.

29. *Ibid.*, Feb. 26, 1797.

30. Biddle, *Extracts*, pp. 292-93.

31. Ms. Journal, Apr. 5-8, 1795.

32. *Ibid.*, June 14, 1796.

33. *Ibid.*, Oct. 23, 1799.

34. *Ibid.*, Dec. 20, 1798.

35. *Ibid.*, Dec. 26, 1794.

36. *Ibid.*, Jan. 1, 1802.

37. *Ibid.*, Apr. 22, 1796.

38. *Ibid.*, 1799 (n.d.).

39. *Ibid.*, 1799 (n.d.).

40. Biddle, *Extracts*, p. 313.

41. Ms. Journal, Jan. 1, 1807.

42. Cecil K. Drinker, *Not So Long Ago* (New York, 1936), p. 10.

43. Elise Pinckney, ed., *The Letterbook of Eliza Lucas Pinckney* (Chapel Hill, 1972), p. 27.

44. *Ibid.*, p. 6.

45. *Ibid.*, p. 7.

46. *Ibid.*, pp. 34-35.

47. *Ibid.*, p. 49.

48. *Ibid.*, pp. 29, 19.

49. *Ibid.*, pp. 39-40.

50. Harriott Horry Ravenal, *Eliza Lucas Pinckney* (New York, 1896), pp. 69-70.

51. *Ibid.*, p. 94.

52. Eliza Lucas Pinckney to Miss Bartlett, Manuscript Division, William R. Perkins Library, Duke University, Durham, N.C.

53. Ravenal, *Pinckney*, p. 90.

54. *Ibid.*, p. 100.

55. *Ibid.*, pp. 115-18.

56. *Ibid.*, p. 245.

57. Pinckney to Miss Bartlett.

58. Pinckney, ed., *Letterbook*, p. 144.

59. *Ibid.*, pp. 100-102.

60. *Ibid.*, p. 168.

61. *Ibid.*, p. 142.

62. *Ibid.*, p. 152.

63. *Ibid.*, p. 181.

64. *Ibid.*, p. 243.

65. *Ibid.*, p. 276.

66. George C. Rogers, *Charleston in the Age of the Pinckneys* (Norman, 1969). The Pinckney Family Papers in the Library of Congress, Washington, D.C., provide ample evidence that the three children of Eliza Lucas Pinckney continued to operate as a family through the rest of their long lives. From Charles C. Pinckney's receipt book we learn that in 1796 Harriott was acting as "attorney for General Pinckney" and paying his bills. It is clear that through the whole time Tom was abroad she took care of both his plantation and his financial affairs. In August 1815 Charles wrote Harriott asking her to look into and inform him about a certain machine he had heard of for the manufacture of cotton goods. As late as 1822 the two of them were cooperating in the search for black-seed cotton to plant. These are only samples of their continued habit of working as a unit. The large number of "My dear Harriott" letters from both brothers would make an interesting book.

67. Fitch is quoted in Edmund Morgan, *The Puritan Family* (New York, 1966), p. 143. The Marshall quotation is found in Frances Mason, ed., *My Dearest Polly: Letters of Chief Justice John Marshall to His Wife* (Richmond, 1961), p. 140.

EMMA WILLARD AND ALMIRA LINCOLN PHELPS

All the women of the "Self-Portraits" were still alive when Emma and Almira Hart were born in 1787 and 1793, respectively. Women of this new generation, however, were destined for a vastly different life experience. Both Harts aspired to be serious scientists; both grew up to become leading figures in the world of education. At mid-century the newspapers referred to "Mrs. Willlard" or "Mrs. Phelps" without finding other identification necessary. Both of these women came across my horizon in the early 1960s as graduates of the Troy Female Seminary turned up in the southern mansucripts, nearly always as leaders in their local communities. Sometime in 1963 I read Almira Hart Lincoln's The Female Student *and completely missed its significance. Over the years I told my students about Troy and remarked that if only we had some way of tracing the lives of its graduates we would be able to say something about the effect of higher education on early and mid-nineteenth century women. But, I always added, of course, that would be impossible.*

In 1976, looking for something else, I stumbled on a fat volume entitled Mrs. Willard and Her Pupils *and discovered that a committee of Troy alumnae had gathered and published biographical data for more than 3,500 women who had spent some time at the seminary between 1821 and 1871. In a few hours I realized that this was the richest source I had yet seen for the life experience of a large number of educated nineteenth-century women; I also recognized that there was far more data than I could comprehend with pencil and notecards. Fortunately at that moment Patricia Hummer, who had recently taken a degree at Duke, agreed to join me, and together we pressed into service her husband, Alfred Pitts, who was, by great good fortune, a trained demographer and knew how to put a computer through its paces.*

In considerable innocence we composed a code sheet and went to work on the bits and pieces of life stories contained in the printed volume. When coding became too tedious, I varied the routine by trying to find out all I could about the two women: Willard and Phelps. Poking around in the basement of the library at the Emma Willard School in Troy, I found the original manuscript questionnaires upon which the published report had been based—and discovered that a good deal of material had been left out of the printed volume. A number of the pupils had attached long letters to their questionnaires. We had to start our coding all over, but the data were now much richer, and our feeling for the individuals was much greater.

"What, Then, Is the American" was the first fruit of this enterprise, followed by "The Ever-Widening Circle," and then by the essay on Phelps. The second won both the Berkshire Prize and the History of Education Society Prize in 1980. Meantime, Patricia Hummer went off to teach in Michigan and, in her almost nonexistent spare time, to begin working on an essay on the Troy women who became teachers.

Writing even a brief biographical sketch of Emma Willard presented certain difficulties, since her official biographer, preparing his book shortly after her death, had apparently destroyed the 10,000 letters to which he had access. The indefatigable Alma Lutz had collected all the surviving manuscripts and deposited them in the Vassar College Library, but the total amount of primary material was disappointingly small. I have repeated some of Lutz's efforts to track down missing data with the same discouraging results.

In the 1930s an energetic student of Thomas Woody made the same effort to collect material for a biography of Almira Lincoln Phelps. She, too, although more successful than Lutz, was doomed to many disappointments. For example, Phelps's journal, covering seventy-five years, had been burned by her son—possibly on her own orders.

These lives, then, had to be pieced together without vital personal documents which might have provided insight into the inner life and motivation of these two powerful women. I also found the conventions of nineteenth-century prose harder to penetrate than the less self-conscious writing of my colonial women. Would I recognize these two if my magic carpet took me back to the mid-nineteenth century? I am not so certain.

Whether I have gotten the personalities just right or not, I have no doubt that a close study of their work must force a revision of the conventional history of education. A curious myopia seems to afflict nearly all historians of American education, whether traditional or revisionist. For most of them education means the education of children (sex not specified) or of men. Three readers designed by distinguished historians (David Tyack, Rush Welter, and Rene Vassar) for students of educational history contain no word of Benjamin Rush's seminal essay on female education nor of Emma Willard's Plan. James McLachlan's excellent and provocative American Boarding Schools—*a title which suggests inclusiveness—deals only with schools for boys and polishes off women in three sentences. In David Madsen's* Early National Education, *said by its editor to be based on "the best recent scholarship," girls rate two pages, in which there are at least six questionable sentences. Clearly Madsen is not much interested in or acquainted with any scholarship, recent or otherwise, which deals with the role of women in expanding American education. Merle Borrowman's* Teacher Education in America *says not a word about Troy or Mount Holyoke or any of their numerous offspring, which were busy training teachers before the first normal school existed. Jonathan Messerli's* Horace Mann *never mentions Emma Willard or Mary Lyon, though they were the contemporaries in whom Mann was most likely to have been interested. Lawrence Cremin's magisterial volumes contain excellent bibliographical references to women's role in education, but the text is thin on the subject. Along the way Cremin edited a reprint series called "Men and Issues in American Education." So it goes. I hope these essays, along with Kathryn Sklar's work on Catharine Beecher and some of the work now in progress, will help turn the attention of historians of education in a new direction to the seminal importance of the early drive to make higher education available to women.*

What, Then, Is the American:
This New Woman?

The selection of Mrs. Emma Willard to occupy a place in this
gallery of eminent American Teachers was . . . because she is
preeminently a Representative Woman, who suitably typifies
the great movement of the nineteenth century for the elevation
of women.[1]

—The Reverend Henry Fowler, D.D., 1861

Something began to happen among American women in the first decades
of the nineteenth century. In 1782 J. Hector St. John de Crevecoeur had
posed the question, "What, then, is the American, this new man?" that
has challenged historians ever since. Few people noticed that new personality types and new forms of behavior were also appearing among
American women; and historians have paid more attention to the social
constraints of woman's role than to the ways in which talented and
ambitious women first began to break through those constraints.

By the mid-1830s two significant kinds of change were going on: able
women, shut out by social convention from leadership, and often even
from participation, in major social structures, were beginning to build
organizations and institutions that they themselves could control; women
engaged in these organizational and institutional inventions were also
establishing bonds with others similarly engaged, creating networks for
communication and mutual support. These developments, originally the
work of a handful of mavericks, in time contributed to the great nineteenth-
century movement for the "elevation of woman" and changed important
aspects of American society.

Reprinted with permission from the *Journal of American History,* 65 (Dec. 1978), 679-
703.

A detailed examination of the career of one of these new women exemplifies both of these major developments and provides a case study in the means by which a determined woman could reach a position of power and influence in a male-dominated society. The woman in question, Emma Hart Willard, created several institutions herself and trained others to be institution-builders as well, developed a significant female network, gained national recognition as a teacher, organizer, and author, and yet never once admitted that she had stepped out of "woman's sphere." The question "How did she do it?" is of considerable interest.

Much depends, in any life, on timing. Emma Hart was born in 1787, the year of the Constitutional Convention. She was fifteen years old when the Louisiana Purchase added the vast trans-Mississippi west to the national domain and was a young wife with her first child in the year the Boston Associates opened their mill. She grew up at a time of active institution-building.

For two centuries Americans had managed with a handful of familial, religious, political, and economic structures appropriate to a society in which change was measured over generations rather than decades. But by 1815 many individuals and groups were beginning to seek organized ways to take advantage of expanding economic and political opportunities and to deal with the social consequences of that growth. From savings banks to historical societies, from canal companies to benevolent organizations, from schools and libraries to antislavery associations, people were associating themselves together in new organizations and institutions. Alexis de Tocqueville's amazement when he witnessed this phenomenon in the 1830s is well known—to him it seemed a new thing under the sun. Americans, he said, had "carried to the highest perfection the art of pursuing in common the object of their common desires, and have applied this new science to the greatest number of purposes."[2] Interested though he was in American women, he seems not to have noticed, as historians after him also failed to notice, that many of these associations were the work of women, and that these usually served two purposes: an announced, substantive purpose, care for widows and orphans, education, temperance, or abolition of slavery, and an unannounced purpose, providing talented women with an opportunity to exercise their ambitions and develop their abilities.

"Mrs. Willard's Celebrated School," like Thomas Jefferson's University, Tapping Reeve's Law School, Lyman Beecher's church, Horace Greeley's newspaper, was an institution that bore the strong stamp of an individual personality. Its formal name was the Troy Female Seminary, and between 1821 and 1872 more than 12,000 pupils spent some time there. The degree to which they were affected by the experience varied widely, but the surviving evidence gives some credence to the judgment of George Combe, the Scottish phrenologist and friend of most of the leading American educational pioneers, when he described Emma Willard as "the most powerful individual at present acting upon the condition of the American people of the next generation."[3]

Her particular choice of career, again, had much to do with timing. Her life had begun at almost the same time as the great educational surge that followed independence. Many people had followed George Washington's advice in his Farewell Address to promote institutions for the general diffusion of knowledge. These institutions were as diverse as the people who founded them: colleges, lyceums, mutual improvement societies, female seminaries. Together they formed a growing structure of American higher education.[4]

The first schools for women had appeared in the mid-eighteenth century, and after 1815 female seminaries multiplied, particularly in New England, but also in middle Georgia, the Moravian settlements, southern Mississippi, frontier Tennessee, and Ohio. Beginning with Benjamin Rush's *Thoughts on Female Education*, published in 1787, the subject of women's education had become a favorite with college debaters, commencement speakers, ministers, essayists, at least one novelist (Charles Brockden Brown), and with women themselves.[5] The new *American Journal of Education* announced in 1826 that female education was among its prime interests, and Sarah Josepha Hale's *American Ladies Magazine*, launched in 1828, likewise devoted much of its space to the pressing need for improved education for women.

The argument was repeated so often it threatened to grow hackneyed. Just as widespread educational opportunity for men was justified in college charters and public orations as being essential to the preservation of republican virtue (Washington had warned that public opinion must be enlightened), so women's education was repeatedly urged as a way to ensure the wise training of young republicans from the cradle. Piety was linked to learning, and education to the formation of moral character. Women were to be turned from frivolity by serious study and be insured against one of the problems of aging, since a well-trained intelligence could rescue a women from oblivion when she was no longer able to attract men by her physical charm.

A complex set of social changes that coincided with Emma Willard's lifetime gave added force to the idea that women should be taught something more than spinning, weaving, food preparation, and piety, which had been the informal curriculum designed to create "notable housewives" in the age of homespun. In New England, particularly, economic development was already making it difficult for a young unmarried woman to pull her own economic weight solely by domestic industry. Urbanization and factory production of cloth were making domestic production less significant for women of all ages. The westward movement was drawing off more men than women, even as it created a series of rough, new communities in obvious need of the civilizing force of schools. A rapidly growing population meant large numbers of children. As opportunities for men to make money in business increased, proportionately fewer were available to teach school. These developments and others yet to be explored were increasing the size of the potential clientele for schools for women.[6]

Thus republican ideology, economic development, and demographic shifts worked together to prepare the way for educational leaders who could begin to press the outer limits of what had hitherto been defined as appropriate education for women. A set of visible social needs made possible the emergence of a woman who wanted to change the shape and nature of women's education.

Emma Willard's personality, and her sense of her own destiny, were central to her work as an institution-builder. The basic elements of that personality became visible early in her life. Most of what is known about her youth comes from her own and her sister's recollections, which suffer from the usual deficiencies of such accounts written long after the fact.[7] Yet even allowing for the rewriting of the past, which is inevitable in later life, the surviving record leaves no doubt that Emma Hart was an unusual young person. Born on a farm in Berlin, Connecticut, sixteenth of seventeen children in the family, she grew up in a hard-working religious household. In addition to his farm her father had public responsibilities in church and town; her mother (his second wife) she would remember and admire as an almost legendary frugal housewife. Two things seem clear from her later recollections: among the children still at home she was her father's favorite, and even as a child she had unusual drive, energy, ambition, and capacity for concentrated effort.

Such a child was almost bound to be bored in school, and Emma Hart was, until she had the good fortune to encounter young Thomas Miner, an able Yale graduate teaching at the local academy while he saved money to study medicine. Miner and an older woman in the neighborhood recognized the girl's ability and encouraged her to use it. Under their combined influence she began to teach at the local school when she was seventeen.[8] A rural New England classroom in 1804 typically contained pupils of many sizes, ages, and degrees of motivation. There is a recurrent story in the folklore of the teacher who by force of personality and sometimes by physical force establishes control over such a school and is thereafter much admired by the pupils who strive to learn in order to please. In Emma Hart's version of this tale, she used a switch to establish her authority on the first day and never found it necessary again.

Whatever that first day was like, she succeeded as a teacher, for her reputation spread rapidly and brought her new opportunities. At seventeen she had a sense that it was important to know influential people; she made friends easily and—as older men found her interesting—she soon attached herself, as a young person seeking their guidance, to several of Hartford's leading professional men. She was careful also to cultivate their wives.

She had already begun to see herself as having a special mission, one that the Almighty had chosen her to accomplish, and one that would take her beyond the ordinary bounds of a "woman's sphere." Such ambition in a woman exacted a price. In a sympathetic letter written in 1824 to a younger contemporary who was suffering from the constraints society imposed on women's talents, she described a youthful nervous affliction of her own that she attributed to the "peculiar organization of my mind," and to agitation brought on by high hopes that she had not yet found a way to achieve. "It requires the nerves of a man to stand undisturbed the conflicts and inward fires of minds like yours and mine. . . . It is the pent-up fire which causes the earthquake." In her case the "pent-up fire" provided the energy to underwrite her ambition.[9] She worked hard to increase her knowledge and improve her pedagogy.

As her reputation for effective teaching spread beyond Connecticut, invitations came from several communities. At twenty she was in charge of a female academy in Middlebury, Vermont. There, she wrote, "My neighborhood to Middlebury College made me bitterly feel the disparity between the two sexes."[10] Women's educational opportunities must have been meager if a raw, new college could hold so much that seemed desirable. In a characteristic reaction Emma Hart, far from accepting the inevitability of "the disparity between the two sexes," set about teaching herself the subjects the college offered to men.

Then, in 1809, under the influence of what she called "an uncommon ardor of affection," she married one of the town's leading citizens, a medical doctor and public official thirty years her senior. Although she once said that for love of him "I gave up my literary ambition and became a domestic drudge," there is considerable evidence that John Willard, like Miner, played an important part in her intellectual development. Many years afterward she recalled that he "sought my elevation, indifferent to his own. Possessing, on the whole, an opinion more favorable of me than any other human being would ever have,—and thus encouraging me to dare much, he yet knew my weaknesses and fortified me against them."[11]

For many nineteenth-century women marriage was a way to improve one's social and economic position, but Emma Willard did not see hers in that light. She told a disgruntled stepson that she had married his father for love, and not for the usual reasons, offering as evidence the observation that "my standing in society was as good as his. My income arising from the exercise of my talents, of which I was fond, was . . . sufficient for my support."[12] She married him less for "standing in society" or money than for intellectual stimulation and the kind of tutoring he was willing to offer so eager a pupil. He was a self-educated medical man of unusual acumen, independence of mind, and information. She was his third wife, and the gap in their ages made his relationship to her somewhat fatherly. For most of their married life both Willards concentrated on her career.

The five years after her marriage were the only ones in her long life devoted exclusively to domestic pursuits. She gave birth to her only child, managed the affairs of both house and farm with considerable administrative skill, carried on as head of the family during her husband's frequent absence on business and political missions, and continued her program of study. She must have welcomed the financial reverses that, in 1814, gave her a socially acceptable reason for opening her own school—to wit, that she could help her husband recover from financial losses.

From this time forward her life is reminiscent of William Herndon's Abraham Lincoln whose "ambition was a little engine that knew no rest." The new school was scarcely underway when she set herself the goal of making it better than "any heretofore known," and to "inform myself, and increase my personal influence and fame as a teacher, calculating that in this way I might be sought for in other places, where influential men would carry my project before some legislature."[13] Enlisting "influential men" continued for the rest of her life to be an important part of her strategy for getting what she wanted.

"My project" was a secret enterprise. She told no one but her husband, thinking she would be regarded as "visionary, almost to insanity, should I utter the expectations which I secretly entertained in connection with it."[14] She drafted a proposal addressed both to the public and to the legislature of some as yet undesignated state proposing a comprehensive plan for the improvement of female education. That giving advice to legislators was not an accepted part of women's role in 1818 did not deter her at all.

The plan in its final form was polished like a first-rate lawyer's brief. She argued the necessity for educating as many as possible of the women of the country, the impossibility of accomplishing such a large undertaking with private means, and the rationale, therefore, for publicly supported female seminaries. Her proposal was carefully designed to prevent "a jealousy that we mean to intrude upon the province of men."[15] Her central argument was the familiar one that educating women would elevate the character of the whole community, since children receive better nurture from educated mothers. To this she added her own conviction that mothers, in order to do their job, needed to be trained in psychology, or, as she phrased it, needed to study "the nature of the mind." She adverted to the familiar statement that the republic must have an educated citizenry to survive and argued that this required universal public education. There were not enough men to staff a system of common schools; hence the only way the state could meet its responsibility for educating all its children was by training women to be teachers. She also suggested that hiring women would save money, since they could afford to teach for a smaller wage—an argument she lived to regret.

The *Plan* was one of those formative documents in the history of American culture that laid out a set of ideals and expectations so persuasively that it set the terms of discussion for half a century. It was destined for a long career, independent of its immediate purpose, and succeeded, as she had hoped it would, in spreading her views and in making its author's name known in distant places. As was her habit, she turned to a knowledgeable man for guidance, and, on the advice of the father of one of her pupils, sent it with a long and somewhat flowery letter to DeWitt Clinton, the governor of New York, who had shown a great concern for education. There is no record of what she was doing, or thinking, during the ten months that elapsed before he replied, praising her work and assuring her that the *Plan* itself was evidence of "the capacity of your sex for high intellectual cultivation." He said nothing about what he might do, but in his next message to the assembly he recommended that it look into legislation for improving women's education in the state.[16]

With this much encouragement, the Willards had the *Plan* printed, distributing copies to a number of bookstores, including some in New York City and Philadelphia, to be sold on consignment. They went to Albany, where Emma Willard read and discussed her *Plan* with any group of legislators who would listen. She solicited letters of support from John Adams, Thomas Jefferson, President James Monroe, and lesser lights. She asked her friends, women as well as men, to write members of the legislature and suggested that they persuade their influential relatives to write also. She assured Clinton that if the money for a model female seminary were to be appropriated nothing would prevent her from "embarking her reputation" on the execution of the project. It was to be simultaneously a great public undertaking and a major personal effort.

This vigorous lobbying was not as successful as she had hoped. The legislature did grant a charter to a female seminary at Waterford, New York, and toyed with the idea of granting it an appropriation from the Literary Fund, but in the end no money was forthcoming. The idea was one whose time had not yet come. Emma Willard thought wildly of appearing before the legislature herself to plead the case. "I felt it almost to a frenzy. . . . Could I have died a martyr in the cause, and thus have insured it success, I would have blessed the faggot and hugged the stake."[17]

The historian, trying to pierce the mist that veils the past to see clearly this able, ambitious young woman behaving in ways so far from those prescribed for her sex, gets a little help from John Lord, her authorized biographer. Lord lectured at Emma Willard's school and had access to her letters and diaries, now apparently lost. On the basis of these he believed that by 1819, at the age of thirty-two, "her soul panted for a wider sphere," and she longed for "some institution which she could direct."[18] The cause of women's education and her own desire for a position of influence in the world were by now closely intertwined.

Though the New York legislature failed to meet their hopes, the Willards did not give up. Instead they moved from Middlebury to Waterford to take charge of the seminary, which did at least have a state charter and which might become eligible for a grant from the Literary Fund. Gathering pupils and teachers as she went along, Emma Willard set out to create a model school, hoping that example would persuade the legislature if argument would not. She was by now developing both a pedagogical and an administrative philosophy. The first was a compound of Johann Pestalozzi and John Locke, with a good many additions of her own. She understood the pedagogical principle that has to be constantly rediscovered by educational reformers: start where the student is. Thus, in her geography classes the first assignment was to draw a map of one's hometown. From Pestalozzi she took the principle of using concrete objects for teaching, and from her own conviction came an emphasis on "order" and "system."[19]

From the most able young women among her pupils she selected assistant teachers and was soon able to create a faculty. Those who, like herself, were seeking an outlet for ambition, were strongly attached to her, and some became lifelong friends and associates in the building of a model school.[20] At Waterford Emma Willard adopted from the men's colleges the practice of holding public examinations. She lured members of the legislature, governors, and Supreme Court justices to attend. The young women were thoroughly prepared and so impressed observers that many were converted into supporters of the *Plan*.[21] To her developing skills as a teacher and organizer she was adding those of public relations.

In the midst of all this activity she did not neglect politics and public policy, an interest she dated from her childhood and her father's knee.[22] In 1820 she published a pamphlet, *Universal Peace to be Introduced by a Confederacy of Nations Meeting in Jerusalem*, a proposal for a league of nations a century before the idea became a staple of western diplomacy.

Though the Waterford school gained rapidly in reputation, the legislature did not provide the expected funds, and the town fathers were not ready to fill the financial gap. Meanwhile, down the Hudson, citizens of the ambitious and growing town of Troy were more alert to the commercial advantage of having a good female seminary and offered to provide both a building and a committee of women overseers if the Willards would move their school there. After some careful negotiations, and encouraged by convincing promises of long-term support, the move was made in 1821. Various teachers and pupils came along, and Troy became Emma Willard's base of operations for most of the rest of her long life.

Like Jefferson's university, chartered by the state of Virginia in the year that Emma Willard's *Plan* appeared, Troy Female Seminary was the founder's mind writ large. Like Jefferson, she planned the layout of the building, organized the curriculum, chose the books, and dictated the diet. Her interest in details extended to the careful placement of roommates. She liked to combine "spoiled and petted misses" with serious young teachers-in-training, saying that the teachers would need soon enough to learn how to cope with spoiled brats, and the latter might (though she was never unduly optimistic about undoing the effects of parental indulgence) be inspired to higher ideals by living with hardworking companions.

Convinced that the only possibility for achieving universal education lay in multiplying the number of women teachers, and convinced, too, though she did not say it so often, that women were usually better teachers than men, she designed a revolving scholarship program. Ambitious young women who could not pay Troy's high tuition were educated on credit with the understanding that they would repay her from "the avails of their teaching." Her part of the bargain was to find them jobs.[23] In addition, a few talented pupils were able to pay their way by working as assistant teachers while they studied, a kind of apprenticeship that was soon recognized by potential employers.

Except for language teachers who were recruited abroad, the Troy faculty consisted of Emma Willard's trainees, who paid as much attention to pedagogy as to substance. Amos Eaton, a self-made botanist, a dedicated Pestalozzian, and a gifted teacher, was building a science curriculum at the new Rensselaer Polytechnic Institute in Troy, and willingly admitted women to his classes. In addition, he gave individual tuition to her younger sister, Almira Hart Lincoln, a widow with two young children who had joined the staff in 1824. Almira Lincoln, under Eaton's tutelage, experimented with inductive methods of teaching science: she and Eaton may have been the first teachers in the country to permit their students to carry out their own experiments. With his help, she prepared for her classes a botany text that became a best seller, used in colleges and schools for nearly fifty years. Troy soon had a reputation unique among female seminaries for its instruction in science. Mathematics was stressed, and the capacity to deal with higher mathematics was offered as evidence of women's intellectual potential.

While her sister wrote textbooks in science, Emma Willard composed books in geography and history (the first in collaboration with William Woodbridge) to suit her own methods of teaching. The search for fame was never far from her consciousness, and the books were one way to achieve it. Nor was the money they brought in unwelcome.[24] Her vision grew. Like Lyman Beecher, who sought to spread his version of New England culture through the union by educating and sending on their way "intelligent and enterprising ministers," Emma Willard aimed to impress her cultural values on the developing society through the agency of well-trained women teachers who would go out, not only nearby but also to the growing South and West and, wherever possible, found schools modeled upon the original.[25]

Troy was to be the fountainhead and her goal was nothing less than to make it the best school for women in the country, with a curriculum equal to that of the New England men's colleges and a pedagogy better than theirs. By 1833 she was convinced that the colleges might learn something from examining her methods. She thought she accomplished more, and in a shorter time, than they did. Troy's reputation grew rapidly, and in due course at least one woman would enroll for a few weeks, solely "for the influence the name would give me."[26]

Part of this growing reputation came from solid accomplishment: teachers coming from the school were so well trained that demand for them soon outran the supply. Some of her time was required each day to answer letters from would-be employers. Troy graduates were taking over or founding schools in various parts of the country and sending back to Troy for staff. In addition, well-educated and confident young women were returning to the towns and cities of New York and nearby states to marry members of the rising professional class. Lawyers, judges, college presidents, and members of Congress found wives among Troy alumnae: William Seward, Eliphalet Nott, Mark Hopkins, Henry B. Stanton were a few of these. Meanwhile, Emma Willard's and Almira Lincoln's textbooks carried their authors' names across the country and occasionally across the sea.

The school's reputation and that of its founder developed *pari passu*. John Willard died in 1825, and Emma Willard took over the business side of the school and the responsibility for her own financial affairs, conducting them with such acumen that her style of life increasingly befitted that of a leading citizen. She continued to recognize the need for good public relations and to coax members of the legislature and the judiciary to public examinations. She admitted daughters of Troy's leading citizens at whatever age their parents wished; she kept in close touch with former pupils.

She was not willing, however, to rest on her laurels. Good as the school was recognized to be, it fell far short of her vision. She wanted to have no pupil younger than sixteen, to have a clearly marked three-year course that all would follow, to have only boarders so that her control could be complete, and to offer only an advanced curriculum. She wanted a permanent endowment and a faculty made up of specialists. Neither the necessary preparatory institutions nor the necessary public understanding and willingness to supply money yet existed to underwrite such ideals. As things were, she had to admit girls of all ages, had to accept pupils for only one year or even one term if their parents insisted, had to admit day students as well as boarders, and had to cope with many who were only prepared for the most elementary course work. She had not yet been able to persuade the legislature to give Troy a charter and provide it with money. Feeling both her success and the great weight of what she had not achieved, she decided in 1830 to go abroad in search of wider horizons. Turning over the management of the seminary to Almira Lincoln, and, taking her twenty-year-old son along for propriety, she set sail for Europe.

She was Edward Gibbon's ideal traveler, displaying "the flexible temper which can assimilate itself to every tone of society from the court to the cottage; the happy flow of spirits which can amuse and be amused in every company and situation."[27] From Paris she sent home careful descriptions of buildings, art works, and the Chamber of Deputies for the edification of her pupils, and she sought out women who shared her interest in education. During her six-month stay she visited every kind of French family, including that of the maid in her pensione; had clothes made so that she could discuss French life with seamstresses; recruited teachers; bought art works for the seminary; and presided over her own salon where politics and education were the central topics. Like other Americans before and since, she was surprised that her schoolbook French served her so ill among the Parisians, but characteristically she began at once to take daily lessons.[28]

A carefully cultivated friendship with the marquis de Lafayette, begun when he had made a ritual visit to the seminary on his grand tour in 1826, opened many doors, including those of royalty. "How differently," she reflected, "at different periods of our lives do similar events affect us. At fifteen I was all in a flutter at the thought of entering on a village ball-room, with plenty of company; how could I then have believed that a time would come when I should enter the court of France alone, pass through a long room . . . without any particular emotion whatever."[29] She examined the state of women's education in France and decided it was deficient and that the country was paying a high price for this deficiency.

Gathering letters of introduction to English educational reformers, she moved on to the British Isles where women's education again seemed to her sadly inadequate, though Scotland appealed to her as the home of "the graves of some of the fathers of my mind." She returned to Troy "not reluctantly, but gladly"—more than ever convinced of the importance of what she was doing there.

The European tour added to her education and to her self-confidence. Elizabeth Cady Stanton, a pupil at Troy at the time, recalled years later her first sight of Emma Willard upon her return from Europe. She had, Stanton wrote, "profound self-respect (a rare quality in woman) which gave her a dignity truly regal."[30] The trip had also improved her credentials in America. Her *Journal and Letters* were quickly copied by a team of Troy pupils and teachers and sent off to the printer. The woman exhibited in its pages was a careful and astute observer, a person who spoke her mind with considerable freedom, and one who—after seeing the best the old world had to offer—was happily returning to continue her mission in the new. She was ready, indeed, to move upon a larger stage.

The opportunity presented itself almost at once. Emma Willard joined many other Americans in the romantic enthusiasm for the effort of the Greeks to free themselves from Turkish rule. She was acquainted with the work of John and Frances Hill, Episcopal missionaries, who were in Athens attempting to set up a school, and was convinced that Greek society was just then "dissolved into its original elements" and hence fluid enough, as France and England were not, to take a truly progressive step by setting up a school to train women teachers who would thus be ready to help shape the society as the new independent nation took form. Her observations on the continent had confirmed her view that what she called "the tone of society" depended very much upon the degree of education among its women.

To carry out her plan for the Greeks, she turned to a tool that she would use increasingly in the years to come: a voluntary association of women. She organized the Troy Society for the Advancement of Education in Greece to raise money for a teacher-training school, which would be supervised by a Troy graduate who, by good fortune, was already in Athens. Willard gave lectures, contributed the royalties from her recently published *Journal*, and recruited to the cause her friends Lydia Sigourney and Sarah Josepha Hale, both influential names among American women. To old friends and Troy alumnae she sent circulars to be spread among "your most influential ladies." In a typical letter she wrote: "Perhaps you will do well to go round and see them, and consult them in the first place, and get them individually stirred up, and then appoint a meeting, which I hope will result in your forming a cooperating society. . . . I hope you will be corresponding secretary; and further (which I take a deep interest in) I hope you will be a delegate to our convention on the 8th of August. I hope to get together at that time a number of the most talented . . . women in the country."[31] The association raised $3,000 for the school in Athens, and, more significant in the long run, Emma Willard had learned something about the potential of the growing network of women, among whom Troy alumnae were key figures, which she had been developing.[32]

Even among the citizens of Troy who knew her well, such aggressive assumption of leadership on the part of a woman was not altogether acceptable. There were, she told Sigourney, "slanderous aspersions" that her work on the Greek project had been less for the benefit of Greece than for her own fame. To diminish this kind of talk, she had declined to take the presidency of the association, but in the end, as she wrote her sister, she got "more praise to my face than even I like."[33] Leadership in public affairs was more and more exhilarating, and her self-confidence continued to grow.

She began to feel herself at a crossroads. Her personal standing and influence in the country at large had never been greater, but for some reason not entirely clear she had not yet succeeded in obtaining a charter for the school from the New York legislature, nor the permanent endowment she felt to be so necessary if the seminary was to have a secure future. She did not think the men who controlled the city of Troy were giving their wholehearted support to the school. With these thoughts in mind, she toyed with several possible lines of action. The University of Vermont was in financial trouble, and it occurred to her that one solution would be to make it into a female university with herself at the head. At the same time, since her textbooks were bringing in a comfortable income and she owned a house in Middlebury, she considered retiring to Vermont to devote herself entirely to writing.

Things came to a head in the spring of 1833 when the time came to renew the school's lease with the Corporation of Troy. She spelled out the issues in a "Memoir" composed for the seminary trustees, who had apparently been troubled by rumors of her flirtation with the University of Vermont, and who wanted to know her future plans. In this carefully drafted if somewhat wordy document, she first laid before them the alternatives open to her: she could retire to Vermont and write, thereby taking better care of her health (a matter she considered of some importance, she told them, to a "mind which fancies itself gifted"). She had no doubt that if she had time to write, her fame would increase.[34] Having established the fact that she had more than one option, she spoke of her sense of duty to the cause of female education and education in general. "I have the satisfaction of believing my past labors have had a beneficial effect upon the general frame of society among us," she observed, indicating that with the right encouragement she would continue such labors.[35] If the trustees were willing to take responsibility for developing stronger support for the seminary among their fellow citizens, above all if they would work to raise a permanent endowment, then she would consider staying after all.

But only, she made clear, on her own terms. She wanted a new building as well as a professor of chemistry and natural philosophy who was also a good classical scholar. To assure them that no part of her demand was for personal gain, she offered to contribute $500 from her own pocket for these improvements. She also wanted a new lease that she, but not they, could terminate at will. The trustees had expressed fear that she might marry again; she assured them that this was unlikely since she had come to enjoy her independence. Admitting that her demands were a bit one-sided, she nevertheless jusitifed them. How could she run a school if she never knew when the Corporation of Troy might unexpectedly cancel the lease? On the other hand, if she should choose to leave they should have no complaint since "it is the spirit within me which has wrought to do what I have already done, so it is only by giving that spirit its play by confidence and encouragement that you can expect me to do things, whereof your city may be glad hereafter. It is that spirit you want, not me without it. Depress it by want of confidence and encouragement so that I lose hope of accomplishing what I desire, and the sooner you are rid of me the better."[36]

Did they find this peculiar? Well, she concluded, "If I had not been somewhat of a peculiar woman I should not have been here at this time negotiating as I am."[37] And indeed the "Memoir" showed her to be a tough negotiator in her own interest. Communicating with a group of men whom she knew well, she spent no time in ritual obeisance to the idea of woman's sphere or male superiority. Instead, she laid out the issues as she saw them and stated her demands boldly.

Unfortunately, at this exciting moment, the record becomes obscure. What the trustees said to her or she to them at the meeting is not known. One can only infer that since she did not leave, and since four years later the long-awaited charter was achieved, she got her way.

The events of 1838-39 marked a break in Emma Willard's life to be followed by a series of new directions. Before analyzing these changes, one of the techniques she developed in a continuing quest to increase her influence in promoting women's education and women's progress must be examined: the building of a female network. Similar networks developed in increasing numbers as the nineteenth century passed, and by 1900 there were dozens of interlocking ones, some visible, some obscure, which provided women with powerful tools available for many different purposes. As far as it can be determined, Emma Willard and her younger contemporary, Catharine E. Beecher, were the first to grasp the possibilities inherent in such networks and the first to experiment with institutional links among women going beyond a single community.[38]

In Emma Willard's case the beginnings were not planned. As soon as a few pupils of her Middlebury School were trained to be teachers, she found places for them and encouraged them to take charge of schools whenever possible. An illustration of the almost inadvertent way the network began can be found in the biography of Julia Pierpont, whom Emma Willard sent to Sparta, Georgia, to open a school in 1819. Sometime in the following five years, Pierpont married and had a child, but by 1824 both husband and child were dead, and the young widow came to Troy for further training. In 1832 she married Elias Marks, an unusual schoolman from South Carolina who had first studied medicine and then had become interested in women's education. He had once laid before the South Carolina legislature a proposal quite similar to Emma Willard's *Plan*. By the time of his marriage, he had created a school for women in Barhamville, just outside Columbia, South Carolina. When his wife joined him, the school was remodeled to meet Troy standards and renamed the Barhamville Collegiate Institute. Soon it became a center for intellectually aspiring young southern women. Emma Willard and Julia and Elias Marks were in regular communication. A South Carolina scholar who studied the history of Barhamville found himself tracing the second generation of

Willard influence. "The far reaching hand of the Barhamville Institute in Southern culture in the days of its extension to the Southwest," he concluded, owed "much of its skill and influence to the Northern institution."[39]

Caroline Livy, who studied at Troy for four years beginning in 1837, provides another example of Emma Willard's expanding network. Livy married a minister, J. M. Caldwell, and moved south with him. In 1845 she became principal of the Rome Female Academy in Georgia, and according to her son, presided, in due course, over the education of 5,000 girls. He concluded that the influence of this Troy graduate "in moulding the afterlife of her pupils and thus refining and elevating the community cannot be overestimated."[40]

As time went by, other new outposts were established. Not long after Almira Lincoln married John Phelps, she became head of a school in Patapsco, Maryland. Although modeled on Troy, it was modified by Almira Phelps's mind and character. Younger sisters do not usually care to be complete replicas of their elders.

Sarah R. Foster had taught for awhile before she decided at the age of thirty-one to enter Troy for additional education. Like many others, she admired Emma Willard and "yielded herself implicitly" to her direction, which meant, after her training, being sent to Cadiz, Ohio, to take charge of two schools. At the end of four years, she had established a sufficient reputation to be sought after as principal of the Female Seminary in Washington, Pennsylvania. According to an admiring pupil, she infused a new vigor into the school that was felt throughout the area. Eight years later, she paused to marry a minister, but did not give up her school. On the contrary, she added to her responsibilities the long-distance oversight of two additional schools, one in West Virginia and another in Ohio. Described as having a character that inspired respect, she was reported to have intimidated James K. Polk, who remarked that she was the only woman whose strength of personality ever made him lose his presence of mind.[41] Her executive ability was the source of wonder among her neighbors, and she energetically spread Willard principles in three states. She continued in full charge of the Washington Female Seminary until the age of seventy-two.

The original pattern of deploying young women as missionaries in the cause of women's education began without a preconceived plan; but when Emma Willard sensed the potential influence of her network, she set about systematizing and strengthening the ties that kept it alive and functioning. As early as 1832, she traveled in a private carriage from Troy to Detroit, spending almost every night in the home of a former pupil, reinforcing feelings of loyalty to her and to the Troy idea. She also seized the opportunity to spread her view among parents and friends of alumnae, many of whom were influential people in their local communities.[42] By now Emma Willard was a confident and charming woman in her mid-forties, and the father of one former pupil described her as the most attractive woman he had ever met.[43]

In 1833 the network had successfully campaigned for a teacher-training school in Greece. In 1837 Emma Willard institutionalized network activities in the Willard Association for the Mutual Improvement of Teachers, with nearly 200 members, a list of honorary members, and another list of honorary members drawn from "literary ladies" who approved of her plan for educating teachers.[44] The following year she published a distillation of her years of thought on the subject of pedagogy. Members were reminded that one of the principal objects of the association was to communicate correct views about female education to teachers of different sections of the country and to gather facts that could form the basis for lobbying.[45]

When Emma Willard began in the 1840s to meet with superintendents and teachers in New York State to discuss the work of the common schools, she expanded her network to include women who would agree to form community associations for common-school support. In 1846, with her niece Jane Lincoln, she traveled 8,000 miles to all the states south and west of New York except Florida and Texas. She visited former pupils, collected old debts, lectured on pedagogy, and again tightened the bonds among Troy alumnae, while encouraging them to organize local associations for the common schools. She followed up her visits with extensive correspondence. Thus Troy teachers spread through the republic to train others and to convince community leaders of the importance of women's education. Sometimes Willard's vision verged on hubris, as when she said in an offhand moment that if enough Troy graduates could marry southern leaders perhaps the sectional conflict could be resolved!

The network, as it developed, was made up of a series of concentric circles. At the center was Emma Willard herself. The smallest and most integrated circle was made up of the carefully selected teachers who stayed on at Troy and carried on the seminal work of the seminary under the founder's watchful eye and control. Next was a larger but still well-integrated circle of women who made teaching a lifelong career and who founded or headed schools of their own. This circle was incorporated in the association and strengthened by regular communication. Largest and most loosely attached of the circles contained the thousands of women who had attended Troy for anywhere from one to ten years, who had gone on to domestic lives as wives and mothers or as single women living with parents or siblings. Many of these were active in the local associations for the common schools, and many took part of their adult identity from their association with Emma Willard.

Among the inner circle, one member had been selected to carry on when the founder herself should decide to give up active direction of the school. Sarah Lucretia Hudson came to Troy as a pupil when she was eleven. She became an assistant teacher, a teacher, and then assistant principal. In 1834 she married John Willard, the only son of the principal. (Could this have been simply fortuitous, or was it, too, part of Emma Willard's plan?) Thus it was that in 1838 when Emma Willard decided to take the step the trustees had feared, and engaged herself for a second marriage, Sarah Lucretia Willard became principal, and her husband, as his father before him, took on the task of business management.

The failure of Emma Willard's second marriage[46] had little bearing on her life as an institution-builder. But having given up direction of the seminary, she found herself, in less than a year, looking for a new outlet for her energies. The result was a second career, related to but in some respects quite different from her first. When she left her husband in the spring of 1840, her first stopping place was her old home in Connecticut that was still inhabited by many members of her extended family. There she encountered Henry Barnard, just then in the midst of his crusade to improve common-school education in Connecticut, inspired as he described it "with the zeal of Peter the Hermit."[47] When Emma Willard returned to her hometown to collect her wits and plan her next step, Barnard swept her along with his great enthusiasm and persuaded her to stand for the post of school superintendent for the town of Kensington. Elected overwhelmingly, she set up a model school where she both taught children and conducted a "normal class" for teachers. In addition, she organized the mothers of the community into the Female Association for the Common Schools and encouraged them to undertake a wide variety of responsibilities. First, they were to seek out every "forlorn and neglected" child in order to provide clothing and to ensure school attendance. Then, through a systematic effort, they were to make life for teachers more attractive so that able young women would be willing to accept teaching jobs. Finally, she urged mothers to study with the children in order to "keep up with the improvement of the times." If "you would but try it," she said, "you would find that your mature mind would with little labor master subjects that require pains to teach the young."[48] She encouraged mothers to invite their children's classes to meet in their homes as a way of promoting this adult education. It was her conviction that the more thoroughly the women of the community were involved with the work of the common schools the better those schools would be.[49]

The work of the women she organized, together with a very successful public examination of the pupils, fired the Kensington community with educational enthusiasm. The experiment was widely reported in the educational press, and Willard was soon much in demand for pedagogical lectures. Everywhere she went, she organized women's associations similar to the one in Kensington, and gradually she came to believe that women should take full charge of the educational activities in every community. Her conception of proper behavior did not permit her to lecture in public to mixed groups. Often she wrote out her lecture so that it could be read for her by a male friend, but upon occasion she solved the problem more directly, either by inviting people to meet with her in a private home, where she could cast her lecture in the form of conversation or, even more simply, by sitting instead of standing in a public place, again, so that the "lecture" became merely "conversation."

She was also diplomatic as she actively encouraged women to take on new public responsibilities. Her methods of work and the way she bowed to cultural restrictions without being really limited by them are illustrated by two draft resolutions she suggested whenever she went into a community to work with teachers, superintendents, and parents. The first resolution was to be passed by the men only: "Resolved: That we will forward the cause of the common schools by inviting the ladies of the districts to which we severally belong—as we may have opportunity—to take such action in the common schools of each district, as may seem to us, that they are peculiarly fitted to perform; and such as we regard as properly belong to their own sphere in the social system." For the women she drafted the following: "Resolved: that if the men, whom we recognize, as by the laws of God and man, our directors, and to whose superior wisdom we naturally look for guidance, shall invite us into the field of active labor in the cause of common schools —that we will obey the call with alacrity, and to the best of our abilities fulfill such tasks as they may be judged to be suitable for us to undertake."[50] Having thus taken care of the social mores, she urged the women to take responsibility for everything having to do with the schools.

There was talk of appointing her head of a proposed normal school, and she toyed with the idea of buying an orphan asylum that was on the market in Hartford, thinking she would form the orphans into a demonstration school for teacher-training. She also consulted with friends about founding an educational journal. In the end, however, the pull of Troy proved to be too strong. Her son urged her to return, and in 1844 she moved into a house on the school grounds. Lucretia Willard remained the principal and operating head of the seminary, but Madame Willard, as she was now called to distinguish her from her daughter-in-law, was a powerful presence. She was fully informed of every detail of life at the school, entertained selected pupils at tea, recruited new students from her vast range of acquaintances, tutored some specially favored daughters of old pupils for their exams (while firmly informing their mothers that, of course, nothing could be done to excuse them from those same trials by fire), and presided over the public examination when Lucretia Willard was incommoded by one of her frequent pregnancies. She was also available to lend a hand at the obstetrical event. The former principal continued to write and revise textbooks, composed two scientific treatises, traveled at home and abroad, corresponded frequently and at length with her network of teachers, as well as with Barnard and a large group of other educational reformers. As always, she wrote long letters of advice to political figures.

The events leading up to the Civil War inspired her to one last burst of organizing activity. This time she initiated an association of women to petition Congress for a compromise solution to the slavery conflict; the group gathered 40,000 signatures. The content of the petition did not mark Emma Willard's finest hour, for while she would have been glad enough to see slavery end, she was also willing to make concessions to the South to avoid war, which she considered an evil greater than slavery. Neither the petition nor her *Via Media*, another proposal for compromise, published in 1862, deserve high marks for moral sensitivity. They do represent evidence of her continued vitality and her incorrigible urge to take charge of the world and straighten it out when it was off track.

When the war came, she applied for a federal contract to produce clothing for the army, planning to provide employment for the poor women of Troy, especially for wives of soldiers. She did not get the contract, but if she had it is certain that one part of the clothing for Lincoln's armies would not have been made of shoddy. She had to content herself—at the age of seventy-four—with being president of the General Relief Association of Troy women.

When she died in 1870, the New York *Times* published a somewhat garbled story of her life and called her the most famous teacher in America. She was indeed a fine teacher, organizer, and leader in the evolving movement to offer higher education to women. To be all these things, however, she had to find a way to work within the framework of social expectations about women's proper behavior without allowing that framework to hamper seriously her very large plans or to limit her ambition. The skill with which she did this is attested by the fact that while she achieved a public career stretching over fifty years, she was seldom criticized for stepping out of her place.

Living in an age when American men were busy associating themselves in institutions and organizations to achieve a wide variety of goals, she saw the possibilities in such association for promoting her own central goals. But obstacles stood in the way of an ambitious woman. If a man, for example, wanted to organize a business, all he needed in order to borrow money was a good name for credit, something for collateral, and a friend or two who had money to lend. A woman with similar ambition found herself at once embroiled in legal complexities, especially if she were married. Similarly, a man who wanted legislative support for some enterprise, business or eleemosynary, could go to the legislature, make his wishes known, trade favors perhaps, wine and dine if necessary. Women's methods in such a situation had to be more roundabout. Men wishing to build public support for any idea could take to the platform and the newspapers to persuade the public of the wisdom of their plans. Such avenues were virtually closed to women.

A close study of Emma Willard's projects and methods shows how a determined women dedicated to bringing about change could overcome these complexities and obstacles, without alienating the men who controlled the money and power she needed, and how she could build a highly successful career by using for her own ends social stereotypes about women's place. Her *Plan* was the first public call for the state to support the higher education of women. In the pursuit of this goal she developed ways of dealing with male politicians, whether in the legislature or in the Corporation of Troy.

Getting the political support she wanted took a long time (Troy

Female Seminary was not incorporated and made eligible to receive money from the Literary Fund until 1837), but in the meantime she created and staffed her school and began to use her growing network of teachers trained at Troy to spread her ideas from one end of the country to another. The result was a significant change in the patterns of women's education. Along with her younger contemporaries Catharine Beecher and Mary Lyon, she initiated a movement that, by the end of the century, would see 50,000 women enrolled in some institution of higher education each year.

She also played a significant—and almost unremarked—part in the common-school crusade and in the movement for normal schools in Connecticut and New York. Combining her experience in teacher-training with her firm belief in women's voluntary associations, she went about giving lectures to teachers and superintendents, and at each persuaded the men to "invite" the women in their communities to take a larger role in running the common schools. This allowed her to teach women the possibilities inherent in voluntary associations. In all her activities she provided her pupils and the women whom she brought together in these associations a striking example of a woman who had no hesitation about undertaking large projects and administering large enterprises; watching her, they could learn something of the techniques for effective functioning in a male-dominated society. Few lessons could have been more useful to an ambitious nineteenth-century woman.

NOTES

1. Henry Fowler, "Educational Services of Mrs. Emma Willard," in Henry Barnard, ed., *Memoirs of Teachers, Educators, and Promoters and Benefactors of Education, Literature and Science* (New York, 1861), p. 167.

2. Alexis de Tocqueville, *Democracy in America*, ed. Henry Steele Commager (London, 1946), p. 377.

3. Quoted in Alma Lutz, *Emma Willard: Daughter of Democracy* (Boston, 1929), p. 193.

4. For some provocative thoughts on this development, see Douglas Sloan, "Harmony, Chaos and Consensus: The American College Curriculum," *Teachers College Record*, 73 (Dec. 1971), 221-51.

5. Thomas Woody, *A History of Women's Education in the United States*, 2 vols. (New York, 1929). Though now outdated in many ways, this monograph was in its time a monumental accomplishment and so far no modern scholar has

had the courage to undertake a thorough revision. For information about many long vanished schools, see I. M. E. Blandin, *Higher Education of Women in the South prior to 1860* (New York, 1909). On the post-Independence ferment on the subject of educating women, see Linda K. Kerber, "Daughters of Columbia: Educating Women for the Republic, 1787-1805," *The Hofstadter Aegis: A Memorial*, ed. Stanley Elkins and Eric McKitrick (New York, 1974), pp. 36-59.

6. For essential background on the developments in the men's colleges in the first half of the nineteenth century, see David Allmendinger, *Paupers and Scholars* (New York, 1975).

7. Emma Willard's sister, Almira Lincoln Phelps, recognized this deficicency when she wrote, "Who can describe himself truthfully. . . . Even ourselves, as we were last year or even yesterday, we cannot paint to the life, for the most difficult of all knowledge is that of self." Almira Lincoln Phelps, *Reviews and Essays on Art, Literature and Science* (Philadelphia, 1873), p. 183.

8. F. B. Dexter identifies Thomas Miner as a son of a country parson, graduate of Yale in 1796, who studied law but because of bad health began to teach at Berlin; he later studied medicine. Dexter singles Emma Willard out as one of two pupils of whom Miner was particularly proud. She always spoke of him as her much valued friend. Dexter calls him one of the most learned physicians of his time. F. B. Dexter, *Biographical Sketches of the Graduates of Yale College with Annals of the College History*, 6 vols. (New Haven, 1885-1912), 5:206-10.

9. Emma Willard to Harriet Munford, Dec. 26, 1824, typed copy in the Archives of the Emma Willard School, Troy, N.Y. Mary Lyon and Elizabeth Cady Stanton used similar metaphors. Lyon spoke of a "fire shut up in my bones," and Stanton said: "My latent fires shall sometime burst forth." All three women were behaving in ways that were socially deviant, while maintaining in varying degrees the outward mein of respectable ladies. It was a strain. Marion Lansing, ed., *Mary Lyon as Seen through Her Letters* (Boston, 1937), p. 129; Theodore Stanton and H. S. Blatch, eds., *Elizabeth Cady Stanton as Seen through Her Diary, Letters and Reminiscences*, 2 vols. (New York, 1922), p. 102.

10. John Lord, *The Life of Emma Willard* (New York, 1873), p. 34.

11. Fowler, "Educational Sevices of Mrs. Emma Willard," p. 134.

12. Lutz, *Emma Willard*, pp. 43-44. It may be significant that in no written record was she ever referred to as Mrs. John Willard but always as Mrs. Emma Willard.

13. *Herndon's Life of Lincoln* (Cleveland, 1949), p. 304; Lord, *Life of Emma Willard*, pp. 34-35.

14. Fowler, "Educational Services of Mrs. Emma Willard," p. 134.

15. Ezra Brainerd, "Mrs. Emma Willard's Life and Work in Middlebury," read at Rutland, Vt., Sept. 20, 1893, and printed for private distribution by a member of the Troy Female Seminary, class of 1841.

16. Lutz, *Emma Willard*, p. 644.

17. *Ibid.*, p. 81.

18. Lord, *Life of Emma Willard*, p. 46. Lord's book inadvertently provides insight into the ambivalence of a well-intentioned, even admiring, nineteenth-century man confronted with an amibitious, driving woman. He admired Willard

and so always was at pains to assure his readers that she was indeed a proper Christian lady; but he was also a good reporter, so that his facts sometimes contradict his assertions. Thus he could write that her only purpose in all her work was to make women better wives and mothers (a purpose he could approve), while at the same time he reported in detail her ambition to step beyond the restricted sphere allotted to women, her desire to become a person who influenced legislatures, commanded institutions, rewrote scientific theories, and set public policy. Once, in a forgetful moment, he praised her for her "good sense and masculine force."

19. Willard's pedagogy is too important to be briefly summarized and will be treated in some detail in a separate article. The point here is that its success contributed to the growing recognition of her ability in the community.

20. An example from the brief Waterford interlude was Miranda Aldis, who first studied with Willard and then became her collaborator in the composition of textbooks. She also read law with her father and worked as his legal assistant. Comparatively late in life she married a lawyer, for whom she performed the same office. Willard to Miranda Aldis, Dec. 26, 1824, Archives of the Emma Willard School; see also the files of the Emma Willard Association at the same location.

21. Willard to Sally Russ, Apr. 19, 1820, Archives of the Emma Willard School.

22. Emma Willard, *Journal and Letters, from France and Great-Britain* (Troy, N.Y., 1833), p. 48.

23. In 1839, the first year for which records have been found, half the pupils were receiving tuition on credit. This may have been the highest proportion in any year.

24. William Woodbridge's and Willard's *Geography* was the first of its kind and went through a number of editions.

25. For a discussion of Lyman Beecher's cultural imperialism, see Richard Lyle Power, "A Crusade to Extend Yankee Culture, 1820-1865," *New England Quarterly*, 13 (Dec. 1940), 638-53.

26. Pamelia Murray recollection, Archives of the Emma Willard School.

27. John Murray, *The Autobiographies of Edward Gibbon* (London, 1896), p. 270. Landing at Le Havre her first thought was to observe peasant homes and peasant dress, noting "human beings ever interest me most." Willard, *Journal and Letters*, p. 14.

28. Willard, *Journal and Letters.*

29. *Ibid.,* p. 202.

30. Quoted in Lutz, *Emma Willard*, p. 173. Stanton's recollection was part of a speech she made at the Emma Willard Reunion at the Chicago World's Fair in 1893.

31. Lord, *Life of Emma Willard*, p. 177.

32. The teacher-training program was incorporated into the school run by John and Frances M. Hill, and the association supported young Greek women as students for a number of years. For a brief biographical sketch of Frances M.

Hill, see Edward T. James, Janet Wilson James, Paul S. Boyer, eds., *Notable American Women, 1607-1950*, 3 vols. (Cambridge, Mass., 1971), 2:191-93.

33. Lord, *Life of Emma Willard*, p. 161.

34. "Memoir Addressed by the Principal of the Troy Female Seminary, April 21, 1833, to the Trustees," Vermont Historical Society, Montpelier.

35. *Ibid.*, pp. 4-6.

36. *Ibid.*

37. *Ibid.*, addendum.

38. For a discussion of some of Catharine Beecher's experiments, see Kathryn Kish Sklar, *Catharine Beecher: A Study in American Domesticity* (New Haven, 1973), pp. 168-83. The earliest one is described in Catharine Beecher, *Educational Reminiscences* (New York, 1874), pp. 62-65.

39. Handwritten notes of Henry Campbell Davis, deposited in South Caroliniana Library, Columbia. Davis tried to trace the influence of Troy in the South and West, particularly in South Carolina, and concluded that it was "an important fact in the history of culture in America." Apparently, none of Davis's research has been published. Julia Marks's daughter felt strongly that her mother was "acting in union," as she put it, with Willard and Phelps and that the three together were the leading educators of women in the country. See her letter to the women collecting material for *Mrs. Emma Willard and Her Pupils*, Archives of the Emma Willard School.

40. Mrs. A. W. Fairbanks, ed., *Mrs. Emma Willard and Her Pupils, or Fifty Years of the Troy Female Seminary, 1822-1872* (New York, 1898), p. 45.

41. "Manuscript questionnaire for Sarah R. Foster," Archives of the Emma Willard School.

42. A study of 3,501 Troy alumnae made by the author in collaboration with Patricia Hummer shows at least 268 fathers to have been public officials. There were many daughters of congressmen, governors, and judges among the pupils.

43. Diary of Thomas Bog Slade, Southern Historical Collection, University of North Carolina Library, Chapel Hill.

44. Emma Willard, *Letter Addressed as a Circular to the Members of the Willard Association for the Mutual Improvement of Teachers; Formed at the Troy Female Seminary, July 1837* (Troy, N.Y., 1838).

45. *Ibid.*

46. The strange lapse of judgment which led Emma Willard to marry Dr. Christopher Yates, whose interest in her turned out to be mercenary, has never been explained satisfactorily. Apparently he promised to help her publish what she considered to be her important work on the circulation of the blood, but he showed his hand when he demanded that she pay for the wedding supper. She took the difficult step of going to the Connecticut legislature for a divorce and was given permission to resume her name. Willard merely said that her husband found her fame and sense of own abilities "inconvenient." See Lord, *Life of Emma Willard*, p. 201.

47. See Henry Barnard to Horace Mann, Feb. 13, 1843, Mann Papers, Massachusetts Historical Society, Boston.

48. Letter from Willard to Mrs. Hotchkiss, secretary of the Kensington Female Association in Aid of the Common School, Apr. 20, 1841, Henry Barnard Papers, Library of New York University, New York.

49. The Parent-Teacher Association of modern times is usually believed to have had its origin in the late 1890s with the foundation of a national Congress of Mothers. No reference to Willard's association of mothers has been located, but she founded a great many of them in the two decades after 1840.

50. Willard to Barnard, Nov. 18, 1845, Barnard Papers.

The Ever-Widening Circle:
The Diffusion of Feminist Values
from the Troy Female Seminary,
1822-72

"Should women learn the alphabet?" asked a nineteenth-century feminist, intending irony, and suggesting what we all know, that education can lead to unforeseen and unintended consequences, social and personal. If schools accomplished only their announced purposes, if pupils learned only what they came to learn, the work of the historian of education would be easier than it is.

The Troy Female Seminary, officially opened in 1821 but tracing its roots to 1814, was the first permanent institution offering American women a curriculum similar to that of the contemporary men's colleges. The founder stated her purposes clearly: to educate women for responsible motherhood and train some of them to be teachers. It is only in retrospect that the school can be seen to have been an important source of feminism and the incubator of a new style of female personality.

The development and spread of nineteenth-century feminism represented a major value shift in American culture, the consequences of which reached into almost every aspect of personal and social life. The underlying reasons for this shift, and the mechanism by which new ideas about women's role spread, continue to puzzle and intrigue cultural historians. One reason — there were many others — was a dramatic increase in the number of well-educated women. To examine the mechanism involved, we need first to suggest a way of looking at the distribution of traditional and feminist values in the population.[1]

Reprinted with permission from the *History of Education Quarterly* 19 (Spring 1979), 3-25.

Historians usually divide nineteenth-century women into three groups: a tiny handful of feminists, known to their contemporaries as "strong-minded women," another small group of anti-feminists who were articulate about what they saw as the threat to family life inherent in feminist values, and a large undifferentiated mass of women untouched by feminism at all.

Such a classification is too crude to be useful. Not only does it fail to account for a great many particular cases, but it is also static, except insofar as it assumes that members of one group occasionally go over to another. A different kind of description comprehends a much larger amount of the evidence, provides a more accurate way of describing change, and is helpful in explaining some apparent paradoxes. Let us imagine a continuum that looks like this:

Feminist values

100	90	80	70	60	50	40	30	20	10	0
0	10	20	30	40	50	60	70	80	90	100

Traditional Values

Such a continuum has a place for everybody. At one end were the handful of radical feminists, who began early in their lives to question the whole conception of "woman's sphere" and the old definition of woman as a creature of emotion rather than reason, inherently self-abnegating, born to serve others, and defined by her sex. At the other end were the women who believed all these things and who, comfortable in their assigned role, felt no need to question the underlying value structure. What is more important, this continuum has a place for the very large number of women who were not at either end, but somewhere in between, often holding some part of each set of values simultaneously. It also accommodates those who were in motion, moving toward the feminist end of the spectrum.

Large numbers in the middle or in motion should not surprise us, since changes in the key values of a society or a social group rarely occur as sharp and sudden breaks with the past. When the wind has been blowing from the west for a while, the waves of the sea roll consistently from that direction. If the wind shifts to the south, the ocean waves will continue to roll from the west for a time, but soon, cutting across them, will be waves coming from the south, crisscrossing, and slowly the older

wave system will diminish to be replaced by the new. So it is with broad
social attitudes, the old and new often exist not only side by side, but
also cut across each other. We know from observation that people have
an astonishing capacity to hold ideas which reason and logic would call
contradictory.

In retrospect, the thought and behavior of women who were still
attached to the older values while they were experimenting with the new
has sometimes seemed paradoxical, but they were simply exhibiting the
ambivalence which is common when values are in the process of change.
Indeed, the most effective purveyors of new values were often those who
had some attachment to the old and therefore were not so frightening.
There were also many active feminists who used the old values as a shield
against criticism. In so doing they inadvertently misled historians who are
only beginning to realize that, while radical feminists were few, women
who were to some degree affected by the "woman movement" were
numerous.[2]

If the changing state of women's self-perceptions and value structures
did not simply involve a few radicals, but was rather one of the major
phenomena shaping nineteenth-century social history, it is important to
examine the various ways the new values spread.[3] A good deal of attention
has justly been paid to reform movements and voluntary associations as
seedbeds of feminism, but the early seminaries and pre–Civil War colleges,
insofar as they have been attended to at all, have been seen as bulwarks
of tradition. A close look at the history of Troy Female Seminary and its
alumnae in the framework I have just sketched suggests a different
conclusion.

Like many individuals, Troy as an institution combined an allegiance
to certain well-defined ideas about what was proper for women with
subversive attention to women's intellectual development. Its founder and
head, Emma Willard, provided a powerful example of a "new woman"
whose achievements were made possible because of her ability to integrate
new values with the prevailing ones. Her life work, she always said, was
to further "the progress of my sex," yet she adhered to the ideology of
woman's domestic role (though with a very broad definition of domestic)
and to the idea of separate spheres and spoke highly of the patriarchal
family. By carefully selecting from her own words it would be possible
to paint her as a prime exemplar of "true womanhood," or as a
thoroughgoing feminist. In fact, she was both, and in this fact lay much
of her effectiveness.

Between 1821 and 1871 more than 12,000 women spent some time at Troy, and due to the efforts made by a group of alumnae in the 1890s, biographical data for more than 3,500 of these women were gathered and preserved. From these and related materials it is possible to piece together the process by which Emma Willard made her very proper female seminary into an early source for and disseminator of certain feminist ideas.[4]

Her stated goals show how, almost from the beginning, she deftly combined an appeal to the prevailing view of woman with a revolutionary emphasis upon women's intellectual capacities and with an innovative proposal for broadening "woman's sphere" to include professional work. The educational program and the atmosphere of Troy were quite different from those of most female seminaries, and the process by which Willard spread her message and the ingenious ways in which she institutionalized this process of dissemination are all part of a complex pattern. The biographies of women who attended the school show how the Troy experience affected at least some of them.

Emma Willard's Views and Methods

Emma Hart was born in 1787 in Berlin, Connecticut, next to the last of seventeen children. She was a precocious child who had good luck in her early teachers, and by the age of seventeen was herself teaching in a village school. Her reputation spread, and at twenty she took charge of a female academy in Middlebury, Vermont, where the presence of a new college exacerbated her frustration at being denied higher education. While steadily developing her own affinity for the intellectual life, she began to feel a divine call to improve women's educational opportunities.[5]

In 1809 she married a much older man (who encouraged her ambitions), had a child, and began to formulate a comprehensive plan for the improvement of women's education, which, when it was finished and polished, she presented to the governor of New York, asking him to submit it to the legislature. She proposed that the state provide money for a group of first-rate female seminaries, better than any then existing. Her argument ingeniously combined tradition and innovation; it ran like this: (1) It is the duty of government to provide for the present and future prosperity of the nation. (2) This prosperity depends upon the character of the citizens. (3) Character is formed by mothers. (4) Only thoroughly educated mothers are equipped to form characters of the quality necessary to insure the future of the republic.

After describing the structure and curriculum necessary for such superior schools, Willard went on to argue that the educated citizenry essential to the success of republicanism could only be created by universal primary education. To provide that, women would have to be trained to be teachers, since there were not enough men available to staff common schools for all the children. Earlier republican experiments had failed, she said, because of "inadequate attention to the formation of the female character," and only educated women could prevent the inevitable "destruction of public virtue" when the country—as it was bound to do—grew large and rich.

By adopting her plan, she said, the legislature could bring into being a population of moral, hardworking women, whose taste for intellectual pleasures would prevent them from loving "show and frivolity." Such women, taught to seek "intrinsic merit," would be prepared, whether as mothers or as teachers, to raise children of good character. Further, able women who "yearned for preeminence" could achieve it as administrators of these publicly supported schools for their own sex.

The first nation to give women "by education that rank in the scale of being to which our importance entitles us," she wrote, would add to its national glory. "Who knows how great and good a race of men may yet arise from the forming hands of mothers, enlightened by the bounty of that beloved country,—to defend her liberties, to plan her future improvements and to raise her to unparalleled glory?"[6]

The argument that the preservation of the republic depended upon educated women had been around for decades, but she added three innovations: (1) that the state should spend public money to provide what amounted to colleges for women, something which did not at that time exist anywhere in the world; (2) that women were capable of intellectual excellence in any field; and (3) that women should be specifically trained for a profession. Willard's plans thus went far beyond anything previously proposed.

The idea of teacher-training itself was relatively new. From the beginning the men's colleges had recognized a mission to prepare their graduates for the learned professions, the ministry, law, medicine, or college teaching. Many young men taught school for a while before or after college, but usually as a steppingstone to another career. What Willard proposed was to treat school teaching as a serious profession and to open it to women, who had hitherto gotten much the shorter end of the educational stick.[7]

Troy Takes Shape

Members of the New York legislature spoke in praise of the *Plan*, but did not appropriate any money. It remained for Emma Willard to create from private sources, and with the help of the Corporation of Troy, a school where she could endeavor to approximate her ideal.

For tactical reasons she had distinguished between colleges (which were for men) and a seminary planned especially for women. In fact, however, Troy bore a remarkable resemblance to the contemporary men's colleges. Willard, like her male counterparts, the presidents of Brown, Amherst, Williams, Dartmouth, and Union, used a domestic metaphor, speaking of her pupils as "daughters" as they did of "sons." Like them, she emphasized the building of character as the chief aim of education, dwelt upon the importance of the Christian religion, and gave weekly lectures aimed at instilling moral values. Like them, she taught the senior course in mental and moral philosophy, using Lord Kames, Paley, and later Wayland as her texts. She was, says her first biographer, "one of the first modern educators to dwell on bringing out the latent powers of the mind . . . and this was the great revolution she made in female education."[8]

The curriculum included mathematics, science, modern languages, Latin, history, philosophy, geography, and literature. An early enthusiast for the teaching of science, Willard had the good fortune to become a friend of Amos Eaton (a key figure in the founding of the Rensselaer Polytechnic Institute, also in Troy), who welcomed young women to his classes and helped develop a science program for the seminary. He took Almira Lincoln, Emma Willard's sister and protegé, as a sort of graduate assistant, and together they set pupils to doing their own experiments, perhaps the first teachers in the country to do so. All three were interested in the psychology of learning and were stimulated by the ideas of Johann Pestalozzi.[9]

Although it was difficult for young women to find schools to prepare them for an advanced curriculum, the difference between the Troy students and their male counterparts either in preparation or in the quality of their educational accomplishment was not very great.[10] Indeed, it might be argued that in some ways Troy was leading where the colleges would later follow, in its reliance upon a pedagogy which demanded that pupils think for themselves, in its science program, and in the teaching of modern languages. There can be no doubt of its innovative spirit with respect to women; nowhere else in the country in the 1820s were young women told that they could learn any academic subject, including those hitherto reserved to men, that they should prepare themselves for self-support, and that they should not seek marriage as an end in itself. To underline this last point, Willard provided "instruction on credit" for any woman who would agree to become a teacher, the debt to be repaid from her later earnings. Willard could, of course, find her a job. (See Table 1 for an analysis of the effects of this program.) The school was hardly under way before she was running a flourishing teacher placement agency, and the demand soon outran the supply. Someone commented that Emma Willard's signature on a letter of recommendation was the first form of teacher certification in this country.

In addition to the shaping force of an intellectually demanding curriculum and high expectations, there was the imposing personality of Willard herself.[11] Where else in the 1820s and 1830s could young women daily see one of their own sex, married and a mother, yet founder and administrator of what they all knew to be the best-known school for women in the country, author of best-selling textbooks, advisor to politicians, formulator of scientific theories, a woman unafraid of any challenge, who had, as Elizabeth Cady Stanton remembered when she looked back to her school days at Troy, "profound self-respect (a rare quality in a woman) which gave her a dignity truly regal."[12]

In certain settings Emma Willard was forthright about her feminism. "Justice will yet be done. Women will have her rights. I see it in the course of events," she wrote five years before Sarah Grimké's *Letters on the Equality of the Sexes* and fifteen years before Seneca Falls.[13]

Yet this same woman often presented herself as a model of female respectability who gave voice to traditional values. She wrote Catharine Beecher: "In reflecting on political subjects my thoughts are apt to take this direction: the only natural government on earth is that of the family— the only natural sovereign the husband and father."[14] The early rules of the seminary included the following: "Above all preserve feminine delicacy. Let no consideration induce any young lady to depart from this primary and indispensable virtue. . . . Each pupil must be strictly careful to avoid the least indelicacy of language or behavior such as too much exposure of the person in dress."[15]

TABLE 1. The Revolving Scholarship 1839-63 (based on Annual Reports)

	Instruction on Credit (for those intending to teach)	Number Sent out to Teach
1839	100	43
1840	100	54
1841	36	38
1842	24	28
1843	(not given)	25
1844	30	25
1845	14	12
1846	14	25
1847	14	14
1848	17	17
1849	29 (+4 partial)	31
1850	29 (+9)	24
1851	34 (+6)	27
1852	18 (+5)	35
1853	42 (+3)	36
1854	22	50
1855	22	27
1856	24	34
1857	17	(not listed)
1858	30	12
1859	22 (+5)	12
1860	12 (+1)	12
1861	11	7
1862	3 (+3)	9
1863	5 (+3)	—
TOTAL	669 (+39)	597

NOTE: Annual reports begin in 1839, after Troy was chartered by the New York legislature and thus made eligible for a small subsidy from the Literary Fund, the subsidy being based on the number of pupils receiving full-time instruction. It is possible that instruction on credit was at its peak in 1839. It may also be significant that a normal school opened in that year, and others soon followed, so that women wishing to be trained as teachers had other options. However, note that the largest single group of teachers left the school in 1854. If the average for the years before 1839 was approximately the same as the average for the years for which we have information, the total number of teachers would have exceeded 1,000.

In her the "true woman" and the feminist co-existed, and, however much ambivalence this may have caused her from time to time, it was one source of her influence.

The Uses of a Network

Pupils who began to leave the seminary as early as 1822 to marry or teach, or both, were agents of cultural diffusion, spreading Willard's ideas about women's capacities and about the need for women's education, and often setting an example by their interest in study and learning. George Combe, the phrenologist and friend of Horace Mann, observed what was going on at Troy and labeled Emma Willard "the most powerful individual at present acting upon the condition of the American people in the next generation." She herself hoped that "educated women who are rising up" would prove capable of "investigating our rights and proving our claims . . . it is to the future lives of my pupils, taken as a body, that we must look, as the test of our success."[16] A poem she wrote for a pupil about to take charge of a female academy summed up her philosophy: "Go, in the name of God/Prosper, and prove a pillar in the cause/ of Woman. Lend thy aid to waken her/from the long trance of ages. Make her feel/ She too hath God's own image."

By regular correspondence and visits she bound the alumnae to her and provided support and reinforcement for what, in many parts of the country, were seen as advanced or dangerous views about women's education. Bit by bit she created a network of former pupils spreading to the northwest, the southeast, and then to the southwest, a network held together by a common belief in women's capabilities and by personal relationships. By 1837 when she made part of this network formal by organizing the Willard Association for the Mutual Improvement of Teachers, it had been in the making for sixteen years. In a pamphlet written for members of this group she spoke of guiding them in the execution of their "important duties, that not only yourselves may obtain benefit, but the thousands of the rising generation who are under your instruction."[17]

Several examples show how the network developed. Julia Pierpont, a Willard pupil in Middlebury, had been sent by her mentor to Sparta, Georgia, in 1819. There she opened a school, married, and had a child. Both husband and child died, and in 1824 Julia Warne, as she then was, came to Troy for further study. Afterward she returned South and married Elias Marks, author of a proposal to the South Carolina legislature along the lines of Willard's *Plan*. Together they took charge of the South Carolina Collegiate Institute at Barhamville and endeavored to build a southern version of Troy. They remained part of Willard's closest inner circle.[18] In the 1930s a South Carolina scholar, intrigued by the pervasive influence of Troy in his state, identified more than 100 South Carolina women who had had some connection with the seminary and concluded that directly, and through the agency of Barhamville, Troy's influence had been a major factor in the shaping of southern culture in the years it was spreading to the southwest.[19]

Before Julia Warne left Sparta, a replacement arrived in the shape of Elizabeth Sherrill. Sherrill, whose mother had been Emma Willard's Middlebury housekeeper, had served an apprenticeship as an assistant teacher at Troy. In Georgia she married an army officer whom she induced to resign from the army and join in her educational career. The two went on to take charge of an academy in Augusta and continued part of the network for many years.

Urania Sheldon finished Troy in 1824, taught first as a governess, then set up her own school in Washington County, New York, and was invited to move it to Schenectady. After seven years there her reputation was such that the trustees of Utica Female Academy built a house to induce her to take charge of their school. This she did and administered it until 1842, when she became the third wife of Eliphalet Nott, the almost legendary president of Union College.

Example after example might be described. Caroline Livy, who studied at Troy from 1837 to 1841, married a minister and set out for Alabama. En route, they were persuaded to settle in Rome, Georgia. Her husband found a church which suited him, and she became principal of the local female academy. Rome was then a small frontier community, which had been part of Cherokee Georgia until Andrew Jackson's Indian Removal opened it to white settlement. More than 5,000 girls were said to have studied under Livy's direction (and that of her husband, who later joined her in the enterprise). She had five children along the way. It was her son's perhaps somewhat biased judgment that "her influence in moulding the afterlife of her pupils and thus refining and elevating the community cannot be overestimated."

Other outposts of Troy appeared in many parts of the country. Almira Lincoln Phelps became head of the Patapsco Female Institute in

Maryland and largely modeled her program upon that at Troy. Sarah Foster, described as having "conceived the greatest admiration for Mrs. Willard and yielded herself implicitly to her care and direction," headed schools first in Ohio and then in Pennsylvania. Admiring pupils thought she "infused new life and vigor into the school which was felt throughout the surrounding country."

Jane Ingersoll established a seminary in Cortland, New York, "on the Troy plan" and braved community opinion to follow Willard's example by offering a course in physiology.[20] By the mid-1830s across the country Troy graduates, reinforced by pupils and protegés of Catharine Beecher and Mary Lyon, were busy creating a profession which, from its inception, was open to women.

Of course, the professionalization of school teaching was going on in many places in both western Europe and North America in the early nineteenth century. By the late 1830s Horace Mann, Henry Barnard, and a group of like-minded men were working for the establishment of teacher-training institutions of various kinds, first in Massachusetts, Connecticut, New York, and then elsewhere. It is not surprising to find many Troy graduates taking an active part in the common-school movement when it began to burgeon in the 1830s.[21]

Henry Barnard persuaded Emma Willard herself to run for the office of supervisor of schools in Kensington, Connecticut; the male voters elected her. With the help of one former pupil she developed a demonstration school for training teachers, and with another she organized a Woman's Association for the Common Schools, the purpose of which was to bring the mothers of the community into active responsibility for the school system. It was up to the mothers, she said, to improve working conditions and pay so that the "best women" would be willing to become teachers. She also suggested that they make sure that all the children in the district had proper clothing and books and that classes be invited to meet in homes so that the women themselves could examine the children. "Such a plan would keep the mothers along with the improvements of the time . . . it would set you to review old studies, or look over new ones. And if you would but try it, you would find your mature minds would with a little labor master subjects that require pains to teach the young."[22] In a letter to Henry Barnard written at the same time she said that the more she reflected on "the condition of our country" the more need she felt for the influence of women to set things right.

The Kensington experiment and the work of the association of mothers were reported in the educational press, and Emma Willard was soon being invited all over New York State to conduct teacher institutes, to lecture on pedagogy, and to organize mothers as she had done in Kensington. A former pupil who worked with her recorded that when asked to speak she insisted upon sitting down, since she did not believe it proper for women to speak in public. By remaining in her chair, she could consider her speech to be merely conversation and therefore appropriately feminine.[23]

In 1846 she extended her efforts through the rest of the country, traveling 8,000 miles "by stage coach, packet boat and private carriage" into every state south and west of New York except Florida and Texas, visiting former pupils, lecturing on women's education, conducting teacher institutes, and organizing associations.

By all these means, and by the work of her former pupils, which she continually watched over and encouraged, the "Troy idea" spread through the country. In time there were said to be 200 schools modeled upon the original, each one disseminating by precept and example Willard's view of women's capacities and their appropriate responsibilities.

The census takers in 1870 counted 200,515 teachers of public elementary and secondary schools, more than half of them women. Thirty years of normal school work had had a great deal to do with this change in the composition of the teaching profession as had the fact that women persisted in being willing to work for lower wages than men. But for the sources of the changing social attitudes which contributed to the professionalization of school teaching, and for the willingness of women to enter that profession, we must begin with Troy.[24]

A New Personality?

From a slightly different angle of vision, what did the Troy experience mean to individual women? How did it contribute to changing their self-perceptions and the way they ultimately lived their lives? Such questions present difficult methodological problems and, given the nature of the data, invite speculation rather than solid assertion. Yet this question is both intriguing and important.

In these first generations of educated women, it is possible to discern the emergence of a new type of personality and some new patterns of adult life. The personality was one which, precisely as Emma Willard had forecast in 1819, included an intellectual component, a certain kind of seriousness of purpose beyond the domestic and religious spheres, and a degree of personal aspiration which precluded that tendency to "show and frivolity" the proponents of women's higher education always deplored. The ideal was described in a memorial address given by Lucretia Hudson Willard, Emma Willard's daughter-in-law and successor as principal at Troy, when she said that her predecessor had shown "that young ladies are capable of learning those intellectual subjects which discipline their minds, train their reasoning powers, strengthen and elevate their characters, and make them more permanently attractive than when educated by light and trivial studies."[25]

A handful of Troy pupils left some record of what they thought the long-term influence of the institution and its founder upon them had been. A number who replied to questionnaires sent out in the 1890s responded with long letters, and others, even in brief answers, threw some light on how they recalled the experience. Still others, simply by describing their lives, inadvertently bore witness to the kind of strength of character which Troy reinforced. What stands out in most of these records is the great importance of Willard's personality in providing her pupils with a new image of what woman could be. One, for example, had traveled with her on a steamboat in 1842 and described the experience: Willard had inquired "what object in life I had in mind." "She inspired me with a self-respect and dignity new to me."[26]

The editor of *Mrs. Emma Willard and Her Pupils* was surprised at the outpouring of information about events which had occurred so many years before. "Mrs. Emma Willard's influence is immortal. I am surprised to note even in my sequestered life that I am continually coming upon new clues that lead out to a scholar of the old Seminary."[27] The same woman remarked that she had been "mentally reinvigorated in this daily intercourse with teachers and girls who were once such important factors in my life."[28] Teachers described their schools which had been modeled on Troy and indicated that they had tried to follow Emma Willard's example as closely as possible.

The nephew of a long-dead woman wrote that his aunt had frequently spoken of the "influence exerted on her life and the lives of other pupils by the training they had received under Mrs. Willard's supervision."[29] Several correspondents spoke of being rejuvenated by the call to write about their school days, others referred to the deep impression made upon them by the Saturday morning talks which had been given by Emma

Willard, Almira Lincoln, and later by Lucretia Hudson Willard. "My whole after life (to a certain extent) has been influenced by them," wrote one octogenarian; and another wrote: "Indeed she was the grandest woman America ever produced."[30]

One of the longest letters came from a woman who had spoken at the Chicago World's Fair in 1893 on "Emma Willard and the Troy Female Seminary." She wrote not only of the influence of the school upon herself but also of her perception of its far-reaching social consequences: first, spreading the idea of intelligent study of geography; second, because of its emphasis upon "the importance of women in their own right"; third, because of the pioneering teacher training and systematic study of pedagogy available there; fourth, because of the great influence of Willard and her pupils on the development of the common-school movement; and finally, because she felt that Willard's textbook, *The Republic of America*, did much "toward uniting people into a nation."[31] The daughter of another pupil from the 1820s reported that the Willard name had been a "household word" in her family. Another recalled a picture hanging in her home of "that much loved and honored teacher."[32]

A pupil who had been in the first class, writing in a clear, firm hand, noted that "Mrs. Willard was my ideal of perfection, she was the embodiment of everything that was lovely in both mind and body." "She taught with the enthusiasm of an originator, thus enkindling the enthusiasm of her pupils," said her daughter-in-law.

The alumnae of Troy who survived into middle age and beyond included many examples of what the late nineteenth century called "new women." There was Carolyn Stickney, who, hearing that her brother was on trial for murder in Colorado Territory, came from England and "by personal intervention gained his acquittal" and took him back to England for safe-keeping. Mary Newbury Adams founded a society for the study of the arts and sciences in Iowa with the aim of educating the whole Midwest, women and children in particular. Lucretia Willard Treat founded normal schools in Michigan, while Rebecca Stoneman cultivated her own orange grove in California. Adeline Morse Osborne, self-taught geologist, gave papers to the American Association for the Advancement of Science, and Jane Andrus Jones, widow, ran a large farm "in a very successful way." Miranda Aldis, trained in the law by her father, was her husband's legal assistant; Elizabeth Marshall managed a factory; Cornelia Whipple, wife of the bishop of Minnesota, gave all her time to the cause of the Indians. Elizabeth Mather Hughes helped her husband run the

Minnesota *Chronicle*; and Jane Bancroft Robinson took a Ph.D. in Zurich. Clare Cornelia Harrison wrote a well-known history of French painting; Lucy Marsh dealt in real estate; Dr. Elizabeth Bates delivered 2,400 babies without losing one mother "at the time of delivery," but she added, in the interest of accuracy, she had "lost some cases from diseases incidental to the lying-in-period." Charlotte Henry worked to improve conditions for the freed slaves; Harriet Maria Pettit House translated books into the Siamese language; Sara Seward, seventeen years out of school, undertook medical training so she could become a medical missionary; Sophie L. Hobson taught English to Spanish-speaking youngsters in California. The testimony runs on and on, often in the copperplate handwriting Emma Willard had insisted they learn in the interest of effective communication. Each one in her turn was an example to the young.

That the biographical committee, working twenty years after the most recent boarding pupil had left the school and seeking to find others whose school days were anywhere from seventy to thirty years behind them, was able to secure more than 3,500 responses was itself some evidence of the strength of the Troy tie. So was the fact that so many children and grandchildren, filling out questionnaires for long-dead alumnae, remembered the significance mothers and grandmothers had attached to their schooling. Many of these descendants spoke of the women's intellectual interests. "She [a deceased mother] was a woman of scholarly tastes who read Greek and Hebrew," or, another, "My mother was possessed of greater general information than anyone I almost ever knew." "She keeps herself in touch with the questions of the day and is fond of intellectual pursuits," wrote another.[33] A pupil of the 1850s was said to have read Caesar for recreation and to have kept up her studies in art and modern languages till the last week of her life; another was recorded as "an authority on questions of history, geography and politics." Perhaps one of the most significant comments came from the daughter of an 1829 graduate: "her pupils *and their daughters* scattered over the wide world revere her name."[34] It may be that one of the delayed effects of the Troy experiment, if we could measure it, would be found in the educational expectations among the daughters of the early pupils.

Of course such evidence must be interpreted with care. Obviously, a woman who felt very much attached to Troy would be likely to write a detailed response to the questionnaire; children who remembered such

TABLE 2. Life-Cycle Experience of Troy Women

Troy Women	Life-Cycle Experience					
Decade left school	1821-32	1833-42	1843-52	1853-62	1863-72	Total
Number reporting	372	540	769	975	845	3,501
Never married	49 (13%)	97 (17%)	160 (20%)	210 (21%)	217 (25%)	733 (22%)
Married once	303	413	582	721	611	2,630
Married two or three times	20	30	27	44	17	138
Married but no children recorded	104	141	200	226	183	844
Average number of children of those who had children	4.5	3.8	2.7	3.1	2.6	3.4
Percentage of children dead by 1898	28%	27%	20%	17%	11%	21%
Worked for pay before marriage	39 (12%)	111 (25%)	124 (20%)	166 (21%)	75 (12%)	515 (14.7%)
Number and percentage of all single women who remained single and worked for pay	6 (12.2%)	34 (35%)	57 (35%)	89 (42%)	54 (24%)	240 (38%)
Number of married women who worked after marriage; percentage of all married women	15 (5%)	35 (8%)	29 (5%)	58 (8%)	29 (5%)	166 (6%)
Number and percentage who joined any voluntary association	55 (14%)	90 (16%)	162 (21%)	315 (32%)	224 (26%)	845 (24%)
Founded or administered a school	16	44	36	36	14	146
Created some non-school institution	2	5	2	12	3	24
Coded "unusual": subjective judgment based on biographical data	34 (9%)	59 (10%)	37 (4%)	65 (7%)	27 (3%)	222 (6%)

attachment would be likely to take the trouble to reply. There was certainly a process of self-selection on the part of the women who chose to go to Troy. These fragments do bear witness, however, to the beginning of a new personality type, the educated woman who was not ashamed of learning and who would inevitably have a wider notion of what the world had to offer than her sisters who had not been encouraged to read widely or to think for themselves.[35]

Another way of examining the effects of the Troy experience is through some statistical analysis of the biographical material collected in the 1890s. This analysis is still in a preliminary stage, but the early findings are suggestive.[36]

Table 2 represents a rough systematization of some of the data into what I have called a life-cycle table. Several rather striking conclusions emerge from this table: the rather high proportion of the women who remained single, particularly among those who were at school after 1840. For comparison we may look at the figures for all American women born between 1835 and 1855, of whom between 6 percent and 8 percent never married.[37] When this fact is added to the rather small families of Troy women, compared to those of the average of all U.S. women, a startling contrast emerges. As Table 3 suggests, among Troy women who left school between 1852 and 1863, 21.2 percent had only one child, compared to 10.6 percent of New York women born between 1836 and 1840 and to 7.8 percent of all U.S. women.

At the other end of the spectrum, 19.1 percent of all women were having five or six children, but only 13.7 percent of Troy women were bearing such large families. If we look at those who had seven to nine children, Troy figures drop to 4.7 percent while for the whole country the figure is 21.7 percent.[38] One of Emma Willard's avowed goals was to make better wives and mothers, but her pupils were less likely to marry than women in general and, if married, they bore fewer children than their contemporaries.

Twentieth-century experience is that the more education a woman has, the more likely she is to work for pay, whether single or married. This effect may have occurred among Troy women as well, though comparisons are difficult since our data reveal the number of women who worked at any time in their lives—26 percent—while the census reports all the women who are working at the particular moment the census taker appears. Even so, since most working women in the nineteenth century were domestic servants, factory workers, and agricultural workers,

TABLE 3. Changing Patterns of Childbearing of Those Who Had Children, as Indicated by Percentage Who Had What Number of Children, by Decade (*n* = 1924)

Number of Children	1821-32	1833-42	1843-52	1853-62	1863-72
1	13.7	16.0	18.6	21.2	22.2
2	12.3	16.0	23.2	22.3	27.6
3	16.4	21.8	18.3	20.8	21.1
4	16.0	13.1	15.6	16.3	12.6
5	10.0	10.9	9.5	9.1	8.5
6	7.3	10.3	5.4	4.6	2.7
7	8.2	3.5	2.9	1.9	2.7
8	3.7	2.9	3.2	1.9	1.3
9	5.9	1.3	2.0	0.9	0.4
10	3.2	2.6	0.5	0.4	0.4
11	1.4	1.0	0.0	0.6	0.2
12	0.9	0.3	0.5	0.0	0.0
13	0.9	0.3	0.2	0.2	0.0

that 26 percent of this group of middle-class women spent some time in the labor force may be significant.

Even more interesting is the proportion of married women who worked while they were married (about 6 percent), the proportion of widows who supported themselves in widowhood (more than 10 percent), and the proportion of the teachers who made teaching into a serious career (we estimate about 40 percent). The number of Troy graduates who founded or administered schools is also significant.

In addition to the married women who worked for pay after marriage, there were 202 women who said they shared their husbands' work. Most of these were wives of ministers, missionaries, and teachers, but some were wives of lawyers, who reported learning to write briefs and otherwise acting as aides, or scholars, exemplified by the woman who learned Swedish to be her husband's research assistant, or another "more fond of books than housekeeping" who—with her husband—translated German tales.

It is not surprising to find that 38 percent took part in some kind of voluntary association, but it is surprising that among those who worked for pay the percentage was higher than for those who were not in the labor force. There is as yet no control group to show whether this rate of participation in voluntary associations is higher than among middle-class women in general.

Even in its present primitive state, the statistical analysis strengthens the argument that Troy and by implication similar places, such as Mt. Holyoke, Hartford, Georgia Female College, or Wheaton, despite their emphasis upon the importance of "woman's sphere," were important agents in that development of a new self-perception and spread of feminist values which contemporary observers described as the "great nineteenth century movement for the elevation of women." The process was repeated on a larger scale when the women's colleges got underway in the years after 1865 and initiated what might be called the second great wave of consciousness-raising.[39]

Conclusion

At the broadest level of generality, the evidence presented here suggests that higher education for women, as it began to develop at Troy and spread thereafter, played an important part in the diffusion of feminist values. This was true despite the fact that early and late leaders of educational institutions for women reiterated the traditional values of home and motherhood and accepted the idea that women were destined to spend their lives in a sphere separate from that of men. Feminist values not only coexisted with the more traditional ones but also spread more easily when they were carefully attached to "correct" views of woman.

At a more specific level, it is clear that Emma Willard's role in the social history of the nineteenth century was more complex than has generally been understood. She not only was one of the first to offer young women higher education; along with it she offered a cluster of new values as she encouraged self-respect and self-support and assured her pupils that marriage was not essential to a useful life. She encouraged intellectual development and self-education and built a carefully cultivated network of women through the country whom she had trained and influenced and whom she expected to train and influence others. The result was that schools for women and associations of women to oversee the common schools spread across the land.

Willard was not only one of the first Americans to speak publicly about women's "rights," but also she was among the first to think seriously about the problems and methods of teacher training and to encourage the professionalization of school teaching, a process which opened a new range of opportunities to women. She also understood the virtues of what is now called continuing education, or lifelong learning, and put great stress on it in training her pupils and encouraging the women in her Association of Teachers.

Together with some of her former pupils she played a major part in the common-school movement, especially in New York and New England but to some extent across the Middle West and even in the post–Civil War South—by way of Patapsco and Barhamville.

Although the term has been trivialized, she was certainly a powerful role model—so much so that twenty-five years after her death admiring former students were raising money to place her statue in a prominent place in Troy and gathering themselves in an association bearing her name. There were few women available to be such role models in the early days of Troy. After the first two decades, however, Willard's pupils began to supply such models in many parts of the country. In this, too, the multiplier effect was at work.

Women, education, and the prevailing social values were all parts of a system in which there was constant interaction and feedback. Educated women became carriers of the newer values, and the spread of feminist ideas led more and more women to seek education. In each succeeding generation after 1820 there were a larger number of women enrolled, first in the seminaries, then in the colleges; and each succeeding generation contained more independent women. Education appears to have been a major force in the spread of feminism.

NOTES

1. Essential feminist values include the beliefs that: (1) women should be seen as individual human beings with a range of potentialities which they should be free to develop; (2) men and women should be equal before the law; (3) marriage should be a partnership between equals. There are many specific feminist attitudes, but these three are fundamental. For more detailed statements, see Alice Rossi, *The Feminist Papers* (New York, 1974). Traditional values include the beliefs that: (1) woman, the weaker sex, was created to serve man, and her role and functions in life are defined by her sex; (2) women are feeling rather than reasoning beings; (3) women should be pious, submissive, and obedient,

putting the needs of husband and children ahead of her own. To these basic ideas, which have persisted through centuries, was added in the nineteenth century a cluster of beliefs which laid stress upon the existence of a separate sphere for women in which they were to exercise their moral responsibilities. For detailed statements of the nineteenth-century version of the traditional values, see Barbara Welter, "The Cult of True Womanhood," *American Quarterly*, 18 (1966), 151-75, and Nancy L. Cott, *The Bonds of Womanhood* (New Haven, 1977), pp. 1-2.

2. The existence of a large number of women who combined the old values with the new is amply documented in Karen Blair, *The Clubwoman as Feminist* (New York, 1980). For a useful analysis of the concept of women's consciousness, see Jessie Taft, *The Woman Movement from the Point of View of Social Consciousness* (Chicago, 1915). Other works which have strengthened my conviction that we need to find a new way of describing the distribution of feminist and traditional values in the nineteenth century include Cott, *Bonds of Womanhood*; Susan P. Conrad, *Perish the Thought* (New York, 1976); Daniel Scott Smith, "Family Limitation, Sexual Control and Domestic Feminism," in Lois Banner and Mary Hartman, eds., *Clio's Consciousness Raised* (New York, 1974); Ellen DuBois, "The Radicalism of the Woman Suffrage Movement," *Feminist Studies*, 3 (Fall 1975), and *Feminism and Suffrage* (Ithaca, 1978). I am also indebted to Carl Degler for letting me see the manuscript containing his discussion of the anti-suffragists, which became part of his book, *At Odds: Women and the Family in America from the Revolution to the Present* (New York, 1980). It may be relevant to recognize that holding on to old values and experimenting with new ones is not necessarily comfortable. Ambivalence was common among women in the middle of the scale, as is clear from many biographies. The founder of Troy Female Seminary herself once wrote that women who spoke up for women's rights were accused of having cast off their feminine sensitiveness "and often when such women are found moody and are thought capricious it is this which is the cause of their ill-humor and dejection." See Emma Willard, *The Advancement of Female Education* (Troy, N.Y., 1833), p. 10.

3. Of course, a larger question is where the new values come from in the first place, but for the purpose of this discussion I shall simply assume their existence and pursue the question of how they spread and became gradually acceptable to ever larger numbers of women. As is always the case with documenting a major attitudinal change, the sources are apt to be complex. In this case they included the rapid population growth and economic development of the country, the changing pattern of production, which took many of women's historic functions out of the home, the increasingly pervasive spirit of individualism and egalitarianism among men, the spread of evangelical religion, and—possibly —the romantic movement in art and literature.

4. Mrs. A. W. Fairbanks, ed., *Mrs. Emma Willard and Her Pupils, or Fifty Years of the Troy Female Seminary, 1822-1872* (New York, 1898). The material in this book was gathered by a committee of alumnae of the school who sent questionnaires to every former pupil they could find, and to friends, descendants,

and even postmasters of those who had died. The original manuscript question-naires are in the Archives of Emma Willard School, Troy, N.Y.

5. See John Lord, *The Life of Emma Willard* (New York, 1873); Henry Fowler, "Educational Services of Mrs. Emma Willard," in Henry Barnard, ed., *Memoirs of Teachers, Educators, and Promoters and Benefactors of Education, Literature and Science* (New York, 1861); James Monroe Taylor, *Before Vassar Opened* (Boston, 1914); Alma Lutz, *Emma Willard: Daughter of Democracy* (Boston, 1929); Willystine Goodsell, *Pioneers of Women's Education* (New York, 1931); Ezra Brainerd, "Mrs. Emma Willard's Life and Work in Middlebury," read at Rutland, Vt., Sept. 20, 1893, and printed for private distribution by a member of the class of 1841 at Troy Female Seminary. See also A. F. Scott, "What, Then, Is the American: This New Woman?" *Journal of American History*, 65 (Dec. 1978).

6. Emma Willard, *An Address to the Public Particularly to the Members of the Legislature of New York proposing a Plan for Improving Female Education* (Albany, 1819). Linda K. Kerber, "Daughters of Columbia: Educating Women for the Republic, 1787-1805," in Stanley Elkins and Eric McKitrick, eds., *The Hofstadter Aegis: A Memorial* (New York, 1974), pp. 36-59, found all of these arguments being made in the years immediately after the ratification of the Constitution. Emma Willard drew them together in a logical progression and tied them to specific proposals for state-supported higher education for women and for teacher training. "Nothing in those early days compares in influence . . . with this noble appeal . . . it was far beyond anything then proposed or known." Taylor, *Before Vassar Opened*, pp. 5-6. The Willards had 1,000 copies of the *Plan* printed and bound for sale in bookstores. As I read Willard's early writings, it seems to me likely that she had already begun to observe the general deterioration of the female personality that occurs when prosperity lightens the load of necessary labor and education has not yet provided other things to think about. Novelists from Jane Austen and George Eliot to Elizabeth Gundy have dealt effectively with this phenomenon; historians have tiptoed around it, though it was a familiar theme among nineteenth-century feminists of all degrees of radicalism. See Lord, *Life of Emma Willard*, p. 110, for her advice to a pupil on the importance of self-education: "It will keep you from that desire of gadding about which is so fatal to the improvement of your sex."

7. Merle Borrowman, *The Liberal and the Technical in Teacher Education* (New York, 1956), p. 55, lists three schools which had set out to train teachers before 1821. He seems never to have heard of Troy or Mount Holyoke and, therefore, is under the misapprehension that serious teacher training began with the first normal school in Massachusetts in 1839. Many other historians of American education have been similarly uninformed.

8. Brainerd says that Willard deliberately chose the word seminary, thinking that it would "not create a jealousy that we mean to intrude upon the province of man." See "Mrs. Emma Willard's Life," p. 16. Lord, *Life of Emma Willard*, p. 96. The titles of these books are: Henry Home Kames, *Essays on the Principles of Morality and Natural Religion* (Edinburgh, 1751); William Paley, *Paley's Moral*

Philosophy (London, 1859); Francis Wayland, *The Elements of Moral Science* (1835; Cambridge 1963).

9. Emma Lydia Bolzau, *Almira Lincoln Phelps: Her Life and Work* (Philadelphia, 1936).

10. Before one makes too much of the ambitious college curriculum with its Livy, Tacitus, and Xenophon as daily fare, it is worth listening to President Francis Wayland of Brown, reporting to the fellows of the college of 1841, asking for a tightening of entrance requirements because "students frequently enter college almost wholly unacquainted with English grammar and unable to write a tolerably legible hand." The fellows themselves, a year later, noted that "students are frequently admitted very ignorant of the grammars and are unable to read but a very small portion of Latin and Greek at a lesson." See Walter C. Bronson, *The History of Brown University* (Providence, 1914), p. 217. Willard's pedagogy, more than that pevailing in the colleges, emphasized the development of critical thinking, and, while even Harvard still depended upon the deadly daily recitation as its chief pedagogical tool, she introduced the Pestalozzian dialogue and assured her pupils that, until they had learned a subject well enough to teach it, they could not consider that they had mastered it. The whole question of what constituted "higher education" in the nineteenth century is a slippery one. The quality or difficulty of a curriculum was not necessarily revealed by the label placed upon it, and a wide variety of institutions were engaged in providing some part of what would eventually come to be defined as a collegiate education. The variation in institutions was matched by the variation in students, who might be fifteen or fifty, who might be seeking intellectual, culture, or professional skills, and who, taken collectively, made up a heterogeneous mass of learners. See Douglas Sloan, "Harmony, Chaos and Consensus: The American College Curriculum," *Teachers College Record*, 73 (Dec. 1971), 221-51. Opportunities for women to get serious academic instruction developed in bits and pieces from about 1787 to 1821. Then came Troy, and, until the opening of Mt. Holyoke Seminary and the Georgia Female College in 1836, it provided the best academic opportunity available to women in this country. Lord, himself a Dartmouth graduate, testified, "Whatever name her school may go by, yet in all essential respects it was a college." Lord, *Life of Emma Willard*, p. 51.

11. The head of the Clinton, Georgia, Female Seminary went in 1837 to see for himself what was going on at Troy. He found Emma Willard's personal appearance "very different from what I had anticipated. She is considerably above ordinary size of females, quite corpulent, but dignified and commanding, easy and pleasant in her manners; in her conversation shrewd and intelligent, but fond of adulation and self-esteem. Her dress was more gaudy than my 'beau ideal' of a literary lady and instructress of youth. I witnessed the examination of her pupils —and was much gratified by their proficiency." He heard classes examined in arithmetic, French, philosophy, history and geometry. Diary of Thomas Bog Slade, Southern Historical Collection, University of North Carolina Library, Chapel Hill.

12. Lutz, *Emma Willard*, p. 173, taken from a speech Stanton made at the Chicago World's Fair in 1893. At about the same time a former pupil wrote to Emma Willard's granddaughter, "Your grandmother's great distinction seemed to

me to be a supreme confidence in herself and, as a consequence, a stubborn faith in the capacity of her own sex." Eliza Athrop to Mrs. Scudder, May 9, 1892, Archives of Emma Willard School. Willard herself compared her work in education to that of the Founding Fathers in creating the Constitution!

13. Willard, *Advancement of Female Education*, p. 9.

14. Lutz, *Emma Willard*, p. 121.

15. Typescript in Archives of Emma Willard School.

16. Willard, *Advancement of Female Education*, p. 137. In 1826 she had written a member of the New York Assembly: "I never expect that complete justice will be done our sex until this old set [of legislators] are chiefly with their fathers. But I am confident that our cause is a righteous one." Willard to Mr. Granger, Granger Papers, Library of Congress, Washington, D.C.

17. *Letter to the Members of the Willard Association for the Mutual Improvement of Teachers* (Troy, N.Y., 1838), p. 5.

18. See letter from Julia Marks's daughter: "Mrs. Willard, Mrs. Lincoln Phelps and my mother were three educators acting in union." Archives of the Emma Willard School.

19. Handwritten notes of Henry Campbell Davis, deposited in South Caroliniana Library, University of South Carolina, Columbia. In the 1930s Davis was engaged in tracing the influence of Troy in the South and West and concluded that it was "an important fact in the history of culture of America." As far as I can find out, his research on this subject was not published.

20. Fairbanks, ed., *Mrs. Emma Willard and Her Pupils*, pp. 70, 171-72, 201, and manuscript questionnaires for each of these women in the Archives of the Emma Willard School.

21. The work of Willard and her pupils in the common-school movement is rarely mentioned in the secondary sources dealing with that movement, which is odd since the richest primary sources, the *Annals of American Education*, the *Massachusetts Common School Journal*, and Henry Barnard's *American Journal of Education*, all paid close attention to Willard and her ideas. See Emma Willard to Henry Barnard, Nov. 18, 1845, Henry Barnard Papers, Library of New York University, New York, for an example of the close relationship between them.

22. Emma Willard to Mrs. Hotchkiss, Apr. 30, 1841, and Willard to Henry Barnard, in Henry Barnard Papers. In a letter to Governor William Marcy of New York in 1826 she had said, "My views for the advancement of female education are connected with those I entertain of the improvement of the common schools." Lutz, *Emma Willard*, 194-95.

23. Sketch of Sarah Fisher Hoxie, in Fairbanks, ed., *Mrs. Emma Willard and Her Pupils*, p. 516. At about the same time that she was thus paying tribute to the power of the idea of "woman's sphere," she was writing an article for the *American Literary Magazine* in which she proposed that France, which had recently experienced a revolution, should set up a separate congress of women to deal with those matters for which women should be especially responsible, including education. See "Letter . . . on the Political Position of Women," *American Literary Magazine*, 2 (1848), 246-54.

24. I do not mean to minimize the importance of the other two women

whose contribution to the professionalization of teaching was as important as that of Emma Willard: Catharine Beecher and Mary Lyon. See Kathryn Kish Sklar, *Catharine Beecher: A Study in American Domesticity* (New Haven, 1973), and the "following essay" of David Allmendinger on Mt. Holyoke Seminary. Their contributions come a little later.

25. Memorial of the late Mrs. Emma Willard, *A Proceeding of the Seventh Anniversary of the University Convocation of the State of New York* (Albany, 1871), p. 79.

26. Margaret Stanley Cowles, "A brief sketch of an incident of travel with Mrs. Emma Willard," Archives of the Emma Willard School.

27. Mary Fairbanks to Olivia Slocum Sage, Archives of the Emma Willard School.

28. Fairbanks to Sage, Oct. 14, 1895, Archives of Emma Willard School.

29. Nephew of Ziporah de Camp Jacques, 1823-26, Archives of Emma Willard School; Fairbanks, ed., *Mrs. Emma Willard and Her Pupils*, p. 405.

30. Eunice Samantha Bascom Memoir, Archives of Emma Willard School.

31. Mary Newberry Adams to Olivia S. Sage, Nov. 4, 1893, Archives of Emma Willard School.

32. Daughter of Jane Pelletreau Ashley Bates, replying to questionnaire, Archives of Emma Willard School.

33. Daughters of Elsie Van Dyke, 1827, and Agnes Powell, 1829-32, Archives of Emma Willard School; Fairbanks, ed., *Mrs. Emma Willard and Her Pupils*, p. 399.

34. Daughter of Sarah Serbine Stewart, Archives of Emma Willard School.

35. Almira Lincoln Phelps, *The Female Student or Lectures for Young Ladies* (New York, 1836), contains weekly lectures given to Troy pupils. One continuous thread runs through these lectures: learn to use your mind. Phelps also dwelt upon the need to be prepared for self-support.

36. My collaborator in this venture is Professor Patricia Hummer, presently of the department of history of Michigan State University. She has done a great part of the technical side of the computer-assisted analysis and is planning to write specifically about the Troy women who became teachers.

37. Irene and Conrad Taeuber, *People of the U.S. in the Twentieth Century* (Washington, D.C., 1971), p. 378.

38. Wilson Grabill, Clyde V. Kiser, and P. K. Whelpton, *Fertility of American Women* (New York, 1958), p. 56.

39. Keith Melder in "Masks of Oppression: The Female Seminary Movement in the United States," *New York History,* 55 (July 1974), argued that because of their adherence to the idea of separate spheres, the female seminaries perpetuated the oppression of women. I am persuaded that at least with respect to Troy this is a misapprehension and that many of Willard's pupils, like Willard herself, found it possible to combine the old values and the new in creative ways.

Almira Lincoln Phelps:
The Self-Made Woman in
the Nineteenth Century

The notion of the self-made man is a common one in our culture and was especially so in the nineteenth century. But what of the self-made woman? At first glance it would seem unlikely that such a phenomenon existed in a society committed to the view that woman's appropriate sphere was the domestic one. Yet there were an increasing number of such women as the nineteenth century progressed, and their path to achievement was necessarily different from that followed by men.

Since teaching was the one profession to which women had access, it is not surprising to find a teacher—Almira Lincoln Phelps—not only providing an archetypal example in her own person but also diligently instructing her pupils as to how they might rise in the world through their own efforts.

Though a New Englander by birth and instinct, Phelps made her career and her reputation in Maryland. In 1841 she took charge of the Patapsco Female Institute which she directed until 1856. For the ensuing nineteen years she was a pillar of Baltimore, presiding over a salon devoted to literary and scientific subjects, working for the St. Bartholomew's Mission Church, and founding its women's society as well as a number of other voluntary associations. Her son Charles Phelps, graduate of Harvard Law School, represented Maryland in the Thirty-Ninth and Fortieth Congresses and was thereafter a judge and law professor.

If we look closely at the concept of self-making as it was viewed by restless nineteenth-century Americans, it was not quite what the cliché

Reprinted with permission from *Maryland Historical Magazine*, 75 (Sept. 1980), 203-16.

suggests. The term self-made man usually evokes images of a rags-to-riches career, yet we now know that most of the truly rich did not begin in rags and did not create their success unaided.[1] A much wider definition of the term would encompass not only the tiny handful who began poor and ended their lives rich, but the much larger number who, beginning their lives on farms or in agricultural villages, exerted themselves to acquire some degree of education and became the ministers, doctors, lawyers, social reformers, teachers, public officials, and merchants, often of modest means, who shaped the emerging town and city culture. They used the word *character* to sum up the combination of qualities required for this change.

The process of developing the necessary character and achieving a new status is reported over and over in the biographical sketches in which nineteenth-century men told their stories or those of their contemporaries. The beginning was usually discontent with life on the family farm. Some, of course, chose to find new farms in the West, but the most ambitious turned their feet toward the town or city. The first quality which they found essential was a high degree of adaptability. Self-reliance and perseverance were almost as vital. Character-building, as they saw it, required constant effort, and the capacity to seize each opportunity that presented itself. Neither the training nor the certification for any particular profession was yet firmly fixed: a fact which widened opportunity, on the one hand, but led to anxiety-producing uncertainty, on the other. Disappointments and setbacks were seen as part of the game and were often welcomed as tests of resilience and strength, or at least were said to have been welcomed once they had been overcome. For many men religious commitment reinforced the strength of character they were seeking to develop.

Many began with meager material resources, though the cooperation of members of an extended family might make the most of what did exist. In the process of becoming a professional and attaining some degree of local or even national eminence, a man might try three or four careers. Some practiced more than one profession simultaneously; some kept one foot in the older rural culture by continuing to live on a farm while practicing law or medicine. "Success," when it came, might arrive late in life, and in a field far from the one in which the young man had begun.

Similarities amounting almost to a pattern emerge when one dips randomly into the biographies of nineteenth-century male achievers. Mark

Hopkins worked as a farm hand in order to go to school, then taught in the South to save money for college. He had a go at theology, law and medicine before a tutorship at Williams almost accidentally opened the career in which he became famous. J. Marion Sims began practicing medicine so inadequately trained that his first two patients, both children, died. Yet, braced by the experience, he returned to more diligent study and became in time the leading gynecologist of his generation, founder of the New York Woman's Hospital. Francis Wayland had begun to practice medicine when a religious experience turned him to theology. Poverty forced him out of Andover Seminary and into a menial tutor's job at Brown University, where his own study and reflection launched him on a notable career as a moral philosopher and reformer of collegiate education. William Woodbridge was licensed as a Congregational minister and thinking of becoming a missionary when a trip to Europe turned his attention to geography. He began to search for better methods of teaching geography, which concern led on to an influential career in pedagogical reform. Amos Eaton read law, worked as a land agent for Stephen Van Rensselaer, became interested in plants, began to study botany, and launched a scientific career by the simple expedient of giving public lectures on the subject to anyone willing to pay a small sum to listen. In time he went on to study geology, created the first *Index* to the geology of the northern states, and joined the small group of scientists who were making science a serious field of study in the colleges.[2]

It would be possible to pile up example after example of this pattern of trial and error, resilience in the face of setback, belief in the virtues of adversity, and a strong reliance upon self-education, but enough has been said to show the general pattern followed by self-made men. How did women differ?

"Rising in the world," the stated goal of so many energetic young Americans of both sexes, was, for a woman, most readily accomplished by good sense or good luck in the choice of a husband. If she happened upon a man who had found the complex key to success, she would automatically rise with him, sharing his identity and reflecting whatever glory he might provide. A handful of women, by contrast, set out to achieve eminence on their own. Instead of waiting for fate to provide a husband whose life experience would shape their own, such women boldly set out to shape independent careers by a process of self-making similar to that of ambitious men, but modified by the social constraints summed up in the term "women's place."

The contrast between the social expectations of the two sexes was dramatic. Men were encouraged, applauded, and rewarded for diligent self-improvement. A woman who followed the same pattern ran the risk of being seen as deviant, labeled "strong-minded," caricatured, scorned, or even rejected by respectable society. So powerful were the cultural definitions of woman's role, so fixed the restrictions upon educational and professional opportunity, that an ambitious woman had to become adept at appearing to conform to the cultural prescriptions at the very time she was seeking to defy them. Achieving women often spoke with pain of the deviousness they felt brought on by this necessity.[3]

The career of Almira Hart Lincoln Phelps offers an instructive example of a woman who paid constant lip service to the idea of a special "woman's sphere" while stretching the boundaries of that sphere beyond recognition.

"Mrs. Phelps" as she was casually referred to in the press of her time, upon the evident assumption that her name was universally recognized, provides yet another illustration, if another were needed, of the transience of human fame. One of the best-known women in America during a good part of the nineteenth century, the second woman ever to be elected to the American Association for the Advancement of Science, a textbook author who introduced several generations to the study of botany, an influential pedagogue who played a major role in two pioneering female seminaries and helped to bring Pestalozzian methods into American education, a woman of letters sought after by literary editors—her name now brings blank stares even from American historians. She is known, if at all, as the sister of Emma Willard, whose own fame, though much diminished, has been somewhat preserved by the fact that the school she founded still bears her name.[4]

A sketch of Almira Phelps's life shows how one woman created a career, and from her writings it is possible to discover how she justified her ambitious achievements and attempted to guide young women who might wish to follow her example.[5] She carefully instructed her pupils in the methods of making themselves into strong characters and taught them how to elude the restrictions of "woman's sphere" without ever admitting they had done so.

Almira Hart was the seventeenth and last child in her family, a family descended on one side from the founder of Hartford, on the other from Massachusetts Bay Puritans. Her father had fought in the Revolution. Being seventeenth might have been a disadvantage—the parents were old, money for educating children would have been exhausted—but in her case, it was quite otherwise. Her much older brothers were able to help pay for schooling, and her sister, Emma Hart, already embarked on her own self-made career, was a useful mentor. Both sisters had been precocious children, encouraged by their father who was said to have read Milton and Shakespeare in his spare time, and to have shared his enthusiasm for such reading with his daughters.[6]

Almira was a forceful young person. At fourteen, accused of some dereliction of duty and placed for punishment in the teacher's chair at the district school, she used that vantage point to deliver a spirited critique of a recitation in progress and then wrote her weekly composition, in the form of a protest, on the subject of fitting punishment to crime. The reaction of the teacher to these assaults on his dignity is not recorded, but her behavior was a good forecast of things to come.

Two years later she began teaching in a country school and "boarding around" with local families, few of them as cultivated as her own had been. Though speaking well of the discipline this experience afforded, she decided that she would have to move up in the world to find a more congenial environment. For a young woman setting such a goal in 1810 there were two options: she could marry well, or she could prepare for a more ambitious teaching career. Since no suitable alliance had yet been offered, Almira took the second path and repaired to Middlebury, Vermont, where her sister had just taken charge of a female academy, and where three young men, students at Middlebury College, were willing to include her in their study sessions.

In an effort to go still further in her education, she moved for a while to Pittsfield, Massachusetts, where her cousin Nancy Hinsdale ran a highly respected academy. Living with high Federalist relatives did not prevent her from expressing Jeffersonian convictions in public, sometimes with dramatic intensity. The Hinsdale connection put her in line to be examined for a job as teacher of the winter school at New Britain, the first time a woman had been considered for that post. Confronted with a difficult question in astronomy, she covered her lack of precise knowledge by offering to read to the examiners an original essay on "The Duties and Responsibilities of Teachers." This device, she said, allowed her to exhibit her technical knowledge of reading, writing, and orthography as well as her appreciation of the office for which she was being examined. It need hardly be added that she got the job.[7] After New Britain she briefly conducted a private school in Berlin where she enjoyed a lively social life, but when a better job, the headship of a school in Sandy Hill, New York, was offered, ambition took precedence over pleasure. She moved again, telling herself that it was her duty to do the hard rather than the easy thing. "May the thought of having sacrificed my wishes to a conviction of duty inspire me with that firmness which my situation demands," she noted, somewhat self-righteously, in her diary.[8]

At Sandy Hill she hit upon a new tool for developing her mental skills and took to making written abstracts, "in condensed, logical form" of each book she read. She was soon teaching her pupils to follow her example. It was also about this time that she came across Lydia Sigourney's *Moral Pieces in Prose and Verse*, which inspired her to think that she, too, though a woman, might become a writer.[9]

Thus far her life had been a steady series of small triumphs, as she prepared herself for better and better teaching posts and experienced the excitement that accompanied the acquisition of knowledge, the development of mental skills, and a growing reputation as a teacher.

In 1817, when she was twenty-four, an opportunity for a more traditional female career presented itself in the form of a proposal of marriage from one Simeon Lincoln, editor of a Federalist paper in Hartford. His personal charm and their shared pleasure in literature overcame the disadvantage of his politics, and she retired for the time being to domestic life. Three children were born before her husband's sudden death in 1823 threw her upon her own resources to support herself and the two surviving children.

She returned almost at once to the district school at New Britain, but before many months a better chance came. Three years earlier Emma Hart Willard had opened the Troy Female Seminary in New York State in an effort to provide something closer to higher education for women than anything hitherto available. Now she asked her widowed sister to join the enterprise. In the atmosphere of intense intellectual effort Emma Willard fostered at Troy, Almira Lincoln launched herself upon the study of Latin, French, Greek, Spanish, and higher mathematics. Her greatest excitement came when Amos Eaton invited her to learn botany under his tutelage. "A new world seemed opened to her imagination in pursuit of the natural sciences," she wrote.[10]

Eaton, delighted with so apt and diligent a pupil, was soon calling her his "scientific assistant" and encouraging her to apply Pestalozzi's methods of inductive learning to the teaching of botany. None of the existing textbooks was designed to train pupils to work directly with plants, as Pestalozzian theory required, and so with Eaton's help she began to compose such a book. *Familiar Lectures on Botany* or "Lincoln's Botany," as it was generally called, became a standard text used in schools and colleges in every part of the country for half a century. It was destined to be many times revised and reprinted and to introduce several generations of youngsters to the study of science. In time various college professors of botany, some eminent, would attribute their first love for the field to an early encounter with this book.

Exhilarated by the favorable response to her botany text, she next undertook to translate from the French Vauquelin's *Dictionare de Chemie* and was rewarded with an encomium from Eaton's good friend, Benjamin Silliman, professor of chemistry at Yale, who called her translation "learned, judicious and able." She continued to grow in competence and self-confidence, and doubtless more than family loyalty was involved when Emma Willard left Almira Lincoln in full charge of the seminary when she herself departed for a long visit to Europe in 1830. The acting-principal took to administration as readily as she had to scholarship, and the seminary proceeded on its accustomed way quite as well as when the head was in residence.

People who were not frightened by Almira Lincoln's forceful personality often found her magnetic. In 1831 John Phelps, the widowed father of two Troy pupils, came to visit his daughters and was immediately attracted to the thirty-eight-year-old widow. After a courtship largely conducted by mail, she agreed to marry him, upon the condition that she would continue the various activities she subsumed under the phrase "my literary labors." She moved to Phelps's home in Guilford, Vermont, where the amount of work she accomplished was prodigious by any standard. With full reponsibility for the household, with two children of her own and several of her husband's to care for, she nevertheless revised her botany text, wrote three similar books to introduce students to chemistry, natural philosophy, and geology, edited the manuscripts of the weekly lectures she had given at Troy into *Lectures for Young Ladies*, wrote several articles for the *American Ladies Magazine* and *Godey's Lady's Book*, and organized a new church, a Sabbath school, a library, and a Female Society for the Promotion of Religious Knowledge. She conducted a three-week "normal course" for teachers in her home while she was pregnant. She bore a son in 1833 and a daughter in 1836. During the infancy of the first she kept a meticulous record of his day-by-day development and behavior, which was published as an appendix to a book she had translated from French and which constituted one of the first American contributions to descriptive developmental psychology.[11]

John Phelps was a strong figure in his own right, a self-educated lawyer who had served in the constitutional convention of Vermont and was still a member of its legislature where his involvement on the losing side of a heated argument over slavery increased his willingness to pull up stakes when his wife was asked to take over a female seminary in West Chester, Pennsylvania. She accepted the post with due sensitivity to the mores, writing a friend: "There is great danger that injustice may be done in the public mind to a gentleman whose wife makes herself conspicuous; we must do all we can to prevent this."[12] And lest posterity be misled, she made a note in the family Bible: "He was gratified in seeing his wife successful and honored, never imagining that this could detract from any distinctions to which he felt himself entitled."[13]

The West Chester Seminary fell victim to the panic of 1837 and the Phelpses, after a brief stay at Rahway, New Jersey, moved on to take charge of the Patapsco Female Institute, a faltering school under the control of the Episcopal diocese of Maryland.

While her husband took charge of the business affairs of the school, Almira Phelps ran the educational program, speedily establishing the "order" and "system" which had been her by-words at Troy. She set up a three-year course, required pupils to study mathematics, philosophy, and languages, announced that no one was to enter late or leave early, and established a curriculum to train teachers. As fast as she was able, she tightened requirements, extended the curriculum, provided for instruction for some who were postgraduates, and developed the public examination as a method of encouraging diligence on the part of pupils and respect on the part of the community. In a short time Patapsco was making a name in the South comparable to that which Troy enjoyed in New York, the middle states, and the Ohio valley.

Phelps perceived southern women, especially daughters of slaveholders, as presenting special problems for an educator. She worried lest they never really learn to work and felt she had to cajole them into undertaking the difficult subjects which she held to be essential for the full development of the mind. She never concealed her high regard for New England ways and Puritan values, which did not always endear her to southern pupils or their parents. One disgruntled student accused her of wanting only to make money and of spying on her pupils. A dissatisfied North Carolina congressman whose daughters were enrolled at Patapsco criticized her strong-minded behavior and thought her inadequately attentive to the development of feminine charm. On the second point she would have agreed with him; it was her pride that Patapsco provided women with advantages corresponding to "those enjoyed by young men in the colleges" and she said she was more interested in training good women than fine ladies.[14]

Other pupils praised the school and its preceptress and, though Patapsco's student body was never as large as that of Troy, it was soon sending trained teachers south and west to become part of the spreading women's educational network which Emma Willard had inaugurated four decades earlier.[15]

In 1849 John Phelps died, and for seven years Almira Phelps ran the seminary alone. In 1856, stricken by the death in a railway accident of her oldest daughter, Jane Lincoln, a remarkable young person whose life had exemplified her mother's ideal of what the educated woman should be, she retired from the school. She was sixty-three.

"Retirement" did not connote a diminution of activity. Though Phelps took part in Baltimore high society, she continued to read, write, talk, engage in politics, and take delight in new challenges. In 1870 she addressed a passionate document to the Senate and the House of Representatives urging them to support Cuba's fight for independence. At eighty-one, speaking to the Maryland Academy of Sciences, she made a spirited attack on the theory of evolution, though honoring Darwin for "all the good he had done in the search for truth."[16]

Along the way she organized and presided over various voluntary associations, including the St. Bartholomew's Mission church in Baltimore and its Woman's Aid Society. She firmly excluded the rector from meetings of the latter. This show of sturdy feminism was at odds with her decision to join the anti-suffrage forces and to argue publicly, with her usual vigor, against the wisdom of granting the vote to women. The fear of her influence was enough to inspire the *Woman's Journal* to an acerb comment: "Years of teaching give to dogmatic natures an increase of arrogance, which it is hard to keep in subjection."[17]

She continued to revise her textbooks, except for the one in geology since she felt that field had left her far behind, addressed the American Association for the Advancement of Science twice, supervised the education of her grandchildren, and advised her son, a member of Congress, on matters of public policy. After the Civil War she created a Society for the Liberal Education of Southern Girls to help young women from the impoverished states resume their education. Sixty-seven women were able to go to school under its auspices, a number of whom, in the best Phelps tradition, went back to the South to teach.[18]

The very substantial income from her textbooks provided her with comfortable surroundings: she continued to preside in matriarchal splendor over a three-generational household, and over a salon for the Baltimore intelligentsia, until she died at ninety-one, in full possession of her faculties.

In two published volumes of lectures, as well as in a novel and various essays, Almira Phelps left a record of her efforts to instruct young women on a wide variety of topics, among them the art of self-education and the method of building an autonomous identity. Didacticism was an integral part of nineteenth-century culture, and young men, too, were the recipients of a vast amount of advice on self-improvement. However, the task which Phelps undertook was somewhat more complicated than that faced by the assortment of philosophers, college professors, and medical men who tried to instruct men on the ways and means of getting ahead in the world. Her purpose was to help young women find their way to an independent identity, whether they married or not, and to help them prepare for achievement. In order to do this she had to help them call into question the firm net of cultural doctrines which, on the face of it, were quite at odds with her purposes. These doctrines were based on the assumptions that: (1) Women were created to be wives and mothers, helpmates for men, and took their identity from their relationships to husbands or male children. (2) Women's innate abilities lay in the emotional rather than in the intellectual realm. (3) God had appointed men to be the decision-makers, and fathers were to families as God himself was to believers. (4) Women who did not marry had failed to fulfill their destiny, though this error could be partly rectified if the woman spent her time serving some man, a father or brother, or, in a pinch, a brother-in-law.

How could a woman, surrounded with these cultural restraints, shape herself into a strong character capable of living, if she chose, an independent life? While achieving men were admired and held up as models to the young, women were admired for self-sacrifice and piety and were often despised for asserting themselves. Thus Phelps and others of her persuasion had first to show young women that individual achievement was possible for a woman, then had to help them prepare for intellectual independence by building their own characters, and finally had to teach them to use the cultural expectations to their own advantage. It was a formidable task.

Reduced to essentials, what Phelps offered young women, in three overlapping categories, was first, her understanding of the relationship of education to the process of character development; second, her firm belief that self-education was possible and, indeed, desirable; and, finally, instruction in how to deal with the dangers involved in stepping out of the prescribed "woman's sphere."[19]

Her intellectual starting point was a combination of Descartes and Locke. The mind is the basis of identity; all knowledge comes through the senses. Human beings are born with potential which can only be developed by exercise. Since knowledge is expanded by careful and purposeful observation and minds are developed by use, it follows that each person makes his or her own identity. Perhaps Almira Phelps herself did not realize how radical these assumptions were when applied to women, whose identities had for so long been seen as being formed by a relationship to a man.

She believed the purpose of education was to create an individual equipped to deal with whatever, in the providence of God, life should present. She called this goal "elevation of character." Learning and morality she believed to be complementary necessities: learning without moral principles could be dangerous; morality without an educated mind would be ineffective. Her ideal young woman was both learned and pious.

The process of creating one's own character required unremitting effort. While teachers could be helpful to the very young, self-education was "after all the great business of life," and the sooner a woman cut loose from teachers and took full responsibility for her own education, the sooner was a desirable maturity likely to be acquired. "Think what you want to be and then strive to render yourself such," she told her pupils, advising them to make a written plan for their lives.

Almira Phelps's enthusiasm for intellectual growth was visible despite her conventional nineteenth-century sentimental style. She emphasized the sheer joy of mastery and quoted approvingly a French author who urged women to learn to reason so they could enjoy the greatest minds, though he did suggest that such enjoyment be kept secret. Her recommendations for reading made no concessions to the supposed weakness of the female mind: Gibbon, Hume, Robertson, Voltaire, Locke, and Paley were among the authors she praised. Nor did she believe that any field of study was beyond a woman's range. "No kind of knowledge of literature or science is useless to a teacher. . . . Almost anything you can learn by observation may at one time or another aid in your educational labors," she told them. Formal schooling was the barest beginning: when you leave school "far from considering that you know everything, you must think you have almost everything to learn." She thought the female mind peculiarly suited to developing scientific theories.

Having established the general framework, she proceeded with specific instructions for developings powers of reasoning. Begin by studying mathematics, she said, then learn to observe carefully, make detailed investigations of subjects which interest you, then think, compare, and examine your own judgment. The last was important, for she had a strong belief in the virtue of independent thinking, which, combined with her faith in the potentialities of inductive reasoning, led to her constant emphasis upon self-reliance. For her own part, she did not hesitate to offer a critique of Aristotelian logic or to make emendations to a celebrated work in moral philosophy. None of this advice would have been remarkable had it been directed to young men. Directed to young women in the 1830s, it bordered on the revolutionary.

She stressed the need for women to study psychology ("philosophy of mind") and instructed them to observe carefully the functioning of their own minds in order to work out the general principles of mental operations. She recommended that each keep a private journal "in which the moral tenor of your actions and the bent of your minds should be scrupulously noted. This journal should be for your own inspection only; for such is the deceitfulness of the human heart, that it is very apt to suggest a too flattering picture of itself, where it is made with the design of being seen by any but the original," adding that "Man, know thyself, is a precept as important as it is difficult to practice."[20]

Phelps provided a whole series of precepts on the art of study. Concentration, she told her pupils, was of the first importance. Do one thing at a time, and give it your whole attention. Practice writing concise summaries of books you read. Try to explain what you are learning to other people. And so on. She was a proponent of what is nowadays called the inquiry method. Her stern insistence on concentration was at odds with the whole pattern of the usual female life which perforce called for doing many different things and turning rapidly from one to another. Yet she insisted, "Attention is indeed everything; without it nothing requiring mental effort can be well done." And, in another place: "It is the most difficult task of young students to gain that command of their trains of thought which scientific research requires."

The Greek ideal of the sound mind in the soundy body appealed to her, and in light of the widespread ill-health and physically constrained life of many nineteenth-century women, her preaching about health takes on greater significance. If you want to make something of yourself, she told her pupils, you must get regular exercise, enough sleep, and take food and drink in moderation. She had studied physiology and passed on precepts drawn from that study which, like all the rest of her advice, rested on a bedrock of belief in the possibility of self-control and self-help. She advised her pupils to pay close attention to their own physical natures and their particular reactions to medications in order to take care of their health themselves in preference to depending upon often ineffective medical doctors.

In lecture after lecture she held up an ideal of intellectual growth and character development to be achieved by women's own efforts, an achievement which would not only admit them to the company of the greatest minds, but would help them become strong, resilient individuals capable of dealing with any problem. She was sure life would offer plenty of vicissitudes to test their capabilities.

Indeed, she thought the world was harder for women than for men and that they had greater need for strong characters. But, she assured her pupils, "as an intelligent being woman is not different from man," and she urged them to make their lives a constant refutation of the assertion that a woman must be ignorant in order to be useful.

She assured them that marriage was not essential to a productive life and that they should prepare to be self-supporting. "It is of great importance to our sex, that they be secured against the sad necessity of marrying for the sake of maintenance." In her novel *Ida Norman*, Phelps tended to dispose of husbands so that her exemplary women would have to rely upon themselves and, as she delicately put it, "exhibit masculine resolution at variance with the delicate susceptability of [their] nature [s]." The only women in the novel who demonstrate force of character are those who had applied themselves to serious study and had overcome some obstacle or misfortune.

She offered young women female models to admire and emulate and advised them to search history for strong women. She told them they were responsible for the future of the republic: "On [women] depend in great measure the destinies of nations, as well as of families." She praised famous women who were also distinguished for domestic virtues and bowed regularly in the direction of society's definition of womanhood — "There is also a degree of delicacy expected from a lady in the use of her acquirements, which should not be lost sight of." At the same time, she suggested ways to bypass the constraints of social expectation: "Should you chance to become sufficiently acquainted with any branch of science to enable you to impart information, I know of no law either of morality or propriety, which would be violated by your modestly communicating that knowledge to others, neither do I think any man of real science would be displeased to find a lady capable of supporting conversation on scientific subjects."[21]

Upon one occasion she waxed even bolder and suggested how she had justified her own strong commitment to a public life.

The sphere of woman's duty is to be looked for in private and domestic life; and although she may and ought to do all in her power to elevate, refine, and embellish all that comes within her own circle, she should be cautious of suffering her desires to extend beyond it. If genius, circumstances of fortune, or I might better say, the providence of God, assigns to her a more public and conspicuous station she ought cheerfully to do all that her own powers, aided by the blessings of God, can achieve; and as far as human feelings will allow, act fearlessly of human censure, looking to a higher tribunal for the reward of her labors.[22]

What could be a more effective rationale for leaving the "private and domestic life"? Neither genius nor the circumstances of fortune are easy to define, and the providence of God is almost impossible to argue with.

In the end, at least as important as her precepts was her example. Moving as she did, cheerfully and fearlessly in a "more public and conspicuous station," doing "all that her own powers . . . can achieve," she was still a respected and respectable lady. It was a complicated and demanding prescription she offered young women as she taught them to maintain the outward behavior of perfect ladies while building a strong individual personality, engaging in demanding intellectual endeavor, preparing for self-support, and adopting a life-long commitment to self-education. Few people of either sex have the stamina to live up to all that Almira Phelps thought a woman ought to do.

Her lectures provide insight into the puzzling way many achieving nineteenth-century women tended to present themselves. No reader of the numerous biographical statements such women wrote about themselves and each other can fail to be struck by what seems to be the hypocrisy of the surface presentation in which so many were described as gentle, good, pious, self-abnegating, and an inspiration to those who came within their orbit. Perhaps this relentless facade of propriety and success in the assigned woman's role was necessary protective coloration for any woman who wanted to do more than perform the duties of wife or mother or beloved maiden aunt. Almira Phelps pointed out in one lecture that the social expectations were apt to make women devious. Contemporary biographies of achieving women suggest that the less one lived up to the prescriptions of true womanhood in daily life, the more one claimed to have done so for the record.

Neither in those documents of her own life which she permitted to survive nor in public statements to younger women did Phelps discuss the darker side of this effort to carry water on both shoulders, to be a true woman as society defined that condition and at the same time an independent achiever capable of shaping the society as well as of being shaped by it. Since there was no broad social support for ambition and achievement, women like Phelps and her sister reinforced each other and developed close relationships with younger women who followed their example and their advice. The didacticism and self-assurance noted by her critics may have stemmed in part from the insecurity which goes along with defying the cultural mores. The defensive tone of her notes about John Phelps's full support of her career and the care with which she shaped her biographical materials for public view all point to the high cost of self-making. Yet the surviving evidence also indicates that her zest for life was far from destroyed by the Victorian context, and it seems likely that, whatever the cost, she felt it worthwhile.

About all this, one can only speculate.

What is much clearer is that in her life and teaching she exemplified a truly self-made woman. In order to become one she had fulfilled all the social expectations summed up in the catch phrase "true womanhood": she was a wife and many times a mother; she was kind, compassionate, and intensely pious; she chose outstanding men as mentors and flattered them by close attention. At the same time she had taken her destiny in hand, educated herself, developed administrative skills, created and run several institutions, spoken out on political and social questions, attained recognition from men as well as women, and—to top it off—made a fortune by her own exertions. "What our hands find to do let us do quickly. Let us apply ourselves to the work of improvement," she had told a group of women in Guilford in 1836.[23] It was the theme of her own life.

As a single case Almira Phelps's life would be interesting but perhaps not worth this much elaboration. Its significance lies in its exemplary nature: in the women she and her sister influenced to go and do likewise.[24] Tracing influence is problematical, but we should note that beyond the considerable number of young women whom Phelps reached directly at Troy and Patapsco, *Lectures for Young Ladies* was many times reprinted, was required reading in many female seminaries, and was published in a special edition by the Massachusetts Board of Education for use in the public schools. Those who had ears to hear had a chance to learn what they wanted to know: how a woman could rise in the world. More did than we yet have any notion of, and with consequences for the society we can so far only dimly discern.

NOTES

1. In a number of studies Edward Pessen has demonstrated that most of the well-to-do in New York, Boston, and Philadelphia in the "age of the common man" were far from common men, but had begun life in families of property and standing. See, for example, his *Riches, Class and Power before the Civil War* (Lexington, Mass., 1973). See also Lee Soltow, *Men and Wealth in the United States, 1850-1870* (New Haven, 1975).

2. Brief lives of all these men are in the *Dictionary of American Biography*. See also Jonathan Messerli, *Horace Mann* (New York, 1972); Frederick Rudolph, *Mark Hopkins and the Log* (New Haven, 1956); and for other examples, *The Remains of the Reverend James Marsh D.D. . . . with a memoir of his life* (Boston, 1943); Anne Eliot Ticknor, *Joseph Green Cogswell* (Cambridge, Mass., 1874); Vincent P. Laramie, ed., *Henry Barnard: American Educator* (New York, 1974). Pessen warns me to be aware that I am talking about a tiny minority of all the young men alive in these years, though their part in shaping the emerging culture was out of proportion to their numbers.

3. Numbers of brief biographies of self-made women can be found in Frances Willard and Mary A. Livermore, *American Women: Fifteen Hundred Biographies*, 2 vols. (New York, 1897); in Mrs. J. C. Croly, *The History of the Woman's Club Movement in America* (New York, 1898); and in Edward James, Janet James, and Paul S. Boyer, eds., *Notable American Women, 1607-1950*, 3 vols. (Cambridge, Mass., 1971).

4. One incentive to the examination of Almira Phelps's life is this *sic transit gloria mundi* quality; another is the image created in the mind by her grandson's description of her at the age of ninety-one: "Conscious of her own

rectitude, she was always ready to lay down the law for others: her firmness and strong personality made her a leader in any circle in which she moved." See Emma Lydia Bolzau, *Almira Lincoln Phelps: Her Life and Work* (Philadelphia, 1936), p. 461.

5. The biographical information used here was collected forty years ago by an extraordinarily diligent scholar who compiled as complete a record as the surviving materials permit. See *ibid.*

6. Except where otherwise indicated, the statements of fact in this section came from *ibid.*

7. "Mrs. Almira Lincoln Phelps," *American Journal of Education*, 17 (Sept. 1868), an essay based on Phelps's notes. The distinction between the summer school, usually attended by girls and taught by a woman, and the winter school, attended by boys and young men who had been busy in the fields during the summer, may not be familiar to the twentieth-century reader. In 1814 it was still unusual for a woman to teach the winter school.

8. Bolzau, *Phelps*, p. 38.

9. Almira Lincoln Phelps, *Reviews and Essays on Art, Literature and Science* (Philadelphia, 1873), p. 221.

10. "Mrs. Almira Lincoln Phelps," p. 613.

11. Albertine A. N. de Saussure, *Progressive Education Commencing with the Infant* (Boston, 1835).

12. Phelps to Lydia Sigourney, Oct. 16, 1838, Lydia Sigourney Papers, Connecticut Historical Society, Hartford.

13. Bolzau, *Phelps*, p. 67.

14. Mrs. I. M. E. Blandin, *History of Higher Education of Women in the South prior to 1860* (New York, 1910), p. 177; letters of Congressman David Outlaw to his wife, Southern Historical Collection, University of North Carolina Library, Chapel Hill; A. L. Phelps, *The Educator or Hours with my Pupils* (Philadelphia, 1859).

15. See Anne F. Scott, "What, Then, Is the American: This New Woman?," pp. 37-63 herein.

16. Bolzau, *Phelps*, p. 366.

17. *Ibid.*, p. 454; *Woman's Journal*, 1874, p. 84.

18. Bolzau, *Phelps*, p. 455.

19. The sources for what follows are Phelps's writings in which she offered guidance to young women: first, *The Female Student or Lectures for Young Ladies* (New York, 1836), which was made up of talks given at Troy Female Seminary in 1830-31. This volume was reissued in a series published by the Massachusetts Board of Education for use in all the public schools of that state. It went through nine editions, including three in England, and was very widely read in female seminaries as well. *The Educator or Hours with My Pupils* was composed of similar talks given to her Patapsco pupils. Finally, *Ida Norman or Trials and Their Uses* (New York, 1855) purports to be a novel. Composed originally to be read aloud to pupils, it is a didactic moral tale, ludicrous in many of its characterizations and plot, but revealing of her values and methods.

20. I have had many harsh thoughts about Phelps's son Charles, who, after

her death, burned the diary she had kept for seventy-five years. In light of this passage, however, I must concede that she may have told him to do it.

21. Phelps, *Lectures*, p. 275.

22. *Ibid.*, p. 395.

23. Almira Lincoln Phelps, "The Influence of Women on Society," *American Ladies Magazine*, 9 (1836), 563.

24. Anne Firor Scott, "The Ever-Widening Circle: The Diffusion of Feminist Values from the Troy Female Seminary, 1822-72," pp. 64-88 herein.

Jane Addams

My first essay about Jane Addams was composed for crass material purposes (American Heritage, unlike more scholarly journals, pays for articles). That piece has been reprinted a number of times, so I have not included it here. It represented the beginning of an effort, still not complete, to understand a complex woman living in the midst of rapid social change, who came to symbolize something important to her fellow citizens, both men and women. The essay here was written to introduce the John Harvard Library edition of Addams's Democracy and Social Ethics, and it sums up what I understood about her in 1963. The review that follows indicates what I thought in 1974. The returns may not all be in yet.

When Barbara Sicherman's edition of Alice Hamilton's letters and Kathryn Kish Sklar's biography of Florence Kelley are published, when Mari Jo Buhle and others bring out their collective work on the labor and socialist movements in Chicago, when, indeed, the extraordinary Chicago women's movement of the late nineteenth century finds its historian, then Jane Addams will come to be seen not so much as an individual but as a key member of a very important social group, or even of several social groups, for she moved with astonishing ease from one stratum or grouping to another.

In her lifetime and afterward she was called America's greatest woman. I no longer know what "greatest" means, but she was certainly one of our most interesting women, and will continue to be so, as we assess and reassess the part individuals play in significant social movements.

Working through her papers in 1958 led me to my first reflections on the effect of women's higher education on the social development of the late nineteenth century and introduced me to the significance of women's voluntary associations. Understanding her a little helped me understand the numerous southern women who found her so great an inspiration.

The events of the years from the Civil War to World War I were dominated by the rapid emergence of an urban-industrial society. The nature of this change was far from clear to the participants. Nothing like this had happened before in the United States, and the earlier development in England was only partly understood and assimilated. Inevitably, certain thoughtful people tried to make sense of it. Jane Addams was one of these, and *Democracy and Social Ethics* was one of the most interesting efforts to achieve an intellectual grasp of what was happening. Its thesis was the thesis of her life: that the time had come to add a social ethic to democracy.

To be born in Illinois in 1860 was to bridge two eras. The life of Jane Addams's father, John Huy Addams, symbolized the earlier one. Serving as a miller's apprentice in Pennsylvania, he married his employer's daughter and set out, in 1844, for frontier Illinois. After examining a number of prospects, he chose a spot six miles from Freeport, where he bought a sawmill and a gristmill on a small stream dignified with the name of Cedar River and began to make his way in the world, first as a miller and later as a banker. John Addams was clearly a builder rather than a speculator. For sixteen years a member of the Illinois legislature, he worked for internal improvements which would speed the economic development of the state. In due course he became the leading citizen of Stephenson County. Four of his eight children grew to maturity; of these Jane Addams, born September 6, 1860, was the youngest.

Her father's life stood for the great days of the frontier; her own for the urban age. Her early childhood caught echoes of the great debate over slavery, in which her father's friend Abraham Lincoln was a key figure. "It is curious," she wrote years later, "how children catch the glow of moral enthusiasm of their elders and absorb opinions by listening."[1]

Upon the death of her mother when she was two, the little girl fixed her affection upon her father. It is impossible now to disentangle the real John Addams from her image of him as a being wise and great, of immense personal rectitude, guided by an "inner light." She loved to tell the story of Lincoln's letter to her father, written when both were in the Illinois

Introduction to the John Harvard Library edition of Jane Addams, *Democracy and Social Ethics* (Cambridge, Mass., 1964). Reprinted with permission.

legislature, addressed to "My dear double-D'd Addams" and saying that he knew well that Mr. Addams would vote as his conscience dictated but that it would be a help to know which way that conscience was pointing! "Doubtless I centered upon him," Jane Addams wrote, "all the careful imitation which a little girl ordinarily gives to her mother's ways and habits. My mother had died when I was a baby and my father's second marriage did not occur until my eighth year."[2]

At an age when little girls were commonly expected to model themselves upon housewifely mothers, she was emulating an effective and active father, who had a strong sense of social responsibility. A curious aspect of this relationship was that Jane Addams was convinced that she was herself an ugly duckling. Early pictures show an engaging child, but her own self-image was shaped by a "crooked back"—a spinal defect which made her carry her head slightly to one side. She worried that such a homely child might disgrace her handsome father.

Anna Haldeman, John Addams's second wife, was an energetic woman who knew books and music and shared her knowledge with the Addams children. There were two Haldeman sons. One became Jane's constant playmate; the other later married her sister Alice.

Jane Addams looked back upon her childhood as a time of physical freedom and liberty of the imagination, a wide-ranging outdoor life lived largely in the company of her stepbrother, George Haldeman. After the manner of Victorian fathers, John Addams rewarded her for every "life" from Plutarch read and reported and paid as well for every volume she read of such books as Irving's *Life of Washington*. Although nearby Freeport seemed a true city in contrast to Cedarville, there was little to make her aware of the great industrial society which was coming into being in Chicago and New York. What echoes she caught of this larger and more complex world came from books or from grown-up conversation.

She was aware of the world beyond Cedarville and at seventeen wanted badly to go to Smith College, then recently opened to provide an education for women equal to any available to men. Her father had other plans. Jane was to go to Rockford Female Seminary, as her sisters had, and be "finished off" afterward with a European tour. John Addams's view prevailed, and in 1877 she went off somewhat rebelliously to Rockford.

Life at the seminary was simple and rigorous. Each girl took care of her own room and built her own fire. The intellectual and moral atmosphere was permeated with religious fervor, reflecting the spiritual climate of the Victorian era and the intense idealism of these early college women. The curriculum encompassed Latin, Greek, natural science, ancient history and literature, mental and moral philosophy, and French. The high point of the week for Jane Addams was Sunday morning, which she customarily spent reading the Greek testament with a favorite teacher.

From the fragmentary record of her Rockford years it is possible to catch a hint of a developing personality of more than ordinary force. This slight, shy, provincial girl not only showed signs of being unusually able but also of having unusual personal magnetism. In some mysterious way she became the center of her class — a fact reflected in the reactions to her of both teachers and fellow students. She was dissatisfied with the intellectual range of the curriculum and joined a group of students and teachers who read together Shakespeare, George Eliot, Carlyle, Browning, and Ruskin. From her letters it appears that Carlyle and Ruskin particularly influenced her early efforts to think about herself and her relation to the world.

I, for my part, am convinced that the success of that work [one's calling] depends upon our religion and that I can never go ahead and use my best powers until I do settle it. It seems to me sometimes — I suppose when I am wrought up — could I but determine *that* and have it for a sure basis, that with time and space to work in I could train my powers to anything, it would only remain to choose what. Of course this may be a false stress laid on religion but I don't fuss anymore, since I have discovered its importance but go ahead building up my religion wherever I can find it, from the Bible and observation, from books and people and in no small degree from Carlyle.[3]

Two months later she struck the same note again: "I only feel that I need religion in a practical sense, that if I could fix my relations to God & the universe, & so be in perfect harmony with nature & deity, I could use my faculties and energy so much better and could do almost anything."[4]

At the same time she was plagued by self-doubt. She tried the experiment of not praying for three months and felt none the worse for it. Though there was no touch of arrogance in her letters, there were hints that she occasionally felt that she saw more deeply than other people. Her search for a religious meaning for life was complicated by the fundamentalist atmosphere of Rockford, with which she was not in sympathy, and by the pressure — which she steadfastly resisted — to become a missionary. As a rebel against the prevailing fundamentalism, she was forced to define her own religious position. Her inclination was toward some universal religion, some Primal Cause, of which Christianity was only one manifestation.

At Rockford the hallmark of her adult mind was already beginning to appear: the combination of a mystical-intuitive turn of mind with a down-to-earth interest in how things worked and a fine capacity for observation. Intellectual curiosity she had in good measure, as her wide reading and interest in scientific experiments demonstrated. Spiritual curiosity she had, too, and introspection accompanied observation. In her textbooks she encountered Darwin, whose mark upon her later thinking would be considerable.

If the underlying motif of her college career was one of constant searching for spiritual answers, the surface was one of achievement. She was valedictorian in 1881 and had a hand in almost every student activity. Plans for her own future were vague; she still thought of going to Smith, but at other times she wrote of a desire to go to Edinburgh and study medicine. The summer of 1881, like summers before it, was given over to visiting and being visited, to much reading and discussion of books. In August a great blow fell. Her beloved father, at fifty-nine, died of a ruptured appendix. All hopes, plans, ambitions, fell in a heap. She wrote her closest friend: "I will not write of myself or how purposeless and without ambition I am, only prepare yourself so you won't be too disappointed in me when you come. The greatest sorrow that can ever come to me has past and I hope it is only a question of time until I get my moral purposes straightened."[5] Her search for direction and purpose had been guided by the image of her father; now that he was gone all was confusion. His death brought, she said, "realization of sorrow as the common lot, of death as the universal experience."

Idleness did not help; in the late fall she enrolled at the Woman's Medical College in Philadelphia. Before she was well launched there, the old spinal ailment flared up, and she left the classroom for the hospital. In September 1882 her stepbrother and now brother-in-law, Harry Haldeman, a surgeon, thought he had a solution. An operation ensued, followed by a long convalescence. In January 1883 she spoke of the "lassitude, melancholy and general crookedness" which beset her, but added that she was "emerging with a straight back and a fresh hold on life and endeavor, I hope."[6]

Before the "fresh hold" could become very strong her older brother

James Weber Addams developed a mental illness, and she felt obliged to help out with his affairs. To her surprise she found herself adept at business and wondered if she was about to lose "all hold of the softer graces and refinements."[7] When Weber improved enough to come home from the hospital, Jane Addams and her stepmother sailed for Europe. The purpose was the deferred "finishing" which her father had planned, and perhaps also an effort to shake clear of the melancholy which had dogged her for two years. The prospect was exciting, but she was not altogether happy. Was one really justified in seeking culture and personal pleasure in a world so full of trouble? Once in Europe, she studied art and languages with unusual diligence. She was also very much aware of the life around her: of the inhabitants of London's East End buying decayed vegetables at auction; of the bowed German women carrying heavy loads of hot beer from the brewery to the cooling room. She had a natural affinity for the places where there was want and oppression and yet the more she saw of such things the more the feeling of futility and misplaced energy in her own life increased.

In Italy she was moved by religious painting and the lives of early Christians depicted in the catacombs. The image of the saintly life which had intrigued her years before renewed its fascination. "The grand series of frescoes which carry on a sainted life from one event to another with increasing enthusiasm, until the very apotheosis when they are lost in a cloud of angelic heads never fail to affect me with a tremor and a corresponding desire for the power arising from mere goodness."[8]

The search for a purpose for life went on. Back in the United States, her malaise seemed no better: "I am always floundering when I deal with religious nomenclature or sensations simply because my religious life has been so small;—for many years it was my ambition to reach my father's moral requirements and now when I am needing something more, I find myself approaching a crisis—& looking wistfully to my friends for help."[9] She suffered from paralysis of will. When her stepmother decided to go to Baltimore where George Haldeman was studying at Johns Hopkins, Jane dutifully went along, though "filled with shame that with all my apparent leisure I do nothing."[10]

When summer came, she visited her married sisters and then returned to Cedarville. Nowhere could she find peace. During one of these summers she was baptized, not because of any sudden conversion but because she had concluded that it was conceit to think of "being good in one's own right."[11] Finally, in the fall of 1887, in company with her closest friend,

Ellen Gates Starr, and her former teacher, Sarah Anderson, she embarked again for Europe. Her own self-assessments were harsh at this point. Ellen Starr saw something different, and in a letter from Rome reported:

Jane devoted most of her time at table to an absurd old Missourian who wore a flannel shirt and a paper collar, speared his beard with his fork ... and picked his teeth at the table, and whom nobody else near him would take the trouble to talk to. I never admired her more. She talked to this man as she would have done to a man of the world. I don't know what I would not give to have what prompts her and makes it possible for her to act this way. I suppose what I would not give is the moral effort and self discipline which is required to develop a character like hers. It seems more beautiful to me as I know it better, and would be worth more to me than all Europe if I could become only a little like her. All of which would fairly shrivel her if she could see it and I feel as if I had in some way been unfair to her to write it.[12]

Though their journey was superficially the usual pursuit of art and culture, for Jane Addams it was still a search for the answer to the fundamental question: What is good? Upon this would depend what she was to do with her life.

In the spring of 1888 a revelation came. She was in Madrid and with her friends went to a bullfight. Long after the others had left "in faintness and disgust," she had continued to watch, caught up, she said, "in the vivid association of an historical survival" and not thinking much about the bloodshed. In the evening came a reaction; she was ashamed to have been so carried away by the pageantry as to have been made unaware of suffering and, in a moment of moral revulsion, found herself re-examining her whole way of life. It suddenly seemed that dreams of future greatness had been allowed to substitute for present effort, that she had fallen into "the meanest type of self-deception." In this mood she crystallized a plan that had long been forming in her mind: she would go to a large city, find a house in the middle of the poorest district, and begin to live as a neighbor to the very poor.

William James once described religious conversion as the process "by which a self hitherto divided, consciously wrong, inferior and unhappy, becomes unified and consciously superior and happy."[13] After this experience in Madrid Jane Addams was not a different person, but her seeking, searching, and self-doubt gave way to purpose, drive, conviction, and inner poise. This communicated itself to other people. Ellen Starr wrote in the year Hull-House opened: "She strengthens the weak knees and supports the feeble hands, and has no sense of strength herself. It is a strange and beautiful thing for me to see. Everybody who comes near her is affected by her. It is as if she simply diffused something which comes from outside herself of which she is the luminous medium."[14]

Jane Addams's own forecast of ten years earlier, "If I could fix my relations to God and the universe, & so be in perfect harmony with nature & deity, I could do almost anything," was on the verge of fulfillment. In four years this doubtful girl known only to her family and friends would become a national figure on her way to becoming one of the most famous Americans of her day.

The particular path she chose was the result of the confluence of many forces. Jane Addams's early reading in Carlyle and Ruskin had laid the foundation. In the 1880s she was assimilating the *Fabian Essays* and Charles Booth's *Life and Labor of the People of London*. Positivism, to which she had been introduced by Comte's English disciple Frederic Harrison, appealed to her and for a while she had thought Comte's religion of humanity might be the answer to her long quest for a doctrine sufficiently broad to encompass real life. Echoes of Comte would appear in her writing for years.

Jane Addams's first encounter with Tolstoy may have come at about this time. Toward the end of her life she wrote that his *What To Do Then* had profoundly modified her religious convictions and commented that its power had been greater because of the "widespread moral malaise in regard to existing social conditions" that existed in the late 1880s. Her description of the influence of Tolstoy may be read in the light of the decision she took in Spain: "The doctrine must be understood through the deed. It is the only possible way not only to stir others into action but to give the message itself a sense of reality. 'Certain virtues are formed in man by his doing the action,' said Aristotle."[15]

The specific notion of a house among the poor had been part of her earlier plan of studying medicine and owed something also to the experiments of English college men reaching back to the late 1860s, most strikingly embodied in Toynbee Hall, which she had visited once. She was beginning to formulate what would become one of her central ideas, that of conduct as a means of propaganda.[16] She was much moved by the idea of universal brotherhood, an idea which was also central to Tolstoy's thought.

Once the decision was reached, action seemed easy. Ellen Starr agreed to join the plan. Thereupon Addams left for London, to learn as much as she could from Samuel and Henrietta Barnett at Toynbee Hall, thinking this the best preparation available to her. "We realised that she was a great soul and took pains to show her much and tell her more," Mrs. Barnett wrote years later.[17]

The ideas of Canon Barnett, and of his mentor, Octavia Hill, were influential, but from the beginning it was clear that the basis of this enterprise would be Jane Addams's own convictions. She and Ellen Starr went to Chicago to look for an appropriate location and for people who might help. Starr explained their guiding ideas in a letter to her sister:

After we have been there long enough & people see that we don't catch diseases, & that vicious people do not destroy us or our property, we think we have well-founded reason to believe that there are at least half a dozen girls in the city who will be glad to come & stay for awhile & learn to know the people & understand them and their ways of life: to give them what they have out of their culture and leisure & overindulgence, & to receive the culture which comes of self-denial, poverty & failure, which these people have always known. There is to be no "organization" & no "institution" about it. The world is overstocked with institutions and organizations; & after all, a personality is the only thing that ever touches anybody. . . . Jane's idea which she puts very much to the front and on no account will give up is that it is more for the benefit of the people who do it than for the other class. . . . The truth is, the thing is in the air. People are coming to the conclusion that if anything is to be done towards tearing down these walls—half imaginary between classes, that are making anarchists and strikers the order of the day it must be done by actual contact and done voluntarily from the top.[18]

That there was trouble in the air in Chicago and other large cities by 1889 there could be no doubt. Three years had passed since the Haymarket bombing with its electric effect upon people's thinking about "the social question." Half a century later Jane Addams wrote of "the startling reaction to the Haymarket riot . . . which introduced dynamite into the social conflict and so terrified the entire region that it exhibited symptoms of shell shock for decades afterward."[19]

There was bitterness unlike anything yet seen in America. Henry George had suggested it in *Progress and Poverty* in 1879; it was evident in William Dean Howells's steady progression toward socialism; it would appear in the literature of criticism coming or soon to come from Hamlin Garland, Theodore Dreiser, and Frank Norris. Foreign-born intellectuals such as Emma Goldman and Alexander Berkman tried to lead their fellow immigrants into drastic solutions. In Chicago and New York anarchists, socialists, and communists agreed on one principle—the need for revolutionary change.

In Chicago, where nearly 80 percent of the people were immigrants or children of immigrants, it was perfectly possible for the well-to-do natives to live their whole lives without firsthand contact with the vast population which did the hard, dirty work in the stockyards, on the streets, in the garment trade, work which was making a handful of capitalists very rich, work which accounted for the extraordinarily rapid growth of Chicago in the decades after the Civil War. The immigrants were equally isolated, in their desperate efforts to make a new life in a world that had turned out to be so different from the dreamed-of promised land. The situation was more explosive because of the image of the United States as a place where no man who was willing to work need go hungry. The 1880s and 1890s saw a violence of protest which hitherto had seemed appropriate only to a European despotism.

In choosing to go to live in an immigrant district Jane Addams was taking a practical step, but the main issue was, she felt, a moral one, and the attack on it would come, in her own words, as the result of a "certain Renaissance in Christianity." People's ideas, and ethical values, would have to develop to meet the changing situation. It was no longer sufficient to feel responsible for the well-being of one's own family, friends, and social equals. A new social ethic would have to evolve which would be based on responsibility to the whole community. This in essence was the purpose of Hull-House, and it was to this end that she turned her capacities as a leader and teacher in the broadest sense of the word.

The house itself was found after a long search. It had been built as a country home for a wealthy Chicago real estate man and—symbolic of the rapid growth of the city—in thirty-odd years had become totally surrounded by an immense, closely packed immigrant colony: the nineteenth ward. When Charles Hull's heir gave Jane Addams and Ellen Starr a four-year lease, rent free, the name of the builder was adopted in gratitude.

For a decade both Hull-House and its founder grew remarkably— the house in physical size and variety of function, Jane Addams in purpose and ideas, in depth and breadth of social understanding, and in satisfaction with life. Twelve years later, recovering from a train accident, she could write, "I find this morning, the first downstairs, filled with a content so deep that it reminds me of the early days of H-H."[20]

Other people came to join the venture and to stimulate Jane Addams's development. Julia Lathrop, who eventually became a member of the Illinois State Board of Charities and head of the Federal Children's Bureau, had known Jane Addams at Rockford and had gone on to study at Vassar. A prolific innovator in the new field of social work, she was a wise as well as a witty woman and was greatly valued by all the residents of Hull-House, with which she was associated for forty-three years (1889-1932). One of Jane Addams's last writings was the biography *My Friend Julia Lathrop*, a book that does much to illuminate both their lives.

Florence Kelley had a different style, but she was also a strong and effective woman, with whom life was always interesting and seldom peaceful. Daughter of Congressman William D. ("Pig-Iron") Kelley, she had gone to Cornell when it was first opened to women, studied in Europe, translated Engels, married a European doctor, and borne three children before she appeared at Hull-House in 1893, looking for a base of operations from which to support her children after the failure of her marriage. The most hard-driving of the group, she had a large hand in drafting the first Illinois Factory Law and was appointed Factory Inspector by Governor John Peter Altgeld. When a change of political control led to her dismissal, and the courts annulled the law, she went on to New York and built the Consumers League into an effective tool for improving working conditions. She described her work in a book called *Some Ethical Gains through Legislation*.

Alice Hamilton was younger than the others and came to Hull-House after she heard Jane Addams speak on its work. Trained in medicine, she turned her knowledge to social account in an effort to secure safety regulation in the "dangerous trades." She virtually invented the field of industrial medicine, which the Harvard Medical School would ultimately recognize by making her its first woman faculty member.[21]

The history of Hull-House was related to many significant historical developments. Not least of these was its effect upon the rapidly changing role of women in American life. In addition to the central group of Jane Addams, Julia Lathrop, Florence Kelley, and Alice Hamilton, each of whom was destined to work on the national and international stage, numbers of other women used Hull-House as a base from which to develop significant professional or volunteer careers. Among the best known, Mary Smith, Mary Wilmarth, Louise DeKoven Bowen, and Ellen Starr were Jane Addams's contemporaries, volunteers who helped develop the characteristic Hull-House programs and financed its causes. Later,

Grace and Edith Abbott and Sophinisba Breckinridge combined service at Hull-House with scholarly and professional careers; they all taught at the University of Chicago School of Civics and Philanthropy, and both Edith Abbott and Sophinisba Breckinridge became deans of the school. Grace Abbott headed the Immigrants Protective League, succeeded Julia Lathrop as head of the U.S. Children's Bureau, and ultimately represented the United States in the International Labor Organization.

Jane Addams through her life thought much about the role of women. From her early days at Rockford she aimed toward independence for herself, and she worked in many ways to achieve a new relationship between the sexes in Amerian society. She also spoke frequently of woman's historic role and of the home as the original center of civilization. Much of her social effort was directed toward securing for other women the right to stay at home and care for their children rather than being forced into the labor market. She wanted to preserve what was good in the traditional role and at the same time help society to formulate a new view which would accept a wider range of possible lifestyles for women. Her own example and the encouragement that the Hull-House group offered did a great deal to socialize woman's role and to bring the power of women to bear upon public problems.

The road by which she came to these convictions and to her own life pattern is only partly clear. The six years of freedom in her early life before a stepmother came on the scene may have spoiled her for the deference to men commonly expected of married women in her day. Her admiration for her father and her efforts to imitate him at a formative period shaped her in a different mold from the one traditional for girls. Rockford itself, a pioneering effort for women's education, had provided an atmosphere in which students felt, Jane Addams said, "that each moment of time thus dearly bought must be conscientiously used."

In her surviving correspondence there are only a few references to romance, but there is evidence that she was sought after by several young men, and fifteen years after Hull-House opened she still spoke of love leading to marriage as the "highest gift which life can offer to a woman." Toward the end of her life she explained the fact that she and so many of her friends had remained single:

For a considerable period after the door of opportunity began to be slowly opened to woman, she was practically faced with an alternative of marriage or a career. She could not have both apparently for two reasons. Men did not at first want to marry women of the new type, and women could not fulfill the two functions of profession and homemaking until modern invention had made a new type of housekeeping practicable, and perhaps one should add, until public opinion tolerated the double role.[22]

A post-Freudian age will surely ask "Is this all?" Did her early attachment to the image of a father cast in heroic mold eliminate most of the young men who showed signs of romantic interest? In her sixth decade (by that time a post-Freudian herself) she speculated about the group of women who had been "selected by pioneer qualities of character and sometimes at least by the divine urge of intellectual hunger." Had they, in choosing to be self-supporting and devoting themselves to public affairs, missed the central meaning of woman's life? She consulted her friend Emily Greene Balch, chairman of Wellesley's economics department, who was thinking of the same question. Balch wrote: "Is it compatible with the modern theories about sex that two generations of professionally trained women lived, without vows or outward safeguards, completely celibate lives with no sense of its being difficult or of being misunderstood? Some of them later married; most of them did not. Now they are old or oldish women, how do they feel about it?" She went on to say that they were willing to admit that they had suffered a serious loss, but not at all willing to admit that they were abnormal. "If the educated unmarried woman of the period between the Civil War and the World War represent an unique phase, it is one that has important implications which have not yet been adequately recognized by those who insist upon the imperious claims of sex."[23]

Jane Addams had written elsewhere that as "that modern relationship between men and women, which the Romans called 'virtue between equals' increases, [it] will continue to make women freer and nobler, less timid of reputation and more human."[24] She herself met men on equal terms and developed close and lasting friendships with a wide range of them. John Dewey, William James, Graham Taylor, Henry Demarest Lloyd, William Kent, and Robert Morss Lovett were only a few who gave her not only respect but also admiration and affection.

Yet her own closest affection was reserved for women and children. It was to Ellen Starr, for example, that she unburdened herself in college, and at the time Hull-House began they showed a marked dependence upon each other. "I need you, dear one, more than you can realize." "A day without a letter is blanc, as the French say of a sleepless night. I don't like such a day at all," were typical comments in her letters to Miss Starr.

Mary Rozet Smith, daughter of a wealthy Chicago family, came to Hull-House in its first year and, though she never became a regular resident, was as much a part of its life as if she had been. Younger than Jane Addams, beautiful, and endowed with an extraordinarily warm and generous spirit, she became, in time, in Jane Addams's words "the person I love best." The depth of this affection and the manner of its expression in a long series of letters, many sent only from one side of Chicago to another, are essential to an understanding of Jane Addams. They strike a note of dependency as well as of intellectual comradeship. Mary Smith and her family were large contributors to Hull-House, and since Jane Addams spent her own income for the House, it was Mary Smith who supplied the new dress, the trip to Europe and—later—the summer cottage, such amenities as Jane Addams's busy life left time for.

Close ties bound the whole Hull-House group. Julia Lathrop, Florence Kelley, Alice Hamilton, and Louise DeKoven Bowen were all attracted to Hull-House by Jane Addams, and all went on to far-reaching achievement in their own right. Strong personalities all, it would have been strange if they had always agreed, and in fact their lively discussions were high points in the life of Hull-House. They reinforced each other in a day when independent women were still the exception and developed a strong sense of responsibility for their mutual well-being. The friendship between them was broken only by death.

The first years were exciting. They were also difficult years when it often seemed that the pattern was one step forward, two steps back. In retrospect these years would be seen as misted over with fatigue. There was so much to do, and the means were relatively so small that there never seemed time to rest. The great industrial depression of 1893 brought home the problem of urban unemployment with full force and led Jane Addams to her first serious reading in economics. She became deeply involved in the Chicago Civic Federation and in an effort to mediate the Pullman strike in 1894. The Pullman affair added to the existing unrest and unemployment, and the experience bit deep into Jane Addams's consciousness.

The population of the nineteenth ward was almost totally immigrant: Russian, Italian, Irish, German, and miscellaneous other nationalities. Jane Addams's sensitive observations in many of their native lands prepared her to be almost the first articulate American to understand the feelings of these people, newly uprooted from ancient cultures and thrown willy-nilly into the maw of an American city. She was concerned for the loss of skills and cultural traditions of the homeland, the confusion in family life, and the physical and political exploitation which overcame them. Much of her time and thought was devoted to them.

In the context of the immigrant neighborhood Hull-House set out to find solutions to the problems of a fast-growing city. The residents were prolific social innovators. The first juvenile court in the world grew out of the daily experience of Hull-House with delinquents, and later this same court pioneered in the application of psychiatric treatment of youthful offenders. The first public playground in Chicago was the result of a Hull-House experiment. Baths were provided, and the great use made of them was an argument for municipal bathhouses. Co-operative enterprises ranged from purchasing coal to an apartment house for working girls. The Coffee House offered an alternative, if not a substitute, for the saloon. Spurred on by experience with small children of working mothers, Hull-House worked for mother's pensions. Industrial medicine and the union label were born there. Drama and music were used to integrate immigrants into the community. Investigations of all kinds—into housing, typhoid, tuberculosis, drug addiction, prostitution, truancy—were initiated. *Hull-House Maps and Papers* was an early example of the use of social statistics and now provides a unique source for the social and economic historian of Chicago in the 1890s. The Rockford Summer School for Working Girls provided a brief academic experience for factory workers. Other settlements—the Chicago Commons headed by Graham Taylor, the Northwestern Settlement under Raymond Robins, and Mary MacDowell's University of Chicago Settlement—took inspiration from Hull-House.

Jane Addams was a strong believer in associated effort, so Hull-House experimented with many clubs: boys, girls, Italian, German, Eight-Hour, Plato, Dante, Woman's Club, and—the one she liked best—the Working People's Social Science Club, which gave a platform to any social or economic theory the members wanted to propound. She searched for educational experiments that might reach the mass of factory workers.

Money was scarce in the 1890s, but Jane Addams's own faith in her vision attracted support, and the House grew. The art gallery, the gymnasium, the coffee shop, the cooperative home for working girls, and the Labor Museum were added.

The death rate in the nineteenth ward was much higher than the city average, and at least one obvious source of disease was the poor state of garbage collection. In 1895 Jane Addams began to investigate the problem, with the result that she secured appointment as garbage inspector and rose at six each morning to follow the collector upon his appointed rounds, much to the improvement of the ward and the fury of the collector.

Garbage collection was only one of the urgent problems. It was soon clear that philanthropy could not deal with unpaved streets, nonexistent school rooms, smallpox epidemics, four-year-old thread pullers, and their sweated garment-worker parents. Only the state had the power and scope to be effective. It was natural that the residents of Hull-House should go into politics: ward politics, state politics, and eventually even national politics. Among them only Florence Kelley had ever been a doctrinaire socialist, but experience made the others increasingly radical. In 1904 Jane Addams wrote while on a trip to New York: "We see John Brown's farm and the flag flying over his grave. I have always had a secret sympathy with his impatience and his determination that something should . . . happen. . . . I suppose the first martyrs of economic slavery will come from the city. If it depends on impatience I might be the one."[25]

This was a radicalism that began with experience, not with doctrine. What Hull-House residents saw around them made them early proponents of factory inspection and the regulation of wages, hours, and working conditions. They supported legislation to this end. Jane Addams became a crusader for the regulation of child labor—both state and federal— and made hundreds of speeches on the subject, enlisting support wherever she could find it. Hull-House became a haven for trade unionists and union organizers.[26]

The residents were not long in finding themselves in conflict with the political boss of the nineteenth ward, Alderman John Powers, who stood next to "Hinky-Dink" McKenna and "Bathhouse John" Coughlan in the hierarchy of Chicago political corruption. In 1896 a member of the Hull-House Men's Club was persuaded to run for the ward's second seat on the Common Council, but shortly after his election he was bought out by Powers. In 1898 the residents launched an all-out campaign to defeat Powers himself. They succeeded in scaring him into unaccustomed efforts in his own behalf, and the nineteenth ward was soon sharing Chicago headlines with the sinking of the *Maine* in Havana harbor. Powers won but by a reduced margin. Jane Addams seems to have accepted the general view that her own ward was one of the few in which reform was impossible and thereafter transferred her political efforts to the city school board and state and national reform.

Hull-House became, as Alice Hamilton would say sixty years later, the most exciting place in the world to live. It had a magnetic attraction for foreign visitors, and even Beatrice Webb, who found American society so depressing, noted in her diary in 1898 that Hull-House was "one continuous intellectual and emotional ferment."[27]

In a very short time Jane Addams became a subject of immense interest in Chicago and quickly thereafter in the country at large and in other parts of the world. As early as 1893 on a trip East, she was writing to her sister, "I find I am considered quite the grandmother of American settlements."[28] By the time she went to England in 1896 she was well known to all the leading reformers. After a small dinner at which the Webbs had been the only other guests she noted, "There was a little reception afterward of about twenty people, apparently all distinguished for something."[29] In Paris in 1900 she ruefully reported being treated as a "veteran" in social reform.

A vignette of Jane Addams in 1899 has been preserved in a letter from one of the residents to Mary Smith who was abroad:

She is very tired . . . of course she did not let [that] deter her from tearing about. She preached for the Methodists last Sunday, entertained the Colored Women of the National Council (Mrs. Booker Washington, et al) yesterday & later went to Winnetka . . . she runs over to Mrs. Jones—around to Mrs. Fiellras . . . up to Mrs. Kenyon—off with Mrs. Haldemane, down to inquiring strangers & in and out & around about to Italian Fiestas, forced marriages, rows between scabs & unions etc etc etc until my head spins & I sink exhausted while she poses to Mr. Linden [portrait painter] & discusses the questions of the day with freshness & calmness that put the finishing touches on my amazement. . . . Yesterday a committee from the Building Trades Council waited upon her very courteously to tell her that the mosaic workers now at last engaged on the floor were "each & all" scabs & that the Union plasterers (also working) would have to be called off unless the others were. So I left the Lady starting for Mr. Pond's office while Mr. Linden folded up his tools in despair.[30]

Both to raise money for Hull-House and to promote thinking on the subjects of her concern, Jane Addams lectured frequently in the 1890s to all kinds of audiences. Once these lectures had been tried out a few times, she turned them into articles. In 1902 seven articles, which had appeared in periodicals ranging from the *Atlantic Monthly* to the *American Journal of Sociology* were gathered into her first book. *Democracy and Social Ethics* is a milestone in her intellectual biography; it lays down the general lines of thought which she would continue to develop for another forty years.

The articles reflect in various ways upon the subject which most fascinated Jane Addams, the effort to socialize democracy. Rejecting what she called the inadequate formulation of the eighteenth century, which saw democracy largely in terms of the franchise, she thought the spiritual malaise of her own time called for a broader definition. Her own search had led to a few simple ideas. One was a basic belief in the interdependence of all human beings. Another was confidence in the essential worth of *each* of them. But the individual could only be fully developed and make his full contribution in the framework of a society which recognized interdependence and techniques of associated action. Using her own version of the doctrine of evolution, she reasoned that in an earlier step up from savagery man had evolved an ethic of individual goodness which, at the time, represented progress. Now the social organism had outdistanced ethical development, and a new evolutionary step was demanded. Committed though she was to the idea of evolution, she rejected entirely the Spencerian notion that evolution was automatic or that good automatically came from it. Like Lester Ward she injected mind and will into the process, and occasionally she seemed to suggest that there was no particular virtue in being ethical when it was easy.

The demand for a sense of social responsibility was common in her time. Jane Addams's particular concern was the question of how a social ethic could evolve. With Tolstoy she felt that those who were trying to develop it needed to involve themselves in the social process. Other moralists might sit in their studies and meditate. Jane Addams would go to the corner of Polk and Halstead streets and "drink at the great wells of human experience." By observing and grappling with the hardest practical problems of the confusing new urban society, she believed, one could begin to sense what evolution had in store.

It is legitimate to ask an ethical philosopher "How do we know what is good (or true)?" Jane Addams's response was: from experience. "We have come to have an enormous interest in human life as such accompanied by confidence in its essential soundness," she wrote. "We do not believe that genuine experience can lead us astray any more than scientific data can."

She thought her philosophy came from experience and that her basic drive had always been "the desire to live in a really living world and refusing to be content with a shadowy intellectual and aesthetic reflection of it."

There are several key elements in Jane Addams's thought: Darwinism, experience, pragmatism, and personal value. Like most Darwinians she did not hesitate to impute her own values to the evolutionary process. The concept of experience played a central role in her thinking. It was the medium through which evolution was made clear. From it she was able to perceive certain patterns emerging, replacing others which she designated as "primitive," remnants of an earlier age. It was the idea of experience which allowed her to bridge the gap between fact and value, a use to which Dewey put the same concept. No more than other social Darwinists did she recognize the impossibility of deriving value from fact.

She examined the world about her in the light of a deeply held set of personal values and when she found it wanting worked to change it. For example, the facts of urban life made the increasing interdependence of human beings visible. They did not prove that each member of society was of equal value or had an equal contribution to make to the common life. The first was observable fact, the second Jane Addams's value-laden interpretation. In the same way when she found associative experiments arising among the immigrants or workingmen, she did not hesitate to impute to these people inherently superior wisdom and goodness.

The Darwinian outlook served another and more useful function in Jane Addams's thought. It engendered in her the valuable habit of being alert to the process of social change. When she referred to experience in this sense it was, as in the pragmatism of James and Dewey, a corrective to doctrine. With them she believed that ideas should not be judged true or false in themselves, but only on the basis of whether they worked in practice. There was no such thing as a "good" idea that worked badly. And an idea which might have been good in one set of circumstances might be bad in a new and different set. In this framework she looked at a number of social problems with which she was intimately familiar, and in each case saw the older individual ethical standards at war with a newer, emerging, social standard visible among the poorer people. The recipients of charity rather than the dispensers had developed, she argued, a genuine feeling for their interdependence; the trade unionists were developing techniques of associated action which modern industry so badly needed; hard-pressed factory women were finding ways to do without outmoded domestic service; the political boss rather than the patrician reformer represented the wave of the future in politics. It followed that if the poor were in the forefront of ethical development, social equality was essential to progress. Although in practice she and her associates recognized the need for leadership and that it might come from the upper as well as the working class, there is almost no mention of this in her theoretical analysis.

Through the whole of her early writing the glorification of the working class with its echoes of Comte (who had once written, "The working class, then, is better qualified than any other for understanding and still more for sympathizing with the highest truths of morality")[31] existed side by side with keen observations and devastating realism which saw the failings of her immigrant neighbors as clearly as their virtues. Mysticism and realism combined with a fine sense of style account for some of her fascination.

The key to the chapter called "The Charitable Effort" may lie in a paragraph which appeared in the earlier version published in the *Atlantic Monthly* but was deleted in the book:

> For most of the years during a decade of residence in a settlement, my mind was sore and depressed over the difficulties of the charitable relationship. The incessant clashing of ethical standards which had been honestly gained from varying industrial experience, — the misunderstandings inevitable between people whose conventions and mode of life had been so totally unlike, — made it seem reasonable to say that nothing could be done until industrial conditions were made absolutely democratic.

She then went on to say that after much reflection she had concluded that such direct experience with poverty was in any case the necessary forerunner if "individual sympathy and intelligence are [to be] caught into the forward intuitive movement of the mass. . . . The social reformers who avoid the charitable relationship with any of their fellow men take a certain outside attitude to this movement. They may analyze and formulate it, but they are not essentially within it."[32]

In a complex industrial society, where many people were at the mercy of forces over which they had no control, charity in the traditional sense was really obsolete. Society as it was organized was creating needs greater than individual charity could handle. The crying need was for a new organization of society which would assure every member of it a decent wage and a chance to work. Such a change she suggests here and later in the chapter on "Industrial Amelioration" was likely to be brought about only by the victims of industrialization with the help of people like herself who were willing to immerse themselves in the problems of the masses. This opportunity to learn about the life of the masses was the function which the charitable relationship was still capable of serving.

In this chapter, as in all the succeeding ones, the body of theory was brought to life with material drawn from experience and observation, presented with Jane Addams's considerable talent for identifying herself with any kind of person she was describing.

The essay "Filial Relations" was again presented in the pattern of conflict between an accepted and a newly emerging ethical standard, in this case the one lying at the heart of the woman movement. In the centuries before the industrial revolution the mere maintenance of family life required a woman's best energies. If she had skill at healing, her opportunities were great. Muscle and mind were required to provide food, clothing, shelter, and education for the young. In this social situation the belief that woman's place was in her home was sensible. But one by one meaningful responsibilities disappeared from the lives of well-to-do women. The public school, commercial farming, factory-made clothing, city life: each of these seemed good in itself, but for women the shell of homemaking remained while the substance, except for the care of small children, was removed. It was as if the upper-middle-class woman was herself drained of meaning and remained on the scene as a decorative doll. Thorstein Veblen had described the process from the outside in *The Theory of the Leisure Class*. Jane Addams looked at it from the inside. From her own experience and that of her closest friends she knew the inchoate sense of uselessness which afflicted young women of leisure; at the same time she saw around her endless work that women could and should do to meet pressing social needs. Could the world's expectation of women be modified to admit a new social ethic? She suggested that the needs of a growing community called for women to add to their traditional functions responsibility for social action. From her own experience she recognized that the assumption of community responsibility made emotional as well as intellectual demands and that a woman who attempted to fill her traditional obligations as well as the newer ones might feel a conflict.

To partly solve this problem she put forward William James's notion that an emotion is weakened by each successive failure to act upon it and argued that a girl who felt the impulse to meet social needs but failed to act suffered a net loss of energy. If this happened repeatedly, health might even give way.

The subject of this analysis was clearly the well-educated single girl from a well-to-do family upon whom there was no pressing demand to earn a living and who, as a result of her education, could no longer be content in the restricted traditional sphere of action. The descriptions here were drawn from her own experience and that of Mary Rozet Smith, whose conflict concerning her family ties and her desire to play an active community role had been the subject of much discussion between them.

The chapter called "Household Adjustment" took up the role of women and the ethics of family life versus those of society from another angle. The servant problem was perennially discussed in America, but Jane Addams took hold of it by a new handle. Pointing out that nearly all the industrial functions once carried on by the householder had been transferred to the factory or the skilled outside craftsman, she saw the live-in servant as an anachronism in the twentieth century. Most writers began from the point of how the function of the maid was to be filled in a relatively maidless society; Jane Addams began with the maid's own view of life and asked why she was so reluctant to enter domestic service. She identified herself so well with the servant girl that she often gave the impression that she had been a maid. In her analysis of the servant's discontent she anticipated conclusions, reached in our day by researchers who have explained the lives of factory workers, that not the work itself or even its physical conditions determine satisfaction and output—but the sense of belonging and *esprit de corps*. The social ethic she called for would recognize the human needs of the servant as equal to those of the employer and thus would dictate a determined effort to find new methods of household management which would emancipate the servant.

Early in her career Jane Addams had developed a strong interest in the trade union movement. Union organizers were welcome at Hull-House, and, though she occasionally became exasperated with particular ones, she steadfastly supported the principle of collective bargaining. In it she discerned one of the evolutionary currents she considered most vital, the development of new techniques of associated action.

Modern industry she thought to be on the wrong track because an inherently social effort was used for individual gain. It was not only that the profits of labor went largely to the capitalist, but also even a well-meaning employer who attempted to give his workers certain benefits was going in the wrong direction. Doing things for people did not develop their capacities and contradicted the most basic meaning of social democracy. Experiments were needed to find ways for workers to help themselves. Industry needed to be reorganized so that decisions as well as profits could be shared. Only the unions, as far as she could see, were moving in the direction of a new type of industrial organization.

She did credit private initiative with useful experiments which might otherwise never be tried, but she argued that once successful such experiments must be transferred to an arena in which the workers could take part in the decision-making if they were to have lasting value.

In the chapter on "Educational Methods" Jane Addams offered the extreme statement of her democratic faith when she asserted that not only was it the right of every man to have his full powers "freed" by education but also that society was the loser when *any* citizen was not educated so that the moral power that was in him would be available. It was this moral power in all human beings which in this essay she identified as the engine of social change. Whether this was the Quaker "something of God in every man" or the Comtean insistence upon a mystic source of goodness in the working class, or simply Jane Addams's own faith in innate human goodness is of little moment. The point is that this was her ultimate faith, and it kept her going at times when the concrete evidence might have led to the gravest doubts about human goodness.

It is not surprising, in the light of what has gone before, to find here also the idea that education should consciously train for social action. Educational patterns needed new structure to bring them into coherence with the kinds of lives people really lived. This discussion exposed Jane Addams's deep and often reiterated concern about the meaninglessness of industrial labor. Her observations of the effects of factory life and the division of labor on different personality types were acute. A great concern for production coupled with a lack of concern for the producer seemed to her immoral.

She wanted schools to do two things—first to relate what they taught to the life of the pupil, and second to help him see his place in the world in its relationship to the rest of society. A comparison with John Dewey's *School and Society*, published two years earlier, suggests the high degree of interaction in the thinking of these life-long friends. Dewey had served on the Board of Hull-House and conducted some of his early experiments there. There are striking parallels between his book and this essay.

Jane Addams's theory of education is a natural corollary of her belief that social evolution would come from the working people. Therefore, the educational system had to offer them full opportunity for personal development and a way of connecting themselves with the life of the community. She admitted that the settlement had not yet found techniques of education which were effective with the great mass of factory operatives.

The final chapter, "Political Reform," had first appeared four years earlier, on the eve of the campaign to defeat Alderman Powers, under the improbable title "Some Ethical Survivals in Municipal Corruption." Anticipating Lincoln Steffens, who began his research for *The Shame of the Cities* just about the time *Democracy and Social Ethics* was published, Jane Addams explained the structure of the "boss's" power in an immigrant community, and the emotional and practical basis for it. She demonstrated in detail the ways in which the boss made himself part of the "real life of the community," while the reformer so frequently concerned himself merely with administrative purification. Politics, she said, was not an airtight compartment, unrelated to the community. It was rather one of the modes of expression of the basic moral habits of a group of people. She pointed out that the corporate executive who found it cheaper to bribe the alderman than to pay higher taxes was on the same moral plane as the alderman who used his money in turn to buy the support of his constituents. She asserted flatly that in a democracy "all move forward or retrograde together" and that therefore no single group could be pointed to as the source of community corruption. No one would have been more surprised than Alderman Powers to find Jane Addams saying: "Would it be dangerous to conclude that the corrupt politician himself, because he is democratic in method, is on a more ethical line of social development than the reformer, who believes that people must be made over by good citizens and governed by experts? The former at least are engaged in that great moral effort of getting the mass to express itself, and of adding this mass energy and wisdom to the community as a whole."

The essay concluded with an emotional tribute to democracy, which suggested that she had come to identify it with Christian fellowship.

Taken together these essays illuminate the underlying assumptions upon which Jane Addams's life as a social reformer, as well as her social theory, was grounded. They show how she combined observation and intuition in a framework of almost religious intensity and moral idealism.

They also provide a commentary upon some of the problems of central concern to American progressives and English reformers and offer some illuminating social history.

Though she never felt at home with any single-minded doctrine, Jane Addams was not afraid to be radical. Clearly a child of her times, of Darwin, James, and Dewey as well as of Ruskin, Comte, Toynbee, Frederick Maurice, and Charles Kinglsey, she was also original and had a strong tendency to go to the heart of any problem, by intuition if not by reason. The validity of the questions she asked is suggested by their appropriateness after sixty years in the context of a struggle to move from an individual to a social ethic in race relations.

When the manuscript of *Democracy and Social Ethics* was in the hands of the publisher, Jane Addams wrote to Mary Smith that she was in terrible throes about the "dreadful book" and wishing that she could do it over again. Once out, it received a chorus of praise, some perceptive, some not. Edward T. Devine, writing in *Charities*, took her charity visitor too literally and accused her of setting up a straw man and then "demolishing an enemy that had already been routed." Charles R. Henderson in the *Journal of Sociology* came closer to the mark, and perhaps also answered Devine, when he wrote "The careless reader is likely to miss the point of view in this delicate and indirect treatment of our egoism."

Letters to her were enthusiastic. E. A. R. Seligman said that it was long since he had read "so sane and inspiring a book." Stanley McCormick wrote that he was planning an experiment in profit-sharing. Fellow social workers thought she had said what they all knew but had not formulated, and Canon Barnett thought she helped "us see how if we boldly face what seems evil we see good."[33] The reaction of the general public may be gauged by the fact that 1,676 copies were sold in the first month, and at the end of six weeks a second printing was necessary. The publishers were sufficiently pleased to urge her to write another book as soon as possible.

When *Democracy and Social Ethics* appeared in 1902, Jane Addams was already working in most of the areas which it discussed. In the next dozen years she broadened her activity in many directions. She undertook a larger responsibility for the national woman suffrage campaign, served on the Chicago School Board, which was the center of far-reaching political and educational battles, took a hand in the national as well as the state campaign to outlaw child labor, served as mediator in labor disputes, helped to forge the historic agreement between Hart, Schaffner, and Marx and the Amalgamated Clothing Workers, was the first woman president of the National Conference of Charities and Corrections, helped to found the National Association for the Advancement of Colored People, helped edit the magazine *Charities* and its successor *The Survey*, and took a hand in the organization of the Progressive party. Even this list is not inclusive.

There was a constant interaction between her life and thought, and a stream of lectures and articles ultimately became books. In 1906 she published *Newer Ideals of Peace*, building upon William James's idea of a moral substitute for war. Her approach to peace was indirect; she extended further the idea of a social ethic. She developed again her theory of the nascent social morality to be found in the crowded immigrant quarters and argued that when this development was encouraged and directed, made really operative in society, the need for war would gradually disappear. It is something of a surprise, in view of the title, to turn to the book and find chapter headings such as "Immigrants in City Government," "Industrial Legislation," and "Group Morality." It is, in fact, an extension and expansion of *Democracy and Social Ethics*, with the difference that it projects the ideal of social morality upon the world scene.

Her next book, *The Spirit of Youth and the City Streets* (1909), was a major contribution to urban sociology (which, as a distinct field, did not appear for another sixteen years). It inspired William James to write that certain pages of it "seem to me quite immortal statements" and to add that "the wholeness of Miss Addams' embrace of life is her own secret. She simply *inhabits reality* and everything she says necessarily expresses its nature. She can't help writing the truth."[34]

Hard upon the heels of *The Spirit of Youth* came the autobiographical *Twenty Years at Hull-House* (1910), one of the most widely read of all her books. The impulse to write it, she said, came partly because settlements had multiplied so easily in the United States that she hoped "a simple statement of an earlier effort, including the stress and storm, might be of value in their interpretation and clear them of a certain charge of superficiality." Partly, also, she wanted to forestall two biographies of her which were in progress and which made life in the settlement "all too smooth and charming."

Warning that she was too close to the people and the causes she loved to treat them critically, she nevertheless managed to give a picture of the experiences of her first fifty years which constitutes social and intellectual history of a high order. Her earlier books, she said, constituted an effort to set forth a thesis, while this volume "endeavors to trace the experiences through which various conclusions were forced upon me."[35]

Two years later she published another important piece of urban analysis, *A New Conscience and an Ancient Evil*, a study of the economic origins of prostitution with, again, special reference to the youth of the cities. Published first serially in *McClure's*, it brought a flood of mail.

Until 1914 the development of Jane Addams's life and thought followed a logical pattern. This was still true, but less visibly so, after the outbreak of war. Like many other American liberals she had been horrified to see Europe move toward exactly the catastrophe which was no longer supposed to happen. She had been active in peace movements, and her international ties through the settlement movement were strong. With the outbreak of hostilities she turned all her energy to efforts to bring the war to a speedy end. With Carrie Chapman Catt she issued a "call" for a convention in Washington in January 1915 which led to the formation of the Woman's Peace party, an organization dedicated to finding a way to end the war and bring about an international organization to keep peace. In the spring of 1915 she journeyed to The Hague to preside over an International Congress of Women, made up of delegates from both the warring and neutral nations. This group later organized the Women's International League for Peace and Freedom, of which Jane Addams would be president until her death.

During the next two years she labored unceasingly to bring about a Conference of Neutrals to work out peace terms acceptable to all sides. She traveled with Alice Hamilton and Dr. Aletta Jacobs of Holland to visit foreign ministers and leaders in many countries. She tried to persuade Woodrow Wilson, whose program seemed to parallel that of the Women's International League in many particulars, to seize the initiative in calling for an end to the war. Partly to this end she lent the weight of her name to the Democratic party in 1916.

Jane Addams's concept of pacifism was not a negative one. She was convinced that the horror of the war offered the strategic moment for a new breakthrough, that the time was ripe for an international government which could apply human intelligence to the solution of problems which, unsolved, led inexorably to war. Much of what she was proposing in

1916 and 1917 foreshadowed the economic and social work undertaken by the United Nations since 1945.

To her sorrow and dismay, after Wilson's reelection he seemed less and less inclined to follow the course she thought to be the only one which would help. After the Congress declared war in April 1917, she found herself increasingly unpopular. "Pacifist," which in 1914 had been a term of distinction, was now equated with German sympathizer or traitor. It was difficult for one whose convictions had not been changed as war fever swept the country to find a place to be useful. One by one fellow crusaders for peace decided that, while war in general was bad, this war was necessary. Audiences which had cheered her now sat in stony silence. Old friends and colleagues took pains to dissociate themselves from her view.

Years later Ellen Starr paid tribute to the fact that when every hand seemed against her, and without even the comfort of self-righteousness, Jane Addams had continued to stand for peace in time of war. "All, even the great," Starr wrote, "naturally enjoy the sunshine of approbation and work more easily in its congenial warmth. Jane Addams knew it well, and parted with it under no misconceptions; and what is more remarkable, no bitterness. She could not foresee that it would return."[36]

From two of her books, *Women at the Hague* (1915) and *Peace and Bread in Time of War* (1922), the high tragedy of these years emerges. Her own intelligence told her that human beings who were capable of effecting an international banking structure or the intricate web of international trade were not incapable of developing an international political system — if only they wanted to. Her extreme sensitivity to the value of human life made every death in the brutal and senseless battles a personal agony. Having tried with all her power, and with the support of thousands of women from many countries, to make governments see what she saw, and having failed, she was driven back into a kind of mysticism. The slogans about a war to end wars, to make the world safe for democracy, seemed to her wickedly wrong. How could anyone believe that good could come of such evil? Her old principle that the way in which a reform is brought about is as important as the reform itself was unshaken. It was impossible therefore for her to find the outlet available to most other Americans of throwing herself wholeheartedly into the war effort.

She could be wholehearted about the effort to feed the millions of people to whom war had brought hunger, and it was here that she tried to find some hope for the future. The traditional role of women, she said, had been to provide food for their children. Perhaps in the effort to feed other women's children in the warring countries American women might forge bonds of sympathy and faith which would transcend the enmity of governments and give hope for a new world in which nations would merge into an interconnected world state. It was a slender thread, but it gave her hope and thereby the energy to work unceasingly with Herbert Hoover's food program. Hoover himself was among those who stood by her during these trying years.[37]

To outsiders it probably seemed that Jane Addams's unpopularity dissipated when the war ended, and that in the 1920s she was restored to the position of respect and in some cases almost veneration, which she had enjoyed before. From her own point of view the postwar years still held a good many trying experiences and *The Second Twenty Years at Hull-House* (1930) sounded a note of disillusionment which is different from anything in *Democracy and Social Ethics* or the original *Twenty Years*. To be accused of not being a loyal American because of her interest in developing a wider loyalty to an interdependent society seems occasionally to have caused her to despair of the wisdom of ordinary people in which she had so long put her faith. Few documents give so vivid a picture of the intolerance which followed upon the excitement of the World War and the Palmer Red Scare than her second autobiographical volume.

If she was less optimistic than in the days before 1914, she was not any less willing to engage in thought and action. The chapters in *The Second Twenty Years* range from the woman movement, prohibition, and immigrants to an analysis of the efforts to humanize justice and her old interest in the play instinct. A final chapter is a new formulation of her earlier idea of the propaganda of the deed: she calls it now "Education by the Current Event." Through it all there is no evidence of any diminution of intellectual energy. Nor is there any such evidence in her last volume, published posthumously, *My Friend Julia Lathrop* (1935), which tells a great deal about Jane Addams as well.

She continued to the end of her life a deep concern with international affairs and the effort to build the Women's International League for Peace and Freedom into an effective instrument for peace. In 1931 she shared the Nobel Peace Prize with Nicholas Murray Butler.

The Depression brought new problems to her door. Edmund Wilson went to Chicago in 1932 and wrote of Hull-House:

Inside there is a peace and a sort of sanctity. Jane Addams at seventy-two still dominates her big house among the little ones . . . with her singular combination of the authority of a great lady and the humility of a saint. . . . Through her vitality Hull-House still lives—the expression of both pride and humility: the pride of a moral vision which cannot accept as habitat any one of the little worlds of social and intellectual groupings; the humility of a spirit which, seeing so far, sees beyond itself, too, and feels itself lost amid the same uncertainties, thwarted by the same cross-purposes, as all of those struggling others.[38]

In 1935 to a large gathering held in her honor in Washington, describing the contemporary crisis she used a phrase very reminiscent of *Democracy and Social Ethics*: "The source of our difficulties lies in a lack of moral enterprise."[39] A few days later she died and was honored in death as few private citizens have been.

Jane Addams's seventy-four years, stretching from 1860 to 1934, encompassed the most rapid and acute changes American history had then witnessed. Born a pioneer's child in a simple rural home, she died first citizen of Chicago, which had become a great city in the course of her lifetime.

There are no calipers exact enough to measure a life. Jane Addams was so many-sided that even the close student is apt to feel that he has missed something. But the major lines are reasonably clear. A talented youngster, she early developed a sense of destiny but was not sure what that destiny was. At Rockford she showed signs of unusual personal magnetism. A missionary's life was urged upon her, but while she was deeply concerned with religion she could not accept orthodoxy. She began the long process of working out her own religion which, once accomplished, would provide the framework for her career. The death of a beloved father caused a spiritual crisis, followed by eight years of agonizing indecision. A mystical experience banished the indecision, and afterward she was concentrated and effective, rapidly becoming a leader, a teacher, and a charismatic figure. The missionary career she had rejected was transmuted into a new form, and she became in the broad sense a religious leader and a saint.

In practice and in thought she boldly confronted the nineteenth century's most burdensome legacies to the twentieth: Can human beings live in a rapidly changing industrial society and remain human? Can nations learn to live together in peace? Until she was fifty-four her attention was primarily on the first; for the remaining years on the second.

Herself a thoroughgoing evolutionist, from Hull-House she boldly attacked the dragon of Spencerian Darwinism. To rigid dogma she replied with a call for experience; to fatalism about the condition of the poor she opposed action; turning the Social Darwinians' environmentalism back upon them, she argued that the poor, far from being born "unfit," were a product of their environment. If it could be changed, so could they. The Social Darwinists had no place for ethics; she called for a social morality, saying that an idea had to be judged by its consequences and that there was no such thing as a good idea that brought bad results. And she added for good measure that it was quite as necessary to have good means as good ends. Perhaps more important than anything else she was not content to preach: with her, indeed, preaching followed practice and therefore she could point to concrete accomplishment as proof, by her own pragmatic standard, of the worth of her ideas.

People loved her, and she attracted many disciples. Partly this may have been because saintly figures are always rare, and in them we sense the dimly seen possibilities of the human condition. Partly it may have been her gift for communication and capacity to identify with almost any other person. She dealt effectively with practical questions and things unseen. She managed to encompass qualities which are often separated: she was saintly and an administrator; she was a thinker who was also a doer; a skilled critic who was also capable of constructive thought. She was at home discussing the largest questions of social policy or dealing with the poorest inhabitant of the nineteenth ward, a seeker after truth who did not find the details of garbage collection beneath her.

The pacifism which became the primary theme of her last quarter-century was an outgrowth of her main concerns in the first fifty years. Having worked to help the hungry earn their bread and to save the children from physical and emotional deprivation, she could not quietly watch them sent off to be killed. She saw war as a historical anachronism, a measure of the human failure to develop a full understanding of the social nature of goodness, a lack of moral enterprise. Her rejection of war was basic and not unlike that of the other figures with whom she may justly be compared: St. Francis, Gandhi, and Tolstoy. Tolstoy found the key to life in the single sentence, "Resist not evil." Jane Addams understood this, and practiced it, but added to it, "Love thy neighbor as thyself."

As much as any member of her generation, she contributed to that evolution of social conscience, which she so longed to see take place, as the necessary precondition to social change. This may be her most enduring legacy, though her socialization of women's role and her practical social inventions to meet the problems of the urban world reach deep into contemporary life and have in turn created new questions which this generation must answer.

Her own words written about William Penn form a fitting summary: "Such right thinking and courageous action in the life of one man has an enormous liberating power and taps new sources of human energy. It is doubtless what we need at this moment more than anything else, a generous and fearless desire to see life as it is, irrespective of the limitations and traditions which so needlessly divide us."[40]

NOTES

1. Jane Addams, *My Friend Julia Lathrop* (New York, 1935), p. 25.

2. Jane Addams, *Twenty Years at Hull-House* (New York, 1910), p. 11. This book is a sensitive retrospective analysis of her first fifty years and is indispensable for any one interested in her thought.

3. Jane Addams to Ellen Gates Starr, Nov. 22, 1879, Sophia Smith Collection, Smith College, Northampton, Mass. All letters cited from Jane Addams to Ellen Starr are in this collection. Cf. Thomas Carlyle, *Sartor Resartus* (London, 1838), pp. 169-70.

4. Addams to Starr, Jan. 29, 1889.

5. Addams to Starr, Sept. 3, 1881.

6. Addams to Starr, Jan. 7, 1883.

7. Addams to Starr, Apr. 24, 1883.

8. Addams to Starr, Mar. 9, 1884.

9. Addams to Starr, Dec. 6, 1885.

10. Addams to Starr, Feb. 7, 1886.

11. Addams, *Twenty Years at Hull-House*, p. 78.

12. Starr to Mrs. John H. Addams, Jan. 30 and Feb. 5, 1888, Sophia Smith Collection.

13. William James, *The Varieties of Religious Experience* (reprint ed., New York, 1961).

14. Starr to Mary Allen, Sept. 15, 1889, Sophia Smith Collection.

15. Jane Addams, "A Book That Changed My Life," *Christian Century*, 44 (Oct. 13, 1927), 1196-98. Cf. Carlyle: "But indeed Conviction, were it never so excellent, is worthless till it converts itself into Conduct. Nay properly Conviction is not possible till then; inasmuch as all Speculation is by nature endless, formless, a vortex amid vortices: only by a felt indubitable certainty of Experience, does it find any centre to revolve around, and so fashion itself into a system. Most

true it is, as a wise man teaches us, that Doubt of any sort cannot be removed except by Action." *Sartor Resartus*, p. 201.

16. See Jane Addams, "Tolstoy and Gandhi," *Christian Century*, 48 (Nov. 25, 1931), 1485-88, for one of many statements of this idea. Until she went to Chicago in 1889 the chief intellectual influences seem to have been English and European rather than American.

17. Henrietta Barnett, *Canon Barnett: His Life, Work and Friends* (London, 1921), p. 422. Addams's relationship with the Barnetts lasted as long as they lived.

18. Starr to Mary Blaisdell, Feb. 23, 1889, Sophia Smith Collection.

19. Addams, *My Friend Julia Lathrop*, p. 46.

20. Addams to Mary Rozet Smith, May 19, 1902, Jane Addams Papers, Peace Collection, Swarthmore College, Philadelphia.

21. Alice Hamilton, *Exploring the Dangerous Trades* (New York, 1944).

22. Jane Addams, *The Second Twenty Years at Hull-House* (New York, 1930), p. 196.

23. *Ibid.*, pp. 197-98.

24. *A New Conscience and an Ancient Evil* (New York, 1911), p. 212.

25. Addams to Smith, Aug. 1904, Swarthmore College Peace Collection.

26. See Mary Anderson, *Woman at Work* (Madison, 1952), and Agnes Nestor, *Woman's Labor Leader* (Rockford, 1954).

27. *Beatrice Webb's American Diary*, ed. David Shannon (Madison, 1963), p. 108.

28. Addams to Alice Haldeman, Feb. 23, 1893, Swarthmore College Peace Collection.

29. Addams to Smith, June 27, 1896, Swarthmore College Peace Collection.

30. Gertrude Barnum to Smith, Aug. 16, 1899, Swarthmore College Peace Collection.

31. Auguste Comte, *A General View of the Positive Philosophy* (Paris, 1848), p. 151.

32. Jane Addams, "The Subtle Problems of Charity," *Atlantic Monthly*, 83 (Feb. 1899), 163-78.

33. All these reviews and letters are in the Jane Addams Papers, Swarthmore College Peace Collection, items dated May and June 1902.

34. *American Journal of Sociology*, 15 (Jan. 1910), 558.

35. Addams, *Twenty Years at Hull-House*, pp. viii, ix.

36. Ellen Gates Starr, Tribute prepared for Memorial Service organized by the National Federation of Settlements, June 1935, Sophia Smith Collection.

37. Jane Addams, *Peace and Bread in Time of War* (New York, 1945), ch. 4.

38. Edmund Wilson, *The American Earthquake* (New York, 1958), p. 454.

39. Jane Addams, *A Centennial Reader* (New York, 1960), p. 325.

40. Jane Addams, "The Social Deterrent of Our National Self-Consciousness," *Survey Graphic*, 22 (Feb. 1933), 98-101.

AN AFTERWORD . . .

The new edition of Democracy and Social Ethics *was published in November 1964, and I find on that date the following note in my journal:*

Democracy and Social Ethics *arrived tonight, looking handsome in its new cover and with my introduction. As I re-read it [the introduction] I find it far short of the brilliant piece I had envisioned and can only conclude that I have yet a long way to go before my writing has a distinctive style. I feel a little awkwardness in this piece, as if I am posing for my picture or talking to someone with whom I am not yet at ease. Perhaps I was overawed by the Harvard historians. At any rate it is in print.*

Rereading the essay in 1983 I am no longer so critical of its prose— though I always want to write better than I do—and think the analysis stands up fairly well. I do notice a number of things in light of work I have done since this was written. Jane Addams, like Emma Willard, clearly yearned for an institution that she *could control, and she ran Hull-House her way for more than forty years. I am led to wonder whether powerful women who create institutions have certain characteristics in common that might be identified and compared?*

    I also notice how much Addams depended upon a variety of women's voluntary associations and how she took a hand in forming some of them (as well as in organizing some groups of men and women).

    The final four paragraphs now strike me as oversimple. It is not that what they say is wrong; it is what they do not say, the failure to come to grips with the complexity of Addams's personality. Some of that complexity is revealed in a letter Alice Hamilton wrote in 1926 when Jane Addams was very ill and Hamilton was debating giving up a long planned trip abroad. On the one hand she quotes her sister Norah as saying: "Nothing could quite compare with having J.A. really want me and being able to do things for her." But then she added: "On the other hand, there is my own experience which tells me that I am not at all essential, that a heavy sacrifice made for J.A. is usually a mistake because it proves not to mean very much to her."

Perhaps this was what another friend meant when she wrote that "despite her affectionate warmth and sympathy and understanding there was something impersonal" about Jane Addams. To have known her was "akin to sharing in some blessing of nature, that like the sunlight, shone on the just and the unjust. One shared the gift gladly . . . without a personal stake in it exactly." James Linn, her admiring nephew, said that her closest associates found her sometimes to be a "little withdrawn." Neither Allen Davis, nor I, nor so far as I know anyone else who has written about Jane Addams has yet dealt satisfactorily with this aspect of her personality.

Heroines and Heroine Worship

Allen F. Davis. *American Heroine: The Life and Legend of Jane Addams.* New York: Oxford University Press, 1973. xxi + 339 pp. Illustrations, bibliographical notes, footnotes, and index. $10.95.

Reading *American Heroine*, I found myself thinking of Alice Hamilton's remark that only a person as great as Jane Addams herself would be able to write her biography, and of Gordon Allport's warning about the difficulty we all have in understanding personalities more complex than our own. Biography is perhaps the most difficult of the historian's arts. No biographer worth his salt is content to describe the externals of a life. He wants, beyond that, to discern the influences at work upon that life and to reveal the springs of action. He must have the psychological insight to create a livable, believable human being without falling into the reductionism which turns the person into a small heap of drives, neuroses, and complexes. It is with this last requirement that Allen Davis has most difficulty.

Irony is intended in the title of this book. Davis has in the back of his mind a model of what it is to be a genuine, twenty-four-carat heroine: selfless, unworldly, a great spiritual leader, indifferent alike to praise and blame, a moralist who sees the good and does it; uncompromising in pursuit of moral ends; never calculating, never manipulative; devoid of human frailties. His concept is of the heroine as saint, an ideal type in the Weberian sense.

Since, by this definition, Jane Addams was not a genuine heroine, how did so many people come to regard her as one? Davis offers two explanations. First, people were deceived. Jane Addams, he says, carefully

Reprinted with permission from *Reviews in American History,* 2 (Sept. 1974), 413-18.

nurtured an inaccurate view of herself as "sage and priestess," as a self-sacrificing spiritual leader. And, second, people wanted to believe. By admiring her, by believing that she was engaged, day and night, in trying to solve the human problems of an industrial society, people could go their own selfish ways, comforted by the fact that she was making the sacrifices they were unwilling to make.

The second part of this thesis is provocative and may be sound. Certainly the terms in which she was often described in the popular press were unreal, and certainly she was much *in* the popular press and much admired by a wide variety of people. Though I would hesitate to accept his notion that Addams "fulfilled the need for a female religious figure —a saint, a madonna, even a Protestant virgin," it is with the first part of his thesis that I wish primarily to take issue.

Davis had done a workmanlike job of presenting the events of Jane Addams's life. He is at best when dealing with well-authenticated facts. He has mastered the growing body of Addams materials and used them to retell the story of her life, from her birth on the eve of the Civil War to her death in the third year of the New Deal. He has unraveled a good many puzzles, straightened out some of the confusion left by her own autobiographies and by her nephew's admiring volume, and provided a more accurate and detailed account of where she was and what she did than has hitherto been available. He is, however, more interested in what she did than in what she thought and tosses off the body of her social thinking with the condescending, and debatable, statement that "she was always more important as a publicist and popularizer than as an original thinker" (p. ix).

In the first chapter, covering a period for which materials are relatively scarce, Davis makes skillful use of nearly every surviving document to recreate the small-town and boarding-school experience of an uncommonly talented midwestern girl in the 1860s and 1870s. The floundering and indecision which followed her graduation from Rockford Seminary tempts him to some dubious analysis of the mental and physical health of the first generation of women college graduates, but on the whole he traces clearly the events of the difficult years, which ended with the decisive move to Hull's decayed mansion on the corner of Polk and Halsted in Chicago's nineteenth ward.

Once Jane Addams and Ellen Starr and the young people who joined them are settled at Hull-House, Davis moves back and forth from chronological to topical treatment, describing among other things the development of settlement houses, the variety of reforms in which Jane Addams quickly became a leader, the social justice movement which the Hull-House circle helped to create, her political adventures, her involvement in the peace movement, her personal encounters with the great Red Scare and the Depression, and her last years.

The materials available to the biographer for the years after 1889 are voluminous, and the problem of selection becomes more difficult. As Davis writes, a picture begins to emerge. His Jane Addams is a woman of great intelligence, drive, capacity for leadership, ambition; a skillful conciliator, a highly effective administrator and fund-raiser; a skilled mythmaker. He sees her allaying anxiety and ambivalence about developing all these "unwomanly" characteristics by deliberately creating an image of herself as a kind of idealized mother-figure. His Jane Addams, while secretly eager for power, suffers from a persistent hunger for approval and admiration. This theme is repeated relentlessly: "Jane functioned best when she had an uncritical, loving disciple" (p. 85); "[she] enjoyed and depended on the fantastic praise that was showered upon her" (p. 91); "she accepted the honors and thrived on them" (p. 94); "the praise and adoration . . . gave her confidence and a sense that what she was doing was important" (p. 104); "Jane Addams seems to have been especially dependent on the news clippings" (p. 105). He asserts that she did not become a socialist because "she enjoyed being featured in the drawing rooms of the wealthy" (p. 119). She traveled across the country "glorying in the parties, the adoration, the money she made" (p. 125). "She was ambitious and eager for publicity" (p. 148). "Her autobiography is a conscious attempt to focus the reader's attention on Jane Addams" (p. 159). "She was also aware that anything written on prostitution would sell" (p. 178). "Her 'fan mail' . . . [was] an important factor in her growing self-confidence and sense of identity" (p. 182). "She must have been distressed by the number of letters she received attacking her for supporting Roosevelt" (p. 193). "She was convinced that no one could represent the cause of women and social justice better than she" (p. 192). "Yet there was enough praise and adulation during the campaign to counteract the critical letters" (p. 195). "She helped spread her own reputation through her speaking and writing" (p. 198). "There were many others in the neighborhood, especially men, who came to hate and resent Jane Addams" (p. 204). "[Her colleagues] did not work so hard at promoting themselves" (p. 209). "Jane Addams enjoyed her role of priestess and sage" (p. 211).

"She desperately wanted to be right and to be approved. She grasped at the small amount of adoration left" (p. 236).

In an otherwise carefully documented study, these barbed obiter dicta stand free of supporting evidence. But leaving that difficulty aside, what is the argument? Is it that greatness is incompatible with enjoying approval or attracting admiration? Do we apply this standard to Lincoln, to Schweitzer, to Gandhi? In Davis's oversimple world, if a person with Jane Addams's reputation for goodness is not an ideal saint, then she must be a hypocrite and a fraud. There seems to be no third alternative, such as that she was a complex, interesting, talented, many-sided, sometimes troubled, intensely human being. Yet that would be a far more accurate picture.

She was a person, as he rightly says, who wanted to be right. More, she had a compelling desire to be *good*, and her definition of what that meant changed and developed as she herself grew and matured. She remained throughout her life a seeker after truth, and her models were Tolstoy, St. Francis, and Gandhi. But she was not, nor did she want to be, a plaster saint or a passive self-abnegating woman.

Even in her boarding-school days she had a strong sense of self, which may have been one reason she was a powerful force even in that tiny world. She was, as she grew older, a seeker who was also an activist. She was a reformer who understood that life often offers only half a loaf and that that may indeed be better than no loaf at all. She was a person who understood other people partly because she was self-aware. She taxed herself with both self-righteousness and self-pity and strove to overcome both tendencies. She was a person tough enough to survive in the tumult of the nineteenth ward, who learned from experience, and who lived to see many of the things she set out to do accomplished. When she went to Hull-House, labor unions were an abomination to most right-thinking people, children worked twelve hours a day, there was no provision for unemployment or old age, and women could not vote. When she died all these things had changed, partly through her leadership, through her mix of courage and compromise, of saintliness and worldliness.

In the first eleven chapters of this book Davis portrays a woman to whom approval was an overriding necessity. In the next three he accurately records the fact that in the face of bitter criticism bordering on vilification she stood firm for her pacifist convictions through the whole of World War I, while most of her pacifist friends and associates abandoned those principles once the United States declared war. She was called many ugly names, and aspersions were cast upon her ideals and her loyalty. (Dismissed from the Daughters of the American Revolution, she remarked wryly that she had thought herself a member for life but discovered it was only for good behavior.)

Indeed, the facts of her life as he tells them do not bear out Davis's thesis that the need for approbation as the defining characteristic of her career. When she—a well-educated, ladylike twenty-nine-year-old— went to the slums of Chicago she was, to be sure, admired by a handful of the like-minded, but she was criticized or laughed at by others. The first ten years at Hull-House were filled with difficulty, discouragement, and bitter fatigue. When the depression of 1893 forced Jane Addams to rethink her assumptions about American democracy and to take a radical stand on the rights of labor, criticism fell upon her. Many of the newspaper articles Davis sees as so necessary for her self-esteem were furiously critical of her and all her works. Where was the need for approval when she, along with Raymond Robins, went to the rescue of an innocent anarchist who had been jailed in the aftermath of McKinley's assassination? Where was it when she defied the leaders of the Bull Moose convention to support the rights of the black delegates? Or when she supported the Ford Peace Ship amid cries that she was a fool?

The point is *not* that she did not want to be admired; most of us do. The point is that when her convictions demanded it, she took unpopular stands and suffered whatever abuse came. It is this side of her personality which Davis misses. He should have listened to Alice Hamilton, who knew Jane Addams intimately for forty years:

She had two conflicting traits which sometimes brought her great unhappiness: she was very dependent on a sense of warm comradeship and harmony with the mass of her fellow men, but at the same time her clear sighted integrity made it impossible for her to keep in step with the crowd in many a crisis. Most reformers I have known have enjoyed, more or less, the sense of being in advance of their times, of belonging to a persecuted minority. That was never true of Jane Addams. The famous Pullman strike, the rise of the radical Industrial Workers of the World, the war fever of 1914-1918, the suddenly panicky persecution of suspected disloyalty after the war, to mention only a few instances, were for her the most painful of experiences because then she was forced by conviction to work against the stream, to separate herself from the great mass of her fellow countrymen. Nor did she ever fall into the mire of self-pity or take refuge in the comfort of self righteousness. She simply suffered from the spiritual loneliness which her far sighted vision imposed on her![1]

Ellen Starr, who had known her even longer, said almost the same thing, more lyrically: "All, even the great, naturally enjoy the sunshine of approbation and work more easily in its congenial warmth. Jane Addams knew it well and parted with it under no misconceptions; and what was more remarkable, no bitterness. She could not foresee that it would return."[2]

If Davis's assessment were correct, Jane Addams's career would have been littered with broken friendships, since self-seeking egotists do not wear well. But the contrary is true. Though she had sharp differences with colleagues on matters of ideology and tactics, especially with committed ideologues such a Rosika Schwimmer in the peace movement, not one of Addams's closest associates broke with her, even when they were in deep disagreement over her positions. Indeed, the evidence is strong that their admiration grew rather than diminished over the years.

One of the weaknesses of this book is that while Davis pays a great deal of attention to what people who had never seen her thought of Jane Addams, he pays very little to the opinions of those who worked with her day in and day out for forty years. Did he not stop to ask himself, I wonder, how it could be that the women he admires so much (Florence Kelley, Alice Hamilton, Julia Lathrop, the Abbott sisters, Mary Kenney) themselves thought Jane Addams the greatest of them all? Did he really ponder Francis Hackett's comment, which he quotes: "Hull-House, as one clearly felt at the time, was not an institution over which Miss Addams presided; it was Miss Addams around whom an institution insisted on clustering" (p. 81).

One may speculate as to why Davis, after long and close attention to the evidence, came to misunderstand Jane Addams so badly. For one thing, I suspect, he never understood the need she felt to build support for Hull-House, which led to so many of the public relations activities he interprets as self-serving. For another, it may be that the peculiarly unrevealing nature of her personal correspondence frustrated his efforts to get at the inwardness of the woman, and since he was not especially interested in her thought, he missed the insights which might have come from careful study of her social theory. Most important—and I judge now from the overall tone of the book—Davis came in time simply not to like her. Whether this was conscious or not I do not know, but surely to write a sensitive biography one must avoid actual dislike as much as uncritical admiration.

Whatever the cause of Davis's misunderstanding of the meaning of

Jane Addams's life, the result is that while the record of her magnificent social achievements is here, it is overshadowed by his mistaken version of her personality. The uninitiated reader would, I suspect, come away not so much remembering a woman whose work had an impact on a dozen critical areas of our national life, ranging from the education of children to the building of peace-keeping machinery, as with a picture of an ambitious woman gone astray in search of fame. Knowing and respecting the diligent scholarship which went into this volume, valuing its factual contribution, I must nevertheless conclude that the biography of Jane Addams has yet to be written.

NOTES

1. Alice Hamilton, "Jane Addams of Hull-House," *Social Service: A Quarterly Survey*, 27 (June-Aug. 1953), 15.

2. Tribute prepared for the Memorial Service organized by the National Federation of Settlements, June 1935, Sophia Smith Collection, Smith College, Northampton, Mass.

Making the Invisible Woman Visible:
An Essay Review

Beauty—and much else—is in the eye of the beholder. We see what we are prepared to see, what we expect to see, what we think we ought to see. The absence of women from the written history of the United States is a case in point. Those who write history usually start from two assumptions: that woman's natural place is in the home and that history takes place on the battlefield or in the Congress, the statehouse, the pulpit, the marketplace, or the laboratory. Women, therefore, by definition do not make history, and when they turn up in the sources they are often simply not perceived.

The publication of *Notable American Women*, a biographical dictionary based on the assumption that women *have* played a vital role in the development of American culture, is certain to have far-reaching consequences.[1] The material here provides the basis for a new and more complex understanding of American feminism, and it will also lead, in time, to the rewriting of important segments of American social history. Perhaps, also, these volumes may serve as the first authoritative Female Plutarch, providing those vital models we have long recognized as useful in encouraging aspiration in boys, but which we have seldom troubled to offer to girls.

As the story is told, this impressive work was first conceived when Arthur M. Schlesinger, Sr., reviewing the *Dictionary of American Biography*, was shocked to discover that fewer than one-half of 1 percent of the characters therein were women. He thereupon undertook to persuade the Radcliffe Council that it should sponsor a biographical dictionary devoted

Reprinted with permission from the *Journal of Southern History*, 38 (Nov. 1972), 629-38.

solely to women. Edward T. James, an experienced *DAB* editor, was recruited to direct the project. In time he was joined as associate editor by his wife, Janet Wilson James, author of the first Radcliffe dissertation in women's history. Paul S. Boyer was later appointed assistant editor.

By 1957 the project was underway. The inattention to women in the standard sources posed a formidable problem, but a wide net brought in over 4,000 names. These were classified, scrutinized by experts in various fields, and sifted down to the 1,359 women of "more than local significance" who appear in the finished work. A few (generally wives of presidents) slipped in on the credentials of a husband, and one or two by being mothers of the right people, but the overwhelming majority are women of achievement in their own right. The range of meaning which can attach to that phrase is evident when one finds the owner of a posh Chicago brothel, a lighthouse keeper known for daring rescues, New York's leading abortionist, a successful counterfeiter, three record-holding mountain climbers, a woman who scalped nine Indians, Calamity Jane, and Lizzie Borden. To ensure perspective, only women who had died by 1950 were included. Forty-one were black and fifteen were American Indians.

Every page bears witness to the Jameses' high standards. Not a little of their skill lay in matching authors with subjects. Written instructions called for "solid, dispassionate" accounts, and informal communications left no doubt that high quality was expected. When scholars faltered, the editorial pencil took over. The result is a collection of many excellent essays, a few superb ones, and none that are bad. The excellence of the whole should inspire a perceptive foundation to commission the first supplement at once, so that notable women who lived past 1950 may also receive their due while the editors are still in top form. The extraordinary longevity characteristic of feminists makes this a special problem, since many women who helped shape the first decades of this century lived on into the 1950s and 1960s.

The bibliographies appended to each essay represent a quantum leap in the aids available for the study of women's history. The classified list of topics at the end of Volume III provides an easy entry into one's special interest, and Janet James's introduction will be exceedingly useful to anyone approaching the subject for the first time. Even the proofreading is exceptional.

Among the essays, each reader will have favorites, and no list can be exhaustive. Sydney E. Ahlstrom's "Mary Baker Eddy" is a scholarly tour de force, and Barbara M. Cross's "Harriet Beecher Stowe" not only illuminates its subject but reminds us again of the tragic loss to the profession in Cross's premature death. Jacob C. Levenson makes Maud Howe Elliott come alive, as Donald Fleming does for Ruth Fulton Benedict. Louise C. Wade on Florence Kelley, Barbara M. Solomon on Alice Freeman Palmer, Janet Wilson James on Ellen Richards, Louise M. Young on Belle Case La Follette are all first-rate. So are Lyman H. Butterfield on the Adams women and Douglas Day on Gertrude Stein. Elting E. Morison's evocative treatment of the two wives of Theodore Roosevelt is a little gem . . . and so on and on.

In their original instructions the editors stated their intention to "portray, through individual biographies, the role played by women in the development of American civilization." In the end they did much more. Perhaps biographical history is often, as Claude Lévi-Strauss argues, low-power history, but when the number of cases is substantial, when a significant segment of the population is represented, when the time span covers more than three centuries, when the purposes of the authors are broad and well conceived, then not merely microhistory but macrohistory emerges. Important new lines of inquiry are opened up, and opportunities for comparative analysis are created.

For historians who believe with Rowland Berthoff that social history should be studied "in terms of the development of the social structure and of the functional relationships—or lack of them—among all its parts,"[2] the materials contained herein will be exciting. Not only do these life histories provide new insight into social mobility and family life, but as one reads it also becomes clear that women have been prolific and effective builders of social structures beyond anything we had previously realized.

A striking example can be seen in the area of social welfare. Beginning with the organization by a woman in 1797 of the Society for the Relief of Poor Widows with Small Children, it is possible to trace through women's biographies the development of attitudes and institutions from individual benevolence to systematic programs, from the notion of helping the inevitable poor to the idea of seeking to remove the underlying causes of poverty. Lady Bountiful gave way to the Charity Visitor and the individual gift to the collective purse. Charity Organization Societies (see Josephine Shaw Lowell, Mary Ellen Richmond, Anna Beach Pratt) invented the profession of caseworker and developed university training in social work. The settlement houses (see Jane Addams, Lillian D. Wald, Helena

Stuart Dudley, Katherine Pettit, Eleanor Laura McMain) provided places where concerned do-gooders began to recognize the limits of charity and to probe the underlying causes of poverty, illness, and deprivation.

Women, applying their energies to the tasks at hand, helped build the infrastructure through which an increasingly urban and industrial society sought to deal with mounting social ills. The National Conference of Charities and Corrections, the National Child Labor Committee, the Children's Bureau, and the Consumers League were national in scope. But they were only part of the story: there were also thousands of missionary societies, women's clubs, and Woman's Christian Temperance Union chapters created by women to carry on similar work in local communities.

This outpouring of energy and concern provided much of the drive behind what we call the Progressive movement. There were national reformers typified by Florence Kelley, of whom Felix Frankfurter wrote that she had done more than any other individual to shape the social history of the first thirty years of this century, and hundreds of women working in states and local communities, typified by Minnie Rutherford Fuller, of whom it is said here that she had "written and secured the adoption of most, if not all, of the social welfare laws" in Arkansas between 1914 and 1924 (I: 683). The list of such women is long: Charlotte Stearns Eliot, Hannah Bachman Einstein, Madeleine McDowell Breckinridge, Elisabeth Gilman, Julia Clifford Lathrop, Albion Fellows Bacon, Belle Moskowitz, and Mary Harriman Rumsey provide only a beginning. If Richard Hofstadter had had access to these volumes, his theory of status decline as the root cause of progressivism would have died a-borning. A study of women's experience, indeed, will unquestionably reshape our understanding of that cluster of reform movements as well as provide new leads for specific studies. Is it true, as argued here, that the Women's Trade Union League effectively combined middle- and working-class women? Is it true, as seems evident in these biographies, that women were more effective politically before they were enfranchised?

Organizational and administrative talent was not confined to any one area. The Freedmen's Bureau, the Immigrants Protective League, the Women's Trade Union League, the Amalgamated Clothing Workers, the juvenile court, the San Francisco Children's Hospital, the Southern Sociological Congress, many public libraries, and the Museum of Modern Art are only a few of the diverse institutions which women had a large hand in creating.

It is ironic that the sex which has often been thought to need little formal education should have been responsible for so many educational institutions, but the record is clear. From colonial dame schools to Pestalozzian, Froebellian, and John Dewey–style kindergartens women have been largely responsible for the development of early childhood education, upon which we presume much else is built.

Inspired by their own sense of deprivation Emma Hart Willard, Catharine Beecher, and Mary Lyon invented teacher-training institutions for a developing nation and sent forth a small army of schoolteachers to fight off cultural decline in a time of rapid expansion. Frederick Rudolph argues that Willard's address to the New York legislature in 1819 ranks with the significant contemporary papers of Adams, Clay, or Emerson as a statement of American aspirations (III: 612).

Women played a major part in the founding of the Women's Medical College of Philadelphia, Smith, Radcliffe, Wellesley, Bryn Mawr, Barnard, the Merrill-Palmer Institute, the Chicago School of Civics and Philanthropy, the Milwaukee Normal Institute (later Milwaukee-Downer), Spelman College, the Johns Hopkins Medical School, the Woman's College of Baltimore (now Goucher College), Sophie Newcomb, Agnes Irwin School, the Baldwin School, the Free Night School of New Orleans, the Virginia Industrial School for Colored Girls, the Berry School, and many, many others. Nor did they stop with creating schools. The executive talent which shaped these institutions in their early days was exemplified by such women as Elizabeth Cary Agassiz, Martha McChesney Berry, Agnes Irwin, Alice Freeman Palmer, Sophie Bell Wright, Janie Porter Barrett, and Mary Emma Woolley. No less than sixty-seven founders and administrators of schools are included in *Notable American Women*, ranging from the women who took so large a part in organizing education for freedmen after the Civil War to the superintendents of the entire school systems of Los Angeles and Chicago and to the supervisor of all the country schools of north Georgia.

Similar talents, differently motivated, account for a significant part of our religious history. Thirty-seven founders and leaders of religious groups appear here, including Mary Baker Eddy, Jemima Wilkinson (the Universal Friend), Barbara Ruckle Heck (the "mother of American Methodism"), Ellen Gould White (the co-founder of the Seventh-Day Adventist church), evangelists Phoebe Worrall Palmer and Aimee Semple McPherson, and a host of women leaders in the New Thought movement. And as in the case of women leaders in education, behind whom one glimpses thousands of unknown teachers whose collective hand did so much to mold American culture, so behind these religious leaders can be seen the mass of women organized in missionary societies and Sunday schools, carrying out the day-to-day work. One day a volume will be written on women's missionary societies and their role not only in spreading (for better or worse) many American ideas around the world but in providing a career for talented women, the modern equivalent of prioress of the abbey.

Much notable achievement grew out of the efforts of American women to find a place to use their talents in a society which defined woman's role very narrowly. Along with the explicit desire to solve certain social problems, there was the implicit desire to create a realm of usefulness for themselves. A good deal of their organization-building reflected the absence of opportunity in existing structures. Three examples must suffice: The Women's Educational and Industrial Union of Boston was founded in 1877 to serve both the working girls of the city and women of means. "[T]his universality of needs," wrote one of the first directors, "places all on a kind of equality" (I: 472-73). Through a number of biographies it is possible to watch this organization grow and branch out to meet a variety of women's needs, so that in time it came to provide both vocational training and vocational guidance (publishing six volumes on economic opportunities for women), to offer legal aid, and to create scholarships for advanced students as well as a salesroom for handicrafts. In addition, it was the model for a number of similar organizations in other cities.

The second example is the Women's Medical College of Philadelphia, organized by Quaker women who had encountered the inhospitality of existing medical schools. The importance of this school in training the first women doctors can hardly be overestimated. A third case in point is the Association of Collegiate Alumnae formed by a handful of early college graduates who felt their isolation in the female subculture as well as in the larger society. (Martha Carey Thomas recorded the reaction of her mother's friends who refused to speak her name after she took a Ph.D. with highest honors at Zurich.) Over and over in the biographies of women scholars it is clear that the support of the association was critical to their development. It also worked indefatigably to improve the quality of women's colleges.

Someday a historian may be inspired to undertake a careful analysis of the importance of such organizations to the rapid change in women's position in American society after 1890. As a subordinate group, women had to pursue their goals with tools they themselves fashioned.

So, too, individual women, all but barred from male-dominated professions, were forced to be inventive. Women doctors, frowned on in normal practice, invented new fields of medicine. (See Sara Josephine Baker, Isabel Chapin Barrows, Lydia DeWitt, and many others among the fifty-two physicians.) Ellen Richards pioneered in sanitary engineering and invented home economics as an academic field. Caroline Crane made herself so expert in municipal sanitation that cities paid her the then unheard-of fee of $100 a day to visit and give advice. Myra Colby Bradwell, recognized as the most eminent woman lawyer of her time, invented and published the *Chicago Legal News*, "the most important legal publication west of the Alleghenies" (I: 224). Grace Abbott and Sophonisba Preston Breckinridge followed Florence Kelley's lead in developing the techniques of social fact-finding, and Mary Parker Follett created a new subfield in psychology. So it went. If the professions had been wide open to women, would their social inventiveness have been so great? American women are not the first group to make creative use of adversity.

Other intriguing questions develop as one reads. Why are so many of these women Quakers or descended from Quakers? Why do so many, late in life, turn to some form of spiritualism? Why do they marry late, often choosing men younger than themselves? A high percentage of those who did marry had no children or very few. Was this cause or consequence of their unusual careers? Before one makes the obvious answer, it is necessary to observe that a good many who were childless adopted a child or reared a child of relatives. Why are the marriages depicted here usually either very good or broken?

For the historian interested in quantification there is material here for an experiment in collective biography: a universe of notable women for whom we have information about birth and death, family and marriage, children, social origins and inherited economic position, place of residence, education, wealth, occupation, religion, career choice, and so on. An analysis of this material might yield some enlightening correlations. It should be possible to ask and answer questions about the changes in women's roles over time and the relationship of those changes to other changes going on in the society.[3] It would be enlightening to compare samples of these women with other samples of quite different types (e.g., of wives of men in the *DAB*) to find out on what measures notable women differ from other women. Comparisons between samples of these women and samples of men in the *DAB* would also be instructive.

Is it true, as seems to be the case, that women are often innovative in middle life, while men generally make their mark early? Is there evidence to suggest that the female mind responds to a different biological clock? Is versatility more common among outstanding women than among their male counterparts? Are notable women as likely as notable men to have notable children?

One curious pattern worth examining is the tendency of some women to make themselves purposely invisible. (See Mary Kehew for a particularly striking example.) Why is the pioneering legal research technique worked out by Josephine Clara Goldmark universally known as the Brandeis brief? Why would a woman allow her work to be signed by, for example, Hubert Howe Bancroft or Reuben Gold Thwaites? (See Florence Victor and Louise Phelps Kellogg.) It might be illuminating to find out just how many shared this apparent passion for anonymity.

Subjects for full-scale biographies abound. Albion Fellows Bacon, Grace Abbott, Kate Barnard, Mary Boykin Chesnut, Leonora Barry, Harriet Chalmers Adams—the list is a long one, and, thanks to the excellent bibliographical notes, it will be easier to begin than it would have been in the dark age before the publication of these volumes. The possibilities for family history are also intriguing. Certain families seem to have run to notable women: Flexners, Hales, Howes, Beechers, Bacons, Goddards, Gordons, to name a few.

It would be encouraging if one could conclude after laying down the last volume that the accomplishments of the next few generations will be commensurate, considering the much greater opportunities for education, professional jobs, and public acceptance. I confess to a nagging doubt. When one reads in these volumes of a woman psychologist who not only chaired her association but was honored by a special issue of the association journal; of a woman who was the leading anthropologist of her generation and others of the first rank; of a woman who chaired both the American Psychological Association and the American Philosophical Association; of one who laid the groundwork for the serious study of Roman architecture and another who made the first excavation of a Minoan townsite; of three women awarded the Justin Winsor prize of the American Historical Association; of a marine biologist with 158 articles to her credit; and of the head of an internationally known department of geology—one recalls Marjorie Hope Nicolson's comment that her generation was "the only generation of women which ever really found itself," coming late enough to take education for granted and early enough to secure professional positions. "The millennium had come," she wrote in 1937; "it did not occur to us that life could be different. But . . . the glory is departed. Within a decade shades of the prison house began to close . . . upon the emancipated girl. . . . In the higher professions women reached their peak about 1926, and since that time a decline has set in."[4]

Many lives here represent a triumph over adversity. Was it that by the mid-1920s the battle seemed won and there was no longer the pressure for inventiveness? And that forty years were required before another generation realized that women's autonomy was hardly won? Activists as well as scholars will find food for thought in *Notable American Women*.

My criticims are few. Some minor actresses might have been eliminated to make room for longer treatment of major figures. Despite the editors' thorough search, specialists will miss a few significant figures. The reason for one or two entries is not clear: does Mary Copley Pelham really belong, when her claim to fame is that the stepfather she provided John Singleton Copley was helpful to him? There are the inevitable problems of compression, so that occasionally the reader must take on faith generalizations for which it would be nice to have evidence. The absence of any identification of the biographers is frustrating. But overall the failings are so few that one winds up agreeing with Lyman Butterfield that this work "will promptly take its place among the valuable works of scholarship produced in this century."[5]

Most social historians just now are searching for new ground on which to stand and new ways of understanding the complexity of an American past which included and was shaped by women, black people, poor people, and various other groups to whom attention must be paid. Women's history has badly needed two things: carefully accumulated data and organizing ideas. These volumes, together with the bibliographies attached to each essay, offer the first. The second can only come from historians who see the opportunity and seize it.

NOTES

1. *Notable American Women, 1607-1950: A Biograpical Dictionary*, ed. Edward T. James, Janet Wilson James, and Paul S. Boyer. 3 vols. (Cambridge,

Mass.: Belknap Press of Harvard University Press, 1971). Pp. lii, 687; [vi], 659; [vi], 729. $75.00 per set.

2. Berthoff, *An Unsettled People: Social Order and Disorder in American History* (New York, 1971), p. xii.

3. See Lawrence Stone, "Prosopography," *Daedalus,* 100 (Winter 1971), 46-79, for methodological suggestions.

4. Nicholson, "The Rights and Privileges Pertaining Thereto . . . ," in Wilfred B. Shaw, ed., *A University between Two Centuries: The Proceedings of the 1937 Celebration of the University of Michigan* (Ann Arbor, 1937), p. 414.

5. *Radcliffe Quarterly,* 56 (Mar. 1972), 26.

Notable American Women

During the thirteen years after 1958 as Edward and Janet James labored to produce the first three volumes of Notable American Women, *they probably inspired more scholarship in the history of women than all their predecessors put together. Their monumental work is — I hope — sufficiently appreciated in the article reprinted here.*

For myself, in addition to allowing me to write the essay about Jane Addams, the Jameses also set me to work on a considerable number of southern women. Later, when Notable American Women: The Modern Period *was underway, Barbara Sicherman and Carol Hurd Green similarly were midwives to much important work; in my own case they gave me a long-awaited chance to write about Nellie Nugent Somerville.*

In addition to the overview of the whole enterprise, from which this volume takes its name, I include here four brief biographies, southern women all, which are among those I contributed to the four volumes.

Madeline McDowell Breckinridge

Madeline McDowell Breckinridge (May 20, 1872–Nov. 25, 1920), social reformer, was born at Woodlake, near Frankfort, Ky., the third daughter and sixth of seven children of Henry Clay McDowell and his wife, Anne Clay. Both Clays and McDowells had been leading citizens of Kentucky since its earliest days. Henry McDowell, a veteran of the Union Army, was a lawyer, and Madeline in early girlhood was his close companion. In 1882 the family moved into Ashland, the famous Lexington home of

Reprinted with permission from Edward James, Janet James, and Paul S. Boyer, eds., *Notable American Women, 1607-1950* (Cambridge, Mass., 1971), 1:231-33.

Henry Clay—Madeline's great-grandfather—where she grew up loving outdoor sports. Christened Magdalen, she later adopted the French form of the name, and this, in turn, was usually shortened to Madge. She attended Mrs. Higgins's School in Lexington and Miss Porter's School in Farmington, Conn. (1889-90); and intermittently from 1890 to 1894 she took courses at the State College of Kentucky (now the University of Kentucky) in Lexington. In the mid-1890s intellectual as well as social interests led her into a Lexington study group, the Fortnightly Club. At about this time she contracted tuberculosis, an illness which curtailed her activities for the rest of her life and forced her to take periodic rest cures in the Southwest and at the Trudeau Sanatorium in Saranac Lake, N.Y.

On Nov. 17, 1898, she was married to Desha Breckinridge (1867-1935)—brother of Sophonisba Preston Breckinridge, then on the threshold of her career in Chicago social work. A young lawyer turned newspaper editor, Breckinridge came of a family as distinguished in Kentucky history as her own. His influential *Lexington Herald* and his interest in her social concerns were essential to his wife's career as a reformer. The marriage was childless, and Mrs. Breckinridge soon turned her attention to civic issues. Her first undertaking grew out of a horseback trip into the Kentucky mountains in 1899. Sensing the possibility of a social settlement among the mountain people, she encouraged the Gleaners, a young women's society of the Lexington Episcopal church to which her family belonged, to establish a neighborhood house in connection with an Episcopal mission near the mountain town of Proctor. Similar to the work of Katherine Pettit, this was an early adaptation of the urban settlement idea to a rural area. In 1900 Mrs. Breckinridge was one of a group of citizens who founded the Lexington Civic League, and for many years she was its moving spirit. One of the league's first undertakings was the development of a playground for slum children in the area of Lexington known as Irishtown. From this grew, in 1912, a combined school and social settlement, the Abraham Lincoln School and Social Center, administered jointly by the Civic League and the school board. Seeking to make this a model of its kind, Madeline Breckinridge brought to it the most advanced thinking of John Dewey in education and of Jane Addams in social work. On the practical side, she raised $35,000 to supplement a public appropriation for the school's construction, planned its design, and supervised its staffing.

While spending the winter of 1903-4 in a sanatorium in Denver, Mrs. Breckinridge observed the work of Judge Ben B. Lindsey's juvenile court and also learned more of the woman suffrage campaign, the public health movement, and other reforms of the day. Back in Lexington, she and the Civic League took the lead in securing state legislation in 1906 establishing a juvenile court system and restricting child labor. She was also instrumental in introducing manual training into the Lexington schools, in the establishment of a free public health clinic, in town beautification and park construction, and in securing better care for women offenders. As a founder in 1900 of the Lexington Associated Charities and as a director from 1907 to her death, she worked for higher standards in the care of the needy. Her multipurpose approach to civic responsibility is illustrated by a letter written Aug. 1, 1914, to her friend Mrs. W. W. Anderson, laying plans for opening a new wading pool at the playground, suggesting a boat-building contest for the children, and concluding: "Also, if you're here next week, don't you want to do a little suffrage work at the fair?" Such endeavors soon won national recognition, and Mrs. Breckinridge was invited to address the Conference for Education in the South in 1911 and 1912 and the National Conference of Charities and Correction in 1914. In 1910 she had been elected to a two-year term on the board of directors of the General Federation of Women's Clubs.

Perhaps her most deeply felt crusade was that against tuberculosis, rooted not only in her personal experience but in her admiration for her grandfather William Adair McDowell, a Kentucky physician whose pioneering work, *A Demonstration of the Curability of Pulmonary Consumption*, had appeared in 1843. As early as 1905 she had voiced her concern before the Civic League, and from then until her death she worked through such organizations as the Kentucky Anti-Tuberculosis Society, the Kentucky Association for the Prevention and Relief of Tuberculosis, and the Fayette County Tuberculosis Association to spread knowledge about the malady, to establish a free diagnostic dispensary in Lexington, and to win legislative and public support for a state sanatorium. A monument to her efforts is Lexington's Blue Grass Sanatorium, constructed in 1916 with public funds and the $50,000 she raised through her "genius at publicity and organization" (Breckinridge, p. 140). From 1912 to 1916 she served with distinction on the state Tuberculosis Commission which she had helped to bring into being. An uncharacteristic sentence from one of her letters to a governor on the subject—the last of a series that had begun sixteen year before—suggests the uphill struggle she had waged. "The tuberculosis fight in Kentucky," she wrote, "from the start to finish has been work, persuade, fight, until when you get anything you are so weary you can hardly rejoice in it" (Breckinridge, p. 155).

Believing that the average woman needed "some stimulus to broader interests than she now has," Mrs. Breckinridge in 1905 began a weekly woman's page in her husband's newspaper. To prove her contention that "woman are thinking seriously and to some purpose on a number of subjects not usually considered feminine," she played down fashion news and recipes and treated the important political and social issues of the day. Through the pages of the *Herald*, and as head of the legislative division of the State Federation of Women's Clubs (1908-12), she fought for a variety of legislative reforms, including woman suffrage in school elections, granted in 1912.

She was long the central figure in the Kentucky Equal Rights Association, serving as its president from 1912 to 1915, and again from 1919 until her death. During her first term as president membership rose from 1,700 to 10,000. As a vice-president of the National American Woman Suffrage Association (1913-15) she traveled widely, speaking for suffrage in Missouri, Oregon, Virginia, West Virginia, and the Carolinas. Unlike her fellow Kentuckian Laura Clay, she favored suffrage agitation on the federal was well as the state level and welcomed the Nineteenth Amendment, working tirelessly in Kentucky for its ratification. Of her gift for oratory, one who heard her speak at a Fourth of July gathering in a Kentucky mountain town in 1919 later wrote: "It seemed as if the mantle of 'Harry of the West' [Henry Clay] had fallen on her shoulders, and as she closed, our eyes were filled with tears and I shook hands enthusiastically with a grim-faced mountaineer who said 'By God, that's the best I ever heard, man or woman, and I'm for her' " (Breckinridge, p. 235). Largely through such efforts, the Kentucky legislature ratified the suffrage amendment on Jan. 6, 1920, the first day of its legislative session.

Mrs. Breckinridge was not a pacifist, and she refused to join the Woman's Peace party before World War I. She had high hopes for the League of Nations, however, and in October 1920 undertook an extended speaking tour on behalf of the Democratic party and the League. On Nov. 23 she suffered a stroke at her Lexington home. She died two days later, at forty-eight, without regaining consciousness. Madeline Breckinridge was one of those to whom nothing human is alien. Her rare combination of intelligence, humor, sensitivity, and administrative ability made her an effective reformer and one of Kentucky's leading citizens.

[Sophonisba P. Breckinridge, *Madeline McDowell Breckinridge* (1921), a loving memorial by her sister-in-law, written with a scholar's regard for accuracy, is the chief printed source. A feeling for her extraordinary personality and capacity for work is best gained form her personal papers, which are a part of the voluminous Breckinridge collection in the Library of Congress, Washington, D.C. The *Woman Citizen*, Feb. 19, 1921, contains a moving memorial article by Alice Stone Blackwell. See also Ida H. Harper, ed., *History of Woman Suffrage*, vols. 5 and 6 (1922); and *National Cyclopedia of American Biography*, 29:44-45.]

Sallie Sims Southall Cotten

Sallie Sims Southall Cotten (June 13, 1846-May 4, 1919), leader in the North Carolina woman's club movement, was born at Lawrenceville, Brunswick County, Va., the fifth daughter of Thomas James and Susannah Swepson (Sims) Southall. The families of both parents had settled in Virginia in the eighteenth century; though definite evidence is lacking, her father was probably a planter. While Sallie was still a small child, she was sent to live with an uncle. Here she later attended Wesleyan Female College, and in 1863 she graduated from the Greensboro (N.C.) Female College. On Mar. 14, 1866, after two years of teaching school, she was married to Robert Randolph Cotten, a Confederate veteran who had returned from the war penniless but undiscouraged. Reestablishing financial connections with New York friends, he was able to embark upon a mercantile business in Tarboro, N.C. His ideal, however, was to be a planter, and as soon as he was able he bought land in Pitt County to which he eventually transferred his business. As a prosperous planter-merchant, he several times represented Pitt County in the North Carolina assembly and with his wife became a leader of the community.

The first thirty years of Sallie Cotten's married life were largely domestic. There were seven Cotten children — Agnes LeRoy, Robert Randolph, Bruce, Lyman Atkinson, Sallie Dromgoole, Preston Sims, and Elba Brown — to be reared and educated (two others died in childhood, and the eldest son drowned when he was fifteen). Mrs. Cotten organized a school on the plantation, taught by a succession of teachers who lived with the family. The neighborhood children were invited to participate. Although Mrs. Cotten had servants, she worked indefatigably in house,

Reprinted with permission from Edward James, Janet James, and Paul S. Boyer, eds., *Notable American Women, 1607-1950* (Cambridge, Mass., 1971), 1:388-90.

garden, chicken yard, and kitchen. She entered pickles in the state fair and made twenty-four rugs with her own hands; her common complaint during these years was typified in a postscript to one of her letters, "No time for anything but stitch, stitch, stitch." In spite of this demanding domesticity, which also included visiting sick neighbors, constant super-vision of children, and leadership in the Episcopal church, Mrs. Cotten was essentially an introspective intellectual. Her encounters with female colleges had left her with a love of reading which she somehow found time to indulge. "If you want something full of thought read 'Hamlet,'" she wrote to a friend in 1883, "and if you want a good opinion of the intelligence, wit, nobility, and *ingenuity* of your own sex read 'Merchant of Venice.' *Portia* is grand yet womanly, learned and loving." An excep-tionally able woman herself, she found it difficult to reconcile the role accorded southern women of her day with her own abilities.

The precipitating event in Mrs. Cotten's life came in 1893 when she was forty-seven. Gov. Elias Carr, a friend of the family, appointed her one of North Carolina's "lady managers" for the Chicago World's Fair. In this capacity she traveled over most of the state, and in Chicago she met women from all parts of the country who were active in the burgeoning "woman movement." Electrified by their example, and struck by the number of earnest and struggling woman's clubs which she had seen in many North Carolina towns, trying to improve themselves and their communities, Mrs. Cotten returned home to encourage women in their effort to organize themselves. The result was not only a proliferation of local clubs but also the North Carolina Federation of Women's Clubs, which she helped organize in 1902 and headed until 1913. Convinced that "the new force in modern civilization . . . is educated, Christianized, organized womanhood," she gave her energies over the next twenty-five years to a movement with far-reaching social and political consequences for the life of her state. North Carolina women took a leading part in local civic reform; interested in education, they waged a vigorous campaign against adult illiteracy. The federation also secured passage of a law permitting women to sit on school boards and worked for child labor reform and the improvement of institutions of correction. Though Mrs. Cotten's chief work centered in North Carolina, she was present at the organizational meeting of the National Congress of Mothers (later the Congress of Parents and Teachers) in Washington in 1897 and served from 1898 to 1906 as its recording or corresponding secretary.

Sallie Cotten was a strikingly handsome woman, perhaps most impressive in her later years when she piled her white hair on top of her head. According to her son Bruce, "She possessed none of certain female traits which men so frequently scoff at, but in reality, admire in women, such as feigned helplessness, susceptibility to flattery, small vanities, [or] excessive weaknesses for dress and society"; she used direct rather than "feminine" methods. She lived until 1929, observing with a keen and analytical eye the events of the war and the postwar period. After her husband's death, in August 1928, she joined her daughter in Massachusetts. That winter she was strong enough to attend a great gathering of women in Boston, where she was introduced as the "Julia Ward Howe of the South" and received a standing ovation. This was her last public appearance. She died at the age of eighty-two in Winchester, Mass., of chronic myocardial insufficiency and was buried in the family plot at Greenville, N.C. Both in time and in fact she exemplified the evolution from the southern lady of the old school to the new woman's leader who performed a vital role in southern social and political history.

[Mrs. Cotten's papers, letters and diaries are at the University of North Carolina, Chapel Hill, in the North Carolina Collection and in the Southern Historical Collection; the former also contains many newspaper and periodical clippings. There is a sketch of Mrs. Cotten by Justice Henry Groves Connor of the North Carolina Supreme Court in Samuel A. Ashe, *Biographical History of North Carolina* (1917), 8:122-32; and a privately printed memoir by her son Bruce, *As We Were* (1935). See also *Woman's Who's Who of America*, 1914-15. Sallie Southall Cotten published two books: a verse history of the Lost Colony, *The White Doe* (1901), and *The History of the North Carolina Federation of Women's Clubs, 1901-1925* (1925). Her daughter-in-law, Mrs. Lyman Atkinson Cotten, Sr., was of inestimable help in the preparation of this sketch. Mrs. Alice Troy of the National Congress of Parents and Teachers provided information on Mrs. Cotten's work in that organization. Death record from Mass. Registrar of Vital Statistics.]

Cornelia Ann Phillips Spencer

Cornelia Ann Phillips Spencer (Mar. 20, 1825–Mar. 11, 1908), North Carolina author and educational crusader, was born in Harlem, N.Y.,

Reprinted with permission from Edward James, Janet James, and Paul S. Boyer, eds., *Notable American Women, 1607-1950* (Cambridge, Mass., 1971), 3:333-34.

where her father, James Phillips, son of an Anglican minister of Nevenden, England, had established a classical school for boys in 1818. Her mother, Judith (Julia) Vermeule of Plainfield, N.J., came of a well-to-do family of Dutch colonial descent. Of their three children, Cornelia was the youngest and the only daughter. Her father became professor of mathematics at the University of North Carolina in 1826, and thereafter the family was completely identified with Chapel Hill. Professor Phillips entered the Presbyterian ministry in 1833 and until his death in 1867 combined preaching with teaching, as did Charles, his elder son and successor. Mrs. Phillips for a time ran a small girls' school.

From early childhood, when she eagerly joined her brothers in their studies, trying hard to outdo them though they were older, Cornelia Phillips exhibited unusual force of character. Under the exacting tutelage of her parents, she was taught with her brothers until they entered the university at Chapel Hill (no women were admitted until 1897); thereafter she studied on her own and bemoaned the custom which allowed her only the "crumbs from the college table." On June 20, 1855, she was married to a young lawyer, James Monroe ("Magnus") Spencer and went to live in Clinton, Ala. There her only child, Julia James (June), was born in 1859. Upon her husband's death in 1861 she returned with her child to her father's house and began her long career as one of Chapel Hill's leading citizens.

Well aware that her grief would be helped only by hard work, Cornelia Spencer turned at first to teaching Latin and Greek to village children. The Civil War and the defeat of the South, however, soon set her active mind to appraising the weaknesses of her native state, and, first in letters, then in public print, she began analyzing North Carolina and exhorting its citizens to self-improvement. Her position was that of a proud Carolinian who wanted the state to equal the best in the Union. Her initial venture into journalism came when a former North Carolinian, the Reverend Charles Force Weems, asked her to write for his New York magazine, the *Watchman*, a series of articles describing conditions during the final weeks of the Civil War when the northern armies marched through the state. The accounts were later collected and published as *The Last Ninety Days of the War in North Carolina* (1866). To obtain accurate material she wrote to friends and conferred with many of the state's leading men. She enjoyed a particularly close association with David Lowry Swain, president of the University of North Carolina, and with Zebulon B. Vance, the wartime governor of the state.

For the next nine years Mrs. Spencer concentrated her interests chiefly upon the need for improving educational standards in the South, and especially upon the problems of the University of North Carolina. After the war and the death of President Swain, the Reconstruction government had dismissed the entire faculty and replaced it by men chosen more for their politicial views than for their scholarship, and in 1871 a financial crisis forced the closing of the university. Along with other North Carolinians devoted to the cause of education, Mrs. Spencer joined in the struggle to reopen the university, a project she brilliantly supported in newspaper articles and in letters to friends and persons of influence. When on Mar. 20, 1875, the legislature voted the necessary funds, Mrs. Spencer in her delight climbed the steps to the bell tower and rang the college bell. The new president, Kemp P. Battle, like David Swain before him and George T. Winston after him, looked upon Mrs. Spencer as a close friend and trusted adviser. In 1893-94 the survival of the university was again endangered, by inadequate funds and by militant attacks from sectarian colleges, and Mrs. Spencer once more aided the defense with all the powers of her writing and her ardent personality.

A vigorous and devout member of the Presbyterian church, Cornelia Spencer wrote regularly from 1870 to 1876 for the *North Carolina Presbyterian*, contributing a lively "Young Lady's Column" that still retains freshness and appeal. She continually emphasized the need for education. Constantly urging the girls to set themselves higher standards of excellence, she gave them pungent and often witty advice, as well as reports of what was going on in the great world outside North Carolina. No political or social controversy was beyond her range, and in her comments on the subject of woman's rights she gave her readers considerable insight into the development of her own ideas. Although she maintained a proper southern belief in the natural inferiority of women, she confessed in 1870 her discovery that "the female reformers . . . have really an argument or two on their side," and thereafter she wrote a good deal about the widening opportunities becoming available to women.

Mrs. Spencer played an important unofficial role in establishing the university's Summer Normal School for the training of teachers, which opened in 1877, and was a tireless fund-raiser and writer on its behalf. She made similar contributions to the founding (1891) of the Normal and Industrial School for Women, later the Woman's College of the University of North Carolina, at Greensboro. The educators who began to reform North Carolina's public school system in the 1890s owed much to her encouragement and help; many, indeed (like Charles D. McIver), had known her when they were in college at Chapel Hill. The student body held her in great esteem. "I remember her appearance most distinctly," wrote one student in later years, "and had a feeling that she ought to be addressed in Latin. Her personality was most extraordinary. . . . She simply radiated something invisible and inspiring; a sort of magnetic field. She could furnish an empty room by simply sitting there" (quoted in Russell, facing p. 1). She was the first person honored by the university's LL.D., in 1895.

Cornelia Spencer knew everyone in town and many in the state, and was interested in them all. She felt particular warmth for the hardworking, self-reliant farm people and had a deep concern for the welfare of the freed Negroes. Until the end of her long life she continued to comment with interest and insight not only upon the passing scene but also upon books, men, and history. For two years, 1881-82, she lived in Washington with her brother Samuel, then solicitor general of the United States. In 1894 she left Chapel Hill for the home of her daughter, whose husband, James Lee Love, taught mathematics at Harvard. From Cambridge she continued to carry on her extensive correspondence, and there she reveled in the joys of the Harvard library. She died in Cambridge of influenza shortly before her eighty-third birthday and was buried in the village cemetery at Chapel Hill. Both the University of North Carolina and the Woman's College at Greensboro have named buildings in her honor.

[There is no adequate biography of Mrs. Spencer. Hope S. Chamberlain, *Old Days in Chapel Hill* (1926), and Phillips Russell, *The Woman Who Rang the Bell* (1949), are useful, and Louis R. Wilson has edited the *Selected Papers of Cornelia Phillips Spencer* (1953). Her diaries, journals, and copies of her letters and papers are filed in the Southern History Collection of the University of North Carolina, Chapel Hill. See also Kemp P. Battle, *History of the University of North Carolina*, 2 vols. (1907-12); Rose H. Holder, *McIver of North Carolina* (1957); and Josephus Daniels, *Tar Heel Editor* (1939).]

Nellie Nugent Somerville

Nellie Nugent Somerville (Sept. 25, 1863–July 28, 1952) is known as a suffragist and state legislator.

Reprinted with permission from Barbara Sicherman and Carol Hurd Green, eds., *Notable American Women: The Modern Period* (Cambridge, Mass., 1980), pp. 654-56.

Nellie Nugent Somerville, only surviving child of William Lewis and Eleanor Fulkerson (Smith) Nugent, was of English, Welsh, and Irish descent. Nellie (baptized, but never called, Eleanor) was born on her grandmother's plantation near Greenville, Miss. Her father was in the Confederate army at the time; federal soldiers had shot her grandfather and burned the family home in Greenville shortly before her birth. Her young mother survived barely two years, and, though Nugent remarried, he was widowed again in a few months. Until his marriage to Aimee Webb in 1870, the care of his daughter fell largely to her devout and strong-willed grandmother, S. Myra Smith. In 1872 Nugent moved his family to Jackson, the state capital, where he quickly rose to leadership in the bar and in time became one of the wealthiest men in Mississippi.

By the time Nellie was twelve, five other children had been born, and she was sent to Whitworth College, a boarding school in Brookhaven, Miss., characterized by very plain living. After two years its president confessed that this bright child had exhausted his school's resources, and she went on to the Martha Washington College in Abingdon, Va. She received her A.B. in 1880, finishing with a nearly perfect record. Despite these formal educational experiences, she acquired most of her considerable learning in political theory, theology, history, and public affairs on her own.

After graduation her father suggested that she read law in his office, but she preferred the independence of living with her grandmother in Greenville and earning her keep by tutoring the children of a local banker. In 1885 Nellie Nugent married Robert Somerville, a civil engineer from Virginia whose family's wealth had been destroyed by the war. A mild man of great integrity, Somerville always viewed Mississippi as something of a frontier of civilization. Four children were born in nine years: Robert Nugent in 1886, Abram Douglas in 1889, Eleanor in 1891, and Lucy Robinson in 1895. All but Eleanor were to become distinguished lawyers. Nellie Somerville was close to all her children and remained friend and adviser to them as long as she lived.

Nellie Somerville was an exotic plant among women in the post-Reconstruction South. An iconoclast, she was a voracious reader, an independent thinker, an organizer, a public speaker of unusual power, and a tough-minded politician. When she was thirty-three, she organized and became president of a Methodist association for home missionary work. From this beginning she moved rapidly into a series of major reform efforts.

Stimulus from a larger world came in the early 1890s in the form of encounters, first with Carrie Chapman Catt who, though only four years her senior, was already a national leader in the suffrage movement, and then with Frances Willard, president of the Woman's Christian Temperance Union (WCTU), whom Somerville later called "the greatest woman I ever knew." Somerville took up both their challenges, becoming corresponding secretary of the Mississippi WCTU in 1894 and organizing and chairing the Mississippi Woman Suffrage Association in 1897. Mississippi was probably the most unpromising state in the country for a suffrage organizer, but with intelligence, energy, and organizational skill, she managed to tap a good deal of latent feminism, among men as well as women. She kept her followers hard at work and focused their labors on problems she thought women ought to address: public health, occupational safety, and protective legislation, as well as on the campaign for the vote. In her frequent speeches and newspaper articles, she did not hesitate to attack the double standard. She poured scorn on the prevailing cant about the sanctity and moral influence of motherhood, pointing out that if men did not respect women (and clearly she thought they did not) children would not either, and arguing that "if woman's influence is so stupendous her opinions should have some weight." A devout Methodist, she taught a Sunday school class at a level appropriate for a divinity school. National leaders recognized her as a source of strength in the always fragile southern suffrage movement, and by 1915 she was a vice-president of the National American Woman Suffrage Association.

Both suffrage and temperance work took women to political gatherings — to county and state party conventions and to various legislative bodies. Gradually a few, among them Nellie Somerville, began to take part in the political groups that they had first encountered as lobbyists. Somerville soon displayed a gift for politics. By the mid-1910s she was the recognized leader of one faction in her county Democratic party, which, in a one-party state like Mississippi, functioned in the way a political party did elsewhere. In 1923 she became the first woman to be elected to the Mississippi legislature, where she served until 1927. She also played an important role as a delegate to the 1925 Democratic National Convention.

In the legislature she studied issues and men with equal care. "She knew each political figure," wrote one observer, "his interests, his record, his motivation, his family, his friends, his supporters, and his probable future actions." Such close attention to detail made her an unusually effective legislator. Working for a wide variety of social welfare laws, she brought about a major reorganization of the state mental hospital and also chaired the committee on eleemosynary institutions, which gained stature under her leadership. Her record was such that the newspapers considered it a matter for comment when a bill she supported failed to pass.

The evolution of this able radical (suffrage and many other causes Somerville supported were considered radical in the forty years after 1890) into an equally able conservative, who spoke against pacifism, opposed the federal child labor amendment, and supported the poll tax, parallels that of other southern reformers. A product of her culture, she found many developments of the 1930s and 1940s antithetical. Not only had the major issues changed, but, when the New Deal made the national government an ever more powerful force in individuals' lives, Somerville, along with many Mississippians, drew back. By 1948, at the age of eighty-five, she was an active states' rights Democrat.

Some considered her stern, argumentative, and hard to get along with. She did not suffer fools gladly, and her mind worked rather faster than some people found comfortable. On close acquaintance, however, she was more interesting than intimidating. One clue to her character was the fact that though she had been born with a deformed right hand, she managed so well that many of her coworkers and associates were hardly aware of it. It is recorded that, playing croquet with one hand, she usually won. In business, too, Somerville managed her affairs with consummate skill. After her husband's death in 1925, she began to invest in real estate, and over the nearly three decades of her remaining life she transformed a small inheritance into a substantial property. Her banker thought he had never met so gifted an investor.

In a pattern common among southern women leaders, Nellie Nugent Somerville's distinguished family background and her appearance as a perfect lady permitted her to overcome the hostility often directed against women who entered the public sphere. She was the equal in native ability of such better-known feminist leaders as Carrie Chapman Catt, and given a slightly different setting and cultural context, she would have been a national leader. As it was, she was a major liberalizing force in Mississippi for forty years, setting an example of the "new woman" for thousands of Mississippi women.

She outlived most of her friends and suffrage comrades and was still busily reading, writing, and conducting her business affairs when she died of cancer in Ruleville, Miss., at eighty-eight.

[The basic material for the life of Nellie Nugent Somerville is in the Somerville-Howorth Collection in the Schlesinger Library, Radcliffe College, Cambridge, Mass. The collection includes the diary of S. Myra Smith, Somerville's grand-mother. Other materials are still in family hands. The Archives of the Oral History Program of the University of North Carolina, Chapel Hill, contain a transcript of an interview with Lucy Somerville Howorth, who has also generously supplied additional information. A master's thesis, "Nellie Nugent Somerville" (Delta State University, 1974) by Mary Louise Meredith, covers Somerville's public career. William M. Cash and Lucy Somerville Howorth, eds., *My Dear Nellie: The Civil War Letters of William L. Nugent to Eleanor Smith Nugent* (1977) also contains useful material. There is a brief biographical sketch and information about the Mississippi suffrage movement in *Accomplishments of Mississippi Women*, a pamphlet published by the Mississippi Commission on the Observance of International Women's Year, 1978. Death record provided by Miss. Public Health Service.]

PART II

The South

While *The Southern Lady* was being written, I published two preliminary articles. They are more compact than the chapters to which they gave rise and show in embryo some of the ideas about southern women that later appeared in the book. After the book was out, there were invitations to say more about southern women. Joel Williamson encouraged me to write "Women's View of the Patriarchy" for an annual meeting of the Organization of American Historians; Sam Hill invited ruminations about women and religion. The historiographical essay was composed for the annual symposium of the University of Mississippi in 1982 and is based in part on work done in collaboration with Jacquelyn Dowd Hall that will appear in a festschrift for S. W. Higginbotham. The order of publication is backward in time: I wrote first about the late nineteenth century, went on to the twentieth, and then backward to the 1830s. I have put them here in chronological order, with the historiographical article last.

Women's Perspective on
the Patriarchy in the 1850s

This essay, which first appeared as a paper at the annual meeting of the Organization of American Historians, expands on some of the ideas in The Southern Lady. *Rereading it, I am troubled to observe that I sometimes wrote as if "women" meant only white women. Habits of speech are even harder to change than habits of mind; many of the statements in this piece should be modified to read "white women."*

It would indeed be fascinating if one could reconstruct black women's view of the patriarchy! Perhaps someday someone will do so, using the vast collection of slave narratives from the Works Progress Administration. If it should ever be done, many ironies will emerge.

Southern women were scarcely to be seen in the political crisis of the 1850s. Historical works dealing with that crucial decade seldom mention a woman unless it is in a footnote citing a significant letter from a male correspondent. In women's own diaries and letters the burgeoning conflict between the North and South almost never inspired comment before John Brown's raid and rarely even then.

At the same time women were a crucial part of one southern response to the mounting outside attack on slavery. The response was an ever more vehement elaboration of what has been called the "domestic metaphor," the image of a beautifully articulated, patriarchal society in which every southerner, black or white, male or female, rich or poor, had an appropriate place and was happy in it. "The negro slaves of the

Reprinted with permission from the *Journal of American History*, 61 (June 1974), 52-64.

South are the happiest, and, in some sense, the freest people in the world," George Fitzhugh wrote, describing the happy plantation on which none was oppressed by care.[1] "Public opinion," he stoutly maintained, "unites with self-interest, domestic affection, and municipal law to protect the slave. The man who maltreats the weak and dependent, who abuses his authority over wife, children, or slaves is universally detested." Slavery, Fitzhugh thought, was an admirable educational system as well as an ideal society.[2]

What Fitzhugh argued in theory many planters tried to make come true in real life. "My people" or "my black and white family" were phrases that rolled easily from their tongues and pens. "I am friend and well wisher both for time and eternity to every one of them," a North Carolinian wrote to his slave overseer upon the death of a slave, expressing sorrow that he could not be present for the funeral.[3] This letter was one in a series of fatherly letters to that particular slave, and the writer, a bachelor, offered similar fatherly guidance to his grown sisters, as he doled out their money to them.

Even as planters tried to make the dream come true, they could not hide their fear and doubt. "It gave me much pleasure to see so much interest manifested," one wrote his wife, reporting that the slaves had inquired about her health and welfare, "and I am convinced that much of it was sincere."[4] Quick panic followed rumors of insurrection, and when the war came many planters took the precaution of moving their slaves as Yankee armies approached. For those who enjoy poetic justice there is plenty to be found in the pained comments of loving patriarchs when their most pampered house servants were the first to depart for Yankee camps.

Women, like slaves, were an intrinsic part of the patriarchal dream. If plantation ladies did not support, sustain, and idealize the patriarch, if they did not believe in and help create the happy plantation, which no rational slave would exchange for the jungle of a free society, who would? If women, consciously or unconsciously, undermined the image designed to convince the doubting world that the abolitionists were all wrong, what then?

Some southern men had doubts about women as well as slaves. This is clear in the nearly paranoid reaction of some of them to the pronouncements and behavior of "strong-minded" women in the North. Southern gentlemen hoped very much that no southern lady would think well of such goings-on, but clearly they were not certain.[5] Their fears had some foundation, for in the privacy of their own rooms southern matrons were reading Margaret Fuller, Madame de Staël, and what one of them described as "decided women's rights novels."[6]

Unlike the slaves, southern women did not threaten open revolt, and when the war came they did not run to the Yankees. Instead they were supportive, as they worked to feed and clothe civilians and the army, nurse the sick, run the plantations, supervise the slaves, and pray for victory. Yet even these activities were partly an indirect protest against the limitations of women's role in the patriarchy. Suddenly women were able to do business in their own right, make decisions, write letters to newspaper editors, and in many other ways assert themselves as individual human beings. Many of them obviously enjoyed this new freedom.[7]

Even before the war women were not always as enthusiastic in their support of the patriarchy as slavery's defenders liked to believe. To the assertion that "the slave is held to *involuntary service*," an Alabama minister responded:

So is the wife. Her relation to her husband, in the immense majority of cases, is made for her, and not by her. And when she makes it for herself, how often, and how soon . . . would she throw off the yoke if she could! O ye wives, I know how superior you are to your husbands in many respects — not only in personal attraction . . . in grace, in refined thought, in passive fortitude, in enduring love, and in a heart to be filled with the spirit of heaven. . . . I know you may surpass him in his own sphere of boasted prudence and worldly wisdom about dollars and cents. Nevertheless, he has authority, from God, to rule over you. You are under service to him. You are bound to obey him in all things. . . . you cannot leave your parlor, nor your bed-chamber, nor your couch, if your husband commands you to stay there![8]

The minister was speaking to a northern audience and intended, no doubt, to convince northern women that they should not waste energy deploring the servitude of the slave since their own was just as bad, but surely this Alabama man shaped his understanding of married life in his home territory.

The minister's perception is supported in a little volume entitled *Tales and Sketches for the Fireside*, written by an Alabama woman for the purpose of glorifying southern life and answering the abolitionists. Woman's influence, she wrote, "is especially felt in the home circle; she is the weaker, physically, and yet in many other respects the stronger.

There is no question of what she can bear, but what she is obliged to bear in her positions as wife and mother, she has her troubles which man, the stronger, can never know. Many annoying things to woman pass unnoticed by those whose thoughts and feelings naturally lead them beyond their homes." The writer added that since men were so restless, God in his wisdom designed women to be "the most patient and unretiring in the performance . . . of duties." Weariness almost leaps from her pages. Not only is she bitter about the burdens of woman's lot, she also feels keenly the one-sidedness of those burdens and the failure of men even to notice.[9]

Personal documents provide even more detailed evidence of female discontent in the South of the 1850s. Unhappiness centered on women's lack of control over many aspects of their own sexual lives and the sexual lives of their husbands, over the institution of slavery which they could not change, and over the inferior status which kept them so powerless.[10]

The most widespread source of discontent, since it affected the majority of married women, was the actuality of the much glorified institution of motherhood. Most women were not able to control their own fertility. The typical planter's wife was married young, to a husband older then herself, and proceeded to bear children for two decades. While conscious family limitation was sometimes practiced in the nineteenth century, effective contraception was not available, and custom, myth, religion, and men operated to prevent limitation. With the existing state of medical knowledge it was realistic to fear childbirth and to expect to lose some children in infancy.[11]

The diary of a Georgia woman shows a typical pattern of childbearing and some reactions to it. Married in 1852 at the age of eighteen to a man of twenty-one, she bore her first child a year later. In the summer of 1855, noting certain telltale symptoms, she wrote, "I am again destined to be a mother . . . the knowledge causes no exhilirating feelings . . . [while] suffering almost constantly . . . I cannot view the idea with a great deal of pleasure."[12] The baby was born but died in a few weeks, a circumstance which she prayed would help her live more dutifully in the future. A few months later she was happily planning a trip to the North because "I have no infant and I cannot tell whether next summer I will be so free from care,"[13] but in four days her dreams of travel vanished abruptly when morning nausea led her to wonder whether she was "in a peculiar situation, a calamity which I would especially dread this summer."[14] Her fears were justified, and she had a miscarriage in August. There was no rest for the weary. By January 1857 she was pregnant again, and on her twenty-fourth birthday in April 1858 she was pregnant for the fifth time in six years, though she had only two living children. Diary volumes for the next two years are missing, but in December 1862 she recorded yet another pregnancy, saying "I am too sick and irritable to regard this circumstance as a blessing *yet awhile*."[15] A year later with the house being painted and all in confusion she jotted the illuminating comment: "I don't wonder that men have studys which . . . I imagine to be only an excuse for making themselves comfortable and being out of the bustle and confusion of . . . housekeeping . . . and children."[16] She also expressed bitter opposition to the practice of sending pregnant slaves to work in the fields. By February 1865, after fours years of war, she was writing, "Unfortunately I have the prospect of adding again to the little members of my household. . . . I am sincerely sorry for it."[17] When the child was born prematurely in June, the mother thanked God that it did not live. By 1869 this woman had managed to relegate her husband to a separate bedroom, and, for good measure, she kept the most recent infant in her bed, as effective a means of contraception as she could devise.[18] Later she reflected that she had never "been so opposed to having children as many women I know."[19]

The difference between the male and female angle of vision is illustrated in the life of a South Carolina woman, a niece of James L. Petigru, married to a cousin ten years her senior. She gave birth to six children in the first nine years of her marriage, and her uncle — normally a wise and perceptive human being — wrote to the young woman's mother: "Well done for little Carey! Has she not done her duty . . . two sons and four daughters and only nine years a wife? Why the Queen of England hardly beats her."[20] If the uncle had had access to the correspondence between "little Carey" and her planter husband, he might not have been so quick to congratulate her. It seems likely from the evidence of these letters that her three-month sojourns with her mother in the summers were partly motivated by a desire to prolong the time between babies, but no sooner did her lonesome husband come to visit than she was pregnant again.[21]

This woman had a faithful family doctor who moved into her household when time for her confinement drew near, but even his comforting presence did not prevent her fears of death each time. Mrs. Thomas, writer of the first diary, relied on a slave midwife, her mother, and a town doctor. Both these women loved their children and cared for them, though with ample assistance before the war. Yet each privately insisted that she would have preferred a much longer time between babies. As the Alabama minister quoted earlier suggested, however, a woman could not leave her bed-chamber or her couch without her husband's permission.[22]

Women's private feelings about constant childbearing provide one example of unhappiness which was masked by the cheerful plantation image. The behavior of the patriarchs themselves in other realms of sexual life was another source of discontent. The patriarchal ideal which called for pure, gentle, pious women also expected a gread deal of men: that they should be strong, chaste, dignified, decisive, and wise. Women who lived in close intimacy with these men were aware of the gap between the cavalier of the image and the husband of the reality, and they were also aware that those who had the greatest power were also—by women's standards—the most sinful. A diarist summarized an afternoon of sewing and conversation in Richmond County, Georgia: "We were speaking of the virtue of men. I admitted to their general depravity, but considered that there were some noble exceptions, among those I class my own husband."[23] The entry revealed a certain uneasiness even about the noble exception, since the writer added that if her faith in her husband should be destroyed by experience her happiness on earth would end, and added, "Between husband and wife this is (or should be) a forbidden topic." She was twenty-two.

This notation parallels one in a more familiar diary. Observing the goings-on of the low-country aristocracy, Mary Boykin Chesnut wrote: "Thank God for my country women, but alas for the men! They are probably no worse than men everywhere, but the lower their mistresses the more degraded they must be."[24] Chesnut's comment revealed the dual nature of male depravity: sexual aberration in general and crossing the racial barrier in particular. Concern on this topic was an insistent theme in the writings of southern women and continued to be so long after emancipation. It may be significant that they did not always blame the black women who might have provided convenient scapegoats. The blame was squarely placed on men. "You have no confidence in men," wrote one husband; "to use your own phrase 'we are all humbugs,'" adding that he himself was a great sinner though he did not specify his sin.[25]

Miscegenation was the fatal flaw in the patriarchal doctrine. While southern men could defend slavery as "domestic and patriarchal," arguing that slaves had "all the family associations, and family pride, and sympathies of the master," and that the relationship between master and slave secured obedience "as a sort of filial respect," southern women looked askance at the fact that so many slaves quite literally owed their masters filial respect.[26] "There is the great point for the abolitionists," one wrote.[27] While some southern reviewers blasted "the fiend in petticoats" who wrote *Uncle Tom's Cabin*, southern women passed copies of the book from hand to hand.

Impressive evidence of the pervasiveness of interracial sex and its effects on the minds and spirits of white women, gathered thirty years ago, has recently found its way into print. James Hugo Johnston examined 35,000 manuscript petitions to the Virginia legislature. Among these documents were many divorce petitions in which white women named slave women as the cause of their distress. In some petitions wives told the whole story of their marriages, throwing much light on what could happen to the family in a slave society. One testified that her husband had repeated connection with many slaves, another protested several black mistresses who had been placed in her home and had treated her insolently. Yet another recounted a complicated story in which her brother had tried to force her husband to send away his black mistress, without success. In several cases the husband's attention to his mulatto children, sometimes in preference to his legitimate children, was offered in evidence. The stories run on and on until one is surfeited with pain and tragedy from the white woman's point of view, pain which could doubtless be matched from the black woman's point of view if it had been recorded. Many petitioners candidly described their husbands' long attachment to black mistresses, and their reluctance to give them up. Johnston also adduced evidence of the tortured efforts white men made to provide for their mulatto children, efforts corroborated by Helen Catterall's compilation of legal cases dealing with slavery.[28]

If so much evidence found its way into the offical records of the state of Virginia, how much is there yet unexamined in the records of other slave states, and how much more was never recorded because women suffered in silence rather than go against religion, custom, and social approval to sue for divorce by a special act of the legislature? Johnston, from his close acquaintance with the documents, surmised that there must have been many women who calmly or sullenly submitted to becoming "chief slave of the master's harem," a phrase attributed to Dolley Madison.[29]

Even apart from miscegenation, the general sexual freedom society accorded to men was deeply resented by women. A thread of bitterness runs through letters describing marital problems, the usual assumption being that male heartlessness could be expected. The double standard was just one more example of how unfairly the world was organized: "As far as a womans being forever 'Anathema . . .' in society for the same offence which in a man, very slightly lowers, and in the estimation of some of his own sex rather elevates him. In this I say there appears to be a very very great injustice. I am the greatest possible advocate for womans purity, in word, thought or deed, yet I think if a few of the harangues directed to women were directed in a point where it is more needed the standard of morality might be elevated."[30] Ten years later the same woman had not changed her mind: "It occurs to me that if virtue be the test to distinguish man from beast the claim of many Southern white men might be questionable."[31]

In addition to the widely prevailing skepticism with which women viewed the pretensions of their lords and masters (a label often used with a measure of irony), there was widespread discontent with the institution of slavery. "I never met with a lady of southern origin who did not speak of Slavery as a sin and a curse,—the burden which oppressed their lives," Harriet Martineau observed in her autobiography.[32]

In Virginia, after the Nat Turner rebellion, twenty-four women joined in a petition to the legislature, noting that though "it be unexampled, in our beloved State, that females should interfere in its political concerns," they were so unhappy about slavery that they were willing to break the tradition. They urged the legislature to find a way to abolish slavery.[33] An overseer of wide experience told Chesnut in 1861 that in all his life he had met only one or two women who were not abolitionists.[34] William Gilmore Simms, reviewing *Uncle Tom's Cabin* in the *Southern Quarterly Review*, made clear his understanding of the opposition to slavery among southern women.[35]

Of course Martineau and the overseer exaggerated to make a point, and the Virginia petitioners were unusual. Women of slaveholding families responded ambiguously to the life imposed on them. Some accepted it without question. Others, complaining of the burden of slavery, nevertheless expected and sometimes got a degree of personal service which would have been inconceivable to women in the free states.[36] It was also true that few were philanthropic enough to give up a large investment for a principle. It is further clear that most southern women accepted, with a few nagging questions, the racial assumptions of their time and place.

Even with these conditions many women of the planter class had strong doubts about either the morality or the expediency of slavery, as the following statements indicate. "Always I felt the moral guilt of it, felt how impossible it must be for an owner of slaves to win his way into Heaven."[37] "But I do not hesitate to say . . . that slavery was a curse to the South—that the time had come in the providence of God to give every human being a chance for liberty and I would as soon hark back to a charnel house for health inspiration as to go to the doctrines of secession, founded on the institution of slavery, to find rules and regulations."[38] "When the thunderbolt of John Brown's raid broke over Virginia I was inwardly terrified, because I thought it was God's vengeance for the torture of such as Uncle Tom."[39] "I will confess that what troubles me more than anything else is that I am not certain that *Slavery is right.*"[40] "When will it please our God to enfranchise both the holders and the slaves from bondage? It is a stigma, a disgrace to our country."[41] "In 1864 I read Bishop Hopkins book on slavery. He took the ground that we had a right to hold the sons of Ham in bondage. . . . Fancy a besotted, grinding, hardfisted slave driver taking up a moral tone as one of God's accredited agents!!"[42]

One doubter suggested that she would happily pay wages to her house servants if her husband would agree, and another thought slaves ought to be permitted to choose their own masters. Still another devoted all her time to teaching slaves to read and write, even though to do so was illegal, and to providing a Sunday school for slave children.[43]

Moral doubts were further complicated by strong personal attachments between white and black women. A South Carolina woman went into mourning in 1857 when her favorite slave died, and her sister wrote that "she loved Rose better than any other human being."[44] Another member of the same family insisted that her brother and brother-in-law keep promises made to slaves whom she had sold within the family. A Virginia woman, seeking permission to free her slave woman and keep her in the state, contrary to the law, testified to her "strong and lasting attachment to her slave Amanda."[45] Such phrases were not uncommon among southern women.

For every woman who held slavery to be immoral, or who simply loved individual slaves, there were dozens who hated it for practical reasons. "Free at last," cried one white women when she heard of the Emancipation Proclamation. "If slavery were restored and every Negro on the American continent offered to me," wrote another, "I should spurn them. I should prefer poverty rather than assume again the cares and perplexities of ownership."[46] Such quotations could be multiplied. They are typified by a diary entry in the fall of 1866 expressing relief "that I had no Negro clothes to cut out this fall O what a burden, like that of Sinbad the Sailor, was the thought of 'Negro clothes to be cut out.' "[47]

Motherhood, happy families, omnipotent men, satisfied slaves — all were essential parts of the image of the organic patriarchy. In none of these areas did the image accurately depict the whole reality.

For women as for the slaves, open revolt was made difficult by many constraints. Though women had complaints, they shared many of the assumptions of men and, at least intermittently, enjoyed the role and status of the landholding aristocracy. Discontent does not automatically lead to a clear idea of alternatives, and few, if any, southern women in the 1850s had visions of a multiracial society based on freedom, much less equality. Nor did they conceive of fundamental change in the patterns of marriage and family which bound them so tight. Some, to be sure, found widowhood a liberating experience.[48]

The ideology of woman's liberation, which was being worked out in the North by Sarah Grimké, Margaret Fuller, Elizabeth Cady Stanton, and others, had only begun to take shape in the minds of southern women, but signs of change can be found. A letter written from Yazoo, Mississippi, in 1849 to the *Southern Ladies Companion* complained about an article which seemed to imply that only men were part of mankind: "Woman is not, or ought not to be, either *an article* to be turned to good account by the persons who compose 'this life' [men] nor a plaything for their amusement. She ought to be regarded as forming a part of mankind herself. She ought to be regarded as having as much interest or proprietorship in 'this life' as anyone else. And the highest compliment to be paid her is that she is useful to herself — that in conjunction with the rest of mankind, in works of virtue, religion and morality, the sum of human happiness is augmented, the kingdom of the Savior enlarged and the glory of God displayed."[49]

By the 1850s some echoes of the woman's rights debate, which had erupted in the North in 1848, began to reach southern ears. A violent attack on the Woman's Rights Convention held in Worcester, Massachusetts, in 1851 appeared in the *Southern Quarterly Review,* written by a distinguished southern woman, Louisa Cheves McCord.[50] A closer look at McCord's own history is instructive with respect to built-in constraints.

Daughter of Langdon Cheves, she was outstandingly able both as a writer and as an administrator. Yet she used her ability to defend the whole southern domestic metaphor, including slavery. One has only to imagine her born in Boston instead of Charleston to find in Louisa McCord all the makings of a Margaret Fuller or an Elizabeth Cady Stanton.

What was the significance of this widespread discontent? Public decisions are rooted in private feelings, and the psychological climate in any society is one of the most important things a social or political historian needs to understand. The South by 1860 was in a high state of internal tension, as feelings of guilt and fear of the future mounted. The part played by slaves themselves, as well as by women, in exacerbating these tensions is just now beginning to be examined. Speaking of the American Revolution, Charles Francis Adams once remarked that it "drew its nourishment from the sentiment that pervaded the dwellings of the entire population," and added, "How much this home sentiment did then, and does ever, depend upon the character of the female portion of the people, will be too readily understood by all to require explanation."[51] What Adams called "the home sentiment" was in the South of 1860 an unstable and hence explosive mixture of fear, guilt, anxiety, and discontent with things as they were. How much this stemmed from the unhappiness of "the female portion of the population" is not yet well understood, but it is worth a good deal of study.

NOTES

1. George Fitzhugh, *Cannibals All! or Slaves Without Masters* (Cambridge, Mass., 1960), p. 18.

2. *Ibid.*, p. 25.

3. William Pettigrew to Mose, July 12, 1856, Pettigrew Family Papers, Southern Historical Collection, University of North Carolina, Chapel Hill.

4. Charles Pettigrew to Caroline Pettigrew, Oct. 18, 1857, Pettigrew Family Papers.

5. Anne Firor Scott, *The Southern Lady: From Pedestal to Politics, 1830-1930* (Chicago, 1970), pp. 20-21.

6. *Corinne*, Madame de Staël's famous feminist novel, appeared often in lists of books read by southern women. Even Mary Wollstonecraft was not entirely unknown in the South. See William R. Taylor, *Cavalier and Yankee: The Old South and the American National Character* (New York, 1961), pp. 161-67, for discussion of a pervasive malaise among antebellum southern women.

7. See H. E. Sterkx, *Partners in Rebellion: Alabama Women in the Civil War* (Rutherford, N.J., 1970), for the most recent collection of evidence concerning the extraordinary vigor and range of southern women's activities during the war. It is important to note that this essay does not treat all classes of women. There were 8 million southerners in 1860, of whom the largest part were ordinary farmer folk, slaves, and free blacks. This majority was ruled, politically, economically, and socially, by a small top layer, the large and medium-sized plantation owners who had money, or at least credit, slaves, and power. From their ranks came the proslavery philosophers, the mythmakers, the leaders of opinion. From their ranks came the most visible southerners, the minority which the rest saw and heard. It was members of this minority who consciously or unconsciously clung to the idea of the beautiful organic society so well described in George Fitzhugh, *Sociology for the South: or the Failure of Free Society* (Richmond, 1954). It was women of this minority who were called upon to play the appropriate role, to live up to the image of the southern lady. Other women, farmers' wives and daughters and illiterate black women, were part of society and in some inarticulate way doubtless helped to shape it, but historians have just begun to forge tools which may permit an examination of their role. For insights into southern society, see Steven A. Channing, *Crisis of Fear: Secession in South Carolina* (New York, 1970).

8. Fred A. Ross, *Slavery Ordained of God* (Philadelphia, 1859), pp. 54-56.

9. R. M. Ruffin, *Tales and Sketches for the Fireside* (Marion, Ala., 1858).

10. For other sources of women's unhappiness, especially the desire for education, see Scott, *Southern Lady*. This essay concentrates on areas of complaint directly related to the patriarchal myth. Of course the education some women hoped for, had it been available, would have indirectly undermined the patriarchy.

11. See *Annual Report to the Legislature of South Carolina Relating to the Registration of Births, Deaths and Marriages for the Year Ending December 13, 1856* (Columbia, S.C., 1857). Though the report acknowledges grave deficiencies in its fact gathering, this early venture into vital statistics supports generalizations suggested here. For comparative purposes the report includes some statistics from Kentucky, which are also supportive. Of the deaths recorded in South Carolina in 1856, nearly one-half were children under the age of five and nearly one-fourth were children under one year. Of marriages in the same year, 5.7 percent were of men under twenty, while 40.4 percent of the women were under that age. Nearly one-half of the men and three-fourths of the women who married in 1856 were under twenty-five. One-fourth of the men but only 9.4 percent of the women married between the ages of twenty-five and thirty. A cohort analysis of selected groups of southern women patterned on Robert V. Wells's study of Quakers might be useful, if data could be found. See Robert V. Wells, "Demographic Change and the Life Cycle of American Families," *Journal of Interdisciplinary History*, 2 (Autumn 1971), 273-82. Analysis of the biographical sketches of 150 low-country planters prepared by Chalmers Gaston Davidson provides further evidence of the age gap between husbands and wives. Davidson's study is based on 440 South Carolinians who had 100 or more slaves on a single estate. (Although fifty of the planters were women—a somewhat startling fact—his

information is always about the men these women married.) The majority of the men were one to ten years older than their wives in first marriage. For second marriages the age difference increased, as it did for third and fourth marriages. In cases where the woman was older than her husband (twenty-three in all), the age gap was usually up to five years, though three women were more than ten years older than their husbands. Chalmers Gaston Davidson, *The Last Foray: The South Carolina Planters of 1860: A Sociological Study* (Columbia, S.C., 1971), pp. 170-267.

12. E. G. C. Thomas Diary, June 26, 1855, Department of Manuscripts, Duke University, Durham, N.C.

13. *Ibid.*, May 26, 1856.

14. *Ibid.*, June 1, 1856.

15. *Ibid.*, Dec. 1862.

16. *Ibid.*, Dec. 31, 1863.

17. *Ibid.*, Feb. 12, 1865.

18. *Ibid.*, Jan. 29, 1869.

19. *Ibid.*, Nov. 29, 1870.

20. James Petigru Carson, *Life, Letters and Speeches of James Louis Petigru: The Union Man of South Carolina* (Washington, 1920), p. 441.

21. Letters of Charles and Caroline Pettigrew, 1856-61, Pettigrew Family Papers.

22. The degree to which maternity shaped women's lives emerges from any random examination of family histories. For example, Charles and Mary Pratt Edmonston of North Carolina had their first child in 1812, their last in 1833. During those twenty-one years Mrs. Edmonston bore eleven children, four of whom died in infancy. Mrs. Andrew McCollum of Louisiana bore ten children between 1840 and 1855, including one set of twins. Three died in infancy. During 180 months of married life, she spent ninety in pregnancy and seventy in nursing babies, since she did not use wet nurses. Thus in all her married life there was one month when she was neither pregnant nor nursing a baby. Margaret Ann Morris Grimball, wife of South Carolinian John B. Grimball, married at twenty and had a child every two years for eighteen years. At seventeen Varina Howell of Mississippi married Jefferson Davis who was thirty-five and a widower. Children were born in 1852, 1855, 1857, 1861, and 1864. Georgian David Crenshaw Barrow married Sarah Pope who bore him nine children in seventeen years, then died. John Crittenden's wife bore seven children in thirteen years. Robert Allston of South Carolina married Adele Petigru, ten years his junior. She bore ten children in seventeen years, of whom five lived to maturity. Examples could be multiplied indefinitely, but far more useful would be a careful demographic study of selected southern counties, tidewater and up-country, to give a firm underpinning to this kind of impressionistic evidence.

23. Thomas Diary, Apr. 12, 1856.

24. Mary Boykin Chesnut, *Diary from Dixie*, ed. Ben Ames Williams (Boston, 1949), pp. 21-22.

25. Charles Pettigrew to Caroline Pettigrew, July 10, 1856, Pettigrew Family Papers.

26. Quoted in Severn Duvall, *"Uncle Tom's Cabin*: The Sinister Side of the Patriarchy," *New England Quarterly,* 36 (Mar. 1963), 7-8. This perceptive article deserves serious attention from social historians.

27. Thomas Diary, Jan. 2, 1858.

28. James Hugo Johnston, *Race Relations in Virginia & Miscegenation in the South, 1776-1860* (Amherst, 1970); Helen Tunnicliff Catterall, *Judicial Cases concerning American Slavery and the Negro,* 2 vols. (Washington, D.C., 1926). See also Guion Griffis Johnson, *Ante-Bellum North Carolina: A Social History* (Chapel Hill, 1937), p. 221, for evidence that cohabitation with a Negro was the second most important cause for divorce in North Carolina.

29. Johnston, *Race Relations in Virginia,* p. 237.

30. Thomas Diary, Feb. 9, 1858.

31. *Ibid.,* May 7, 1869.

32. Harriet Martineau, *Harriet Martineau's Autobiography: With Memorials by Maria Weston Chapman,* 3 vols. (London, 1877), 2:21.

33. Augusta County Legislative Petitions, 1825-33, Virginia State Library, Richmond.

34. Chesnut, *Diary from Dixie,* p. 169.

35. William Gilmore Simms, review of *Uncle Tom's Cabin,* in *Southern Quarterly Review,* 8 (July 1853), 216, 233.

36. Their expectations may be illustrated by the E. G. C. Thomas family in its poverty-stricken postwar phase still requiring, so they thought, a person to cook, a person to clean, a person to wash and iron, one to do the chores, and a carriage driver. See Thomas Diary, 1868-69, as Mrs. Thomas details her search for reliable domestic help among the freed people. One complication was that it was considered unethical to hire fine servants who had once belonged to friends.

37. John Q. Anderson, ed., *Brokenburn: The Journal of Kate Stone, 1861-1868* (Baton Rouge, 1955), p. 8.

38. Rebecca L. Felton, *The Subjection of Women,* pamphlet 19, Rebecca L. Felton Papers, Manuscript Division, University of Georgia, Athens.

39. Mrs. Burton [Constance Cary] Harrison, *Recollections Grave and Gay* (New York, 1912), p. 42.

40. Thomas Diary, Sept. 23, 1854.

41. Martha E. Foster Crawford Diary, Feb. 7, 1853, Feb. 3, 1854, Department of Manuscripts, Duke University.

42. Hope Summerell Chamberlain, *Old Days in Chapel Hill, being the Life and Letters of Cornelia Phillips Spencer* (Chapel Hill, 1926), p. 93.

43. John Q. Anderson, "Sarah Anne Ellis Dorsey," in Edward James, Janet James, and Paul S. Boyer, eds., *Notable American Women, 1607-1950,* 3 vols. (Cambridge, Mass., 1971), 1:505-6. There were southern men who opposed slavery, too, but theirs was usually an economic, not a moral critique.

44. Jane P. North to Caroline Pettigrew, Nov. 16, 1857, Pettigrew Family Papers.

45. J. H. Easterby, ed., *The South Carolina Rice Plantation as Revealed in the Papers of Robert F. W. Allston* (Chicago, 1945), p. 149.

46. Caroline Merrick, *Old Times in Dixie* (New York, 1901), p. 19. Mary A. H. Gray of Georgia, quoted in Matthew Page Andrews, *Women of the South in Wartime* (Baltimore, 1920), p. 334.

47. Thomas Diary, Sept. 20, 1866.

48. A study of planters' widows would be interesting. Many of them ran plantations with considerable success, and as they necessarily came in contact with the outside world in business they began to develop more forceful personalities and interest in politics as well. For example, Jane Petigru North, sister of the famous James L. Petigru, was widowed early and ran one plantation owned by her brother and then another owned by her son-in-law, Charles L. Pettigrew. She did not hesitate to take full responsibility, and like her brother she was an outspoken supporter of the Union down to the moment of secession.

49. *Southern Ladies Companion*, 2 (1848), 45.

50. L.S.M. [Louisa Cheves McCord], *Southern Quarterly Review*, 5 (Apr. 1852), 322-41. See also Margaret Farrand Thorp, "Louisa Susannah Cheves McCord," in James, James, and Boyer, eds., *Notable American Women*, 2:451-52.

51. Charles Francis Adams, *Letters of Mrs. Adams with an Introductory Memoir by her Grandson* (Boston, 1848), p. xix.

Women, Religion, and Social Change in the South, 1830-1930

The significance of evangelical Protestantism in southern history and culture has long been a subject of interest. The history of southern women, just now beginning to be studied, may throw new light on this old topic. The personal documents of literate southern women contribute a new angle of vision from which to view the question of the role religion played in the society and in the culture and in the vast social changes which occurrred in the years after 1830.

In antebellum times such women were intensely preoccupied with personal piety, with the need for salvation and for godly behavior. Men of the time had similar concerns, but except for ministers of the church a man's daily behavior was not expected to reflect so fully the depth of his religious commitment. The image of the ideal Christian woman was very close to the image of the ideal southern lady so that religion strongly reinforced the patriarchal culture.

The primary social concern of antebellum southern women, stemming in part from their Christian commitment, was with African slavery. Placed, as plantation wives were, in close juxtaposition to slaves, responsible for their physical and spiritual well-being, many southern women became secret abolitionists. When the Civil War came, it was not uncommon for women to view it as God's punishment of the South for the sin of owning slaves. Women often described emancipation as the will of God.

Adapted from Anne Firor Scott, *The Southern Lady: From Pedestal to Politics, 1830-1930* (Chicago: University of Chicago Press, 1970), and reprinted with permission from Samuel S. Hill, Jr., et al., eds., *Religion and the Solid South* (Nashville: Abingdon Press, 1972), pp. 92-121.

For the rest of the nineteenth century and well into the twentieth religion continued to be a central aspect of many women's lives, but its form gradually changed from intense personal piety to a concern for the salvation of the heathen and for social problems. In their missionary societies and in the Woman's Christian Temperance Union many southern women came bit by bit to develop something which was in practice, if not in theology, a social gospel. In making this transition they also remade themselves. By experimenting with new kinds of behavior they developed new strength of personality and capacity for leadership hitherto not much encouraged by the society. The process is interesting and throws considerable light on the interaction between religion and women's emancipation.

Everywhere in the Anglo-American culture of 1830 "woman's sphere" was sharply defined and very restricted. Nowhere was this more evident than in the American South. When Sidney Mead, a historian of religion, asserts that one of the universal images of the period was that of the "free individual . . . the person with full opportunity to develop his every latent possibility or natural power," it would appear that he is simply asserting that American history is the history only of American men.[1] Certainly no such universal image prevailed with respect to the female half of the population.

Far from being encouraged to develop her latent possibilities, it was the prevailing view that women existed for the benefit of her family and that her life should be conducted in complete submissiveness to the will of her husband. Neither the culture nor the law viewed her as a free individual, nor did many women themselves glimpse such a possibility.

Thomas Nelson Page supposed himself to be writing not fiction, but social history, when he described an antebellum Virginia matron:

> Her life was one long act of devotion, — devotion to God, devotion to her husband, devotion to her children, devotion to her servants, to the poor, to humanity. Nothing happened within the range of her knowledge that her sympathy did not reach and her charity and wisdom did not ameliorate. She was the head and font of the church. . . . The training of her children was her work. She watched over them, inspired them, led them, governed them; her will impelled them; her word to them, as to her servants was law. She reaped the reward . . . their sympathy and tenderness were hers always, and they worshipped her.[2]

The southern women who left a record, the women who wrote letters and diaries, stories and poems, to whom sermons were addressed and eulogies written were expected to be meek, mild, quiet outside their homes, self-abnegating, kind to all, and to accept their husbands as lord and master.

The imagery is plain. Precisely the virtues which were attributed to the perfect woman were those demanded of the perfect Christian. The church effectively reinforced the cultural image of woman. Christian perfection was seen as obedience to the will of God—and women were frequently reminded of the necessity for inhabiting the "sphere to which God had appointed them." "All sin consists in selfishness and all holiness or virtue in disinterested benevolence" seems to have been the operative theology of many antebellum southern women.

The demands for Christian perfection were transmitted largely through the evangelical churches. Baptists and Methodists together claimed over a million members in the South in 1855, so that with some help from Presbyterians they clearly dominated the religious life of the section. The mechanisms were familiar ones: Sunday church, midweek prayer meetings, revivals, and periodic love-feasts. That these gatherings served many functions in addition to religious ones we take for granted: In a thinly populated society everything from horse trading to courtship was conducted at church, as well as simple sociability, gossip, and politics. In addition to all these things, however, women communicants seem to have absorbed a common theological outlook. This point of view was reinforced by the religious periodicals, including some written expressly for women. The themes which recur in the diaries and letters of antebellum southern women are familiar to any student of evangelical religion: the emphasis upon prayer, contemplation, and Bible reading; the need for constant cultivation of submissiveness to the will of an all-powerful God; the need for subduing the self and practicing goodness to others; the importance of raising children to fear God; the achievement of conversion and secure salvation; and a strong sense of one's own innate wickedness. For salvation both faith and works seem to have been required. Whether they were aware of the label or not, most southern women were Arminians who believed in man's participation in his own salvation. Add to this a firm belief in life after death, and the constellation of generally accepted beliefs is complete.

A mosaic constructed from letters and diaries is revealing. "I feel this day heavy and sad and I would ask myself why and the answer is I feel cold in religious matters oh why am I thus?"[3] "I feel that I am worthless and through the merits of Christ's all-atoning blood alone can I be saved."[4] "Mr. B. [her husband] says we must try to live holier. Oh that I could. Spent some time today reading, weeping and praying."[5] "Help me O Lord for I am poor and weak, help me for I am desolate, in Thee alone have I hope."[6] "As for myself I find my heart so full of sinful feelings that I am ready to say 'I am chief of sinners.' "[7] "Lord I feel that my heart is a cage of unclean beasts."[8]

In a time when infants and children died very easily, women found comfort in the assurance that God had some purpose in these deaths. "As you say we have been greatly afflicted," wrote a mother whose two children had died, "we dare not ask *why* but strive to say to our crushed hearts 'Be still and know that I am God. . . .' I trust our Gracious God will preserve me from the slightest rebellion against his holy will—will you pray for me?"[9] "I see so much of sin, so many things to correct, that I almost despair of being a perfect christian."[10] "Oh! for an increased degree of peace to know and do my redeemers will, to live more as I should."[11] The biblical verse most frequently quoted in southern women's diaries was from Jeremiah: "The heart is deceitful above all things and desperately wicked: who can know it?"[12] There are references to sins too awful even to be recorded in a private journal, accompanied by allusions to cold hearts.

Many women assumed that if they were not happy and contented in the "sphere to which God had appointed them" it must be their own fault and that by renewed effort they could do better. "My besetting sins are a roving mind and an impetuous spirit," wrote one woman whose diary is filled with admonitions to herself to be systematic, diligent, prudent, economical, and patient with her servants.[13] In another context she might have been proud of her imaginative reach and her spontaneity.

Josephine Clay Habersham, a gentle and gifted woman who presided with skill and dignity over a large plantation in eastern Georgia and whose fitness for the role society offered her might be measured by her spontaneous notation, "I wish always to have a sweet babe on my lap," still felt it necessary to cultivate constantly a cheerful spirit and to ask God for help with her "dull and wayward heart."[14] She continues, "The Summer is over! Have I improved it as I should have done? Have I improved my children? Let me put these questions to myself in the privacy of my room and ask God's forgiveness that I am not a *more faithful* servant."[15]

A young girl was already well on the way to the typical woman's view of life: "Oh, we young ladies are all so surface like, so useless; I pray God I may be useful, only useful, I feel that I can say with Evangeline often, 'I have no wish nor desire but to follow meekly with reverent steps the footprints of my Redeemer,' and yet how I fail oh so sadly, many are the vain desires that every now and then trouble this prevailing one, and my flesh is so weak, I am always failing."[16]

Women whose families and friends would have credited them with a "spotless life" were themselves convinced that their souls harbored serpents. "Oh that I might be delivered from the serpent's power—that God—would put enmity between me & the serpent—his folds are around my limbs; his sting in my heart. Today has not been without profit. I have reviewed my besetting sins—repented—and resolved this week at least to make battle against them. How proud & happy I could feel at the close of it, to find that in God's strength I have opposed my foes successfully."[17] Or, "My way of late has been hedged up and my mind has seemed sunken with a state of apathy from which I can with difficulty arouse myself. I feel sure that my present state is owing to my own neglect of duty and fearful transgression of God's Holy law. And although the desire of my heart is to love and to serve him yet I am conscious of the world and its cares have too large a share of my time and affections."[18]

Sudden death was not confined to children and the necessity for being ready to die at any moment was deeply felt. For religious women this meant one had to be "saved." The concern was not only for themselves but for all the members of the family, especially those who had not yet felt the experience of religious conversion.

After church I partook of the Lord's supper and benefited to an unusual degree. Oh! for an increased degree of peace to know and do as my redeemer wills, to live more as I should. More to the glory of God and the advancement of that holy cause of which I profess to be an unworthy disciple . . . how fervently do I desire to bring her [a sister] and my husband to the throne of peace and pleading only the shed blood of our Lord and Savior obtain pardon and redeeming love."[19]

For many people what really mattered was the afterlife—what went on during the brief span of earthly life was merely preparation—and it required constant effort to avoid eternal damnation. Nor was it possible ever to rest assured that one was saved; the self-exhortation continued through life.

I am much too prone to allow the passing and vexatious scenes of this life to interrupt my religious enjoyments and for the time to impede my preparation for that life which is eternal. Oh My Divine Master, be pleased for the time to come to grant me Grace sufficient to help in every trying hour to overcome every evil propensity of my nature, so that I may be calm and collected at all times and ready . . . at a moment's notice . . . to depart in peace.[20]

Another minister's wife put the matter much more succinctly: "I am not as much engaged in religion as I should be. . . . Too worldly."[21]

Occasionally piety might even be seen as a competitive accomplishment, as in the case of one bright young lady in Alabama, who determined early in her life to become a missionary (and did, in fact, become Alabama's first woman missionary), who remarked, "I have established a reputation for piety and considerable intelligence. I am mortified when I hear of others doing better than I."[22] Often these women were cast into deep depression because they had slapped a child or whipped a slave. A woman who could hardly bear the sound of her husband tuning his violin gritted her teeth and said nothing, dedicated as she was to the ideal of self-sacrifice.[23] There was no rest for the conscience. "We owe it to our husbands, children and friends," wrote Caroline Merrick, "to represent as nearly as possible the ideal which they hold so dear."[24] " 'Tis man's to act, 'tis woman's to endure," Caroline Hentz reflected in the midst of some of her more difficult trials with a husband she did not much respect and financial problems that were beyond her power to solve.[25] Women were made, Ella Thomas was sure, "to suffer and be strong."[26] "Give me a double portion of the grace of thy Spirit that I may learn *meekness*," wrote another.[27] "Your mother seems to brood much," wrote Joseph LeConte to his daughter.[28] "I looked into that young patient face and busy thought went far into the future," wrote a woman meditating upon her young daughter, "and all that women must here feel and suffer."[29] "The task of self-government was not easy," said Caroline Gilman.

To repress a harsh answer, to confess a fault, and to stop (right or wrong) in the midst of self-defence, in gentle submission, sometimes requires a struggle like life and death; but these *three* efforts are the golden threads with which domestic happiness is woven; once begin the fabric with this woof, and trials shall not break or sorrow tarnish it.

Men are not often unreasonable; their difficulties lie in not understanding the moral and physical structure of our sex. . . . How clear it is, then, that woman loses by petulance and recrimination! Her first study must be self-control, almost to hypocrisy. A good wife must smile amid a thousand perplexities, and clear her voice to tones of cheerfulness when her frame is drooping with disease or else languish alone.[30]

Elizabeth Avery Meriwether stood practically alone among the diary keepers and memoirists when she asserted in her *Recollections of 92 Years* that at an early age she had rejected immortality on her own initiative. "It seemed to me preposterous to imagine that a *good* God would create a human being with the power to feel and to suffer if He knew before creating that being that its fate was Hell for all eternity. . .—and I then came to the opinion I still hold, viz., that the Hell we mortals get is of our own making and that we get it on this earth and not in a future life."[31] Perhaps such independence of mind was of a piece with her decision to send all her husband's inherited slaves to Liberia.

Mrs. Meriwether and a few sophisticated ladies of Charleston and New Orleans stand as exceptions. The overwhelming majority of southern women who have left records at all reveal their preoccupation with religion and its demands for self-denial. Women made up more than 60 percent of the membership lists of various churches.[32]

What function did these stern demands upon oneself for piety and goodness serve? In an uncertain world, full of change, economic insecurity, and sudden death, did the search for perfection help to give some steady center to life? Certainly the constant reiteration of "God's will be done" helped to relieve the burden of understanding as well as the burden of dealing with recurrent crises. Observing the kinds of sudden disasters which were commonplace: the dry summer which destroyed a crop, the epidemic which killed a third of the slaves and half the children in the family, the sudden bankruptcy caused by external economic conditions, or by the simple generosity of having gone on someone else's note; the unexplained deaths of adolescents who were well and active one day and dead three days later, it is no wonder that a woman might feel herself to be not an actor but a pawn in some giant game she could not possibly understand. To assume it was all meaningless would be a prescription for insanity.

Perhaps, too, by being good one could make secret bargains with God or Fate. Yet the bargains didn't work, the children died anyway, health disappeared in spite of them, husbands were sometimes hardhearted or dissipated.

Perhaps the diaries are misleading. It may be that one way to manage fears and anxieties is to write them down, after which one can then go on to live a reasonably normal life. Some hint of this is contained in a huge collection preserved at the University of North Carolina, wherein a woman's religious diary is as perfervid as any to be found, while her daily letters to sons away at school are matter-of-fact and down to earth, with only the normal amount of reference to salvation, church attendance, and the like.[33]

It seems possible that the demand for Christian perfection that so many women internalized, while it laid great burdens upon them, also enabled the strongest to become truly remarkable mainstays of family life. The paradox is that the faith which sustained them added new burdens and increased the level of anxiety. Perhaps the vision of heaven was comforting (weary women often spoke of the longing for death and peace), but the price of admission was high. Here were excellent women, thousands of them, whose sins were of the most minor kind. Yet they carried constantly with them the conception of a jealous, wrathful God, capable of punishing by eternal damnation their innate corruption, whom they were yet supposed to love. Because of their understanding of what salvation required, they were persuaded to apologize abjectly for the very qualities which make a woman (or a man for that matter) an interesting and rich personality—for spirit, for a roving mind, for pride to think well of themselves.

How this anxiety would have been resolved had there been no upheaval such as the Civil War, it is impossible to know. But the war came, and self-abnegating southern women were put to sterner tests than they had previously imagined existed. With many men gone submissiveness was no longer a functional virtue. Once the war was over, slavery was also ended, and a new phase of women's relationship to the church began. In the on-rushing industrialization of the late nineteenth century many of the traditional economic tasks which women had performed in the recent rural past began to disappear. Even in the South, towns were multiplying and the urban population steadily increasing. The story is too familiar to require much repetition: smaller families, better health, canned food, store-bought clothes, all combined to reduce the time required for necessary household functions and to expand the leisure time of urban wives. The presence of many Negro women willing—or compelled—to work for very low wages reduced still further the necessary tasks of many wives and mothers. Added to the economic facts was a certain psychological malaise, the key, perhaps, to much of the postwar development: "Women who had been fully occupied with the requirements of society and the responsibilities of a dependency of slaves, were now tossed to and fro amidst the exigencies and bewilderments of strange and for the most part painful circumstances, and were eager that new adjustments should relieve the strained situation, and that they might find out what to do."[34]

In direct contradiction to the old saw about Satan finding work for idle hands, it was the firm conviction of many women that if their families needed them less, the Lord had work for them to do. An energetic Alabama woman foreshadowed the future when she wrote Bishop James Andrew in 1861, pointing to the immense amount of work southern women were then engaged upon, and saying that surely women loved God as much as country, if only the church would offer equally specific tasks to be done.

Here and there women's missionary societies had existed long before the war. At the first Baptist convention in Alabama in 1823, when Alabama was still a frontier, half of the small number of delegates present were sent by missionary societies, and "stranger still, every one of these missionary societies was a little organization of women that had been formed in obscurity, none knowing of the existence of any other, and thus without concert of action."[35] A female missionary society in Columbus, Mississippi, was said to have had continuous existence from 1838, but before the war it always sent a man as its delegate to various conventions.[36] The records of these early societies are all but lost to history—and thus the societies themselves are only dimly remembered.

What came to pass in the 1870s was of a different order of magnitude. In that decade Methodist, Baptist, and Presbyterian women all over the South, released from the responsibilities of slaveholding and plantation administration, seemed to have received a simultaneous impulse which set them to organizing missionary societies, studying geography, raising money, and recruiting people to go to foreign shores.

The prevailing doctrine of these churches with respect to women was extremely conservative. Church publications were full of praise for ladylike women, and expressions of horror at "unsexed" females. The erudite *Quarterly Review* of the Methodist Episcopal Church South examined the question "May Women Preach?" and stood firmly with St. Paul who was presumed to have forbidden it. "So in Sunday-schools and Bible classes, and Missionary Societies, great caution is needed—more, perhaps, than is always shown—in utilizing the gifts and graces of pious, zealous, and intelligent women. Nothing can compensate for the sacrifice of feminine modesty: this must be guarded, though the heavens fall!"[37]

Baptist editors agreed completely, nor did their opinions change much with the passing of decades. In 1868 the Baptist *Religious Herald* asserted:

"As the rival of man, in the struggle for place, power and prominence, she, as the 'weaker vessel', is doomed to defeat. From such a contest, she must inevitably come forth, not with modesty, delicacy and loveliness which impart a charm and influence to her sex, but soiled, dishonored and disappointed."[38] Thirty-one years later the same paper was saying: "When . . . woman becomes *emancipated* from the care of the young and the making of the home, she has entered into the worst of all bondage, which comes always to every one who disregards the law of his own life. They only 'walk at liberty' who have learned to obey the divine precepts, as written in their being."[39] Within the church itself Baptist men were very slow to grant new privileges to women. There, too, St. Paul's injunction to "let the women keep silent in churches" was sternly applied. "We do not propose to be persuaded, cajoled, or drawn by the force of public or private opinion, into adopting this unscriptural and foolish practice. . . . Let *all* our people *positively* refuse the use of our churches to such an unscriptural and dangerous innovation. . . . 'From womanly men, and from manly women, good Lord deliver us.' "[40]

The Baptist church maintained an even more conservative stance vis-à-vis its women than did the Methodist. Baptist ministers firmly opposed any southwide women's organization for fear it would become a front for dangerous feminism. "An independent organization of women," wrote the Reverend Tiberius Jones of Virginia, "naturally tends toward a violation of divine interdict against a woman's becoming a public religious teacher."[41] It was 1888 before Baptist women were strong enough to insist on their right to a southwide organization, but in the meantime they carried on within their missionary societies the same kinds of programs—and the same kind of self-development—as their Methodist sisters.

It was no wonder that one Mississippi Baptist woman, praying for the enlightenment of the heathen added to her prayer, "I pray God to enlighten the minds of our benighted husbands, and show them their error."[42]

Yet these same Baptists, while officially opposing women's rights in any form, encouraged the expanding role of women in benevolent causes and encouraged participation in the temperance crusade "as long as these efforts remain dissociated with the feminist agitation and politics."[43]

The Methodists, too, were happy to turn over to women not only the responsibility for raising money for foreign missions, but responsibility for furnishing and taking care of parsonages and for local philanthropy. In meeting these responsibilities the women began to revise their self-image and ultimately found themselves to be part of the feminist movement which the church so deplored. In due course they would begin to demand more power within the church itself. The church fathers were not as foresighted as a certain antebellum minister who had refused permission for a woman's prayer meeting on the ground that if women were alone "who knows what they would pray for?"

The tendency of women to form themselves into religious societies was present in all the denominations. The introspective piety of the early decades of the century turned outward, the desire to do good in society increased, and a missionary spirit directed both to foreign lands and to social problems closer to home developed very rapidly.

Groups of women had hardly begun to realize that their own experience was being duplicated in many places when they began to think of setting up up a southwide organization. The Methodists were first to achieve this goal. In 1878 the Methodist General Conference, after some debate, authorized a Woman's Board of Foreign Missions, and at the close of its first year of existence the board counted 218 societies, 5,890 members, $4,000 in the treasury, and one missionary in China. Ten years later there were 2,399 societies, 56,783 members, and missionaries in dozens of places. The women were learning to administer programs and to handle large sums of money. By 1890 the Methodist Woman's Board of Foreign Missions owned almost $200,000 worth of property and had responsibility for ten boarding schools, thirty-one day schools, and a hospital.[44] Three years later the organization had grown to 76,000 members. Actual service in foreign lands offered a new form of work for women and a new opportunity for women whose religious zeal did not find adequate outlets at home.

While saving the heathen had a very strong emotional appeal, one which returning missionaries developed fully, women in the missionary societies were also becoming aware of needs nearer home.

In the process of carrying out what appeared on the surface to be rather traditional philanthropic work among the poorer people, church women came into direct contact with social problems which led them to a new interest in home missionary work, so great that some leaders worried for fear the foreign missions would be neglected. As early as 1882 Miss Laura Haygood organized the Trinity Home Mission of Atlanta, having for its purpose the "physical, mental, and moral elevation of the poor of the city, and especially of our own Church and congregation."

By the end of the first year this society had established an industrial school and a home for dependent and helpless women.[45]

Southern church women were observing, as many of their secular counterparts in the northern settlement-house movement had observed, the social consequences of industrial development. In Chicago the most obvious victims of the factory were foreign immigrants; in the South they were poor white people. In 1899 the general secretary of the Methodist Board of Home Missions told her sisters that they were standing on the threshold of a great opportunity as the southern states began to develop manufacturing. She called upon them to be farsighted, to move at once "to ameliorate existing conditions, to see that laws to protect helpless childhood are created and enforced."[46] By 1908 local church women were studying industrial relations in their regular meetings and passing resolutions of concern. The concern did not stop with resolutions but issued in a widespread network of settlement houses in industrial communities.[47]

In 1899 Southern Methodist women took the first tentative steps toward corporate concern with the problems of black people. In 1900 the Women's Missionary Council urged women throughout the South to "do all in their power in their own communities to help and uplift the Negro race," and a year later the council began to raise money to add an annex for girls to the Paine Institute, a school which the Methodist Church had established in Augusta, Georgia, to train Negro leaders. Ten years later a young Alabama woman, Miss Mary DeBardelben, began her missionary work, not in a foreign land, but in a Negro settlement house in Augusta.

Meantime the Methodist women established a Bureau of Social Service with Mrs. J. D. Hammond as its superintendent. Mrs. Hammond, whose husband later became president of Paine Institute, published in 1914 a book called *In Black and White*, which laid out a program for ameliorating the conditions of southern Negroes. Read in the context of its year of publication, and with the realization that the author was a southern woman whose parents had been slaveowners, the book is an astonishing document. Social equality aside, Mrs. Hammond tackled nearly every hard problem which vexed race relations in the South. She announced that she did not believe Negroes to be inferior. In her cosmos God had put them on earth, even as he had white people, to fulfill some destiny. In a series of hard-hitting chapters, she held a mirror to southern society, which must have caused some soul searching among such of her readers as did not throw the book away in disgust. Taking her stand firmly on the Christian ethic, she castigated her fellow white southerners for permitting Negro slums, for sending youngsters to jail whose home experience had prepared them for nothing but deliquency, for permitting inequity in the courts of law, for accepting stinking Jim Crow cars, for failing to educate talent when it came in a black skin, for failing to set an example of honesty and fair dealing, for hypocrisy and insensitivity.[48] The book provided a blueprint for much of the work which would develop in the 1920s under the leadership of a group calling itself the Commission on Inter-racial Cooperation, headed by Will Alexander.

Among the three leading Protestant denominations, women in the Methodist Church moved furthest in the direction of a social gospel. It is also noticeable that many of the women who led secular reform movements in the South were members of the Methodist Church. The reasons for this are not clear, though some speculations are possible. Connectionalism was a Methodist concept. Unlike the Baptists, who were congregational in church government, the Methodists had a higher layer of organization, which meant not only that the experience of joint decision-making existed in that church but also that members of various conferences could sometimes move beyond what members of local church groups might have sanctioned. This pattern, as we have seen, was reflected in the fact that the Methodist women had a southwide missionary organization somewhat earlier than the Baptists. Further, the Methodists had a good communication network—the publishing house was founded before 1800.

Wesleyan theology tended toward a this-worldiness and an emphasis on doing good here and now. The evangelical denominations shared certain concerns, but Methodist women seem to have reached out ahead of the others in matters such as child labor reform, prison reform, and especially in the effort to improve race relations.[49]

The mushrooming of women's organizations in the churches had consequences quite beyond the number of missionaries supported, schools founded, hospitals inaugurated in foreign lands, or even the social settlements closer to home. Church work was the essential first step in the emancipation of thousands of southern women from their antebellum image of themselves and of "woman's sphere." In 1879 a prominent North Carolina minister assured his daughter that membership in a missionary society would be "no compromise of female modesty and refinement,"[50] and no doubt many other men gave the same assurance. What these admirers of ladylike women did not foresee were the psychological consequences of the missionary society experience. The historians of South Carolina Presbyterianism remarked that at the beginning the women in the missionary society were so shy that they contented themselves with reciting the Lord's Prayer in unison. From this they progressed to sentence prayers, delivered seriatim, and finally (they triumphantly noted) 60 percent were prepared to lead the prayer![51] It was said that a statewide meeting of the South Carolina Methodist Women's Missionary Society was the first public meeting in the state to be presided over by a woman—this in 1880. "With experience and a growing and compelling sense of mission women in the church began to gain confidence and slowly emerge from the self-consciousness and fear which had bound them," observed the historian of Methodist women.[52] The public life of virtually every southern woman leader for forty years began in a church society. "The struggle that it cost the women to attain to the ultimate goal, in satisfaction of a conviction that the right was theirs to labor for the Lord, only served to qualify them the more for greater success, when once the end sought was reached," concluded the historian of the Alabama Baptists.[53]

As women gained self-confidence and felt pride in their achievements, they began to push harder for independence and greater rights within the church structure. A bitter battle took place in the Methodist Church in 1906, when, without consulting the women who had built both organizations, the men in the General Conference decided to combine the Foreign and Home Missionary Societies and put them under the control of a male-dominated Board of Missions. One woman missionary was so incensed that she resigned forever from the Methodist Church, though she continued her work.

As late as 1910 one worried Methodist woman was writing to another that she feared the women would "lose their independence of thought when they lost responsibility for, and management of their own affairs. . . . I fear the future will see the most intelligent women seeking a field of usefulness elsewhere and leave the less intelligent lacking the leadership that leads to enthusiasm and fuller development. . . . We are in a helpless minority in a body where the membership is largely made up of men opposed to independence of thought in women."[54] From long experience the women decided they had no choice but to keep their tempers and try again. Finally, after repeated rebuffs, Methodist women were granted laity rights—in 1918.[55] In spite of, perhaps in part because of, the difficulties they encountered women learned in the churches to be leaders. As individual women developed purpose and capacity and were frustrated in their plans by unsympathetic males, they came more and more to desire independence and to take responsibility for their own thinking.

In the meantime another development, which sprang from somewhat the same sources as the women's missionary societies, was the rapid growth of the Woman's Christian Temperance Union (WCTU). In the early 1880s Frances Willard, the extraordinary national president of the WCTU, made the first of a series of southern forays. In New Orleans in 1881 she addressed a large audience in the Carondelet Methodist Church. A year later she returned and drafted Caroline Merrick, wife of a prominent judge, to be president of the New Orleans WCTU. Mrs. Merrick thought temperance a thankless reform, but she found herself unable to refuse Miss Willard, who, she thought, had done more than any other person in the nineteenth century to "widen the outlook and develop the mental aspirations" of women.[56] Thereafter Mrs. Merrick spent ten years as president of the organization, and as a result was said to have been the first woman in Louisiana to speak in public on public questions.[57]

In 1883 a "few brave souls" summoned a convention of Christian women in North Carolina, and with Miss Willard's aid launched the union in that state. Six years later the scene was Jackson, Mississippi, where Frances Willard drafted a woman, who had not until that moment known of the organization's existence, to become an organizer. Belle Kearney, the woman in question, felt after prayerful meditation that she had heard God's call; in any case she had heard the call of Frances Willard.

Miss Willard's astonishing personal effectiveness was one reason the WCTU spread so rapidly in the South. A southern woman who later became prominent in national work said that "the first time I heard her I lay awake all night for sheer gladness. It was such a wonderful revelation to me that a woman like Miss Willard could exist. I thanked God and took courage for humanity."[58]

It is clear from the publications of the southern WCTU that many women had fastened upon alcohol as the root cause of a number of related things that bothered them about southern men and southern life, and in their fanatic insistence upon its eradication (even to the point of advertising flavoring in crystal form to avoid the alcoholic solvent and eschewing brandy in puddings), they managed — at this remove — to make themselves and their cause quite ridiculous. To see them as a joke is to miss the point.

Drinking was then virtually a male prerogative. It had long been a significant part of the life of many southern men. While temperance as a cause dated back to the 1830s temperance as a practice was not widespread among antebellum men. Eliza Frances Andrews, editing her Civil War diary for publication in the 1890s, commented in the preface:

In fact, I have been both surprised and shocked in reading over this story of a by-gone generation, to see how prevalent was the use of wines and other alcoholic liquors, and how lightly an occasional over-indulgence was regarded. In this respect there can be no doubt that the world has changed greatly for the better. When "gentlemen" . . . were staying in the house, it was a common courtesy to place a bottle of wine, or brandy, or both, with the proper adjuncts, in the room of each guest, so that he might help himself to a "night-cap" on going to bed, or an "eye opener" before getting up in the morning.[59]

Miss Andrews's reminiscence is borne out by the sentimental fiction of the antebellum years, which is filled with drunken husbands (only dis-covered to be such after marriage) and disillusioned wives. In the social circles somewhat less exalted than that of the Andrews family the frontier's rough-and-ready pleasure in hard drink was widespread, a fact recognized by the evangelical churches which early began to preach temperance as necessary to salvation. The war appeared to have killed the temperance societies and to have fostered the drink habit. Observers thought that social drinking and tippling were prevalent everywhere in Reconstruction, and that the rise of commercial villages and the multiplication of country stores made alcohol more accessible. Drinking was thought to have been stimulated, too, by the despondency with which the future was regarded. Saturday afternoons were scenes of alcoholic confusion in many villages.[60] The Negroes, whose access to hard drink had been carefully regulated in slavery, were now able to join their white brothers in weekend orgies, though some observers thought them less given to drunkenness than white men. For both races there was an intimate relationship between alcohol and crime, particularly violent crime.

   Such behavior was troublesome to women for a number of reasons — not only because it seemed to lead to a threatening social instability, but because it led to hardship in many individual families. In antebellum days much had been made by men and women alike of the power of "woman's influence" to bring men, not naturally so inclined, to virtuous habits. But "influence" was a chancy tool at best, and even a casual student of personality psychology would guess that it often worked in ways quite remote from the goal of the person trying to exert the influence. Total abstinence pledges and statewide prohibition were more likely to be effective, or at least it was possible to hope so.

There was also a strain of crusading revivalism in the organization which may have appealed to some women whose churches forbade them the privilege of preaching. In this wholly female organization women could, and did, preach—though perhaps not from a pulpit.

The union women did not stop with prohibition and total abstinence. They soon developed a broad educational program on the physiological effects of alcohol and went to work to make its teaching mandatory in the schools. This was the beginning of a good deal of public school teaching of health education. The WCTU may well have been the first group in the South to speak openly of the need for sex education.

An interest in prison reform and the demand for juvenile reformatories also grew directly from women's work with alcoholics among convicts. Mrs. L. C. Blair of the Raleigh, North Carolina, WCTU told a state legislative committee in 1905: "As superintendent of prison work for the W.C.T.U. I have for ten years studied this subject in our county jails and state prisons, and if I had time and language to portray to you, sirs, the dreadful effects I have seen arising from our methods of dealing with youthful criminals, I would have but little doubt of getting a reform school."[61]

In 1889 Mrs. Sallie Chapin, a talented Charleston aristocrat, was president of the South Carolina WCTU and spoke to the annual convention. In the course of her speech she referred to the convict lease system ("a disgrace to the civilization of the nineteenth century"), to a plan for educating mothers and reducing infant mortality, to the concern she felt for reducing the normal work week of laboring men. Discussion at the same convention revealed the fact that the Spartanburg union was running a woman's exchange to aid women who needed to earn a living.

The notion of the WCTU as in part an organization motivated by a desire to control male behavior is borne out by the emphasis its members put on what they called "social purity," the accepted euphemism for elimination of venereal disease. One approach to eliminating venereal disease was to attack that ancient bogey of women—the double standard.

Like the women in the churches the women in the WCTU in many cases underwent a personal transformation, as they learned to think for themselves, organize programs, assume leadership; as they met—in national conventions—women from other parts of the United States. Belle Kearney was a case in point. In the first year of her "ministry" she traveled all over Mississippi and organized hundreds of unions among young women and children. She held business meetings and discussed the methods of work best suited to forward the interest of the societies she was organizing. In 1889 she went to a national convention in Chicago and gained, she said, "a new vision of woman's life."[62]

Mrs. Lide Meriwether of Memphis, Tennessee, who had been born in 1829, recorded of herself that after the war she lived a simple home life, devoted to husband and children. Then, when "most women are only waiting to die, their children reared and the tasks of the spirit largely ended, began for her a life of new thought and activity." A friend in Arkansas asked her to help in a WCTU convention, where she discovered an hitherto unrecognized talent for public speaking. Under her leadership the Tennessee WCTU grew and flourished, and from this work she was led into an even more ardent interest in woman suffrage.[63]

Like the church women these women were also by their choice of subjects brought into direct contact with many of the social problems of their communities and decided that they could and should do something about them. Because they wanted temperance education in the schools and prohibition for their states they found themselves, willy-nilly, in politics. The frustration they felt when members of legislatures listened politely and voted as they pleased led WCTU women to become the earliest southern suffragists. "They see the solution of the drink problem lies to a great extent in woman's ballot; and, looking deeper, they find that the key to the whole situation. Not only in political and philanthropic circles have women been brought to realize these restrictions, but in ecclesiastical as well."[64]

One theme running through the essays in *Religion and the Solid South* is that of religion reinforcing southern culture. Looked at through women's lives the theme becomes more complex. The antebellum church by its doctrines reinforced the most limited and restricted role for women while it also provided a source of personal strength. The postwar church, still preaching Paul's doctrine that women should be silent in the churches and holding firmly to the antebellum image of the southern lady, inadvertently provided Christian women with a road to emancipation. Timothy Smith has argued that in the United States generally the revivalism of the early nineteenth century laid the foundation for social reform. While southerners took part in some aspects of the prewar reform movement, the presence of slavery and the link between reform and abolitionism often worked to limit practical applications of Christian perfection in the antebellum society.

Furthermore, while slavery existed, many southern women of the class discussed here were fully occupied with what could legitimately be called the extended family of the plantation. Not only their own children and relatives, but all the slaves were their responsibility, and if there was one thing no plantation mistress complained of it was not being needed.

Emancipation at one stroke pushed many southerners for the first time into a nuclear family. The economic stringency of the immediate postwar period reduced the amount of social visiting and perhaps even of kinship responsibilities. It was precisely when these old functions were disappearing that women in all the evangelical denominations began to develop their intense interest in foreign missions, and then in reform closer to home. In the beginning they used the institution most familiar to them, in which they felt most at ease — the church. The WCTU was almost a church, and it was only after two decades of experience with these familiar institutions that the more innovative women's clubs and suffrage societies began to appear.

The study of southern religion has assumed, as is customary among American historians, that men spoke for the whole society. Even the fragmentary evidence here is enough to make it clear that women had their own voice, though possibly its tone concealed its substance. Much more work must be done before it will be possible to say how many southern women were actually involved in serious social reform. Certainly there were some. Southern women cheered Frances Willard enthusiastically when, speaking in Atlanta in 1890, she announced that the wage system was certain to pass away, that labor unions were the hope of the future, and urged upon industry a consideration of profit-sharing. "If to teach this is to be a socialist," Miss Willard had said, "then so let it be."[65] It might be difficult to find an assemblage of southern men of the same social class and economic status cheering, or even listening to, such a speech at that time.

If the degree of female radicalism needs more study, one other thing is inescapably clear. Whatever function they served initially, the missionary societies and the WCTU (and the women's clubs and suffrage organizations for which they paved the way) provided a school for women leaders of considerable significance in the shaping of southern society and even southern politics in the ensuing decades.

NOTES

1. Sidney Mead, *The Lively Experiment* (New York, 1963), p. 92.

2. Thomas Nelson Page, *Social Life in Old Virginia* (New York, 1898), pp. 38-42.

3. Diary of Myra Smith, Apr. 17, 1851, Sommerville-Howorth Papers, Schlesinger Library, Radcliffe College, Cambridge, Mass.

4. Smith Diary, Jan. 1852.

5. Diary of Fannie Moore Webb Bumpas, Mar. 5, 1842, Southern Historical Collection, University of North Carolina, Chapel Hill; hereafter cited as SHC.

6. Diary of Charlotte Beatty, 1843, SHC.

7. Sarah Wadley Journal, Feb. 4, 1863, SHC. She was eighteen at the time!

8. Lucilla McCorkle Diary, May 1846, SHC.

9. Lizzie Smith to R. L. Felton, June 22, 1876, Felton Papers, University of Georgia, Athens.

10. Annie to Lollie, Dec. 14, 1859, in Lucy Cole Burwell Papers, Duke University Manuscript Department, Durham, N.C.; hereafter cited as Duke.

11. E. G. C. Thomas Diary, Apr. 8, 1855, Duke.

12. Jeremiah 17:9.

13. McCorkel Diary.

14. *Ebb Tide: Diary of Josephine Clay Habersham*, ed. Spencer B. King, Jr. (Athens, 1958), pp. 103-4.

15. *Ibid.*, p. 77.

16. Wadley Journal, Aug. 20, 1863.

17. Diary of Mrs. Isaac Hilliard, Apr. 21, 1850, Louisiana State University Department of Archives, Baton Rouge; hereafter cited as LSU.

18. Smith Diary, Dec. 15, 1850.

19. Thomas Diary, Apr. 8, 1855.

20. Diary of Anne Beale Davis, Aug. 14, 1842, SHC.

21. Bumpas Diary, June 26, 1842.

22. Martha E. Foster Crawford Diary, 1850, Duke.

23. Thomas Diary, Nov. 30, 1858.

24. To "my dear friend," May 23, 1857, LSU.

25. Caroline Hentz Diary, Mar. 5, 1836, SHC.

26. Thomas Diary, New Year's Day 1859, Duke.

27. McCorkle Diary, July 12, 1846.

28. Joseph LeConte to Emma, Apr. 25, 1869, LeConte Papers, SHC.

29. Beatty Diary, Mar. 21, 1843.

30. Caroline Gilman, *Recollections of a Southern Matron* (New York, 1838), p. 256.

31. Elizabeth Avery Meriwether, *Recollections of 92 Years* (Nashville, 1958), p. 35.

32. This estimate is based on a study of membership lists of over 100 churches made by Professor Donald Mathews of the University of North Carolina.

33. Beale-Davis Papers, SHC.

34. Caroline E. Merrick, *Old Time in Dixie Land* (New York, 1901), p. 172.

35. B. F. Riley, *A Memorial History of the Baptists of Alabama* (Philadelphia, 1923), pp. 35-36.

36. Z. T. Leavell and T. J. Bailey, *A Complete History of Mississippi Baptists,* 2 (Jackson, 1904), p. 415.

37. July (1881), 478-88.

38. Feb. 20 (1868), 2.

39. Jan. 5 (1899), 1.

40. *Biblical Recorder* (Raleigh, N.C.), Feb. 10, 1892, p. 2, quoted in Rufus B. Spain, *At Ease in Zion* (Nashville, 1967), p. 169.

41. *Minutes of the 65th meeting of the Virginia Baptist Association* (1888). In addition to the quotation given here, pp. 42-43 include a long diatribe about the danger to society of any talk of "women's rights" and an urgent recommendation that no separate women's organization be permitted in the church.

42. Leavell and Bailey, *Mississippi Baptists*, p. 1417.

43. Spain, *Zion*, p. 168.

44. *Twelfth Annual Report*, Woman's Board of Foreign Missions, Methodist Episcopal Church, South (Nashville, 1891).

45. Noreen Dunn Tatum, *Crown of Service: A Story of Woman's Work in the Methodist Episcopal Church, South, from 1878-1940* (Nashville, 1960), p. 26.

46. *Ibid.*, p. 349.

47. *Ibid.*, pp. 352-53. For general background see Broadus Mitchell, *Rise of Cotton Mills in the South* (Baltimore, 1921).

48. Lily Hardy Hammond, *In Black and White: An Interpretation of Southern Life* (New York, 1914).

49. See Anne Firor Scott, *The Southern Lady: From Pedestal to Politics, 1830-1930* (Chicago, 1970), pp. 135-63, and *passim*, for the secular reformers. In gathering evidence about women reformers I began to notice the disproportionate number of Methodists. Careful statistical studies need to be made to check this impression. Various theologically trained friends have helped me speculate about the possible causes, especially Professor Thomas Langford of the Duke University department of religion, and Professor Samuel Hill, the editor of this volume.

50. A. W. Plyler, *The Iron Duke of the Methodist Itinerancy* (Nashville, 1925), p. 166.

51. F. D. Jones and W. H. Mills, eds., *History of the Presbyterian Church in South Carolina since 1850* (Columbia, 1926), p. 442.

52. Tatum, *Crown*, p. 37.

53. Riley, *Memorial History*, p. 164.

54. Mary Helm to Nellie Nugent Somerville, Somerville Papers, Schlesinger Library, Radcliffe College, Cambridge, Mass.

55. Tatum, *Crown*, pp. 34-40.

56. Merrick, *Old Time*, pp. 143-45.

57. Obituary in New Orleans *Times-Picayune*, Mar. 30, 1908.

58. Quoted in Anna A. Gordon, *The Life of Frances Willard* (Evanston, 1912), p. 102.

59. Eliza Frances Andrews, *Wartime Journal of a Georgia Girl* (New York, 1908), pp. 7-8.

60. Francis B. Simkins and Robert H. Woody, *Reconstruction in South Carolina* (Chapel Hill, 1938), pp. 322ff.

61. *North Carolina White Ribbon*, 1906.

62. Belle Kearney, *A Slaveholder's Daughter* (New York, 1900), pp. 167-68.

63. Frances Willard and Mary A. Livermore, *American Women: Fifteen Hundred Biographies* (New York, 1897), 2:499.

64. Kearney, *Daughter*, p. 174.

65. Address by Frances E. Willard to the Seventeenth Convention of the WCTU, Atlanta, 1890.

The "New Woman"
in the New South

In 1884 a distinguished lady in New Orleans was made chairman of a committee of the New Orleans Education Society. When she came to make the report of her committee, over which she had labored long, the society decreed that it must be read for her by one of the male members. The lady resigned in protest—but even her protest required male cooperation: "I requested my husband," she recorded, "to cease paying my dues!" Here, in miniature, was the "woman problem" as it began to take shape in the post–Civil War South.

Northern women had begun in the 1830s to raise their voices against legal and social discrimination, to protest the lack of equal educational and professional opportunity. In the South the institution of chivalry had held firm. It seems to have been characterized by a widespread legal and theoretical acceptance of the premise that woman was an inferior creature and a widespread practical expectation that she would perform as a superior one. The acceptable goals for southern women were to please their husbands and to please God, and to this end they were supposed to be beautiful, mildly literate, gracious, hardworking, and church going. "Woman's sphere," as they called it, was well marked out. This description applies to the minority of women who belonged to the pace-setting plantation families. For the rest, our information is small, but such as we have indicates that they worked hard and knew their place.

Testimony is unanimous that slavery did not make for leisure as far as plantation mistresses were concerned. They carried large responsibilities and did as well much physical work. Open protest against their disabilities

Reprinted with permission from the *South Atlantic Quarterly*, 61 (Autumn 1962), 417-83.

was infrequent, and genuine rebels such as the Grimké sisters found it necessary to leave the South altogether.

Then came the war. Southern women were thrust into new public and private responsibilities, ranging from running whole plantations to providing food, clothing, bandages, and nursing care for the Confederate army. With the men away "woman's sphere" suddenly became very elastic. If the fire-eaters had foreseen this particular consequence, perhaps they would have been less eager for secession—for as far as women were concerned Pandora's box was opened. Reconstruction offered other challenges, including for many the necessity of making one's way in a world in which women outnumbered men. With the whole South to rebuild, every pair of hands was needed, and while the legend of the southern lady was tended along with other more or less accurate legends of the old South, the lady herself had not much time for acting her prescribed role. In addition, the whole structure of women's lives was being changed by the multiplication of factory-made products which lightened domestic burdens immeasurably. The single invention of the sewing machine was an immense emancipation of mothers. For southern women there was an additional emancipation in the freeing of the slaves. Nearly all who recorded their opinions rejoiced that slavery was ended.

The culture pattern, of course, remained strong and was faithfully reflected by the law. In some southern states a married woman could not make a will, collect her own wages, or claim possession of any property, real or personal. Guardianship rights were often vested wholly in the husband. In 1879 Louisiana women were outraged when a generous bequest by a woman to an orphan asylum was lost because all the witnesses to the will were women. They were, declared the Chief Justice of the North Carolina Supreme Court, "slaves of despots."

There was plenty of evidence that any change would be difficult. A traveling organizer for the national woman's suffrage organization found her way to Mississippi and found discouragement on every hand. In some towns she was not permitted to lecture on suffrage at all and had to content herself with a discourse on "Literature and Modern Tendencies" into which she bootlegged as much talk of the forbidden subject as she dared. "Death and education have much to do to redeem the southland," she concluded. A prominent Baptist minister declared that a woman who went into politics "violated the womanly instinct and defied God's law as certainly as did the painted woman who walks the streets and invites the noonday sun to witness her shame." The University of Georgia trustees found a petition for the admission of women so unfitting that they agreed to expunge all mention of it from the record. In Louisville Henry Watterson announced that votes for women would imperil the whole human species.

The contrary forces stirred up by the war, reinforced by material and intellectual influences from the North, would not have an easy time. They were too strong, however, to be downed. The end of slavery and intellectual and material influences from the North were catalytic forces. They could not have had a significant influence without a corresponding change in the way southern women were viewing the world. Here and there such a change was taking place. In Kentucky in 1874 a twenty-five-year-old daughter of the Clay family recorded her "rebelliousness to the inequality set between men and women in this world" and decided that God had called her to help further women's rights. In North Carolina a busy planter's wife, with a house full of children, was writing that "the greatest need in the world is educated, vigorous and unhampered womanhood." In Mississippi a planter's daughter, forbidden by her father to undertake a career, felt "a constant and unceasing rebellion" at "the injustice that had always been heaped upon my sex." Another Mississippi woman mocked the favorite male palliative for discontented women — "the hand that rocks the cradle is the hand that rules the world" — as nonsense, saying that if men did not respect women, children would not either.

These were the women who now began to emerge as leaders in the southern version of what was inelegantly called the Woman Movement. Most of them were women of such impeccable family that they could, as it were, afford to be radical. They were generally in outward appearance the very model of Southern Ladies, described by their contemporaries as beautiful, charming, poised, intelligent, and brave. They were educated women, and not solely because they had been to school. All were voracious readers and writers. A long intimacy with the English classics had produced in them a pungent English style. Many were married and had children. They were women with enough energy to travel outside the South, who very early established contact with women leaders in other parts of the country, as well as with each other. They listened to and were influenced by Frances Willard, Susan B. Anthony, Elizabeth Cady Stanton, and later Anna Howard Shaw and Carrie Chapman Catt. All of them were deeply religious. Perhaps most significant, all were women of talent who had at some time in their lives felt that their talents might well be wasted for lack of opportunity to use them. As one of them put it: "Of all the unhappy sights the most pitiable is that of a human life, rich in possibilities and strong with divine yearnings for better things than it has known, atrophying in the prison house of blind and palsied custom."

Leaders are indispensable, but to produce a major social change many ordinary people must also be involved. In the face of the strong cultural pattern with its narrowly defined role for women, how could anything in the way of a following emerge? Not for southern women was any such blatant call to action as the "Declaration of Sentiments" flung to the shocked world by the Woman's Rights Convention at Seneca Falls in 1848. On the contrary, to the eye of the casual observer the southern home and fireside seemed as safe from radical modernism and the dangerous "new woman" in the 1880s as it had been in the 1840s.

An acute observer, however, might have been led to look closely at such respectable and safe groups as the women's missionary societies of the various churches. It was here that many women first had a taste of running their own affairs. The minister who had opposed the organization of a separate prayer meeting on the grounds that if they were alone "who knows what the women will pray for?" was perhaps more prescient than he seemed. For it was in precisely such groups that the intense soul searching which had characterized southern religion before the war began to be transformed into a demand for social reform. In what was euphemistically called "home and foreign mission work" women encountered the disinherited of the postwar world and began to question the political and social arrangements which permitted them to exist. In these church societies natural leaders had a chance to lead, to learn to stand on their feet and make speeches, to keep records, and to organize. Yet because they were doing "church work," it was all very respectable and the most suspicious husband or father could hardly forbid attendance.

Equally respectable—for what could be more proper than a concern for Christianity and temperance?—was the Woman's Christian Temperance Union (WCTU). Yet no group did more to subvert the traditional role of women, or to implant in its southern members a sort of unself-conscious radicalism which would have turned the conservative southern male speechless if he had taken the trouble to listen to what the ladies were saying. Between efforts to secure prohibition laws, the women of the WCTU worked in various southern states for prison reform, child labor regulation, shorter hours of labor, compulsory education—and cheered Frances Willard to the echo when she announced that the industrial revolution must be made to benefit the average workingman and added, "If to teach this is to be socialist, then so let it be."

Part of the influence of the WCTU in the lives of emerging southern women came from the quality of its national leader. Frances Willard was one of the most magnetic personalities of the nineteenth century, and her tours of the South, during which she expounded a comprehensive program for reform (for which, one is tempted to think, demon rum was only a respectable front), were vastly influential. "For the local and denominational," one southern woman wrote, "she substituted the vision of humanity." "The W.C.T.U.," said another, "was the generous liberator, the joyous inconoclast, the discoverer, the developer of southern women."

The woman who penned this flowery description of the WCTU spoke from personal experience. Belle Kearney had been born into an aristocratic Mississippi family which had been so impoverished by the war that for a time she and her mother did sewing for their former slaves. She yearned for education, but the idea of a girl working her way through school was so foreign to her father's view of life that it was never even discussed. Over his vigorous protests she opened a school in her bedroom and attained thereby her first small measure of independence. Public opinion and family pressure were so strong, however, that she succumbed to the accepted pattern, hating herself for her weakness and abhorring the way her time was spent. Then came Frances Willard, whose ability to identify potential leaders was considerable. Before long "Miss Belle" was organizing the WCTU in Mississippi, and from her success in this endeavor she moved easily into the national suffrage movement. When women were finally enfranchised, she crowned her career by being elected first woman senator in the Mississippi legislature. "The Woman's Christian Temperance Union," she recorded in her autobiography, "was the golden key that unlocked the prison doors of pent-up possibilities."

Hard upon the heels of the missionary societies and the WCTU came the women's clubs. This movement, which began spontaneously in many parts of the country, mushroomed in the South in the 1880s after the pioneer organization in New Orleans announced its purpose to assist "the intellectual growth and spiritual ambition of the community." Literary societies, Browning and Shakespeare clubs, Daughters of the American Revolution, and village improvement societies began to dot the landscape. Some began wholly as cultural groups—what husband could object to the ladies gathering to read Shakespeare or study Dante? And how was he to know if they moved along to John Stuart Mill's "On the Subjugation of Women" or read Margaret Fuller or discussed, as the Portias in New Orleans were wont to do, the problems of organized labor?

As every authoritarian regime knows, association can be dangerous. From discussion it is only a few steps to action, and by 1900 the list of things that women's clubs were doing or trying to do in the South was staggering. They organized libraries; expanded schools; tackled adult illiteracy; organized settlement houses; fought child labor; supported sanitary laws, juvenile courts, pure water, modern sewage systems; planted trees; and helped girls to go to college. Doubtless many of these groups would have inspired the pen of an earlier Helen Hokinson, but it is impossible to overlook their record of achievement or the spirit in which they began to attack the problems with which their native region was so plentifully supplied. One has only to read their diaries and scrapbooks to catch a sense of the seriousness of purpose and the broad ambitions which motivated these women.

In North Carolina Governor Elias Carr appointed a personal friend, Mrs. Sallie Southall Cotten, to be North Carolina Lady Manager for the Chicago World's Fair of 1893. Mrs. Cotten had lived a quiet life as a planter's wife, raising six children, and spending most of her spare time reading and thinking, thinking especially about the need for better educated and more independent women. The World's Fair responsibility took her to Chicago, where she met outstanding women from all over the country. It also took her over the whole state of North Carolina from New Bern to Asheville, and in many towns she found small clubs working away at village improvement or self-improvement. She came back after the fair determined to unite the women of North Carolina in their efforts, and by strenuous personal effort managed to bring the local groups into a statewide federation, which she then proceeded to lead into one battle after another for the improvement of North Carolina.

In the nature of things it would not be long before such groups began to have political significance. It is rare to find these women speculating upon any philosophical analysis of the proper relationship of government to the people. But in a pragmatic way they discovered more and more that the things they wanted to accomplish could only be achieved through political action.

As a lobbyist, the southern lady turned new woman proved herself ingenious. The principle enunciated by one Arkansas lady, "If you don't make a friend at least don't leave an enemy," might have stood for most of these women as they journeyed to city council and state legislature armed with facts and figures to be presented with quiet dignity. "An unpleasant aggressiveness will doubtless be expected from us," a Mississippi leader told her group. "Let us endeavor to disappoint such expectations and spend the year in learning what to do and how to do it." One indignant Alabama legislator announced that the ladies had "apparently hypnotized some members of the Senate."

Occasionally more direct methods were possible, as when Miss Kate Gordon of New Orleans discovered that taxpaying women could vote in New Orleans when a question of taxes was involved. New Orleans suffered from a shortage of good water—the poorer people relied entirely upon cisterns—and an absence of a municipal sewage system. Wakened to their danger by a yellow fever epidemic, more farsighted members of the community were anxious to acquire both a water system and a sewage system, but the weight of opinion appeared to be of the "what was good enough for father is good enough for me" variety. Then Miss Gordon, with the Equal Rights Association (a pioneer woman's club) behind her, undertook to ferret out and register every woman taxpayer. The proposition to raise twenty million dollars for sewage and drainage passed handily.

It was experiences such as these, added to many others when women could *not* vote and felt the consequences, rather than an abstract belief in "women's rights," which was the real impetus behind the suffrage movement in the South. Miss Jean Gordon, a sister of the redoubtable Kate, put the case pungently in recording her battle for a Louisiana child labor law: "The much boasted influence of the wife over the husband in matters political is one of the many theories which melt before the sun of experience. The wife of every representative present was heartily in sympathy with the child labor bill, but when the roll was called the husbands answered 'no' and in that moment were sown the seeds of a belief in the potency of the ballot beyond that of woman's influence."

In 1910 Miss Mary Partridge of Alabama recorded a similar experience. "After seeing the defeat of the constitutional amendment for prohibition despite the earnest but ineffectual effort of women who besieged the polls," she decided the time was ripe for a suffrage organization. She walked out of the hall and began organizing. Seven years later she counted eighty-seven suffrage societies in her state and remarked that she had also converted thirty-two newspapers.

A year later Mrs. Patty Blackburn Semple of Kentucky made the same point in a speech to the National American Woman Suffrage

Association: "Last year an appeal came to the Woman's Club—to the women of Louisville—to take our schools out of politics. It was a gigantic fight but we won. As the climax of our struggle we spent the greater part of election day at the polls and I think at the close of that day every one of us had exhaused all the joys of 'indirect influence,' which is supposed to satisfy the craving of every female heart. Our club will be twenty-one years old in November, and we want to vote!"

By 1910 the woman movement in the South was moving out into the open. The missionary societies and the women's clubs, the Browning groups and the village improvement societies had laid the groundwork and had afforded an essential period of security during which leaders were developed and followers gathered. Now the time had come to throw down the gauntlet and wage an open battle for suffrage and for equality in the eyes of the law.

The dividing lines were not those of sex. In many states able and progressive-minded men took an equal part; Desha Breckenridge in Kentucky, Luke Lea in Tennessee, and Walter Clark and Josephus Daniels in North Carolina were among the best-known champions of women's rights, and in every state there were public men and newspapermen supporting the movement. On the other hand, multitudes of southern women were afraid of change and believed emancipation of women to be a threat to the stability of the home. The "new women" were asking not only for rights, but also for responsibilities, and there were plenty of women who found the older system perfectly comfortable and satisfactory. Others were sympathetic in their hearts, but had not the courage to do battle with public opinion or to face ridicule.

From 1912 onward southern newspapers were publicly rubbing their eyes in astonishment at some of the accomplishments of the women's groups. Women were credited with "the improvement of health; the betterment of morals, the modernizing of education and the humanizing of penology." "Persistence is what carries them along," wrote another editor. "These women will secure every one of the things demanded in their program and will be no fifty years about it, either . . . their aims can no more be resisted than the tides. We believe they are really unconscious of their tremendous power to affect conditions." "Woman's day has arrived," said another, "never to depart. From the back seat of obscurity she has stepped . . . to the front rank of world activities . . . and the world is going to be a happier and brighter place because of her coming."

In spite of such recognition, and in spite of a steady increase in the number of converts to the suffrage cause, the cultural pattern in the South remained the most rigid in any part of the country. In 1919 the seventy-year-old national battle to persuade Congress to initiate a constitutional amendent for woman suffrage was finally won, and the amendment sent to the states for ratification. In every southern state there was a battle royal. The victorious opposition in North Carolina even sent reinforcements to Tennessee to encourage the opponents there. Only Tennessee, Arkansas, and Texas of the states of the former Confederacy formed part of the required three-fourths of the states who ratified the amendment.

Despite the recalcitrance of southern legislatures, there were—because of the developments which have been related here—plenty of southern women ready to take advantage of suffrage when it came. Not only Miss Kearney, but Mrs. Somerville was soon sitting in the Mississippi legislature. In Georgia the ladies reported that they hardly recognized their hitherto hostile and chilly legislators who now suddenly found they had plenty of time to listen to their women constituents. In many states the suffrage groups were promptly converted to Leagues of Women Voters to finish the battle, as Carrie Chapman Catt put it, and to educate other women to their responsibilities.

The achievement of suffrage was symbolic and important, but it was only part of the larger story of the transformation, in the years after 1865, of the southern lady into the "new woman." Like the lady the new woman represented only a small minority of all women in the South. Unlike the lady she did not become the universal ideal. At her best, she maintained the graciousness and charm which had been the sound part of the chivalric ideal and, without losing her femininity or abandoning her responsibility for the propagation of the species, became an important force in public as well as in private life.[1] She made it possible for the young women who came after her to begin at once to develop whatever talent they might have, without having first to fight a long battle for the right to education and opportunity.

This change was brought about by the unremitting efforts of a few women who longed for a chance to develop as individual and independent human beings, and who felt a responsibility for improving the quality of the larger society in which their children would grow up. For themselves and to some degree for the society at large they evolved a new conception of the proper role of women. Their efforts were reinforced by a changing economy, by the influence of the modern world, and by what that first woman's club in New Orleans in 1884 had rightly called "the irresistible spirit of the age."

In an environment basically hostile southern women had taken on various protective colorations in their initial efforts to develop independence and maturity. In the name of temperance, or Shakespeare, or the church, they had resolutely set out to work, for themselves and for their communities. In many cases they were led into a pragmatic radicalism and had tackled problems which, had they been more sophisticated, might well have frightened them.

This analysis ends, except for an occasional glance ahead, in 1920. Whether southern women with the long-sought nineteenth amendment in their hands would live up to the promise of their accomplishments when they had no vote is another tale, for another time.

NOTE

1. In introducing Mrs. Cotten in 1913, the president of the North Carolina Federation of Women's Clubs made this point: "Probably the ideal woman is the one who combines all the graces of the golden days gone by with the highest type of the woman of the present time. She has caught step with the broadening and mighty influences which characterize her age. . . . Such a woman we have with us tonight."

After Suffrage: Southern
Women in the 1920s

In few parts of the country was the nineteenth amendment awaited with higher expectations than among an earnest group of southern women. Not unlike the present-day southern liberal who yearns for a federal civil rights bill because the road to state and local legislation is so long and rocky, southern women who had labored for state suffrage and for social reform against an opposing tide looked to the federal amendment for help. For them the vote had also become a symbol of something much larger—the image of the "new woman." Long constrained by southern tradition about woman's place in southern life, they saw the amendment as a grant of freedom and a new measure of independence.

One of these women remarked in a private letter in 1920 that she was planning a trip to Europe because "once we *really* get into politics (i.e., once the suffrage amendment is ratified) I will never be able to get away."[1]

Another, in North Carolina, thought "the advent of women into political life" would mean "the loosening of a great moral force which will modify and soften the relentlessly selfish economic forces of trade and industry in their relation to government. The ideals of democracy and of social and human welfare will undoubtedly receive a great impetus."[2] For many years these earnest women had organized themselves, talked to legislators, worked for or against congressmen in their home districts, testified at hearings, haunted the polls on election day, cajoled money, written newspaper articles, watched the progress of more advanced northern and western women—and now, at last, had the federal help that promised to open the way to substantial achievement.

Reprinted with permission from the *Journal of Southern History*, 30 (Aug. 1964), 298-318.

By 1920 southern women had come to exert increasing influence in public affairs, but many of the problems that concerned them were still unsolved: the dislocations caused by industrialization, the conditions of work for women and children, the inadequacies of the educational system, the lack of opportunity for many children, prison conditions, the ravages of alcohol and disease, injustice to Negro citizens. To all such problems, and some new ones they would discover along the way, the newly enfranchised women now addressed themselves with renewed hope. Their successes as well as their failures have tended to vanish—in C. Vann Woodward's phrase—in that twilight zone between living memory and written history. An examination of what they tried to do, of the goals reached, the obstacles encountered, the failures endured, throws new light on the South in the 1920s and upon the springs and motives behind the emancipation of southern women.

What this record shows will depend upon the questions we ask. If we ask whether woman suffrage led to progress in social reform in the southern states and to a more active political life for women, the answer is clearly that it did. If we ask in addition whether the broader hope, the dream of a new life for southern women in which their independence, their right to think for themselves, to work for the things they believed in, to be respected as individuals regardless of sex, was accomplished, the answer must be much more qualified.

It may be worth recalling at the outset that early in the nineteenth century the South had adopted a more rigid definition of the role of women than any other part of the country and had elevated that definition to the position of a myth. There were inherent contradictions in the elements of women's role as the culture defined it: women were supposed to be beautiful, gentle, efficient, morally superior, and at the same time, ready to accept without question the doctrine of male superiority and authority. On matters not domestic they were to be seen and not heard, while in the domestic sphere it was taken for granted that a women would rule. For those without inherited means, marriage was the only road to economic security (as for inherited wealth, its control passed at marriage into the hands of the husband). For those who did not marry, the only acceptable pattern was to become the pensioner—and often *de facto* servant—of some male relative. Hints that some women felt the contradictory nature of these expectations, and resented them, appeared from time to time before the Civil War. After the war, changes which seemed likely to alter the culture pattern appeared on all sides; but, as

part of the comforting glorification of the past with which the South
tended to evade present problems, the image of the Southern Lady—
whatever the reality—survived relatively unchanged.[3] The force of this
cultural image was so strong that southern women had to follow a more
devious road to emancipation than those elsewhere. It was only after long
apprenticeship in such outwardly safe organizations as church societies
and the Woman's Christian Temperance Union that they began to venture
into women's clubs and suffrage organizations.[4]

From this process a few women emerged as recognized leaders. These
few had in common impressive social standing and family background,
intelligence, courage, and a degree of inner security that permitted them
to survive criticism. Such were Madeline Breckinridge in Kentucky, Mary
Munford in Virginia, Nellie Somerville in Mississippi, Sallie Cotten in
North Carolina, Pattie Jacobs in Alabama—each highly respected in her
own state by men as well as women.[5] Now, with the power of the ballot
and the new freedom it symbolized, they hoped not only to be more
effective in public life but also to modify significantly southern thought
about the proper role of women.[6]

They were well aware that the older image of the Southern Lady,
although undergoing modification in a number of ways, was still very
much alive in 1920. The image was, of course, made up of a number of
components, some external: beauty, gentleness, winning ways. Other
components related to appropriate behavior: modesty, domesticity, chastity,
and submission to male opinions. It was a lovely image that could be
maintained with a minimum of strain whenever the woman in question
was lucky enough to be well endowed with the outward qualities (the
proportionate number so endowed was doubtless about the same in 1920
as in 1820). But it was the definition of appropriate behavior that women
were most anxious to modify. In earlier years the effective leaders of the
movement had had to conform behavior to the image. As a Virginia
woman remarked in 1918, "The wise suffrage leaders here have realized
. . . that success depends upon showing their cause to be compatible with
the essentials of the Virginia tradition to womanliness, and both instinct
and judgment have prevented the adoption here of the more aggressive
forms of campaigning."[7]

In the 1920s maintaining the ladylike image was still considered to
be good politics, but the active women continued to alter behavior
remarkably. A few of the more radical wanted to dispense, once and for
all, with what they called the "chivalric nonsense" that put woman on a

pedestal in order to keep her out of the affairs of the real world. A young North Carolina woman, for example, reflected:

Last year I travelled from one end of our State to another. I saw thousands of women, old and young, mothers and little girls, working in stores and factories ten or eleven or twelve hours a day; or worse, working in the factory all night, and taking care of their homes by day. And I asked, where is this chivalry that so protects women? And I saw working in the fields, hoeing cotton and corn and doing all kinds of hard labor, women and children, white as well as black. And again I asked, whom does chivalry protect? In the last session of the legislature, I heard arguments about a bill which would have raised the amount allowed from the estate to a widow and her children for the first year of widowhood. And many were the jokes made and the slurs slung about mothers who would spend the amount for silk stockings instead of on the care of children. Respect for motherhood, reverence for womanhood, was not the ruling thought when the bill was considered, for it was voted down. It was not the political rights nor any of the deeds of the "new woman" who took the working women from their homes and made them labor as if there was no such thing as chivalry and pedestals. . . . Genesis says that after the Lord had created male and female, he gave them dominion over the earth and then he rested. The two were created to work out welfare for all on earth. Why not go on with the work and stop babbling about chivalry when there is no chivalry except for the small class whose financial conditions prevents their needing it.[8]

The older ideal of the Southern Lady cropped up in another way when the opponents of reforms for which women worked used it as a weapon. It was hardly politic to argue in public that one believed in child labor or enjoyed the profits that stemmed from women laboring long hours into the night, but—given the southern frame of reference—it was quite possible to attack the proponents of reform on the ground that they were "unwomanly" and thus to discredit the cause for which they fought. This was done repeatedly, and the cry was often echoed, of course, by other men who feared for their own domestic comforts.

Even before the nineteenth amendment was ratified state suffrage organizations began to turn themselves into Leagues of Women Voters with the announced purpose of educating newly enfranchised citizens and working for "needed legislation." Leaders gathered in Chicago for intensive training, organized by a political scientist from the University of Chicago, and went home with instructions to pass along all they had learned. "Citizenship schools" blossomed over the southern landscape, and courses with reading lists worthy of graduate instruction in political science were found side by side with mundane classes in election law, registration procedures, and How to Mark a Ballot. The troops were receiving basic training.[9]

At the same time every state had its legislative council in which women's groups of the most diverse kinds joined together to work for legislation. The Alabama council was typical; it was made up of sixteen organizations, ranging from the Women's Trade Union League to the Methodist Home Missionary Council. Despite their diverse origins the organized women were in surprising accord on legislative goals.

Whether the goal was a social reform such as the abolition of child labor, or a political one such as the reorganization of the state government, veterans of the suffrage movement were political realists and skilled lobbyists. Their lobbying technique, developed before they had any votes to deliver, was based upon tact and superior information rather than upon threats. Though they were trying to throw off the shackles of chivalry, women voters were not above appealing for chivalric responses in a good cause.

An example of typical methods may be seen in a letter from a Virginia lady of the old school describing her efforts to persuade Congress to adopt a child labor amendment: "I got busy about the child labor amendment and stirred up the Virginia Federation of Labor and the Ministerial Union of Richmond which means all the Protestant clergymen of the city . . . the Federation of labor sent official communications to all senators and all congressmen and our papers have given us good notices. . . . I carried your summary of the situation to our leading morning paper and he promised to use it and comment on it editorially."[10]

A favorite device was the publication of complete lists of legislators with their views on various issues presented for the voters' information. Indeed, education of the electorate was a basic technique, and there was always an effort to develop support for their programs among "the people back home." The experience of the suffrage campaign came into play at every turn.

The ideological milieu of the 1920s was nowhere conducive to social reform. The Red Scare had affected every part of the country, and programs considered mild in 1912 were now labeled Bolshevik.[11] The reform-minded women in the South were little disturbed at the outset by the fact that many of the causes in which they had long been interested were now termed radical. The president of the Tennessee League of

Women Voters remarked mildly, "Some good souls are pleased to call our ideas socialistic. They are indeed uncomfortable often for some folk. Some timid souls of both sexes are only half converted to the new order . . . [yet] every clear thinking, right feeling and high minded man and woman should consecrate his best talents to the gradual re-organization of society, national and international."[12]

The ink was scarcely dry upon the suffrage amendment before legislatures began to realize that women now expected more respectful attention than in the past. "The men were scared to death of what the women might do," one North Carolina woman recalled.[13] In that state, as a measure of insurance against reprisal for having rejected the suffrage amendment, the governor and legislature agreed to appoint the president of the Federated Clubs as commissioner of charities and public welfare, one legislator being overheard to remark that she was "pretty, anyway, and won't give us any trouble." The insurance turned out to be inadequate, for in short order North Carolina women, abetted behind the scenes by the same pretty welfare commissioner, were demanding that the Woman's Bureau of the U.S. Department of Labor be invited to survey the working conditions of women in North Carolina textile mills.

Textile manufacturing was a major economic interest in the state, and working conditions in the mills were frequently bad, wages were low, and many children were employed. The millowners reacted strongly. The women were accused of being unwomanly to mix in things about which they knew nothing, of being dangerous radicals or at the very least dupes of northern manufacturers bent on spoiling the competitive advantage that child labor and cheap female labor gave the South. The YWCA, one of the groups joining in the request for a survey, was threatened with a loss of contributions. The state president of the League of Women Voters was hailed before a self-constituted jury of millmen and lectured severely. The suggestion reached her that her husband's sales of mill machinery would diminish rapidly if she and the league continued their interest in women's working conditions. Families divided as wives argued with husbands about the survey. Textile men brought pressure upon the governor and upon agencies of the state government. In 1926 the governor, while standing firm against allowing "outsiders" to meddle in North Carolina's business, agreed to order his own Child Welfare Department to make the study—but nothing happened. In 1929 when the Gastonia strike became a national issue, the North Carolina League of Women Voters, in publishing an explanation of the strikers' side of the argument, remarked that if the women's request for a survey of working conditions had been granted the problems that had led to a bloody strike might have been ameliorated.[14]

North Carolina women were more successful in their efforts to bring about stronger state child labor laws.[15] In every southern state, in fact, women worked strenuously against the use of child labor. Many of them supported the federal child labor amendment that Congress adopted in 1924 and then went on to work for its ratification by their state legislatures. In the meantime, an intensive effort to establish broad programs of child welfare took shape. In Virginia, for example, the women urged the legislature to set up a Children's Code Commission and, having secured it, persuaded the governor to appoint five of their number to it. When the commission brought in twenty-four recommendations for new laws, ranging from a statewide juvenile court system to compulsory education, the women turned their attention once more to the legislature, and as a result of their unceasing toil eighteen of the twenty-four recommendations became law in the 1922 session.[16]

That same year a combination of women's groups in Georgia secured the passage of a children's code, a child-placement bill, and a training school bill but failed when they joined forces with the Georgia Federation of Labor for a legislative limitation on hours of work for women. The hearing on this last proposal brought out "every cotton mill man in Georgia," and, while the eloquent testimony of Mrs. Elliott Cheatham persuaded the committee to report the bill, the millowners' influence in the legislature prevented it from being brought to a vote. Two years later efforts to secure ratification of the federal child labor amendment also failed in the Georgia legislature, and women in the state then turned to efforts to strengthen state laws.[17]

Similar issues, all of them demonstrating the increasing influence of women, appeared in the other southern states. In Arkansas, where as early as 1919 the suffrage organization had come out for minimum wages and maximum hours in all cotton mills, the federal child labor amendment was ratified by the legislature. Credit was given jointly to a woman legislator, the Arkansas Federation of Labor, and the women's organizations. The wife of the man who had led the floor fight against the amendment was reported to be delighted that he had failed; of her it was said, "She expressed the spirit of Arkansas women in politics."[18]

One result of the growing movement against the exploitation of women and children in the mills was an increasingly close association between southern women and the labor movement. Lucy Randolph Mason, bluest of Virginia bluebloods, who was to become an organizer for the Congress of Industrial Organizations, noted in 1930: "For a number of years many of us southern women have been concerned over the lack of social control in the development of southern industry. Vast numbers of southern women are becoming more acutely conscious of the need of safeguards, which have already been supplied by most of the states."[19] Association with labor unions actually had begun during the fight for suffrage when trade unions, along with the Farmers Alliances, were virtually the only male organizations to support women suffrage. As early as 1910 the Georgia Suffrage Association reported holding its convention in the halls of "the Federation of Labor, *its true friend*."[20] Now, in the 1920s, women's interests were in line with labor concerns, and they not only found a good press in liberal journals such as the *New Republic* but also cooperated with labor unions.[21]

Particularly important in deepening women's concern for industrial labor was the work of the YWCA. Even before World War I, the YWCA had undertaken to bring college students in touch with the facts of industrial life, and in the 1920s a student-industrial movement flourished. Its legislative program included the abatement of poverty, abolition of child labor, a living wage as a minimum in every industry, an eight-hour day, and protection of workers from the hardships of continued unemployment. Through the YWCA, students at Randolph Macon were studying the problems of coal miners, while those at Converse delved into social legislation, and at Westhampton, unemployment. Girls from these and other colleges served on a regional committee for student-industrial cooperation, seeking, as they put it, to Christianize the social order.[22] Part of this program included a series of summer institutes for factory girls that by 1927 had evolved into the Southern Summer School for Women Workers in Industry, directed and financed by southern women. The school grew steadily through the 1920s and early 1930s. The nature of its sympathies was evident in 1928, when strikers from the Marion Manufacturing Company were invited to the campus to tell their story and were afterward joined by students and faculty in a march through Marion. It was the opinion of the *Nation* that "this small group of women . . . are playing an important part in the fight against economic slavery in the South."[23]

When unionization became a genuine possibility during the New Deal, a large proportion of the women graduates of the Summer School became active organizers. There is something appealing in the picture of a group of well-to-do southern women, of ladylike mien, busy training labor organizers. Nor is there the least doubt, from the record, that they knew what they were doing. They were not innocent philanthropists taken in by hardbitten radicals.[24]

The Southern Council on Women and Children in Industry, organized in 1931 to bring about a shorter working day and an end to night work in all the textile states, was another joint effort growing out of the experience of women in their separate states. The council hired Lucy Mason to organize their campaign. Calling to the colors a few progressive-minded millmen who agreed with her objectives, she then set out to convert some of those who did not agree, recognizing clearly that pressure on the legislatures could not succeed without the support of some of the millowners.[25]

From a national point of view the concern for child welfare was reflected in the passage in 1921, largely due to the work of women over the nation, of the Sheppard-Towner Act for maternal and infant health. Nineteen of twenty-six southern senators voted for the bill. In the house ninety-one of the 279 votes in support of the bill came from the South and only nine of thirty-nine votes against it.[26] This support for a federal welfare program from southern members of Congress is less impressive than the enormous amount of follow-up work that southern women undertook to secure appropriation of the required matching funds from state legislatures and then to report on the actual results of the public health work thus instituted. It is not too much to say that the cooperative state work within the framework of the Sheppard-Towner Act brought about a revolution in maternal and infant health.[27]

In some ways the most intriguing of all the public activities of southern women in the 1920s was their racial work. The roots went back at least to 1901 when Miss Belle Bennett encouraged the Woman's Board of Home Missions of the Methodist Episcopal Church, South, to undertake work among Negro girls and offered a personal contribution to that end. From that year forward the board annually appropriated money in behalf of work among Negroes. In 1910 another Methodist, Mary DeBardelben of Alabama, volunteered for missionary service, not in far-off lands but among southern Negroes. In 1915 yet another Southern Methodist, Mrs. Lily H. Hammond, published a pathbreaking book in which she pleaded for a permanent burial of the "old Negro mammy" and some sensible attention to the needs of Mammy's daughters.[28]

The real breakthrough came in 1920 at an extraordinary meeting of southern churchwomen in Memphis at which four Negro women spoke forthrightly of the needs of southern Negroes. One of them told of having been forcibly removed by twelve white men from a Pullman car while on her way to Memphis. In the emotion of the moment, the ninety-odd white women, representing a number of churches, agreed that talk was not enough and constituted themselves the Woman's Department of the Commission on Inter-racial Cooperation. Headed by Mrs. Luke Johnson of Griffin, Georgia, and supported by leading women in every state, units of this organization set up interracial committees to attack common social and economic problems.

When the National League of Women Voters decided in 1924 to establish a Committee on Negro Problems with membership from every state that had more than 15 percent Negro population, members from eight southern states accepted appointment. Many of these women had been active in their local interracial committees, of which there were eventually some 800 functioning in the South. In Tennessee white women organized a special citizenship school for Negro women. Many of the committeewomen took personal responsibility for their Negro fellow citizens, as did Mary Cooke Branch Munford of Richmond, who made a room of her house permanently available to Negroes for public meetings, or a busy doctor's wife in Alabama who waged a one-woman campaign for better Negro education. When the Richmond city council considered a segregation statute in 1929, it was Lucy Randolph Mason, almost singlehandedly, who brought about its defeat.[29]

The most spectacular work in this field began in the 1930s. It started with the organization in 1930, under the imaginative leadership of Jessie Daniel Ames, a Texas woman who had been active in a dozen reform movements, of the Association of Southern Women for the Prevention of Lynching. At its peak this organization had 40,000 small-town and rural churchwomen enrolled in an effort to put an end to the most spectacularly disgraceful aspect of the southern race problem. While the federal antilynching law was blocked in the U.S. Senate, this band of southern women took upon themselves the sometimes heroic responsibility of opposing any specific threat of a lynching in their own towns or counties.

The crusade against lynching was the most dramatic aspect of women's interracial work. Less visible, but of great significance, was the way in which groups of white and Negro women in the 1920s were sitting down together to tackle common problems in an atmosphere of forthright

discussion. Though a few Negro women were careful publicly to eschew
any desire for social equality, most of them hammered away on equal
rights in court, an end to segregation and discrimination in transportation,
the Negro's need for the ballot, and every other sensitive issue that stood
between whites and blacks in the South during this period of the resurgent
Ku Klux Klan.[30]

Although women's interests tended to center upon measures that
had a humanitarian element, especially those affecting disadvantaged groups
and children, they devoted much time to more strictly political questions.
After learning the mechanics of government, they turned their efforts to
the improvement of governmental organizations. Studies of local and state
governmental structure were published and used in schools and by other
organizations. In Virginia in 1922 women's groups worked for an executive
budget and improved election laws. A year later the state legislative
chairman of the Virginia League of Women Voters reported that she was
in daily attendance at budget hearings.[31] In 1924 her organization concentrated its attention on the improvement of tax administration and
reported it had won an initial skirmish in the legislature by securing active
consideration of the question, despite orders from the Democratic machine
that the subject was not to be raised. In the same legislature Virginia
women voters worked for a bill to create a uniform fiscal year and were
successful in their effort.[32] The league had also supported bills which
failed to pass, for civil service, creation of a conservation department,
county government reform, and reforms in the state educational machinery.

Similar interests and similar campaigns developed in other states.
Women in Georgia and Tennessee, after initial forays into the question
of more efficient government, became convinced that the supreme obstacle
lay in outmoded state constitutions; and in both states campaigns for
constitutional reform were launched in the 1920s and were eventually
successful.[33] Kentucky women in 1927 began to work for home rule for
cities, improvements in local charters, and the adoption of city manager
government.

To an interest in the structure of government was added a concern
for making government more democratic. Because of their long exclusion
from politics, women were sensitive to the implications of "consent of
the governed." It was they who invented the now commonplace idea of
"getting out the vote." In some places women's work led to spectacular
increases in the percentage of qualified voters going to the polls. In
Alabama 54.4 percent of the qualified voters went to the polls in 1924

after women sponsored a get-out-the-vote campaign, compared to less than 30 percent in 1920. One county, where the women had been particularly active, got out 84.1 percent of its qualified voters.[34] Florida in the same year reported a 65.9 percent increase over 1920 in the qualified voters going to the polls.[35]

The poll tax was the subject of dual concern. Women's groups opposed the tax, but in the meantime they set out to collect money for the payment of poll taxes in order to increase the number of qualified voters. In 1925 Louisiana women collected $30,000 to this end. The work of North Carolina women for the Australian ballot, which finally succeeded in 1929, was part of the same interest in making the operation of government more democratic.

Close to home, yet a long way from women's traditional concerns, were two other political issues that developed strength in southern women's groups in the 1920s: government ownership of Muscle Shoals and the regulation of utility rates. Interest in both these questions developed from studies of the cost of living, and women in Alabama and Tennessee became enthusiastic supporters of what was to become the Tennessee Valley Authority. On these as on other questions the politically active women seem to have taken a pragmatic view without much concern for traditional free enterprise arguments.

In all their enterprises, political or social, women knew that the main road to influence lay through political parties. Interest in partisan politics antedated suffrage, and unofficially some women had long taken an interest in party fortunes. It had been the accepted doctrine that the national suffrage organization should be nonpartisan, since it hoped to get support from both parties for the national amendment. That this principle was occasionally honored in the breach is made clear when we find Jane Addams trying to recruit Jean Gordon of Louisiana for the Progressive party in 1912 or discover Mrs. Breckinridge on a speaking tour for the Democrats in 1916. A keen interest in party methods and organization had been one of the by-products of the highly organized national suffrage campaign.[36] Carrie Chapman Catt, the commanding general of the final suffrage drive, was intent that women should find their way not just to the outskirts but to the center of power in the political parties. At the Victory Convention in Chicago in 1920 she had told them:

The next battle is going to be inside the parties, and we are not going to stay outside and let all the reactionaries have their way on the inside!

Within every party there is a struggle between progressive and reactionary elements. Candidates are a compromise between these extremes. You will be disillusioned, you will find yourselves in the political penumbra where most of the men are. They will be glad to see you, you will be flattered. But if you stay long enough you will discover a little denser thing which is the umbra of the political party—the people who are picking the candidates, doing the real work that you and the men sanction at the polls. You won't be welcome, but there is the place to go. You will see the real thing in the center with the door locked tight. You will have a hard fight before you get inside . . . but you must move right up to the center.[37]

At the outset, a considerable number of southern women set out to become active in party politics. Party organizations welcomed them, if not with enthusiasm at least with a realistic appreciation of their potential voting power. Some states began at once the custom that has since become standard of appointing a woman as vice-chairman of the state party committee. A considerable number of southern women showed interest in running for elective office; and, though numerous obstacles lay between almost any woman and nomination, enough persisted so that by 1930 only Louisiana had yet to have women in the state legislature. But only a few, a very few, southern women seem to have made their way to that mysterious center of power to which Mrs. Catt had directed them.

One of these was Mrs. Nellie Nugent Somerville of Greenville, Mississippi, whose political influence preceded the nineteenth amendment. As soon as it was legal to do so, she ran for the state legislature in a campaign that was a model of thorough organization and was elected. She had been observing party organization long enough to know the ropes, and she hoped the newly enfranchised women would be similarly observant. She advised them to be certain they had a hand in choosing county committees and reminded them: "It now becomes the duty of women voters to take lively interests in the details of political machinery. When any meeting or election is ordered by your political party be sure you take part in it."[38]

The chief obstacle to following such advice was the unwillingness of male politicians to promote women of independent mind and political skill. They preferred more amenable females, and hence the forthright and well-trained suffrage veterans often found themselves at odds with the entrenched politicians.[39] Mrs. Somerville herself managed to surmount the obstacles, and in 1924 Mississippi Democrats were divided into

Somerville and Percy factions. At the showdown, hers won. She also served as a member of the committee on permanent organization of the 1924 Democratic National Convention and marshaled William G. McAdoo supporters in imposing array.[40] Her record in the legislature suggests that she understood the effective use of political power. When a bill she had initiated failed to pass, the fact was reported as news — as a rule anything she offered did pass — and her colleagues were frequently quoted in praise of her hard work and effectiveness as a lawmaker.[41]

Another politically minded woman who reached a position of genuine power in the party was Sue Shelton White of Tennessee, an independent court reporter, secretary to members of the Tennessee Supreme Court, and from 1920 to 1926 secretary to Senator Kenneth McKellar. In 1915 she drafted the first mother's pension law to be presented to the Tennessee legislature, finally passed in 1920. She went from Senator McKellar's office to practice law in Jackson, Tennessee, and was sufficiently effective in Democratic politics to be invited to work for the Democratic National Committee. With Nellie Davis (Tayloe) Ross she helped lay the groundwork for the extensive women's program of the party during the early Franklin D. Roosevelt years. A fellow lawyer, who was general counsel of the Federal Social Security Board, said at her death: "Sue knew politics from the inside and from the outside. Politics were more than a game to her, though I think she relished the intricacies of the game. She used her political acumen as an instrument for the promotion of the general welfare. And she wielded the instrument with a grace and effectiveness that delighted the wise and distressed the stupid."[42]

Mrs. Somerville and Miss White were exceptional rather than typical, but women in politics ranged from those who were effective politicians in their own right to those who blamed the men for not permitting them to gain nomination. The success stories make good reading, but the overall picture of women's efforts to exercise real influence in the political parties, South or North, was not one to gladden Mrs. Catt's heart. Sue White analyzed the southern situation in 1928 in a letter to Mary Dewson of the Democratic National Committee:

Women have been discouraged by the rank and file of the party organization. . . . We still have the old anti-suffrage attitude in the south, women have been indifferent, and their indifference has been preached to them, aided, abetted, and encouraged. They have viewed politics as something they should stay away from. They have been told so and have believed it and the few feminists who have tried to push in have been slapped in the face. . . . And the few women who have been artificially reared up as leaders are not leaders of women and have been reared not to lead women but to fool them.[43]

Miss White's analysis was confirmed by Emily Newell Blair, the national vice-chairman of the Democratic party in the 1920s. In Mrs. Blair's view, at the very beginning, competent women—the genuine leaders—had essayed party politics, but when they showed themselves unwilling to be rubber stamps they were replaced by women more willing to be led. These were the artificial leaders to whom Miss White referred.[44]

An increasing number of southern women did undertake simple party work of the doorbell-ringing and envelope-stuffing variety—a trend that still continues. And whether they helped make policy or not, women voters as voters affected the outcome of elections. Women claimed to have defeated James E. Ferguson and elected William P. Hobby governor of Texas in 1920. In Mississippi Henry L. Whitfield, former president of Mississippi State College for Women, was elected governor in 1923, largely through the efforts of alumnae of the college. South Carolina women thought they had a large hand in the defeat of Cole Blease. One South Carolina woman who worked through the whole campaign remarked innocently, "We made no partisan stand, we merely got out the vote." Tennessee Democrats, perhaps looking for a scapegoat, blamed the women for the Republican victory in Tennessee in the 1920 election. The women themselves claimed credit for the return of Cordell Hull to Congress three years later.[45]

Evidence of the increasing effectiveness of women voters may be deduced from the vituperative attacks leveled at them. In addition to the accusations that they were being used by northern manufacturers, they were accused of being radical and unfeminine, of organizing Negro women, and of using "illegitimate pressure" to put across the measures of a "feminist bloc." David Clark, perhaps the South's bitterest enemy of child labor regulation, went so far as to claim that more babies died after the Sheppard-Towner Act was in operation than before. His *Textile Bulletin* attacked women harshly. The Associated Industries of Kentucky circulated a condemnation of "political women" reprinted from the Dearborn, Michigan, *Independent*. The Louisville *Herald* suggested the reason: "As we have said, the woman voter is making herself felt in ways not chartered for her. We will not go to the length of saying she is always welcome in these channels, but there are times when one may gauge the need for one's activity and curiosity by the ungracious manner of one's reception."[46]

Many of the women who undertook a more active role in southern politics in the 1920s had encountered this ungracious reception. But their motivation was deeply rooted. Those who had been trained during the two or three decades before suffrage were eager to move into a more active and effective political role in 1920. By then their general goals had been formulated. Their underlying motivation is complex, but at least two main drives seem clear: first, the drive to assert themselves as individual human beings with minds and capacities that could be used; and, second, the drive to improve the world in which they lived. The balance of these motives varied from person to person. Some, like Lucy Mason, were primarily interested in social reform: "When I was fourteen, a missionary's sermon made me want to be a missionary myself. Later I recognized that religion can be put to work right in one's own community. It was this belief that took me into the Equal Suffrage League, and later the League of Women Voters, both of which were interested in labor and social legislation."[47] Others thoroughly enjoyed the game of politics and the feeling of power that might occasionally go with it. Nearly all felt that significant reforms would be more easily achieved with women's help.

The nineteenth amendment changed a good many things, but it brought only a partial modification in the southern culture pattern, and the difficulties in the way of women's full participation in public life were considerable. One major obstacle, in addition to the demands of home and family, was the flat opposition of many men. Equally important was the unwillingness of many women to assume and carry through large responsibilities. From the record it seems that numbers of women had a vague desire to "do something" but needed leadership in finding what to do and how to do it, and the leaders were never sufficiently numerous to tap all the potential resources. A good example, no doubt an extreme one, was a Virginia town of which it was reported that when a certain Miss Terry was at home the town was jumping with women's political activities but when she went to Europe all was quiet.

Around the handful of leaders there gathered a slowly growing number of supporters and workers, and when this support was effectively channeled specific goals were achieved. In almost every instance groups of men were working to the same ends, and frequently there was cooperation. It is impossible to say what would have happened without the women's efforts, but it does seem clear that in the two areas of race relations and factory regulation much less would have been accomplished without them.

Through it all the outward aspect of the Southern Lady was normally maintained as the necessary precondition of securing a hearing. For some women, this was a perfectly compatible role, so long as they could change its behavioral aspects. Others impatiently called for an end to pedestals, but even they found it more effective to operate within the ladylike tradition. The other side of the coin was that the image of the proper Southern Lady was used effectively as a weapon by those who objected to the substantive goals for which women were working, hoping thus to discredit the goals themselves.

No one would argue that the southern states became a progressive paradise in the 1920s, but it is impossible to study the history of the welfare movements of the time without being surprised by the degree to which the spirit of progressivism was still in flower, and the amount of hopeful optimism about the future of reform that animated women in the face of the general spirit of reaction which is said to have permeated political life. Professor George B. Tindall has adumbrated the "business progressivism" of southern state governments in the 1920s.[48] To the picture he drew must now be added the decided growth through the decade of the conception of state responsibility for public welfare, not in the old custodial sense, but in the newer sense of ameliorating the underlying conditions that created serious human problems. To the growth of this idea and its application in law, southern women made a considerable contribution.

When all this has been said we are left with the most troublesome questions still unanswered. In spite of the impressive record of accomplishment, the high expectations of the women who had led the suffrage movement did not come to pass. What happened to the verve and enthusiasm with which the suffrage veterans set about to reorganize society? That it did not all vanish is evident from the southern scene today, but that it did not lead to a clear-cut image of a New Woman to replace the Southern Lady is also evident. The numbers of women in public life, in proportion to the population, are probably no more today than in 1925. While the number of women in labor force climbs—some say alarmingly — the number of women in responsible jobs of leadership, policy-making, or in the professions is still not large. To these difficult and intriguing questions historians of women must now begin to turn their attention.

NOTES

1. Madeline McDowell Breckinridge to Allie S. Dickson, Mar. 20, 1920, in Breckinridge Family Papers, Manuscript Division, Library of Congress, Washington, D.C.

2. Notes for speech in Mary O. Cowper Papers, Manuscript Department, William R. Perkins Library, Duke University, Durham, N.C.

3. W. J. Cash goes so far as to argue that woman's role was more rigidly defined after Appomattox and emancipation than before. *The Mind of the South* (New York, 1941), p. 131. He cites no evidence; and, on the basis of much reading in diaries, letters, newspapers, and church and organization records, I think he overstates his case.

4. Anne Firor Scott, "The 'New Woman' in the New South," *South Atlantic Quarterly*, 61 (Autumn 1962), 473-83.

5. The obituaries upon Madeline Breckinridge's untimely death in 1920 suggest she was Kentucky's leading citizen as well as its leading woman. Certainly she had a hand in almost every reform movement in that state for twenty years; and, by way of the Lexington *Herald*, her voice was widely heard. A close study of her biography reveals all the elements that created the southern "woman movement." See Sophronisba Preston Breckinridge, *Madeline McDowell Breckinridge, a Leader in the New South* (Chicago, 1921), and Breckinridge Family Papers.

6. Madeline Breckinridge, for example, regularly advised every woman to read Margaret Fuller, John Stuart Mill, and Olive Shreiner. The private papers of the women upon whom this study is centered reveal their vision of an ideal woman, educated and fully developed and free to undertake the work that interested her most. They were so often criticized for wanting to "be like men" that it is worth pointing out that their ideal human being was not a man but some other woman (Jane Addams, Anna Howard Shaw, Frances Willard, for example) and that they did not think men were doing a very good job with politics and government or in shaping society generally. What they aimed for was not freedom to be like men but freedom to be themselves. Economic independence loomed large in the minds of the pioneers—they had nothing against marriage, and most were married, but they objected to it as an economic necessity. It is interesting to find exactly the same arguments in the most recent comprehensive work on the subject, Simone de Beauvoir, *The Second Sex*, trans. and ed. H. M. Parshley (New York, 1953). Mary Johnston and Ellen Glasgow were active suffrage women, and their novels are rich in oblique attacks on the existing system. See especially Glasgow, *Virginia* (New York, 1913), and Johnston, *Hagar* (Boston, 1913). Both novels will repay careful reading for anyone interested in the inner springs of the woman movement.

7. Orie Latham Hatcher, "The Virginia Man and the New Era for Women," *Nation*, 106 (June 1, 1918), 651.

8. Mary O. Cowper, "That Pedestal Again," North Carolina League of Women Voters, *Monthly News*, Nov. 1927. See also the very interesting series

of articles by Nell Battle Lewis in Raleigh, N.C., *News and Observer*, May 1926, in which she discusses the question thoroughly and perceptively.

9. Charles E. Merriam, "The Chicago Citizenship School," *Journal of Social Forces*, 1 (Sept. 1923), 600.

10. Kate Pleasants Minor to Mrs. John J. O'Connor, Apr. 18, 1924, in League of Women Voters of the United States Papers, Virginia file, Manuscript Division, Library of Congress.

11. Note, for example, the comment of the foremost woman progressive of the day: "Social progress during the decade from 1919 to 1929 was conditioned at every turn by the fact that we were living in the midst of post-war psychology. . . . Any proposed change was suspect, even those efforts that had been considered praiseworthy before the war. To advance new ideas was to be radical, or even a bolshevik. . . . Throughout the decade this fear of change, this tendency to play safe was registered most conspicuously in the fields of politics, but it spread over into other fields as well." Jane Addams, *The Second Twenty Years at Hull House, September 1909 to September 1929, with a Record of a Growing World Consciousness* (New York, 1930), p. 153. Or this characterization from the center of Southern liberalism: "Besides there is mighty little freedom of opinion anywhere in the old South as you know." E. C. Branson to R. W. Hogan, Dec. 17, 1922, in Eugene Cunningham Branson Papers, Southern Historical Collection, University of North Carolina Library, Chapel Hill.

12. Report of the President, Tennessee League of Women Voters, Jan. 1923, in League of Women Voters Papers, Tennessee file.

13. Interview with Mrs. Kate Burr Johnson of Raleigh, N.C., Nov. 1, 1963. See also comment of the Georgia women who drew up a bill in 1921 to remove the civil disabilities of women: "These legislators were so courteous and obliging the women could scarcely believe it was the Georgia Legislature. They gave everything asked for and asked 'is there anything more we can do for you?' " Elizabeth Cady Stanton et al., eds., *The History of Woman Suffrage*, 6 vols. (New York, 1881-1922), 6:142.

14. The story of the long fight between millmen and North Carolina women's groups is covered in detail in Mary O. Cowper Papers. Mrs. Cowper was executive secretary of the North Carolina League of Women Voters. The outlines as given here are confirmed by Mrs. Kate Burr Johnson, who was commissioner of welfare during the 1920s and was working behind the scenes with the women's groups. For contemporary analysis, see Nell Battle Lewis, "The University of North Carolina Gets Its Orders," *Nation*, 122 (Feb. 3, 1926), 114-15. Nora Houston of Virginia who was active in the effort to improve working conditions was also a painter and left at her death a dramatic painting of the Gastonia strike.

15. North Carolina League of Women Voters, *Monthly News*, 1922-26.

16. Adele Clark Papers, Virginia State Library, Richmond. Miss Clark helped organize the campaign. See also Eudora Ramsay Richardson, "Liberals in Richmond," *Plain Talk*, 6 (Feb. 1930), 213-19.

17. Mrs. E. B. Chamberlain to Mrs. Solon Jacobs, Oct. 25, 1922, and Report to Director of Southeastern Region, Jan. 10, 1924, in League of Women Voters Papers, Georgia file.

18. Miss Earl Chambers to Marguerite Owen, Oct. 2, 1924, League of Women Voters Papers, Arkansas file.

19. Lucy R. Mason to Henry P. Kendall, Dec. 31, 1930, in Lucy Randolph Mason Papers, Manuscripts Department, Duke University Library.

20. Stanton et al., eds., *History of Woman Suffrage*, 6:125.

21. There is ample evidence for this in League of Women Voters Papers, state files, and Mary O. Cowper Papers. Common interests made inevitably for cooperation.

22. Gladys Bryson to Lucy Somerville, Mar. 23, 1923, in Somerville Family Papers, Schlesinger Library, Radcliffe College Library, Cambridge, Mass.

23. Marion Bonner, "Behind the Southern Textile Strikes," *Nation*, 129 (Oct. 2, 1929), 352.

24. See Lucy P. Garner, "An Education Opportunity for Industrial Girls," *Journal of Social Forces*, 1 (Sept. 1923), 612-13, and Alice M. Baldwin Papers, Manuscript Department, William R. Perkins Library, Duke University.

25. Lucy Randolph Mason Papers, box 1.

26. *Congressional Record*, 67 Cong., 1 Sess., 4216, 8036-37.

27. This story is reflected in detail in League of Women Voters Papers, state files. See especially all the state-by-state reports on the operation of the law and the collection of letters from Texas women who benefited from it. Reports of the Children's Bureau (National Archives, Washington, D.C.) also contain details of the actual workings of the law.

28. Noreen Dunn Tatum, *A Crown of Service: A Story of Woman's Work in the Methodist Episcopal Church, South, from 1878-1940* (Nashville, 1960), pp. 32, 65, 234; Lily Hardy Hammond, *In Black and White: An Interpretation of Southern Life* (New York, 1914). See also Wilma Dykeman and James Stokely, *Seeds of Southern Change: The Life of Will Alexander* (Chicago, 1961), pp. 82-96.

29. Norfolk *Journal and Guide*, Feb. 2, 1929. See also Katherine Du Pre Lumpkin, *The Making of a Southerner* (New York, 1947), for evidence of the significance of the YWCA in breaking through traditional racial barriers.

30. The story of women's interracial work is in the Jessie Daniel Ames Papers, Southern Historical Collection, University of North Carolina. Ames pioneered the antilynching group and was for twelve years executive secretary of the Woman's Department of the Inter-Racial Commission. See Jacqueline Dowd Hall, *Revolt Against Chivalry* (New York, 1979), for a splendid story of Ames and the Association of Southern Women for the Prevention of Lynching.

31. Nora Houston to Maud Wood Park, Dec. 12, 1923, in League of Women Voters Papers, Virginia file.

32. Miss M. E. Pidgeon to Belle Sherwin, 1924, League of Women Voters Papers, Virginia file.

33. League of Women Voters Papers, Georgia and Tennessee files.

34. Report on the Get Out the Vote Campaign, Nov. 29, 1924, League of Women Voters Papers, Alabama file.

35. Mrs. J. B. O'Hara to Ann Webster, Sept. 2, 1924, League of Women Voters Papers, Florida file.

36. See Carrie Chapman Catt and Nettie Rogers Shuler, *Woman Suffrage and Politics: The Inner Story of the Suffrage Movement* (New York, 1924), and Maud Wood Park, *Front Door Lobby*, ed. Edna Lamprey Stantial (Boston, 1960).

37. Mary Gray Peck, *Carrie Chapman Catt, a Biography* (New York, 1944), pp. 325-26.

38. Article in Jackson, Miss., *Woman Voter*, Nov. 19, 1923. For the details of Mrs. Somerville's campaign, see letters of her daughter, Sept. 1923, in Somerville Family Papers.

39. See analysis of first woman vice-chairman of the Democratic National Committee, Emily Newell Blair, "Women in the Political Parties," American Academy of Political and Social Science, *Annals*, 143 (May 1929), 217-29.

40. Clippings and note in Somerville Family Papers.

41. Somerville Family Papers, clippings. She had the additional distinction of providing the state with another successful woman politician, her daughter Lucy who followed her in the legislature in the 1930s and ultimately became a federal judge.

42. Jack Tate in Sue Shelton White Papers, Schlesinger Library, Radcliffe College.

43. Sue Shelton White to Mary Dewson, Nov. 23, 1928, Sue Shelton White Papers.

44. Blair, "Women in the Political Parties."

45. These claims appear in letters and reports to the National Office of the League of Women Voters in League of Women Voters Papers. The information about Governor Whitfield is contained in Lucy Somerville Howorth to author, Feb. 5, 1964.

46. Louisville, Ky., *Herald*, May 9, 1923.

47. Lucy Randolph Mason, *To Win These Rights: A Personal Story of the CIO in the South* (New York, 1952), p. 4.

48. George B. Tindall, "Business Progressivism: Southern Politics in the Twenties," *South Atlantic Quarterly*, 62 (Winter 1963), 92-106.

Historians Construct
the Southern Woman

Human beings have a strong tendency to create a past for themselves. When we have no evidence we make up stories—and indeed sometimes when we *do* have evidence, we still make up stories. Psychologists tell us that such myths respond to important human needs, the need to think well of ourselves, the need to explain the mysteries and tragedies as well as the triumphs of human experience. Literary critics tell us that the stories we tell reveal our unconscious selves. We also observe that some groups of people are more given to myth making than others—just as some individuals have a rich fantasy life while others get along with what we might call the bare facts.

We southerners, perhaps more than other Americans, enjoy making up stories about ourselves, and in the process we have created an array of mythical characters. We have been egged on by people in other parts of the country who for some mysterious reason take particular satisfaction in the mythic images of the southern past . . . and who have added some of their own, which do not always please us when they leap out from the television screen.[1] Some of our myths have been translated into high art, not least by Mississippians.

I speak as one who grew up believing in a good deal of this mythology. I can remember as a small child regretting that I had not been born in slavery times (this was after reading a book called *The Little Colonel*) and more or less believing in that golden age that had presumably existed

This essay was given as a lecture at the 1982 Chancellor's Symposium on Southern History at the University of Mississippi, and it is reproduced here by permission of the University of Mississippi. The article was originally published in Joanne V. Hawks and Sheila L. Skemp, eds., *Sex, Race, and the Role of Women in the South* (University: University Press of Mississippi, 1983), pp. 95-114.

before the war. (When I tell you that my great-grandmother enrolled me in the Children of the Confederacy the day I was born, you can imagine the ambience of my childhood.)

As a consequence of this early conditioning, my working life has been, in part, a thirty-year effort to come to terms with a historical reality that is very different from what I grew up believing—a long exercise in learning to look for evidence. I have had to learn that damn-Yankee is not one word, that Confederate soldiers on the rampage were no less destructive than Federals in similar conditions, that black people did not like being poor, outcast, or enslaved any better than I would have liked it in their place, that those fabled antebellum planters were not very different, and no less various, than the farmers I knew in middle Georgia in the 1930s, that historians' views of what we were carefully trained to call the War between the States depend heavily upon the latitude in which their holders were born. In particular, I have spent a great deal of time trying to untangle the reality of southern women's lives from the multiple myths that surround them, condition them, and sometimes unhinge them completely.

"Southern women," of course, come in a variety of shapes: The lady, to begin with: that wonderful creature epitomized for posterity by Thomas Nelson Page:

Her life was one long act of devotion,—devotion to God, devotion to her husband, devotion to her children, devotion to her servants, to the poor, to humanity. Nothing happened within the range of her knowledge that her sympathy did not reach and her charity and wisdom did not ameliorate. She was the head and font of the church. . . . The training of her children was her work. She watched over them, inspired them, led them, governed them: her will impelled them; her word to them, as to her servants, was law. She reaped the reward. . . . their sympathy and tenderness were hers always, and they worshipped her.

Then, the black mammy, that creature of such impeccable virtue, administrative skill, power, and nurturing ability, who yet inexplicably remained in bondage. . . .

Then, the poor white woman whether described by William Byrd in the eighteenth century or Frederick Law Olmsted in the nineteenth or Erskine Caldwell in the twentieth. . . .

Then, a host of all-but invisible women black and white who were artisans, managers, factory workers, teachers, and heads of families. . . .

Finally the new woman of the post-Reconstruction South whose existence began to be recognized by her contemporaries in the 1890s but who was hardly noticed by any historian until 1960.

All these and others have been the subject of myth or neglect, and finding evidence to construct their reality is a long, slow task. But many hands, they say, make light work, and sometime in the late 1950s a few stirrings of interest in the history of women began here and there; by the 1970s this interest had swelled into what must be seen as a major intellectual revolution, as a resurgent feminism inspired many young historians to take up the challenge of shining a light upon the hitherto almost invisible female half of the population. It is also an impressive case study in the sociology of knowledge. In a little over two decades a brave beginning has been made, and we are now on the verge of a great advance, as much of the work that has been underway comes to completion and begins to appear in print. When you have another symposium like this in 1992 the person who stands where I stand today (or, with a little luck, even I myself) will have a more complete and a more complex tale to tell.

This, then, is in the nature of a progress report. I shall try to outline how the history of southern women has come gradually to be written, and to sketch for you as well as I am able the real southern woman (or women) as she, or they, have emerged from the work of historians so far.

We will recognize at the outset that this work is just beginning—that of the millions of women who have lived in the South since Mistress Forrest and her maidservant Ann Burras turned up in Jamestown in 1608 (not to mention the other millions of Native American women who had lived here, unrecorded, for tens of thousands of years before that date) we have so far been able to reconstruct the merest handful. We will also recognize the difficulty of the task, the fact that women have been less likely to create records and have been less confident of the value of those records even when they existed. Many have lived and died and left not a trace. Many others survive only in parish records of birth, marriage, or death, or on the tax collector's rolls, or in probate and court records or in the manuscript census. Still, historians have always had to live by their wits, and by the time this subject has attracted as much historical energy as, for example, the battle of Gettysburg, we shall know quite a lot about the southern women who went before us.

Before we leave the matter of records, a word about what we are looking for and at. When women are literate, they are apt to write letters;

indeed, one of their self-defined functions has been to keep family communications going. In the nineteenth century they also tended to keep diaries, not at all because they could envision you and me coming along a century later in search of historical data, but because they often needed someone to talk to. A surprising number of women spoke of their diaries almost as if they were human. Thus women's letters and diaries crowd our manuscript depositories. One recent Ph.D. claims to have read through 500 collections, and doubtless there are still cellars and attics which would yield more documents if we went searching.

Then there are the memoirs, most often written in the late nineteenth century and centered on the lost world of the Old South. These are less immediate and direct, more artful, more likely to embellish myths than are the diaries and letters. They are useful, nevertheless, if only for acquainting us with the fantasies and romantic images with which people tried to comfort themselves in the hard times after the Civil War.

Slave women and antebellum free black women have been even less likely than white women to create a record of their lives, but others have sometimes created one for them, in a wide variety of slave narratives, some of them recorded by abolitionists, in plantation records, travelers' observations, in tales handed down in families, in the massive slave narrative collection of the Works Progress Administration. As one would expect, records for black women increase in quality and quantity after emancipation, especially records of schools and voluntary associations. Like white women, black woman may often be traced in manuscript census records and legal documents.[2]

Also in the 1930s sociologists and anthropologists turned their attention to southern women—and in so doing created an invaluable record of a society which was destined to disappear very rapidly during and after World War II.[3]

These, then, are the basic materials from which historians over the years have begun to reconstruct the real lives and worlds of southern women. It is always dangerous to take any point as a beginning—one is sure to find next day that something came earlier—but so far as I know the first small piece of what might be called modern scholarship in the history of southern women was a well-documented article published in 1928 in the *South Atlantic Quarterly* by Virginia Gearhart Gray. Gray was far in advance of her time; she used the manuscript census, city directories, and the like to put together a persuasive narrative dealing with women's work and organizations in the antebellum period. A few years later the same quarterly published "Southern Women of the Lost Generation" by Marjorie Mendenhall—an excellent analysis of what happened to southern women after the Civil War. But these articles dropped into a void. No one was yet listening.[4]

Then in the late 1930s two studies appeared, both written by women living in Chapel Hill, both destined to become classics. One was Guion Griffis Johnson's *Antebellum North Carolina*, an extraordinary and so far unreplicated social history based on a firm understanding that there were two sexes, and the other was Julia Cherry Spruill's *Women's Life and Work in the Southern Colonies*.[5] Each was the outcome of years of work in many varieties of primary sources: Spruill, for example, had examined every extant colonial newspaper, as well as deeds, wills, census records, and travelers' accounts. Indeed, except for slave interviews and the contemporary sociological studies she made use of every kind of source I have described. Johnson had been equally thorough in combing the records of North Carolina. Together these books allow us to see a wide variety of southern white women—at work, in families, in court, in politics, in trouble with the law, seeking education—over almost two and a half centuries. In other words, together they had covered more than two-thirds of the time since the first Europeans settled in the South.

Nowhere in either book does one catch even a whiff of magnolia blossoms. Ironically, in precisely the years these books were published *Gone with the Wind* became a national best-seller and then an immensely popular film.[6]

The woman who emerges from Spruill's and Johnson's pages is a hard-working farm wife or plantation mistress, one who could, if occasion demanded, help to clear land, contrive ways of bringing in some cash to the family economy, raise a garden and chickens, manage a dairy, help an artisan husband in his shop, or run an inn, a tavern, a newspaper, or even a ferry. If she survived she was pregnant or nursing for twenty years and doubtless agreed with an eighteenth-century Philadelphia Quaker woman who wrote: "I have often thought . . . that women who live to get over the time of Childbaring if other things are favourable to them, experience more comfort and satisfaction than at any other period of their lives." Like other American women her formal legal status was extremely limited, especially if she was married, but sometimes her actual legal situation was shaped more by common sense than by common law. This was especially true in the early days, when lawyers were few.

Spruill also adumbrated the effect of the rapid growth of affluence

and the development of a seaboard society with strong ties to England —
what John Murrin has more recently described as the general anglicization
of colonial society. Then came the Revolution, and even fine ladies were
put back to work.

From Johnson we learn about continuities and about change in the
first half of the nineteenth century with respect to women's work, family
life, education, and legal status — nearly all the subjects which presently
make up the substance of women's history are within her purview.

One would expect that two such excellent books would have inspired
a stream of follow-up studies; but alas, neither of these women was able
to secure a regular academic appointment. Neither had graduate students.
Spruill's book disappeared to library shelves to be rediscovered with
enormous enthusiasm in the 1960s. Johnson was read, but more as a
historian of North Carolina than as a historian of women.

In the 1940s only an occasional article broke the utter silence about
women in the southern past.[7] As late as 1965 a massive volume on the
historiography of the South mentioned three works about women in all
its 461 pages.[8]

Even as that book made its way to the bookstores and libraries,
things were beginning to happen which would soon make it, in that
respect, an anachronism. My own experience is illustrative. In the mid-
1950s, as I searched the sources in order to write a dissertation on the
Progressive movement in the South, I began bit-by-bit to find women
initiating or participating in nearly every one of the specific reforms which
made up that broad phenomenon we call Progressivism. No hint of this
fact had appeared in any of the standard works on the subject, and it
was with some uneasiness that in the early 1960s I sent — by coincidence
to the *South Atlantic Quarterly* — an article called "The 'New Woman'
in the New South." When it was accepted for publication, and when a
paper on the same subject delivered at the Southern Historical Association
elicited some interest, I was emboldened to plunge into the history of
southern women as a major preoccupation.

At about the same time in other parts of the country a considerable
number of young women scholars were making similar discoveries and
similar commitments — the silence about women's past was about to be
broken. Beginning in the early 1970s publications of many sorts began
to appear; two or three journals were founded; women's history began
to form a regular part of the sessions of the historical associations; in
less than a decade it became a respectable field of study. The tiny Berkshire

Conference of Women Historians, organized for mutual protection in the 1920s, suddenly found itself burgeoning in size, and when it sponsored a conference on women's history more than 1,000 people turned up.

Although—as we have seen—some of the most important early work in women's history had been done in the South, the surge of growth after 1962 tended to take place in the Northeast and Middle West, and studies of women in those areas multiplied. A comparatively small part of the significant work of the past two decades deals with the South, but it is that part which concerns us here. Using a rough chronological framework, let me try now to sketch "the southern woman" as the historians have begun to construct her.

We can begin with the earliest settlements on the Chesapeake shore in the seventeenth century. Lois Green Carr and Lorena Walsh tell us that the majority of early women settlers were indentured servants, that a high proportion of them died young, and that they were replaced by still other immigrant servants. There were more men than women, so any woman who wished to marry could do so, but a high deathrate worked against stable family life. For example, a woman might marry, have some children, die, and be replaced by a second wife who would also bear some children. Then the husband might die, and the second wife would take a second husband, perhaps bearing children by him as well. Nothing that we see around us in this age of high divorce rates compares in complexity with the variety of sibling relationships in seventeenth-century Maryland![9]

In time, of course, people developed some immunity to the diseases they encountered in the new world, a native-born generation took shape, more stable families began to develop, and kinship gradually came to be the major support system of individuals and families.

As we move into the early eighteenth century, we can turn again to Spruill's book where we find a hard-working, prolific housewife with her servants and her children, meagerly educated (unless she was tutored by her father and brothers) but possessed of numerous practical skills. Spruill's chapter on legal status (supplemented by more recent work) demonstrates that while the common law certainly followed women to this continent, frontier conditions did provide a bit more freedom of action than was the case in England. And to fill in the great gap in Spruill's book (for she hardly deals with the life experience of slave women), we can use Allan Kulikoff"'s study of colonial Chesapeake slave family life, which pays special attention to slave women.[10] Like the women who came as indentured servants the first generation of slave women worked hard and died young.

The historical reconstruction of women's lives in what the political historians long ago labeled the early national period—that is, from the end of the Revolution to about 1820—is so far painfully thin. Catherine Clinton's study of the plantation mistress has added a large amount of corroborative data which tends to show that continuity was more significant than change in the lives of women married to planters, even though these years witnessed the massive westward movement into Alabama, Mississippi, Tennessee, and Louisiana, and repetition of the cycle of development.[11]

The most important and original addition to our understanding of women in these years is a book about the free women of Petersburg, Virginia, black and white. Suzanne Lebsock has made a fine-grained study of a single, rapidly growing commercial community during the years 1784 to 1860. Using a wide variety of sources and making especially imaginative use of legal records, Lebsock documents a high degree of continuity as well as some very interesting and not always explicable changes in women's economic experience. On balance, she found that white women and free black women in these years moved steadily toward more independence with respect to the ownership, use, and management of property. On the other hand, she found them in some ways moving to a more subservient position in public life, especially in their voluntary associations which early in her period were thoroughly independent and later came somewhat under the control of parallel male groups. Overall this book adds to our understanding in half a dozen different areas of women's lives. It should give rise to many similar studies which taken together will gradually begin to permit some generalizations.[12]

Chronologically the first half of my book, *The Southern Lady*, covers the same years as the last half of Lebsock's study. Completed a decade earlier, it paints on a wider canvas and is less methodologically sophisticated. I worked largely from diaries, letters, fiction, and the periodical press to reconstruct the inner world of plantation women who turned out to be—very much like Lebsock's Petersburg women — mostly hardworking, often skilled managers of plantation and business affairs, usually pious and somewhat masochistic Christians. I also found evidence for certain profound discontents with life as they experienced it, particularly discontent with constant childbearing, with the double standard, with the limited access to education, and with the institution of slavery, as it bore upon white women.[13]

The recent developments in women's history have been paralleled by a new wave of slavery studies. As the history of slavery comes to be written with more attention to the slave's point of view, we might expect women to emerge as historical actors in their own right. To some extent this has been true, especially in the pathbreaking works of Eugene Genovese and Herbert Gutman. However, in their zeal to establish the pre-emancipation existence of a black family Gutman and Genovese perhaps inadvertently created a family which, with respect to the father's role, tended to mirror white norms.[14] In 1978 Deborah White completed a dissertation called "Ain't I a Woman," which takes direct issue with the assumptions of Genovese and Gutman. In a convincing reading of the same sources, she describes a matrifocal black family in which work roles were not sharply different nor the work of one sex more highly valued than that of the other. Since, because of the very nature of slavery, black women could not rely upon husbands for protection, they had to depend upon their own ingenuity—and thus created quite a different psychological structure from that of white families. White's study will, I think, quickly become the prevailing view and will inspire research to carry her analysis forward into the post-emancipation period.[15]

Along with work, slavery, and childbearing, religion was a major force in southern women's experience. Personal piety was highly valued, and more women than men were church members. So far the only study which begins to deal with this phenomenon as a major social force is Donald Mathews's *Religion in the Old South*.[16] Mathews found women to be the majority of communicants in most southern churches and found their values and concerns to be a central force in shaping religious life.

When we contemplate the quantity of fiction, memoirs, and myths associated with women's part in the Civil War, we would expect this to be one of the most profoundly analyzed of historical phenomena. In fact, serious historical treatments are still few—beginning with James Patton and Frances Simkins's *The Women of the Confederacy* published in 1936, which dwells overmuch on the sad woman in widow's weeds.[17] In 1966, as part of the Civil War Centennial, Mary Elizabeth Massey published *Bonnet Brigades*, a study of women's part in the war on both sides. Her southern women are far more active and play a more important part in sustaining the Confederacy than those perceived by Patton and Simkins. A chapter on the war in *The Southern Lady* sustains Massey's description and interprets the wartime experience as a major turning point in the evolution of women's roles in the South. A book about Alabama women reenforces this interpretation, as do a number of important primary sources recently published: for example, the massive collection of Jones's family letters from the Georgia coast, the Hammond letters from South Carolina, the new edition of Mary Chesnut's diary-novel, and Catherine Edmonston's diary to name only a few.[18]

Whether from convenience or habit, or because a real and significant break with the past took place in 1865, most southern history tends to divide at the Civil War. Whether this kind of periodization has an internal logic for women's history will depend upon what we have yet to learn about the actual experience of women in the immediate postwar years.

So far there have been no historiographic arguments centering on women's wartime experience; this is not so true with respect to what happened next. In 1970 I argued that women who lived through the war continued into the postwar period to behave more independently, to seek self-support, and to take initiatives which they would not have dreamed of earlier, and that this change in the culture affected the following generations. I also thought that since 350,000 men died in the war— even given a large number of civilian casualties—there would have to be a generation of women with a high proportion of widows and single women and that many of these would inevitably be heads of families.

Jonathan Wiener, studying a small number of wealthy Alabama counties, took issue with this view since he found fewer female planters after the war than before; Lebsock in a provocative epilogue to her book also raises some questions about the notion that women were more independent after the war.[19]

However these differences may be resolved by further research, there can be no doubt that southern women as a group evolved in important ways in the last half of the nineteenth century. The most important agents of this evolution were religious and secular voluntary associations. Women's missionary societies were not altogether new in the 1870s but in all the Protestant denominations they grew rapidly, and in addition to their concern for foreign missions developed what were called "home missions," to carry on and expand the responsibilities of the prewar benevolent societies. John McDowell's study of the Methodist women's societies as the agents of the Social Gospel in the South points the way for a thorough analysis of this phenomenon.[20] Women essentially invented the welfare state.

Even more interesting in its far-reaching social consequences was the Woman's Christian Temperance Union, which has lately been the subject of three good studies, none of which, unfortunately, pays much attention to the South.[21] Yet this organization, as Belle Kearney once put it, was "the golden key which unlocked the pent-up possibilities of southern womanhood." No one has yet studied the burgeoning woman's club movement, which spread rapidly across the South after 1880, or the YWCA, or the United Daughters of the Confederacy or—for the twentieth century—the League of Women Voters. Only the suffrage movement has found its historian.[22]

It would be difficult to overstate the need for a great deal of serious research centering on voluntary associations. Like women themselves their associations have tended to be overlooked or misunderstood. They were used by southern women, and by American women generally, to circumvent legal and social barriers that prevented them from exercising political and social power. They were a major social tool. In the South women's groups brought about the abolition of the convict-lease system, helped create public schools, built libraries, cleaned up the milk supply, promoted public health measures, created opportunities for women's higher education, and attempted to ameliorate the harshest aspects of industrial development. Black women formed associations for self-help and mutual aid and to improve life among their own people. Women's associations created the southern suffrage movement. These groups were the nurseries for leadership, the incubators of the "new woman." Yet their history has barely begun to be written.

Historically speaking, southern women in the century since 1880 scarcely exist. A. Elizabeth Taylor's suffrage studies, the second half of *The Southern Lady*, two excellent articles by an Australian scholar dealing with white and black women's work in two world wars, an article on working women in Atlanta in the 1930s, an article about the North Carolina women's group devoted to building school houses, Cynthia Neverdon-Morton's article on black women's struggle for equality, Sharon Harley's essay on black women educators: these about sum up the published scholarship.[23]

Several dissertations have recently made significant additions to what we know about early twentieth-century southern women. Dolores Janiewski used working-class women in Durham, North Carolina, as a case study in an effort to trace the relationships between the growth of industrial capitalism and women's work and family life. Marion Roydhouse and Mary Frederickson, from different angles of vision, have been interested in the relationships between middle-class and working-class women. Roydhouse's work centers on North Carolina women's voluntary associations in the 1920s, especially on their concern for the wages, hours, and working conditions of mill women. Frederickson wrote about the Southern Summer School for Women Workers, where middle-class women attempted to train mill women to become labor organizers.[24]

Any catalog of important work waiting to be done must include the whole subject of women's education. The upsurge of interest in improved education before the Civil War has been carefully described by several historians, but so far there has been no serious analysis of the meaning of this development in the context of a rural, plantation-dominated society. For the later years the possibilities for description and analysis are enormous. I can envision, for example, a book on the role of the normal school in changing career options for women and in changing the nature of public education. There is another book to be written on the work and influence of the Southern Association of College Women and books on each of several influential women's colleges. I think particularly of Spelman College in Atlanta, Wesleyan in Macon, of Sophie Newcomb, Randolph Macon, Sweet Briar, Hollins, and Goucher, each of which had its peculiar clientele and sent out graduates whose lives were to an important degree shaped by the collegiate experience. Mississippi created the first state-supported college for women. Then there is the whole question of coeducation in the South, pioneered by Atlanta University and the University of Mississippi, and coming, finally, to Virginia in the mid-twentieth century.[25]

Until Martha Swain wrote her paper for this symposium, no one had tackled the large and complex subject of southern women in politics, which begins even before the ratification of the nineteenth amendment and comes down to the present time. In the decade after 1910 certain women began to be powerful in the Democratic party, both nationally and in their local communities. In the first elections held after suffrage women were elected to many local offices and to a number of state legislatures. Many came in full of zeal for improving the political system, and especially for improving the quality of welfare administered by the states. How it worked out we have no idea, yet the possibilities for research and analysis in this area are extremely tempting.[26]

But along these lines — of the possibilities as yet untouched in the study of southern women — one could go on for many hours. Perhaps the important thing is that a beginning has been made. Some of you may remember a childhood toy in the shape of an unusual kind of coloring book in which the pages appeared to be blank but when one dipped a brush in water and began painting, bit by bit a picture emerged. So it has been for the past fifteen years or so with respect to the history of southern women: The blank page is slowly filling up with figures, and the more we paint the more complicated the relationships between them becomes.

We have realized that there is no such thing as "the" southern woman, for she came in many varieties of class, race, and ability. The reality, we have discovered, is neither so simple nor so glamorous as the myth. People have a disconcerting ability not to fit into the historian's categories, much less to fit the legends their descendants like to relate. The reality, when it finally emerges, is no less interesting and far more helpful in understanding ourselves than all the myths and fiction ever were.

NOTES

In the composition of this essay I was greatly helped by Jacquelyn Hall with whom I was at that time collaborating on a much longer historiographical article.

1. William R. Taylor in *Cavalier and Yankee: The Old South and American National Character* (New York, 1961) speculates upon the way northerners have reinforced certain images of the South.

2. Years ago Professor Willie Lee Rose began suggesting that Helen Catterall's five volumes, *Judicial Cases Concerning American Slavery and the Negro* (Washington, D.C., 1926-37), would prove useful to historians of black women. Perhaps someone will soon take up this suggestion.

3. See particularly Margaret Hagood, *Mothers of the South* (Chapel Hill, 1939; reprint ed., 1972). See also Hortense Powdermaker, *After Freedom: A Cultural Study in the Deep South* (New York, 1939; reprint ed., 1969); John Dollard, *Caste and Class in a Southern Town*, 2d ed. (New York, 1949).

4. Virginia Gearhart Gray, "Activities of Southern Women: 1840-1860," *South Atlantic Quarterly*, 27 (July 1928), 264-79; Marjorie S. Mendenhall, "Southern Women of a 'Lost Generation,' " *South Atlantic Quarterly*, 33 (Oct. 1934), 334-53.

5. Guion Griffis Johnson, *Ante-bellum North Carolina* (Chapel Hill, 1937); Julia Cherry Spruill, *Women's Life and Work in the Southern Colonies* (Chapel Hill, 1938).

6. There are different ways of reading *Gone with the Wind*; for most people doubtless the romantic story is the main thing. However, Mitchell did a

great deal of careful research and in many respects Scarlett embodies the qualities which historians are describing in some antebellum plantation women.

7. Eleanor Boatwright, "The Political and Civil Status of Women in Georgia, 1783-1860," *Georgia Historical Quarterly*, 25 (Dec. 1941), 301-24; A. Elizabeth Taylor, "The Origin of the Woman Suffrage Movement in Georgia," *Georgia Historical Quarterly*, 28 (June 1944), 63-79.

8. Arthur Link and Rembert Patrick, eds., *Writing Southern History* (Baton Rouge, 1965).

9. Lois Green Carr and Lorena S. Walsh, "The Planter's Wife: The Experience of White Women in Seventeenth-Century Maryland," *William and Mary Quarterly*, 3rd Ser., 34 (Oct. 1977), 542-71.

10. Allan Kulikoff, "The Beginnings of the Afro-American Family in Maryland," in Aubrey C. Land, Lois Green Carr, and Edward C. Papenfuse, eds., *Law, Society, and Politics in Early Maryland* (Baltimore, 1977).

11. Catherine Clinton, *The Plantation Mistress: Woman's World in the Old South* (New York, 1983).

12. Suzanne Lebsock, *Free Women of Petersburg* (New York, 1983).

13. Anne Firor Scott, *The Southern Lady: From Politics to Pedestal, 1830-1930* (Chicago, 1970), pp. 45-79; Scott, "Women's Perspective on the Patriarchy of the 1850s," pp. 175-89, herein.

14. Eugene D. Genovese, *Roll Jordan Roll: The World the Slaves Made* (New York, 1974); Herbert G. Gutman, *The Black Family in Slavery and Freedom, 1750-1925* (New York, 1976).

15. Deborah White, "Ain't I a Woman?" (Ph.D. diss., University of Illinois at Chicago, 1978).

16. Donald Mathews, *Religion in the Old South* (Chicago, 1977).

17. James W. Patton and Francis B. Simkins, *The Women of the Confederacy* (Richmond, 1936).

18. Mary Elizabeth Massey, *Bonnet Brigades* (New York, 1966); Scott, *The Southern Lady*, pp. 80-102; H. E. Sterkx, *Partners in Rebellion: Alabama Women in the Civil War* (Rutherford, 1970); Robert M. Myers, ed., *The Children of Pride* (New Haven, 1972); Carol Bleser, ed., *The Hammonds of Redcliffe* (New York, 1981); C. Vann Woodward, ed., *Mary Chesnut's Civil War* (New Haven, 1981); Beth Crabtree and James W. Patton, *Journal of a Secesh Lady* (Raleigh, 1979).

19. Jonathan M. Wiener, "Female Planters and Planters' Wives in Civil War and Reconstruction: Alabama, 1850-1870," *The Alabama Review*, 30 (Apr. 1977), 135-49; Lebsock, *Free Women*, epilogue.

20. John Patrick McDowell, *The Social Gospel in the South: The Women's Home Mission Movement in the Methodist Episcopal Church, South, 1886-1939* (Baton Rouge, 1982).

21. Ruth Bordin, *Woman and Temperance* (Philadelphia, 1981); Barbara L. Epstein, *The Politics of Domesticity* (Middletown, 1981); Mari Jo Buhle, *Women and American Socialism, 1780-1920* (Urbana, 1981), see especially pp. 49-103.

22. A. Elizabeth Taylor has published numerous articles and one book, building a state-by-state description of the southern suffrage movement. She plans

eventually to write an interpretive volume covering the whole South. See, for example: "A Short History of the Woman Suffrage Movement in Tennessee," *Tennessee Historical Quarterly*, 2 (Sept. 1943), 195-215; "The Woman Suffrage Movement in Arkansas," *Arkansas Historical Quarterly*, 15 (Spring 1956), 17-52; "The Woman Suffrage Movement in Mississippi, 1890-1920," *Journal of Mississippi History*, 30 (Feb. 1968), 1-34; "The Woman Suffrage Movement in North Carolina, Part l," *North Carolina Historical Review*, 38 (Jan. 1961), 45-62; *The Woman Suffrage Movement in Tennessee* (New York, 1957); "The Woman Suffrage Movement in Texas," *Journal of Southern History*, 17 (May 1951), 194-215. Anastasia Sims, a graduate student at the University of North Carolina, is working on the North Carolina Federation of Women's Clubs.

23. In addition to Taylor and Scott, already cited, see William J. Breen, "Southern Women in the War: The North Carolina Woman's Committee, 1917-1919," *North Carolina Historical Review*, 55 (July 1978), 251-81; Julia Blackwelder, "Quiet Suffering: Atlanta Women in the 1930s," *Georgia Historical Quarterly*, 61 (Summer 1977), 112-24; and Julia Blackwelder, "Women in the Work Force: Atlanta, New Orleans and San Antonio, 1930-1940," *Journal of Urban History*, 4 (May 1978), 331-58; Cynthia Neverdon-Morton, "The Black Woman's Struggle for Equality in the South, 1895-1925," in Sharon Harley and Rosalyn Terborg-Penn, *The Afro-American Woman: Struggles and Images* (Port Washington, N.Y., 1978); Sharon Harley, "Beyond the Classroom: Organizational Lives of Black Female Educators in the District of Columbia, 1890-1930," *Journal of Negro Education*, 51 (Summer 1982), 254-65. See also Gerda Lerner, *Black Women in White America* (New York, 1972); Gerda Lerner, *The Majority Finds Its Past* (New York, 1979), chs. 5-7; Edward James, Janet James, and Paul S. Boyer, eds., *Notable American Women, 1607-1950*, 3 vols. (Cambridge, Mass., 1970); Barbara Sicherman and Carol Hurd Green, eds., *Notable American Women: The Modern Period* (Cambridge, Mass., 1981); Thomas C. Holt, "The Lonely Warrior: Ida B. Wells-Barnett and the Struggle for Black Leadership," in John Hope Franklin and August Meier, eds., *Black Leaders of the Twentieth Century* (Urbana, 1982), pp. 39-62; Terra Hunter, "Charlotte Hawkins Brown" (Honors paper, Duke University, 1982).

24. Dolores Janiewski, "From Field to Factory: Race, Class, Sex and the Women Workers in Durham, 1880-1932" (Ph.D. diss., Duke University, 1980); Marion Roydhouse, "The 'Universal Sisterhood of Women': Women and Labor Reform in North Carolina, 1900-1932" (Ph.D. diss., Duke University, 1980); Mary Frederickson, " 'A Place to Speak Our Minds': The Southern Summer School for Women Workers" (Ph.D. diss., University of North Carolina, 1981).

25. Christie F. Pope, "Preparation for Pedestals: North Carolina Antebellum Female Seminars" (Ph.D. diss., University of Chicago, 1977). For some preliminary thoughts on the subject, see "Education: The Ambiguous Reform" and "Becoming a Notable Georgia Woman," pp. 298-322, herein. For the entry of women into the University of Georgia, see Sara Bertha Townsend, "The Admission of Women to the University of Georgia," *Georgia Historical Quarterly*, 43 (June 1959), 156-69; for the long battle to gain admission to the University of Virginia, see Mary G. Newell, "Mary Munford and the Higher Education for Women in Virginia,"

in Patricia A. Stringer and Irene Thompson, eds., *Stepping Off the Pedestal: Academic Women in the South* (New York, 1982), pp. 26-40. For an excellent bibliographical article, see Virginia Shadron et al., in *ibid.*, 145-68.

26. See my essay, "Nellie Nugent Somerville," p. 168-72, herein, for an exemplary case, and the bibliography attached to the essay. Women's political activities in certain cities, especially Atlanta, New Orleans, and Richmond, would also yield interesting insights.

PART III

Voluntary Associations

Women's voluntary associations—as the introduction to this volume makes clear—have been part of my life experience for a very long time. In spite of this fact, it took me awhile to begin to realize the importance of such associations for the development of a public role for women in the nineteenth century. Perhaps the realization that early members of the Woman's Christian Temperance Union (about which I had the usual stereotypes) saw it as a force for liberation of women jolted me into examining all my preconceived views about women's groups. Perhaps it was the relationship between the Chicago Women's Club and Hull-House. Whatever the precipitating moment, since 1958 or so I have been increasingly aware of the significance of all kinds of voluntary associations: missionary societies, clubs, suffrage organizations, patriotic organizations, the WCTU itself, the Women's Trade Union League, and many others.

My early interest was in the way such organizations permitted women to do things they were not otherwise able to do. In time I came to the even more fundamental question: What did the work of all these associations have to do with the development of American social history? That question leads into others so complex that I am not sure I shall live long enough to work out an answer.

What appears below are my first tentative efforts to do so. I have decided to publish them because many scholars are now at work on particular associations, and even work as incomplete as mine is, so far, may contribute something to this rapidly growing body of knowledge.

"As Easily As They Breathe" was conceived as the first chapter in the book on voluntary associations still under construction. "Women's Voluntary Associations in the Forming of American Society" began as the Bunting Institute twentieth anniversary lecture ("When Outsiders Become Insiders, What Then?") and has gone through several stages of development since it was first presented in 1981. It incorporates the ideas in the first piece and suggests a conceptual framework for the book.

As Easily as They Breathe . . .

"This people associate as easily as they breathe."
—Fredrika Bremer, *Homes of the New World*

About the middle of the 1790s what would in time become a vast and all-pervasive social movement began to take shape as American women of all ages began to form voluntary associations. Along with the revolution in women's education that was taking shape at the same time, this movement was destined to bring about far-reaching changes in social values and social structures, not least in the values that defined women's social roles.

In some sense the principle of voluntarism had been at the root of the American enterprise from the beginning, since (except for Africans and convicts) one defining characteristic of the settlers had been that they chose to come. From the Mayflower Compact onward, despite the generally hierarchical assumptions of the seventeenth century, the tendency of Americans to associate themselves for common purposes had developed steadily. By the end of the eighteenth century this tendency had become a fixed pattern; a careful scholar concluded that in the years between 1783 and 1815 the new nation was "blanketed with organizations created to secure a variety of progressive ends."[1]

By the time Alexis de Tocqueville composed his outsider's analysis in the 1830s nothing was more striking to him than the habit Americans shared of creating associations for a wide variety of purposes. His comments on the subject are well known and much quoted; what has not been so much noticed is that he wrote as if only men were given to joining together.

Yet from the beginning of colonization there had been an occasional association of women. In Massachusetts in 1635, for example, Anne

261

Hutchinson had taken to inviting women to her house to discuss the week's sermon, although such an intellectual enterprise was unusual for her sex. This informal voluntary group, short-lived though it was, exhibited a number of the characteristics which would appear over and over in the future. (1) It was an all-woman group. (2) The women were seeking to educate themselves. (3) The leader was a woman of unusually powerful personal qualities. (4) The substance was religious. (5) The original purpose widened as time went by (from a simple analysis of the weekly sermon to a critique of the prevailing theology).

The rest of this particular story is familiar. For her initiative Hutchinson was accused of heresy, tried by an all-male General Court, found guilty, and was banished. She went eventually to Long Island where she and her family were killed by Indians, an event some of her accusers attributed to God's displeasure.[2] Hutchinson's fate was more extreme than that of any of her successors, but she would not be the last to feel the sting of male disapproval or to be accused of doing things not proper for a woman.

Except for the Women's Meetings instituted by the Society of Friends in 1681, the next hundred years yields no further record of regular gatherings of women for purposes other than the traditional ones of shared work or shared prayer. There was a flurry of organization at the time of the Revolution, when women formed groups to support the cause by eschewing tea, wearing homespun, sewing uniforms, caring for the families of soldiers, and raising money.[3] In 1778 a Female Humane Society in Baltimore organized and ran a charity school, and in the same year in the midst of the conflict with Britain, Hannah Mather—age twenty-five —gathered a group of her Boston friends to form what she called a Woman's Lodge for the purpose of improving their minds.[4] Mather's marriage, followed by the births of ten children, brought an end to this effort, but late in life she made clear in print her profound concern for women's education. Like Hutchinson she insisted that women's intellectual capacities were not inferior to those of men.

None of these early associations appears to have lasted very long or had many imitators. Then, suddenly, by the end of the eighteenth century as the embers of the Great Awakening came to life and the evangelical revival spread across the country, women in many parts of the country suddenly took to organizing themselves with great energy.[5]

The speed with which women's organizations multiplied and spread in new states as well as old ones suggests that we should look for predisposing changes in the rapidly developing society. There was no single cause, but a number of factors combined to bring about a situation in which women found it more and more natural to form their own associations as American men had done for so long.

Women who had been young children during the Revolution had seen the widespread use of association for political purposes during the conflict and had grown up at a time when state-making and formal constitutions were much on people's minds. When they came to form their own groups, they nearly always began with a constitution upon which members voted; they carefully followed parliamentary procedure, kept records, and published reports. By this means women created groups which could survive the particular individuals who started them.

Communication and transportation were improving, and with that the flow of ideas increased. Very early in the nineteenth century national religious and reform associations began to support organizers who went about initiating new groups, including auxiliaries for women.[6] By the 1840s Fredrika Bremer observed:

Whenever any subject or question of interest arises in society which demands public sympathy or cooperation, a "Convention" is immediately called to take it into consideration, and immediately, from all ends of the city, or the state, or from every state in the Union, all who feel an interest in the subject or question fly upon the wings of steam to the appointed place of meeting . . . they come together . . . make speeches . . . vote . . . carry their resolutions. And forth upon the wings of a thousand daily papers flies that which the meeting or the Convention has resolved.[7]

From such gatherings women as well as men came back to their local societies with new ideas and new inspiration, and with a sense that the world did not end at the borders of their own communities. Both the growth of old towns and the rapid creation of new ones brought needs which women sought to meet. With growth came complexity and, for reasons not entirely clear, a heightened perception of poverty. New communities required institutions, and there seems often to have been a tacit division of labor: men associated themselves to establish government, business, and commerce, women to initiate churches, schools, welfare institutions, and ways of regulating behavior.

In addition to the external conditions that encouraged women to form associations, there were various internal motives, not all of them fully conscious.

For instance, the demands evangelical Christianity placed upon the individual were more easily met if they were shared: women saw themselves as watching over one another and helping each other "heavenward." It was not only the desire to do good which brought women together but also the need to be good. In addition to the deeply felt desire for goodness and piety, there was also a growing desire for learning. A little education seemed to beget the desire for more. The leading female seminaries stressed the importance of lifelong learning, and, increasingly, as the century went along, women found ingenious ways to work together for self-education as well as to provide education for others. Collectively women tried to attain the ideal of the educated republican mother who could train citizens.

Other inner needs may be inferred from the record. In their own groups women who yearned to be leaders, to exercise ability, and even to acquire fame had a chance to do so. The more we study the records of nineteenth-century women, the more we are able to identify latent or covert feminism, much of it in the context of group activity.[8] This reason suggests another: a woman who wanted to engage in activities beyond those sanctioned by the prevailing mores was safer if she acted in concert with others.

Other factors await careful quantitative study. We know that at least in New England by 1800 the average age of marriage was rising, as was the ratio of women to men, and everywhere the birthrate was beginning to decline. Even in the absence of firm statistical evidence, common sense suggests that a woman who raised four children had more time to devote to community affairs than a woman who raised ten. Women who never married had a particular incentive to find significant ways to use their time.

The academies and seminaries with their goals of educating mothers and teachers were also, whether they planned to or not, educating potential volunteers. Women who had attended such institutions and especially those who spent some part of their lives teaching constituted an important source of leadership for the multiplying associations.

In addition, the accumulation of resources as the economy grew began to provide even some village women with a little leisure and some access to money. That so many associations were able to support themselves with contributions and by selling products of their own labor was in part a function of the shift from a subsistence to a cash economy even in the smaller centers of population.

The beginning of the sustained development of women's organizations was signaled by the formation in Philadelphia in 1793 of a Female Society for the Relief and Employment of the Poor and of a Quaker women's group which established a free school for female children.[9] Together they foreshadowed the principal directions women's benevolent work would take in its early stages.

In 1797 a widowed schoolmistress living in New York organized the Society for the Relief of Poor Widows with Small Children.[10] The Widow's Society, as it was called, demonstrated the opportunities women could find for exercising their abilities in a rapidly growing urban area where both resources and potential leaders were plentiful. Isabella Graham, the founder, was herself a prototype—albeit an exceptionally able one— of the women across the country who initiated benevolent societies. She was, to begin with, well educated, confident, and experienced, and had managed to support her own family during widowhood. Had she been a man she would doubtless have been a minister; as it was she liked to write voluminously on theological issues. Yet she was fundamentally an activist, and the number of lasting organizations and institutions she managed to create, beginning when she was fifty-five, made her an early heroine of the benevolent movement.[11]

No sooner had the women of the Widow's Society received a charter from the state legislature than they "engaged in plans for extending their usefulness." They quickly concluded that the simple provision of material aid made no lasting improvement in the condition of dependency among their chosen recipients (widows with small children), and so they established schools in various parts of the city in which some of the indigent women could work as teachers. Other women were put to work running soup kitchens.

Members of this and nearly every other benevolent society shared the fundamental evangelical assumption that ignorance leads to vice and vice leads to poverty. To prevent or cure poverty, they reasoned, children must first be taught to read and write and then guided to read properly improving books. The Widow's Society continued to spin off one educational program after another. In 1804 Graham organized a group of young women "of the first rank in the city" to teach poor children. After giving them some initial instruction in pedagogy, she launched the endeavor with a stirring exhoratory speech in which she compared their decision to do the work themselves (rather than simply paying someone else to do it) with Hernando Cortez's decision to burn his ships after his troops had landed in Mexico.

Two years later members of the Widow's Society organized an Orphan Asylum Society for the purpose of creating a permanent institution. Orphans were their particular concern, the women noted, because "crime has not been the cause of [their] misery and future usefulness may be the result of [their] protection."[12] This new society bought four lots in Greenwich Village and built an orphan's home which flourished for thirty years. By that time the city had expanded; the women sold their appreciated property and used the proceeds to build a new and larger institution at what is now Riverside Drive and Seventy-third Street. In 1902, still thriving, the asylum moved again to Hastings-on-Hudson.[13]

Counterparts of the New York Widow's Society with various long-winded names appeared in one after another of the older towns and cities. Their patterns of development and even the words they used were startlingly similar, though it seems unlikely that there was much direct communication, for example, between Graham's women in New York and those of a feisty association in Petersburg, Virginia, or others in Savannah, Georgia, and Raleigh, North Carolina.[14]

Doing good is never easy. Thoroughly imbued with the values of the Protestant middle class, ignorant of the first principles of economics, inexperienced, for the most part, with respect to being poor, the women of the benevolent societies had set their feet on a rocky path. One troublesome obstacle was the concept of worthiness. On the face of it there would seem to be no problem: aid should go to those who were trying to live decently, observing the accepted notions of good behavior. But firsthand experience led at least some of the women to note uneasily that being good while being poor was not so simple. Was it conceivable that people drank or robbed because they were poor and not the other way about?

The idea of "the worthy poor" was easier to sustain in the abstract than in the particular. The managers of benevolent societies were charged with making sure that recipients of aid were of high moral character, neither "vicious" nor "idle," but in practice it was sometimes difficult to make these distinctions. The Raleigh Female Benevolent Society, for example, noted in 1823 that "the most deserving may not be the most necessitous; and although evil may previously have been committed, yet who shall say what has been resisted?" Bit by bit it is possible to see women beginning to wonder whether vice, as they defined it, might be more the result than the cause of poverty.

Further perplexing issues arose when the women's benevolent societies began experimenting with work relief. Graham's straightforward plan of paying widows to teach needy children and to take charge of soup kitchens accomplished two ends at once and worked fairly well. But beyond that troubles appeared. The skills accepted as "women's work" were few: laundering, cooking, child care, or teaching. Who were to be the customers, and who was to pay for the work done? Should they be paid the going wage (which was often too little to provide subsistence for a woman with any dependents), or less (since need always outran the resources of the benevolent societies), or more (so they could live decently)? Wrestling with these issues took benevolent women into the analysis of economic and employment issues and stretched their capacity for innovation.

Two critics tried to suggest better ways of dealing with work relief. Sarah Josepha Hale who helped to found the Boston Seaman's Aid Society hit upon the idea that poor women should sew for other poor people: that is, widows, wives, and daughters of seamen should sew good, substantial clothing for seamen who needed it rather than fancy work for do-gooding ladies to buy. She also figured wages on the basis of what was needed for a decent standard of living. And Matthew Carey, one of the earliest champions of wage-earning women, argued that philanthropy should depart from the normal notion of paying the lowest wage that would still bring the woman to work and attempt to prepare women for higher skills that would allow them to live decently. Neither Hale nor Carey managed to change the prevailing pattern.[15]

More numerous and more typical than these increasingly sophisticated and innovative urban societies were those in small towns and villages where most Americans lived. Like their big-city sisters, women in the smaller communities took responsibility for poor women and children and faced, on a smaller scale, some of the same dilemmas.[16] The records of three societies—in Morristown, New Jersey, Hopkinton, New Hampshire, and Shrewsbury, Massachusetts—exhibit characteristics common to many of these smaller groups.

In Morristown, for example, seventeen Presbyterian women of the leading families joined together in 1813 and by pooling their own resources and appealing to the community began to meet the needs of "poor and needy persons within the city and neighborhood who do not come under the care of the Overseer of the Poor." Dividing their small town (population

3,753 in 1810) into districts, they appointed one member as manager for each district and agreed that only sickness or absence from town should excuse these managers from regular attendance at the meetings. Like their counterparts elsewhere they sought to establish principles of worthiness for recipients of aid, but widows and children could easily be seen as victims of circumstance rather than of their own wickedness. It is of interest, too, that the "worthy" were not confined to their own denomination or ethnic group. In 1858, for example, the society reported helping twenty-five families: "7 Irish, 5 colored, and the remaining our own people."[17]

In Hopkinton (population 2,455) the relentless spirit of self-improvement was embodied in the constitution of the Chesterfield Female Benevolent Society. Article 8 stated: "The foul voice of slander shall never be heard in any of our meetings against any person or persons whatsoever and if it should perchance creep in unawares it shall be the duty of the presiding officer to reprove the one so offending by referring her to the 8th Article of the Constitution." Most of the signatures to this constitution displayed the precise and elegant penmanship taught in female seminaries, and a desire for further education was embodied in another constitutional provision, requiring serious reading and discussion at each meeting. At the end of their first three years members voted to use all the money on hand to create a lending library, which they organized and administered for the use of the whole town.[18]

The smaller societies found a variety of ways to raise money for charitable work. In Hopkinton members wove straw into hats which they sold in the local market. Since this was one of the common forms of home manufacture in New England, they were directly competing with women who needed income for their families. Nothing in their records suggests any awareness of the ambiguities involved in this method of raising money.

In the Shrewsbury Charitable Society, founded in 1832 by forty-four women, principally wives of leading citizens, members sewed articles for sale as well as for direct use, combining the older subsistence methods with the newer cash economy. They, too, made "an energetic and apparently successful attempt to . . . focus collective attention on serious subjects." Topics were given out for discussion at each meeting, and the reading of the Bible was part of their regular program. In addition one member read from some improving work while the others sewed. In 1841 this society adopted a set of resolutions which suggested a concern similar to that exhibited in Hopkinton about gossip.

Feeling the worth of our time, the importance and weight of our example, the necessity of improving it for our own benefit and well as others:

1st Resolved, therefore, that we will endeavor to have our "conversation as becometh the Gospel" that the world may take knowledge that we possess as well as profess, the religion of our divine master.

2nd Resolved, that our select reading shall be chaste and sentimental, that will improve the heart and instruct the mind and lead us to the contemplation of the great duties of religion.

This group, too, undertook to provide a library for the community when it presented a set of books to the Congregational Sabbath School, among them a life of Walter Scott and the works of John Milton.[19]

Benevolent societies were only one of the forms of association which began to proliferate in order to "imitate the blessed Master." The opening of the nineteenth century had witnessed a sudden efflorescence of missionary zeal for the threefold purpose of converting American Indians, carrying Christianity to the "heathen," and evangelizing the frontier. Since the seventeenth century Protestant missions had been the province of men; now—in this latest period of enthusiasm—women began to take part.

In 1800 a woman named Mary Webb organized fourteen Baptist and Congregational women into the Boston Female Society for Missionary Purposes and set off a chain reaction which spread through New England and into the West and South. Women's missionary groups took a number of different names: Cent Societies, Fragment Societies, or Maternal Associations, but, whatever the name, the patterns of development were similar.

One historian calls missionary groups "the font of all organized women's activities in the churches and to some extent in the community." He could have added that they also had provided a significant stimulus to the development of higher education and created one of the first professional careers open to women.[20]

In the very early stages women met to pray for the salvation of the world and to raise money which they turned over to the men's missionary organizations. Ministers and laymen welcomed their contributions, while reminding them that the Bible did not confer on women the right to be "public teachers." However, like the women in the benevolent societies, the members of missionary associations grew rapidly in confidence and independence and demonstrated great facility both in developing varieties of organizations and multiplying goals.

No sooner had the first group of missionaries departed for India in 1812 than women at home began to educate themselves and teach their children about that distant part of the world. Overlapping memberships provided them with links to many other women's groups, so the missionary impulse spilled over into charitable societies while missionary groups sometimes undertook local benevolence. Almost at once this integration of women into the missionary enterprise led to the unanticipated consequence that some of them began to express a desire to go beyond supporting male missionaries and to become missionaries themselves.

Men who ran the various missionary boards shook their heads at the suggestion that unmarried women might become missionaries, but expressed themselves as heartily in favor of missionary wives. Not only did they agree that a male missionary could hardly be expected to carry out his heavy responsibilities without the support of a homemaker, but in the relentless ethnocentrism of the time they felt that the example of Christian home life could be an important contribution to "civilizing" the heathen. Thus while the administrators of the various missionary societies refused to accept single women as independent applicants, these same women were encouraged, even directly helped, to find missionaries to marry.

What must have been the thoughts of two young missionary brides, whose only route to their chosen career had been through matrimony, as they listened to a farewell sermon exhorting them to "enlighten" the women of India: "Go then, and do all in your power, to enlighten their minds, and bring them to the knowledge of the truth. Go, and if possible, raise their character to the dignity of rational beings, and to the rank of Christians in a Christian land. Teach them to realize they are not an inferior race of creatures but stand upon a par with men."[21] Whatever their private thoughts, they and others like them soon marked out a distinctive role for wives in the missionary endeavor, for they began almost at once to create schools for the women and children in the communities to which they were sent.

As they did so their work became the focus for their sisters at home who prayed and raised money specifically for these female endeavors; "women's work for women" became the slogan of women's missionary societies. A body of evangelical literature grew up around these presumably self-sacrificing wives who, however indirectly, were forging a new career for women. Abroad they could do much that was still forbidden at home.

The first woman to be allowed to go overseas as a missionary in her own right was a widow, who was presumed to have profited enough from her years of marriage to present a smaller risk than a young single woman. Even so, her appointment was the subject of anxious correspondence among the men in charge of the American Board of Foreign Missions, who breathed a collective sigh of relief when she married a British missionary in India and assumed a more acceptable role as his assistant. By the late 1820s—after missionary wives in various places had demonstrated their ability to organize and administer schools for girls— single women who had been trained as teachers began to receive appointments in their own right.

The other areas of missionary concern, the western Indians and the frontier settlements, were more available for single women. Indeed, preparing teachers for the West was a central purpose of the first teacher-training seminaries, so much so that they became to some extent a part of the missionary enterprise. As more and more women found a vocation in teaching and headed west, some traveled explicitly under missionary auspices; others, going on their own or sent by Catharine Beecher or Mary Lyon, saw their task in a missionary light.[22]

By the 1830s a pattern of establishing voluntary associations for various kinds of self-help had developed among the more than 300,000 free black people in the United States. While black men created various societies for mutual improvement, as well as to work against slavery, for moral reform, and to distribute Bibles and tracts, black women in Philadelphia, New York, Buffalo, Rochester, and Boston initiated literary societies. Records of these groups are scanty, and much of the evidence for their existence must be drawn from the files of the *Liberator*, but as far as can now be determined their original purpose was educational, though some—like their white counterparts—slipped over into political action as well as into philanthropy.

Black women also formed benevolent societies, which in form and substance were indistinguishable from those of their white counterparts. In 1839 the Abyssinian Benevolent Daughters of Esther Association adopted a constitution and by-laws as a mutual aid society which could provide sick benefits for members "provided the sickness is not a result of immoral conduct."[23]

While charitable, benevolent, and missionary societies were first on the ground, in short order a bewildering variety of women's associations became a standard part of life in almost every part of the country. By the late 1840s moral reform, education, temperance, antislavery, and women's rights societies existed along with the older benevolent and charitable groups, and with various more ephemeral groups. In addition there were auxiliaries of the national Tract Society, Bible Society, and Sunday School Union. Among the women in the early textile mills female labor reform associations foreshadowed the movement for labor organization.[24]

Mary Ryan's careful study of the moral reform associations in Utica, New York, in the 1840s turned up more than a dozen women's groups in that comparatively small city of 12,000. An old filopietistic volume called *Women of Cleveland* shows clearly a frontier town developing into a settled community, knit together by an expanding web of women's associations providing welfare, policing behavior, and initiating reform on every hand.[25]

In these places as in so many others there was so much overlapping membership and convergence of purpose that it is impossible to devise neat categories. In retrospect the proliferation of groups seems on the surface at least to have been wasteful of time and resources. Why should a flourishing missionary society, for example, establish a separate maternal association in which young mothers could provide support to one another in the difficult challenge of raising Christian children? Why should the same women join four or five associations instead of concentrating their energies? What behooved a woman such as the implicit heroine of *Women of Cleveland*, Rebecca Cromwell Rouse, to lead not one but half a dozen societies?

One might speculate that multiplying societies gave more women a chance to learn the skills of leadership, but such a possibility would not explain the tendency of the same woman to join a number of societies. Whatever the anwer to those questions, Rouse was enough of a type to warrant a closer look. Coming along two generations after Graham, she represented much the same type of leadership in a frontier community that Graham had exhibited in New York. Rebecca Cromwell had been born in Salem, Massachusetts, in 1799, converted in 1810, and married in 1817 to a veteran of the War of 1812 who had begun life as a mason. In 1825 the Rouses moved to New York, where they came under the influence of Arthur Tappan, and began to work as tract distributors for the Sunday School Union, visiting "the byways and worst localities of the metropolis." In 1830 the union sent them to Cleveland as missionaries. When they arrived in 1830, the town contained about a thousand inhabitants, and during their first week Mrs. Rouse "gathered about her several good women" and launched a Women's Union for Gospel Work and a Ladies Tract Society.

For the rest of her long life this woman assumed leadership of one group after another. Thirty years of constant activity prepared her to take on a large part of the responsibility for organizing and administering the Soldiers' Aid Society of Northern Ohio at the outbreak of the Civil War, an organization which finally gave to her the opportunity to use her executive abilities: "Once she had three gunboats at her service on the Ohio River, and was aboard one of them when mattresses were hung about the pilot house to shield the pilot from rebel bullets."[26]

Rouse was not the only leader among Cleveland women, but she epitomized a common phenomenon—the capable executive who galvanized many women into action. A male doctor who gathered material for a volume entitled *Heroines of the Rebellion* identified this recurrent pattern when he wrote, with normal nineteenth-century hyperbole: "In the ten thousand Soldiers Aid Societies which at one time or another probably existed in the country, there was in each some master spirit, whose consecrated purpose was the staple in the wall, from which the chain of service hung and on whose strength and firmness it steadily drew. I never visited a single town however obscure, that I did not hear some woman's name . . . round which the rest of the women gladly rallied."[27]

Rebecca Rouse's diary, which might have told us something of how she perceived her vast range of activities, appears to have been lost, but another diary, that of the wife of an early Illinois governor, provides some insight into the part associations played in the life of one who was a member rather than a leader.

Elizabeth Smith Duncan, born in 1808 and educated in Newark, New Jersey, had been a Sunday school teacher. In the same year the Rouses went to Cleveland, the Duncan family settled in Jacksonville, Illinois, where ten children were born before Mrs. Duncan was widowed at thirty-five. She went regularly to a women's prayer group, a missionary society, a maternal association, and a sewing circle as well as to the Society for the Education of Females. Occasionally she also attended meetings on abolition and colonization. All of this was, of course, in addition to regular church attendance.

She often noted in her diary that the discussion in one of her societies had been interesting or that she had enjoyed the female prayer meeting. Occasionally she noted her fund-raising efforts on behalf of "the education of Females." She also helped raise money for a circulating library.

While her husband lived she was almost continually pregnant or nursing, a fact reflected in many notations of ill health, but she was rarely too ill to attend meetings, which were her chief source of intellectual and moral stimulation. Upon one occasion she "reflected considerably about the trials of the Missionarys and asked myself whether I would be willing to let my children go to the heathen & I could not but say I felt reluctant." When, in her widowhood, bad weather or bad health prevented her from going to meetings of her societies she recorded her disappointment in terms of missing the religious conversation of friends.[28]

Institutional and personal records document the same fact: by 1860 most American communities of any size, particularly in the North and Middle West, had developed a dense web of women's associations for a wide variety of formal purposes. These groups displayed a marked tendency to multiply their responsibilities over time. Missionary societies undertook local welfare work, benevolent associations built libraries, antislavery societies engaged in philanthropy, moral reform groups established magazines, city missions, and orphan asylums, and temperance societies organized reading rooms with tea and coffee for those who needed an alternative to the saloon. This fluidity of function permitted a general convergence of purposes, which was further reinforced by the shared leadership and overlapping membership.

Whatever their original or acquired goals, nearly every group developed an educational component. Members sought to educate themselves, or other people, or both. All agreed that education was the basis for creating a moral and a prosperous society, and only a virtuous republic was apt to survive. "True knowledge inspires the love of virtue," wrote an educational reformer in 1848, who could have been speaking for any of the woman's associations, all of which shared an extraordinary reliance upon the printed word as an instrument of salvation.[29]

Improved technology had reduced the cost of printing and made possible an outpouring of inspirational biographies, moral tales, and juvenile literature for distribution by various groups. The demand for such works had the further consequence of offering employment to a host of aspiring women writers. Bible societies aimed to put a Bible in every hand, temperance societies exhorted citizens in print as well as in person, antislavery associations encouraged former slaves to set down their life histories, which could serve as propaganda for their cause. Not only the effort to convert individuals but also the effort to reform the society came to depend upon literacy. This dependence had far-reaching consequences for the education of women upon whom the responsibility for creating a literate population would come to rest.

The assumptions and activities of the Ladies' Education Society of Jacksonville, Illinois, founded in 1833 when the town itself was new, provide a case in point. A group of women, many of whom were already members of various religious associations, began to worry about the children in the still undeveloped parts of Illinois who were growing up illiterate. Their response to this concern was to "assist young ladies to qualify themselves for teaching." They took the ambitious step of bringing into their association women from other parts of the state and set out to raise money for scholarships and to identify possible recipients. They got off to a fast start: by the third year they had not only found forty-five young women to educate, but also they had somehow created an auxiliary society in the East to help raise money. In twenty years time, with help from their eastern supporters, this group raised and spent more than $7,000 for the education of more than 500 women. Most of these young persons justified the aid they had received by becoming teachers, and a number became home or foreign missionaries.[30]

In their own time most of the women's associations would have subscribed to the purpose offered in one benevolent constitution: "Feeling the obligation binding upon us as Christians to help those that are needy and destitute . . . that we may hereby in some degree imitate our blessed Master . . . do hereby mutually agree to form ourselves into a society for the furtherance of our blessed cause."[31] With the advantage of hindsight we can see that they were also initiating a broad social movement which, once begun, would roll on through the century, picking up momentum until it could be described, in the words of a nineteenth-century man, as "the great movement for the elevation of woman."[32]

In the shorter run they were also shaping community values by their own lights, lights sometimes shared with the army of benevolent men but which were sometimes very much their own. Women's voluntary associations pervaded community life and thus helped to form the developing republican culture. They represented a mix of localism and nationalism. Many were concerned only with one community, but, while "American society" was still a congeries of local and regional societies, women were creating networks that brought them in touch with one another across considerable distances.

Unknown to themselves they were preparing the way for a great flowering of women's associational effort during the crisis of the Civil War and throughout the last half of the nineteenth century.

NOTES

1. Frank Warren Crow, "The Age of Promise: Societies for Social and Economic Improvement in the U.S., 1783-1815" (Ph.D. diss., University of Wisconsin, 1952), introduction.

2. Lyle Koehler, *A Search for Power: The "Weaker Sex" in Seventeenth-Century New England* (Urbana, 1980). Ch. 8 provides a convenient summary of the familiar Hutchinson story.

3. Gertrude Bosler Biddle and Sarah Dickinson Lowrie, *Notable Women of Pennsylvania* (Philadelphia, 1942), pp. 59-60 and passim.

4. Crow, "Age of Promise," p. 475; "Hannah Mather Crocker," in Edward James, Janet James, and Paul S. Boyer, eds., *Notable American Women, 1607-1950* (Cambridge, Mass., 1971), 1:406-7.

5. The work of a number of historians has provided the basis for my thinking about the interaction between voluntary associations and women's education. Donald Mathews, "The Second Great Awakening as an Organizing Process," *American Quarterly*, 21 (1969), 23-43, provides the context for the epidemic of women's associations. Among the most useful monographs and articles are Crow, "Age of Promise"; Keith Melder, "Ladies Bountiful: Organized Women's Benevolence in Early 19th Century America," *New York History*, 65 (1967); Carroll Smith Rosenberg, *Religion and the Rise of the City* (Ithaca, 1971); Nancy L. Cott, *Bonds of Womanhood: "Woman's Sphere" in New England, 1780-1830* (New Haven, 1977); Gerda Lerner, *The Majority Finds Its Past* (New York, 1979). In *The Remembered Gate: Origins of American Feminism* (New York, 1978), Barbara Berg builds upon and extends Rosenberg's pioneering work on the moral reform societies but for some reason treats them as solely an urban phenomenon. R. Pierce Beaver's *All Love's Excelling: American Protestant Women in World Mission* (Grand Rapids, 1968) is indispensable for the early missionary societies. Anne Mary Boylan, " 'The Nursery of the Church': Evangelical Protestant Sunday Schools, 1820-1880" (Ph.D. diss., University of Wisconsin, 1973), provides good background for the Sunday School Union. Janet Wilson James gives much useful material in the book of which she is editor: *Women in American Religion* (Philadelphia, 1980). See especially the chapter by Barbara Welter, "She Hath Done What She Could: Protestant Women's Missionary Careers in the Nineteenth Century." Florence Hayes's *Daughters of Dorcas* (New York, 1952) complements

Beaver's work and has a helpful list of charitable, benevolent, and missionary societies in the first half of the nineteenth century.

6. Arthur M. Schlesinger, Sr., "Biography of a Nation of Joiners," *American Historical Review*, 50 (Oct. 1944), 1-25. Schlesinger is especially useful on the subject of the national associations which organized local units.

7. Fredrika Bremer, *The Homes of the New World: Impressions of America*, trans. Mary Howitt (New York, 1854), 2:153.

8. See Linda Kerber, *Women of the Republic* (Chapel Hill, 1981); Berg, *Remembered Gate*; Karen Blair, *The Clubwoman as Feminist* (New York, 1980); and Anne Firor Scott, *The Southern Lady: From Pedestal to Politics, 1830-1930* (Chicago, 1970), for evidence and examples of women of ambition.

9. Crow, "Age of Promise," pp. 459-61.

10. Joanna Bethune, ed., *The Power of Faith Exemplified in the Life and Writings of the Late Mrs. Isabella Graham* (New York, 1843).

11. It is indicative that books about Isabella Graham (and many another benevolent woman) were published by the American Tract Society.

12. Bethune, ed., *Graham*, pp. 249-51.

13. New York *Times*, Dec. 6, 1959, 91, carried a half-page story on the Graham Home for Children in Hastings-on-Hudson, the most recent permutation of the Orphan Asylum. The institution had moved to Hastings in 1902 and in 1959 was appealing for public support to enable it to survive. The *Times* mistakenly identified it as the first orphanage in the country. In fact, women in Savannah, Boston, and Baltimore had founded earlier ones.

14. Professor Suzanne Lebsock of Douglass College supplied information about the Petersburg Orphan Asylum. For Raleigh, see *Revised Constitution and By-Laws of the Raleigh Female Benevolent Society, with Reports of the Society from Its Commencement* (1823); for Savannah, see Mrs. B. F. Bullard, "The Savannah Female Asylum," manuscript in the Georgia Historical Society, Savannah.

15. Mary Bosworth Treudley, "The 'Benevolent Fair': A Study of Charitable Organization among American Women in the First Third of the Nineteenth Century," *Social Service Review* 14 (1940), 509-22. In this thoughtful analysis Treudley analyzes the difficulties which arose almost from the beginning as women tried to provide work relief and shows how the first efforts at social investigation grew out of the work of the benevolent societies.

16. *Ibid.*, 513; see also Rosenberg, *Religion and the Rise of the City*, p. 158, where she argues that women were less likely than men to blame the poor for their poverty.

17. Mary F. Kihlstrom, "The Morristown Female Charitable Society," *Journal of Presbyterian History*, 58 (Fall 1980).

18. Minutes of the Chesterfield Female Benevolent Society, Hopkinton, N.H., Feb. 23, 1844–Sept. 22, 1847, mss. volume in the Schlesinger Library, Radcliffe College, Cambridge, Mass. The Female Missionary Society of Rindge, N.H., in 1814 agreed "to expose one another's infirmities, and not to talk about trifling things . . . unless such talk contributed to God's glory." Another group in Batavia, N.Y., agreed to "avoid all evil speaking against one another, whether they be present at the time or absent." See Hayes, *Daughters of Dorcas*, p. 13.

Daughters is particularly valuable for its list of more than 100 female societies organized between 1803 and 1853, a list which Hayes says "cannot possibly be complete." The list includes "interesting items and anecdotes that have come to us from the old records and other sources."

19. Jack Larkin, "An Extended Link in the Great Chain of Benevolence, the Shrewsbury Charitable Society, 1832-1842," Oct. 1979, Community in Change Interpretive Paper, Old Sturbridge Village, Mass.

20. Beaver, *All Love's Excelling*, pp. 11-19.

21. *Ibid*, p. 82.

22. Kathryn Kish Sklar, *Catharine Beecher: A Study in American Domesticity* (New Haven, 1973), ch. 12.

23. Daniel Perlman, "Organizations of the Free Negro in New York City 1800-1820," *Journal of Negro History*, 56 (July 1971), 181-87. See also Dorothy Porter, "The Organized Educational Activities of Negro Literary Societies," *Journal of Negro Education*, 5 (Oct. 1936), 555-76.

24. Thomas Dublin, *Women at Work* (New York, 1980), pp. 100-1, 108-9, 116-17, 121, 204-5. For women's antislavery activities, see Lerner, *The Majority Finds Its Past*, ch. 8, and Judith Wellman, "Women and Radical Reform in Antebellum Upstate New York," in Mabel Deutrich and Virginia Prudy, eds., *Clio Was a Woman* (Washington, D.C., 1980), pp. 113-27.

25. Mary Ryan, "The Power of Women's Networks," *Feminist Studies*, 6 (Spring 1980), and Mrs. A. W. Ingham, *Women of Cleveland* (Cleveland, 1893).

26. Ingham, *Women of Cleveland*. Ingham was herself a case study in the relationship between voluntary associations and education. A teacher, she had joined the Women's Missionary Society soon after it was founded, and her educational career developed *pari passu* with her work in associations. Rebecca Rouse's papers are in the Western Reserve Historical Society, Cleveland, Ohio, as are those of the Soldier's Aid Society of Northern Ohio.

27. L. P. Brockett, *Heroines of the Rebellion; or Woman's Work in the Civil War* (Philadelphia, 1888), 43.

28. "Diary of Mrs. Joseph Duncan," *Journal of Illinois Historical Society*, 21 (1920), 1-88. See p. 65 for her reflections on missionary life.

29. Lawrence Cremin, *American Education: The National Experience, 1789-1876* (New York, 1980), ch. 2.

30. Clara Moore, "The Ladies Education Society of Jacksonville, Illinois," *Illinois State Historical Society Journal*, 18 (1925), 196-200.

31. Minutes of the Chesterfield Ladies Benevolent Society.

32. Henry Fowler, "Educational Services of Mrs. Emma Willard," in Henry Barnard, ed., *Memoirs of Teachers, Educators, and Promoters and Benefactors of Education, Literature and Science* (New York, 1861), p. 167.

Women's Voluntary
Associations in the Forming
of American Society

This essay began as a lecture in honor of the twentieth anniversary of the Mary I. Bunting Institute at Radcliffe College, Cambridge, Massachusetts. It was called "If Outsiders Become Insiders, What Then?" and stirred considerable controversy, which it has continued to do as I have modified and presented it to various audiences. I think it now has the germ of a useful idea, but it needs more development. I am more convinced that women's associations constituted the social justice wing of the Progressive movement than I am of the argument that we are in danger of losing "outsiders." No matter how many barriers women break—and they have broken a good many lately—women will for a long time be outside the main centers of power. Furthermore, one consequence of the hard times of the 1980s has been a resurgence of voluntarism, so it may be that the next chapter in women's history will include new ways of using voluntary associations to circumvent the existing structures.

"When the history of the nineteenth century comes to be written," wrote Mrs. J. C. Croly in her massive *History of the Woman's Club Movement*, published in 1898, "women will appear as organizers, and as leaders of the great organized movements among their own sex for the first time in the history of the world." More than eighty years later the subject of women's voluntary associations has yet to be treated as an integral part of nineteenth-century social history. So far no one has asked and tried to answer the question: How did these thousands of associations shape social development in the United States? Indeed, this critical question has not been asked about voluntary associations in general, of which women's groups were a special case. This is all the more surprising, since this particular form of social organization was identified more than 150 years ago as central to the development of American society. Alexis de Tocqueville is often quoted: "The Americans make associations to give entertainments, to found seminaries, to build inns, to construct churches, to diffuse books, to send missionaries to the antipodes; in this manner they found hospitals, prisons, and schools. If it is proposed to inculcate some truth or to foster some feeling by the encouragement of a great example, they form a society."[1] But this insight has not led to much serious historical analysis.

His observations, and similar ones coming from Americans, were made at a time when the social force of voluntary associations was in its infancy compared to what it would become as the nineteenth century wore on. Yet scholars in various disciplines have been slow to examine this institutional form in any depth or to formulate the theoretical issues it presents. Sociologists, though they have written voluminously on the subject, have been chiefly concerned with establishing typologies. Political scientists have praised the voluntary association for its presumed contribution to democratic practice and have assumed that the right of free association is basic to our political system, but they, too, have been slow to pay sustained attention to the internal dynamics of associational life or to the way voluntary groups function as part of the political system.[2] With one or two exceptions, historians until quite recently simply ignored the whole subject.[3] A multidisciplinary bibliographical survey conducted in the late 1960s led its authors to conclude that the whole field of study was "in great disarray" and that there was little agreement upon categories for analysis or even upon what questions ought to be asked.[4]

Now a change is in the making, and voluntary associations are beginning to receive long overdue scholarly attention.[5] Some of this change is the work of historians interested in urban development or community development (I think particularly of Richard Brown and Don Harrison Doyle), but much of it is coming from historians of women. Here as in so many other places we find that by asking "what were women doing" we uncover important social forces which have hitherto been overlooked. Studies of particular groups and organizations are multiplying: It was particularly noticeable at the Berkshire Conference at Vassar where I found myself rather desperately hopping around the campus trying to tune in on all the voluntary association talk.

What I would like to do here is to offer first a sketch in broad strokes of the way women's voluntary associations developed as part of the American social scene before 1920 and then to suggest some of the ways in which that development affected both women and the society.

Discussing nineteenth-century social history without analyzing the effect of women's voluntary associations is somewhat akin to discussing plant growth without mentioning photosynthesis. Many other elements went into the making of American society, of course, but if women's associations had not existed much would have been different. One startled student of early benevolent associations remarked that it was as if a clock had struck in 1800 and suddenly women everywhere were forming organizations. Both in established settlements and in the new ones just coming into existence such groups began to meet a wide variety of community needs. Particularly in new settlements there was often a rough division of labor: men associated for one set of purposes, women for another.[6] As the embers of the Great Awakening began to come to life, evangelical women seemed to find organization the natural way to seek salvation and to try to save others. Charitable, benevolent, and missionary societies expressed evangelical zeal and were soon followed by a variety of moral reform and welfare groups: temperance, abolition, education, health reform, employment societies, prison reform, and many others. At a time when no government at any level took much responsibility for what we now call human services, women's groups set out to fill these needs. Sometimes they cooperated with men; sometimes they worked alone.

With the coming of the Civil War, women's habit of organizing for social ends came into bold relief as thousands of soldiers' aid societies erupted, in the North and South. It is particularly notable to find so much of this sort of activity among southern women scattered as they were, for the most part, in small communities and rural settings. In the North women's groups in hundreds of towns and cities organized and ran the local units of the giant Sanitary Commission and raised money to keep the work going. When the war ended, they rapidly converted themselves into agencies for serving the needs of returning veterans (again, the government had not yet assumed much of this responsibility). The woman in Cleveland of whom it was said that she "put on her hat and shawl the instant Sumter was fired upon, and scarce took them off until the Rebellion was subdued" may be taken as typical. The records of the Soldiers' Aid Society of Northern Ohio, which happen to be well preserved, provide an illuminating case study of the growth of female leadership and responsibility under the exigent pressures of a Civil War.[7]

Whether it was the memory of the excitement they had experienced during the war or a response to the needs growing out of the rapid urban growth which followed — or other causes not yet clearly understood — the last thirty years of the nineteenth century witnessed an exponential growth in women's organizations. By 1900 they formed a dense network which spread through every town and village and embraced millions of women.[8]

These associations fall roughly into categories: first, church-related groups, which were a direct descendant of the prewar missionary and benevolent societies; second, the Woman's Christian Temperance Union, which was also a direct descendant of the evangelical movement and which under the national leadership of Frances Willard and the local leadership of hundreds of extraordinary women trained thousands of self-styled "home-loving, law-abiding women" to be social activists. Women's clubs, of several different kinds depending upon location and local leadership, made up a third category, and, finally, the two national suffrage associations with their hundreds of local affiliates were a fourth.

Periodization for this subject is fairly clear-cut at one end: there were no significant number of women's voluntary associations in 1790 (at least that we yet know about), and by 1800 the numbers were growing rapidly. At the other end there is, of course, no end. In various forms women's voluntary associations are a major part of American life in the 1980s. However, for the purpose of manageability, this article does not look much beyond 1920. The passage of the suffrage amendment did mark something of a turning point: after they were enfrancised women formed new kinds of groups and when they had direct access to the political process, methods changed somewhat.

In the first two decades of the twentieth century almost every woman who had attained a degree of visibility in local, state, or national affairs had either gotten her start in a voluntary association, been supported by one, or belonged to several for prudential reasons. This was just as true of women professionals and scholars as it was of reformers — something which is not so often the case today.

The most obvious way in which voluntary associations had brought about social change was by creating a public role for women who, deprived by custom and law of access to the formal, male-dominated institutions — government, politics, the church, business, the universities, law, and medicine—had slowly worked their way to social power by organizing and operating their own groups. Forming societies came as naturally to enterprising nineteenth-century women as creating business firms or organizing railroads did to amibitious men. While the social shibboleth was that "woman's place" was in the home, the fact was that for a certain kind of woman (generally, but not always, of the middle class) "woman's place" was clearly in the voluntary association.

This process of inventing a public role in a setting which, in theory, did not permit them to have one, had considerable influence upon the personalities and life experiences of individual women. Women activists and those who observed them testified to the growth in self-confidence that came as a result of their experience within all-woman groups. Together with the women's colleges, voluntary associations were the most significant incubators of the new woman.

In addition to what the voluntary associations did for women we must ask: What effect did their existence and their method of operating have upon the developing society?

This is clearly a very complex question and one that requires many hours to answer convincingly. Generalizing rather broadly, I would suggest, first, that all-women groups, when they began to work on community or public problems, inevitably brought into the mainstream some of the values which the society had for so long imputed to women and which so many women had internalized. Women's groups also provided one important conduit through which evangelical Protestantism became inextricably interwoven with social reform. Women were expected to be compassionate and to be preservers of social order. They were also expected to be good Christians.

One consequence of this application of what were usually considered to be typically female values to problems outside their own homes was that some women came gradually, explicitly or implicitly, to question the prevailing value structure of the society. As outsiders they often had what Robert Merton in his well-known essay "Insiders and Outsiders" called the "special perspective and insights available to that category of outsiders who have been systematically frustrated by the social system" and who as a result of that experience were sensitized to "the workings of the culture that were more apt to be taken for granted by the Insider."[9]

Women taking responsibility for charity were inevitably brought in touch with the people who were suffering rather than benefitting from the great American success story, and whether they planned to or not, at

least some of these women began to analyze the problems they encountered, began to ask themselves why the needs they sought to meet had
come into being. Without ever formulating the idea in words, they began
to undertake the task of humanizing the rapidly growing industrial society.[10]

I should stop a moment to say that while I intend to describe the
ways in which certain women's groups raised significant social issues and
at least implicitly questioned the prevailing assumptions of society I do
not intend to celebrate them as always right. Like all of us, they were
creatures of a particular time and place. We are all limited by our own
capacities; we all reflect to some extent the values and prejudices of our
particular reference groups. Furthermore, while women may have had the
clarity of vision which comes from not sharing the benefits of a particular
social system, they also had the disadvantage of inadequate access to
education and to the kinds of experience which might have improved
their analysis of social and economic problems.

So I do not come here to tell you that women on their knees praying
in saloons fully understood either the psychological roots of alcoholism
or the economics of the distilling business; I will not argue that the ideal
of converting the world to Christianity was the most appropriate alternative
to the ideal of turning the globe into a vast source of raw materials and
markets for a growing capitalist economy. Nor do I intend to suggest
that all the important challenges to the status quo came from women.
There were plenty of men whose ethical commitments and attachment
to Christian ideals led them to question the prevailing values. There were
important male critics in the ranks of socialists, anarchists, or single-
taxers. However, the history of the male critics has been well documented;
that of the women, not so well. Until we understand both, and the ways
in which they differ, our analysis of social change and value shifts is
bound to be incomplete.

In their earliest associations some women moved from simply providing aid to the needy to asking questions about the causes of poverty.
Their analysis was a simple one: ignorance leads to vice and vice leads to
poverty. Therefore, they undertook to go to the root of the matter by
creating a wide variety of educational opportunities for the young,
especially among the poor. They also became strong proponents of
universal public education as basic to the survival of the republic.

Some of my colleagues argue that the interest in universal education
was a defensive maneuver on the part of well-to-do people who sought
to control the lower classes by putting their children in school and

inculcating the virtues of industry, punctuality, and self-control, which would make them peaceful citizens and good factory workers. I think that is oversimple. It is true that most nineteenth-century community leaders, women as well as men, were concerned about social order. But it seems important to note that the virtues women hoped to promote through education were precisely the ones they themselves sought to live by, which means that the individual goal was moral behavior and the social goal was a virtuous society. "Aha," says the critic, "you have just admitted that the middle-class women were trying to impose their values on the poor." To which one can only respond, yes, to be sure—but with the purpose not of keeping them in their place but of helping them cease to be poor. Breaking the cycle of poverty was a phrase which came into use in Lyndon Johnson's day, but this idea was formulated a century earlier in certain women's benevolent societies.

If we turn from the charitable societies to the parallel development of women's missionary societies, we see again some of the consequences of the difference between women's world view and the dominant one.

The nineteenth-century missionary movement began when an enthusiastic group of young college men dedicated their lives to evangelizing the frontier and the world. Missionary boards, made up—of course—of men, were created to oversee the enterprise. These boards encouraged the women's missionary associations to raise money, while at the same time constantly reminding them of their inferior status in St. Paul's scheme of life. The men were shocked, however, when one result of the women's intense interest in the cause led young single women to volunteer to serve as missionaries. They hastily advised these upstart women to fulfill their ambitions by finding a male missionary in need of a wife.[11] A good many took this advice and once overseas found that they were able to carve out a special role for themselves in societies where the female subculture was inaccessible to male missionaries.

The missionary wife, who had often been a school teacher, was imbued with the notion that there were womanly concerns which were common to all cultures (bearing and raising children, for example). She went to work with the local women to organize schooling for the young, especially for girls. I do not want to make more of this than the evidence will yet bear, but it seems to me at least worth examining the hypothesis that the nature of her experience was such that the missionary wife had a better chance than her husband did to be shaken out of ethnocentrism—to begin to understand a foreign culture in its own terms.

We do know that the "women's work for women" of missionary wives, stoutly supported by the missionary societies at home, proved so important that in time the barriers were lowered and single women were permitted to go as missionaries. Whether in Oregon or China such women had more scope for an independent career than would have been possible at home. Women doctors, for example, pioneered the role of medical missionaries wherein they could practice medicine with fewer constraints than their counterparts in New York and Boston.

Benevolent societies and missionary societies were the beginning; they were quickly followed by more specialized groups. By the 1830s and 1840s temperance organizations, Bible societies, tract societies, antislavery groups, and women's education associations were to be found all over the Northeast and Middle West, and some parts of the South. Some were independent and of local origin; others were auxiliary to male groups or were creatures of a national organization. But whatever their nature and purpose the evidence suggests that women's groups developed a slightly different angle of vision from that of their male contemporaries.

Take the abolitionists. While the men (when they were not arguing about women's rights to speak in their meetings) were thundering about the sins of southerners, members of the female antislavery society were announcing their conviction that actions spoke louder than words. We must, they said, show our good faith "by sitting with [black people] in the churches, appearing with them on the street . . . visiting them in their homes and encouraging them to visit us, receiving them as we do our fellow white citizens." Certainly all abolitionists were outsiders, but women were doubly so since they were often denigrated even within the antislavery movement. They responded in part by working harder and in part by putting their fingers upon a most vulnerable point: the actual treatment of black people by the men who were so concerned about ending their slavery.[12]

In the realm of education obstacles again led to innovation. The female seminaries, which were themselves a form of voluntary association, tried to contradict the conventional wisdom that women's brains could not cope with mathematics or Greek. They did this in part by pedagogical and curriculum innovation. While the faculties of Harvard, Yale, and Brown (to pick examples at random) were still relying on the deadly system of a memorized daily lesson recited to the teacher, their female counterparts were studying Johann Pestalozzi and experimenting with what today is labeled the inquiry method. They inaugurated laboratory science for undergraduates and led the way in introducing modern languages. I am not sure that the faculty in men's colleges would have admitted to learning anything directly from the women's example, but it is instructive to read the comments of the professors who conducted public examinations at various female seminaries as they note surprise that the young women seem genuinely able to think out answers to questions in math or science and do not seem to be depending upon rote learning. Comments such as this from one examiner—"I do not hesitate to say that the young ladies possess as thorough an acquaintance with the subject (in this case philosophy) as the graduating class of any college in the country"—suggest that attention might have eventually been directed to the pedagogy in use.[13]

By 1848 one small group of women was bold enough to launch a critique of the Constitution itself, demanding the right to vote. Harking back to the Declaration of Independence and the slogan of "no taxation without representation," they initiated a battle that lasted for seventy-two years. When the nineteenth amendment was finally ratified, Carrie Chapman Catt summed up the cost. I will not take time to repeat her whole text, but here are some of the statistics: 56 state referenda . . . 480 legislative campaigns . . . 277 party conventions . . . 19 campaigns with 19 successive congresses. It was, she said, "a continuous and seemingly endless chain of activity. Young suffragists who helped forge the last links were not born when it began. Old suffragists who helped forge the first links were dead when it ended."[14]

Perhaps her recital only makes you weary. From another angle, however, one might say: How better to keep alive the basic discussion of the meaning of political participation which must go on if a democratic society is to flourish? Of course, I will not carry that to the absurd length of wishing that our grandmothers had not won the vote for us, but I offer the suffrage campaign as another piece in this mounting pile of evidence that women as outsiders were through the whole century providing vital criticism of the status quo.

Paralleling the long travail of the suffragists there was almost an explosion of women's groups raising questions about a host of fundamental issues. By the 1890s there were so many that even a selective list is in danger of growing unwieldly.

I have said before that education was at the heart of much of women's work, and so it continued to be as kindergarten associations inaugurated early childhood education, as ladies library societies dotted

the Middle West with libraries, as education societies helped to create
(among others) Radcliffe, Pembroke, and Goucher, as literary societies
provided women with some of the higher education they had missed.
Numbers of museums, art galleries, and symphony orchestras, as well as
colleges, hospitals, and a host of other institutions, were the work of
women's groups.

Then there was what we call "community improvement"—the first
group with this as its stated purpose seems to have appeared in Stockbridge,
Massachusetts, in 1853. From creating parks and playgrounds to inspecting
milk or renovating slum housing, women in thousands of communities
were involved in what today would be labeled improving the quality of
life.

I want to include, in their own words, a description of one such
group because I think that this presentation tells you more about a
number of aspects of this phenomenon than I could do with the most
careful paraphrase.

The Woman's Health Protective Association, New York, began in
the autumn of 1884, with a simple morning call made by one woman
upon another in the neighborhood of Beekman Hill: a high bluff over-
looking the East River, and forming a residential district of exceptional
beauty.

The locality, in many respects so desirable, was so polluted with foul
odors that it was impossible to keep the windows open even in the
warmest weather: and the conditions which caused them became the
subject of conversation. The result was a meeting by invitation of a
number of the women whose homes were in the immediate vicinity, and
a subsequent tour of the adjacent neighborhoods in order to discover
exactly what the causes were that produced this state of things.

It was found that the region on First Avenue from Forty-third to
Forty-seventh Street was occupied by slaughter-houses—old wooden
structures reeking with filth, and made up of refuse and the blood of
animals, all mingling in streams in which the children of the streets
revelled and played, as other children play in the grass and under green
trees.

The horrors of this state of things were intensified by the use of the
docks to harbor stationary scows, in which the excrement and offal were
collected and kept, a perpetual threat to the health and comfort of the
crowded quarter.

The report to others of what they had seen increased the number
of the group to fifteen women, and it was these ladies who took the
initiative in organizing, in the drawingroom of one of them the Ladies'
Health Protective Association of New York.

The first effort of the new society was against the scow nuisance. The accumulation of manure was 20,000 tons, 30 feet in height and 200 feet in length. It was maintained by a brother-in-law of a senator in Albany, who was able by political backing to defy law and decency.

The manure in its decayed state was of much more value as a fertilizer, and the revenue was largely increased by letting the stuff remain there to rot, while an entire community was made to suffer. The first step was to obtain an indictment against the owner for maintaining a public nuisance. He cared very little for this action, as he had several indictments holding over him, which had always been pigeon-holed, and he thought this one would travel the same road. But it was his first experience with women, and he did not realize what that meant. He was tried before a Judge Barrett in the Court of Oyer and Terminer, and after a trial lasting for four days he was convicted, and found guilty of maintaining a public nuisance. Judge Barrett gave him thirty days in which to remove accumulation, and he was obliged to do it. Constant vigilance has been necessary since that time to prevent evasion of the law.

This was the beginning of the work. On the 9th of December, 1884, a State charter was secured, and the Ladies' Health Protective Association became a recognized organization for the sanitary improvement of the city. The signers of this charter were Mathilde F. Wendt, Mary E. Trautman, Cecelia Fendler, Hedwig Wile, and Irene E. Harland.

In those days officials were very indifferent, and looked with great disfavor upon any attempt to "interfere" with their neglect of duty. Antagonism met the women at every step, and the admission was made by the then president of the Health Board that he had neither visited nor had a report from that section of the city for six years.

The verdict obtained against the owner of the manure heaps was a great surprise, and a member of the Health Board remarked that the ladies "were not to build upon it, that it was very unusual, and they had better go home now, and not meddle any more in matters that did not concern them."

The next movement was against the slaughter-houses, which consisted of fifty-five rickety, tumbled-down wooden sheds.

The slaughtering was done in the presence of children, who stood before the doors, and became so utterly demoralized that the sight of blood was no more to them than so much running water. The walls and floors of these pens reeked with filth, and the meat, when slaughtered, was hung on large hooks over the curbstone, there to swarm with flies and catch all the dust and dirt of the neighborhood. The cattle were driven through the streets in droves, and when they reached the slaughter-houses were confined in cellars, the air of which was so stifling and fetid that the poor creatures could be seen clambering over each other in frantic efforts to reach up to the grating for a breath of fresh air. In the bone-boiling works, the odors were overpowering, and on investigation it was found that the bones were collected from the retail butchers whenever it best suited convenience regardless of whether they had remained a week or a month in the shops.

It took years of persistent and energetic work on the part of the Health Protective Association, now largely increased in numbers, and divided into legislative and other committees, to remedy this disorder. Bills brought before the Legislature were defeated, but it cost the Butchers' Association so much to do that the president finally said, "Gentlemen, if we have to pay out all this money we may as well put it into what the women want, for it is the thing that ought to be done."

The Executive Board of the Ladies Health Protective Association was invited to meet the executive of the Butchers' Association, and the result was the system of magnificent abattoirs that now exist on the East Side, and have rescued that entire district from conditions that were a disgrace to the metropolis.

The later work was greatly helped by the installation of a new president of the New York City Health Board, Mr. Charles G. Wilson. This gentleman was not only a conscientious, but practical business man, working hard himself, and requiring thorough work from his inspectors. His aid was given at every step, and he inspired confidence to such an extent that a complaint was all that was necessary, if it was based on a real evil, to have it remedied.

The later efforts of the Health Protective Association were directed to the odors from gas houses; the condition of the streets; the disposal of garbage; the blocking of the streets by trucks at night, and their use as a harbor for tramps; the condition of surface and elevated cars, owing to the habits of expectoration of men and boys; and other matters of detail.

Schools have occupied much time and thought, and the question of police matrons and women inspectors has received important aid and consideration.

These matters were greatly helped by the reorganization and better equipment of the street cleaning and police departments of the city. But it is not too much to say that the movement even in this direction was inspired by the practical, persistent effort, the wise judgment, and the genius for detail exercised by the Ladies' Health Protective Association.

During President Wilson's administration there was constant cooperation, and a spirit of reciprocal helpfulness exhibited between the Health Board of the city and the association. This was a marvelous change from the old days, and a great advantage on both sides. Every one who knows anything about municipal affairs knows that eternal vigilance is the price of order and decency. The Ladies' Health Protective Association finds plenty of ways in which to exercise its functions, but it has a right to satisfaction in the work it has accomplished and the respect it has won.

Eleven Health Protective Associations in other cities have grown out of the mother one in New York, all of them more or less inspired by its success, and the energetic leadership of its president, Mrs. Ralph Trautman, the vice-president for New York of the Woman's Auxiliary to the Columbian Exposition. Of these the associations of Brooklyn and Philadelphia are, perhaps, the most energetic, but the work and methods of all adopt themselves to environment, and show excellent results. They have usually preceded the formation of civic clubs, and embody more or less literary and social club features.

In 1891 a national charter was granted in the District of Columbia to the "Woman's" National Health Protective Association of the State of New York, signed by Clara Barton, Jane H. Spofford, Alice C. Fletcher, and Emily L. Sherwood, of the District of Columbia, and Margaret W. Ravenhill, Fannie I. Helmuth, and M. Louise Thomas, of the city of New York. Mrs. Mary E. Trautman, the president, Mrs. Mathilde F. Wendt, honorary president, and ten committees reported in active service.

The change from "Ladies" was made in accordance with a desire long existent, but suppressed in the beginning as a concession to the conventional spirit of the time.[15]

From the concerns which created the Woman's Health Protective Association, it was a short step to the reform groups that filled the landscape in the 1890s and after. The focus of attention nearly always began with women and children—sweatshop workers and children in the textile mills—and led steadily in the direction of ameliorative legislation. The intellecutal seedbed for the social welfare agenda of the Progressive movement lay in the woman-dominated settlement houses. When Jane Addams was criticized for seconding Theodore Roosevelt's nomination in 1912, she replied that she could not fail to support a party whose platform included nearly every one of the causes to which she had devoted her life. When Felix Frankfurter remarked that Florence Kelley was probably responsible for more social change than any other person in her generation, he could have added that from beginning to end her career was built on the support of women's voluntary associations.[16]

I have dwelt on the nineteenth century, but it would be easy to extend this analysis into the twentieth—we could examine, for example, the women's societies of the Southern Methodist Church, which as early as 1902 offered the first outspoken critique on the part of any white southerners of southern racial patterns. Or we could look at the Woman's International League for Peace and Freedom audaciously launching a peace movement in the midst of World War I. We could ask whether it was because women had less stake in the industrial system that the Women's Trade Union League and the Women's Educational and Industrial Union were able to cross class barriers with a degree of success. We could ask whether it was outsider status which permitted women in the YWCA and later in the League of Women Voters to advocate reforms which would adversely affect the business interests of their husbands. We could undertake some narrowly focused community studies to trace the web of women's groups meeting a wide variety of community needs. The historians who care about this subject have their work cut out.

A brief summary of the late nineteenth-century women's effect on social values would go something like this: Beginning in a period characterized by high immigration and proliferating urban problems, when economic theory justified subsistence wages and treating workers as expendable, when race relations were governed by the assumption that white Protestants of northern European origin occupied the top rung of the evolutionary ladder and therefore deserved to be on the top of all other ladders, the society came gradually to accept the need for collective responsibility for those least able to help themselves and came gradually to widen political participation to include first women and then blacks.

Bit by bit the questions first raised by women have found their way to the national agenda—issues of social justice, of preservation of the environment, of equal opportunity, and of international peace. I am constantly surprised anew to find how early women began to ask questions in these areas, questions which we are still struggling to answer.

This has been a very swift tour through a complex and intriguing aspect of our social history, one which is only beginning to receive the kind of detailed and meticulous scholarly attention that should precede the confident enunciation of a thesis such as the one I have offered. Perhaps it is, after all, not a thesis but an hypothesis to be tested. I hope the testing will go forward apace.

NOTES

1. Alexis de Tocqueville, *Democracy in America*, ed. Phillips Bradley (New York, 1960), 2:106.

2. For a useful survey, see David Sills, "Voluntary Associations," in *International Encyclopedia of the Social Sciences* (New York, 1968), 16:362-79. For an interesting, if highly speculative, general discussion, see Arnold Rose, *Theory and Method in the Social Sciences* (Minneapolis, 1954). See also J. Roland Pennock and John Chapman, *Voluntary Associations* (New York, 1969), a

collection of provocative theoretical essays with commentary, written by political scientists.

3. The rare exceptions to this generalization include Arthur M. Schlesinger, Sr., whose "Biography of a Nation of Joiners," *American Historical Review,* 50 (1944), 1-25, should have stimulated research, but for some reason did not. Schlesinger's student Oscar Handlin did examine certain types of voluntary associations in *Boston's Immigrants* (Cambridge, Mass., 1941) and much later in *Dimensions of Liberty* (Cambridge, Mass., 1961). Neither paid much attention to women's associations. Merle Curti, in his pioneering work *The Making of an American Community: A Case Study of Democracy in a Frontier County* (Stanford, 1959), devoted a few pages to voluntary associations in Trempealeau County, Wisconsin, but made no effort to analyze their role in making the community and barely mentions women's groups.

4. Constance Smith and Anne Freedman, *Voluntary Associations: A Perspective on the Literature* (Cambridge, Mass., 1972).

5. One sign of this interest is the inauguration at Yale University of a research program on non-profit organizations, though so far it has only a marginal interest in history. There is also an Association of Voluntary Action Scholars with offices at 1785 Massachusetts Avenue, N.W., Washington, D.C. 20036, which publishes a *Journal of Voluntary Action Research.*

6. Mrs. W. A. Ingham's *Women of Cleveland* (Cleveland, 1893) is a revealing primary source, once the reader decodes the sentimental language. The division of labor emerges from her record.

7. *Ibid.,* and the records deposited in the Western Reserve Historical Society, Cleveland, Ohio. See also the Adele Prentiss Papers in the same depository.

8. See Mary I. Wood, *The History of the General Federation of Women's Clubs: For the First Twenty-Two Years of Its Organization* (New York, 1912); Mrs. J. C. Croly, *The History of the Woman's Club Movement in America* (New York, 1898); Frances Willard and Mary Livermore, *American Women: Fifteen Hundred Biographies,* 2 vols. (New York, 1897); Ruth Bordin, *Women and Temperance* (Philadelphia, 1981); Mary E. Beard, *Women's Work in the Municipalities* (New York, 1915); and many essays in *Notable American Women* (Cambridge, Mass., 1971, 1980).

9. Robert K. Merton, "Insiders and Outsiders," *American Journal of Sociology,* 78 (July 1972), 9-47.

10. Mary Bosworth Treudley, "The 'Benevolent Fair': A Study of Charitable Organizations among American Women in the First Third of the Nineteenth Century," *Social Service Review,* 14 (1940), 509-22; Eleanor Flexner, *A Century of Struggle,* rev. ed. (Cambridge, Mass., 1975); Noreen Dean Tatum, *Crown of Service: A Story of Women's Work in the Methodist Episcopal Church, South, from 1878-1940* (Nashville, 1960); Anne F. Scott, "The 'New Woman' in the New South," pp. 212-21, herein; Keith Melder, "Ladies Bountiful: Organized Women's Benevolence in Early 19th Century America," *New York History,* 65 (1967), 231-54.

11. R. Pierce Beaver, *All Love's Excelling: American Protestant Women in*

World Mission (Grand Rapids, 1968); Joan Jacobs Brumberg, *Mission for Life: The Story of the Family of Adoniram Judson* (New York, 1980), esp. ch. 4.

12. Gerda Lerner, *The Majority Finds Its Past* (New York, 1979), ch. 8.

13. Anne F. Scott, "The Ever-Widening Circle: The Diffusion of Feminist Values from the Troy Female Seminary, 1822–72," pp. 64-88, herein.

14. Mary Grey Peck, *Carrie Chapman Catt, a Biography* (New York, 1944), pp. 5-6.

15. Croly, *Woman's Club Movement*, pp. 919-22.

16. Allen F. Davis, *American Heroine* (New York, 1973); Josephine Goldmark, *Impatient Crusader: The Life of Florence Kelley* (Urbana, 1953), introduction by Felix Frankfurter.

PART IV

Lectures

Interest in women's history reaches beyond history departments and often beyond the academy. Observing my willingness to travel about the country giving lectures on the subject led one of my brothers to remark that he'd always known I was born to be an evangelical minister. But in addition to the desire to make converts, I find these opportunities to talk to widely diverse audiences a liberating experience, and I can try out ideas which may later be subjected to more rigorous study. Questions from audiences often open up new lines of thought and sometimes help to curb my flights of fancy. The reader will recognize—and perhaps forgive—a certain amount of repetition from one lecture to another and will recognize, too, how I have drawn on earlier work. A number of these lectures were exploratory, but I hope they were also responsible, telling the truth so far as I knew it at the time.

EDUCATION AND GEORGIA WOMEN

The following two essays were the Eugenia Blount Lamar Lectures delivered at Wesleyan College in Macon, Georgia, in 1974; they were subsequently published by the college. The phenomenon of the scholarly lecture series, which permits one to present his or her current research in a form that ultimately becomes a short book, is familiar and has given rise to some of the seminal works in American history. I do not remember why I decided to compose these lectures with at least as much attention to the audience that would hear them (undergraduate students and the faculty and citizens of Macon) as to the audience of my colleagues in the field. Perhaps it was not even a conscious decision but the reflection of what had become a kind of two-track life, in which stirring up a broader audience to think about the history of women was one track and breaking new ground in the field, the other. At any rate each of these lectures was related to the hostess institution: Wesleyan considers itself to be the oldest woman's college in the nation, and many of its graduates have been notable Georgia women.

Education of Women:
The Ambiguous Reform

American women's educational progress since that day in 1838 when Georgia Female College opened its doors has been impressive. There was then not a single woman college graduate in the United States. Sixty-two years later the number of women enrolled in some kind of post-secondary educational institution approached 100,000; by the middle of the twentieth century, women were taking a third of all the bachelors and first-level professional degrees, and today there are over three million women in undergraduate colleges.

Women have overcome formidable obstacles to bring about this vast change, to get themselves admitted to colleges, and, once there, to perform so as to take, on the whole, a disproportionate share of academic honors. One would expect, looking at this astonishing educational record, that such progress would naturally be followed by rapid increase in the number of women achieving status, recognition, and posts of responsibility in American society. Yet we all know that this has not been the case, and I believe that certain characteristic ideas and attitudes which were part of this educational revolution contributed to its incommensurate outcome.

In the decade since the revival of feminism, a good many arguments have become familiar; none more so than one litany we have heard over and over. It goes something like this: the proportion of women among doctors and lawyers has not grown remarkably since 1910, the number of women medical students actually declined after 1900, as did the proportion of Ph.D.'s after 1930. Fifty years after woman suffrage no woman sat in the U.S. Senate, and the number in the House is deplorably small; no woman has yet been president of a major coeducational university; only two have ever served in the cabinet . . . and so on and on.

The implications drawn from this recital vary. Some feminists offer these facts as evidence of intransigent discrimination which has prevented women, however strongly motivated, from achieving places of power and prestige in this society. Anti-feminists sometimes have another explanation: that there is a built-in biological limit to female achievement, that nature itself has determined that the number of women in the highest positions in any society will always be very small.

I am a long way from being ready to say that I have a complete and convincing explanation for these often-cited statistics (which, be it noted, are now in the process of changing dramatically), but it is possible to speculate that the attitudes and assumptions shaping many of the institutions devoted to women's education have had something to do with the small number of women college graduates who have fulfilled their promise as scholars, scientists, artists, political leaders, or business executives.

At the outset, of course, various explanations leap to mind; certainly the most obvious is that college women, like other women, marry and have children, and, given the way American society has been organized, marriage and children have been considerably more likely to hinder female achievement than male.

On the other hand, we know that some women do not marry, many are widowed or divorced or never have children, and even a certain number of happily married mothers have, in spite of social handicaps, gone on to major intellectual or political achievements. So we must ask the further question: what, beyond the well-known effects of marriage and motherhood, has inhibited college graduates from developing their abilities and talents and filling important roles in the public life of this society?

For men, achievement, on the whole, has been quite closely related to educational opportunity. Few experienced teachers would deny that the visible talent in any given class of freshmen is quite equally distributed between the sexes. Yet for women the relationship between education and achievement is not at all clear. It may be that for able women higher education is a necessary condition, but not a sufficient condition, for achievement. Some other factor, some X factor, has kept the number of achieving women lower than their proportionate share of talent and education would lead us to expect.

What is that X factor? We may find the missing ingredient in the attitudes toward women abroad in the land at any given time—attitudes which inevitably affect many of the people who administer educational institutions.

In order to develop this analysis I want to look at several things:

1. Changing ideas about the education of women

2. The way these changing ideas presuppose a certain "role" for women in American life

3. The way the development of women's education in the United States reflect both these factors

4. The way in which educational experience and the accepted defintion of women's social role combine to influence the social contribution of women

Historians know that human activity does not take place in a vacuum but is conditioned by the culture of the time and place in which that activity occurs. Three main sets of assumptons have been at work during the two centuries when the education of women has been an issue in America, and the interplay between these assumptions, their success in attracting adherents, is an important part of the history of women's educational experience.

The first set of assumptions is age-old, familiar, and has been part of American culture from the beginning. Its propositions are quite simple: women's minds are different from those of men and are inherently inferior in capacity to reason. This inherent inferiority sets limits to what women are able to learn, and what they are likely to do in the world. Women were not created to be persons-in-themselves but to serve men, and they need only such education as will make them more useful in that function. A variation on this argument is that when women become scholars (thus going against nature) they "unsex" themselves and become somehow monstrous.

A more sophisticated variation on this theme holds that male and female capacities are indeed *different*, but that there is no implication of inferiority or superiority—male and female minds are separate but equal. The catch in this argument is that it always turns out that the things at which women are said to be good or even superior are activities society *defines* as of less importance than the things men are said to be good at, so the net result is the same: women are to be confined to certain aspects of the intellectual world.

A second set of propositions begins with the ideas that intellectual ability is not sex-related, that there is no sexual difference in minds, that therefore women can study anything and should study whatever they want to and excell if they are able, *but* they should expect to use what they have learned in the particular sphere to which God has appointed them: that of the home.

A third point of view agrees with the second that intellectual capacity is not sex-related, but adds the further proposition that since this is so, women should study whatever they want to study, and use their knowledge to do whatever they want to do.

All three sets of ideas have coexisted at least since the fifth century B.C.; the first has been by far the most common over most of western history; the second has been accepted from time to time (and gradually came to be the general view in this country beginning about 1820); the third, though it has had very distinguished adherents (Plato, Erasmus, and John Stuart Mill, for example) has nonetheless been held by only a tiny minority of people and has sometimes disappeared from view for centuries at a time.

It is a critical matter which of these sets of assumptions young women encounter as they go in search of education. Psychologists have begun to explore the effects of expectation on the self-image of individuals, and the consequences for child development of the messages children get from significant adults. Taking a cue from them, historians may usefully ask: what messages about their own capacities and prospects did women students receive from the people who made up institutions of higher learning?

The earliest as well as the most pervasive message was the first I have described: that men had powers to reason while women, instead, were endowed with empathy, insight, and intuition. Since book learning—history, philosophy, theology, mathematics, and languages—required strong minds, women could not be expected to undertake such studies without damage to their minds. And since they were peculiarly fitted for domestic responsibilities, why spoil them by introducing them to things they could never do very well anyhow? Men, according to one somewhat acid sixteenth-century feminist, thought a woman needed only to know enough to distinguish her husband's bed from that of another. Perhaps the classic statement came from that very influential romantic Jean Jacques Rousseau: "A woman's education must therefore be planned in relation to man. To be pleasing in his sight, to win his respect and love, to train him in childhood, to tend him in manhood, to counsel and console, to make his life pleasant and happy, these are the duties of woman for all time, and that is what she should be taught while she is young."[1] Rousseau then proceeded to outline a plan of education that would insure the docility which, he said, "woman requires all her life long, for she will always be in subjection to a man, or to a man's judgement, and she will never be free to set her opinion above his."[2]

Most of the Englishmen who came to settle in North America in the seventeenth century brought with them these general assumptions about women's mental capacities. Though the Puritans prized literacy in both sexes, the governor of Massachusetts Bay expressed a general view when he wrote of his pity for a man whose wife had addled her brains by too much reading and writing of books. In the more southerly colonies women were clearly prized for other things than book learning, as we can see from the pitiful plea sent back to the Virginia Company in England that they should promptly send over some women since the men in Jamestown were having great difficulty getting their laundry done and had no one to nurse them when they fell ill.

Given such views it is not surprising that though Harvard College was founded as early as 1636, no one suggested that women should study there, nor in any of the other colonial colleges which were founded later: Yale, Princeton, William and Mary. To be sure, in 1783 a twelve-year-old Connecticut girl was examined by the president of Yale who admitted that she was prepared to enter the college but pointed out that because of her sex she could not do so.

It was late in the eighteenth century before secondary schools especially for girls began to become common — and even then they usually provided more in the way of lessons in embroidery, music, and French than in the ancient languages or philosophy — clearly reflecting the social view of women's limited capacity. Nevertheless, the Revolutionary period saw a considerable amount of discussion of the need to educate women in a new republic, and the growth of public education in the second quarter of the nineteenth century created a demand for women who were trained to be teachers.

Beginning with Emma Willard's petition to the New York legislature asking for money to found a first-class school for young women, the nineteenth century witnessed recurrent debates about the need for and wisdom of educating women. In these debates men who opposed spending money on schools for women dwelt upon their mental inferiority. A member of the Georgia legislature, opposing the original bill to set up the Georgia Female College announced that "all a young lady needs to know is how to weave clothes for her family and how to paint a daisy in water colors," while another pronounced it "unwomanly for a girl to be educated beyond the ability to read the New Testament." William Gilmore Simms, the antebellum South's best claim to a significant novelist, spoke out against "women clamoring for equality and close companionship with men in all the sterner duties of life" and urged them to "seek education suited to the duties of wife, mother, and housekeeper."[3] Another southerner was even more vehement, arguing that since women were not to be navigators, or doctors, "Why give them a half or quarter proficiency in that of which a whole knowledge would be useless to them? . . . Metaphysics, Logic, Political Economy, belong to the masculine offices and pursuits only, and cannot be brought into female education without wasting the time and injuring the perception, which should be employed in the feminine things."[4]

When it was proposed that women be admitted to the University of Michigan, the faculty unanimously rejected the idea, and the president argued that such a step would lower academic standards.[5] Coming closer to home we find the trustees of the University of Georgia, to whom the Daughters of the American Revolution made the radical proposal that they adopt coeducation, voting to expunge all mention of the subject from their minutes.

A variation on the theme of women's mental incapacity, one which gained a wide hearing in the late nineteenth century, was the idea that women, because of their peculiar biological construction, should not be encouraged to study hard since the use of the mind was detrimental to the reproductive system. The best known proponent of this curious thesis was a medical doctor named E. H. Clarke, whose book *Sex in Education* was widely read and quoted. Probably the most influential psychologist in the country at the turn of the century, G. Stanley Hall, held somewhat similar views.[6]

As recently as 1950 a distinguished historian, then president of a woman's college, published a book called *Educating Our Daughters* in which he offered a very sophisticated argument for confining women's education to those things for which (in his view) women's minds were best suited (though he said that a woman who was absolutely determined to become a physicist should, of course, be encouraged to do so).[7]

The pervasiveness of such attitudes must have had a disturbing effect upon the young women seeking an opportunity to do just what all these respectable gentlemen were saying was impossible, or unnecessary, or dangerous. Think of the ambivalence women students must have experienced as, on the one hand, they began to understand the excitement of using their minds and on the other hand were told that they couldn't or shouldn't be doing so. What is the effect of being threatened with the entire loss of one's female sexuality as a consequence of learning Latin, for instance? What effect must such a system of values have had upon women's self-images and aspirations?

To confuse matters further, from other people came other messages.

The second message was a set of assumptions which also has existed from the beginning of this country's history, and long before, to wit: that women's minds are quite capable of intellectual development, and, indeed, that it is rather fun to help them develop if one happens to be a father, brother, lover, or husband of an intellectually talented woman—or president of a woman's college—but of course, once the mind is developed, it is not to be used outside the home or, at most, a classroom for young children.

In the eighteenth century Aaron Burr seemed intent upon making his daughter Theodosia the best educated person in America. He sent her reading assignments, essay topics, language requirements. His standards were inflexible—all he asked was perfection. In due course, Theodosia married a wealthy young South Carolinian and had a son. It would be a matter of great interest to see how such a superb academic education affected a woman living in that time and place, but alas she and her infant child were lost at sea, and Burr's fascinating experiment thus came to an untimely end.

A handful of other colonial women had similar opportunities provided by a male member of the family or by their own diligent efforts. Jane Colden studied botany (though her father had to translate the Latin texts for her), made some botanical discoveries of her own, and corresponded with a number of European scholars. Eliza Lucas studied everything from languages to horticulture and used John Locke's *Essay on the Human Understanding* as a manual for raising her children. Abigail Adams taught herself French so that she could teach her children and, though she always bewailed the inadequate educational opportunity for women, was a fine example of a self-educated person.

A landmark along the road to higher education for women was the founding in 1820 of the Troy Female Seminary in Troy, New York—an institution firmly based on confidence in the capacity of women to learn hard subjects and on the belief that women should be trained as teachers. But even there, Emma Willard, and even more her sister and assistant Almira Phelps, mindful of the expectations of parents, took care to make it clear that their students, though trained to be teachers, were ultimately destined for domestic roles. This point of view pervaded many of the pioneering institutions for women's higher education. Your own school provided an excellent example.

Chartered by the Georgia legislature in 1836 partly in response to the need for teachers (one member of the legislature argued that people were leaving the state in search of better education for their children), the Georgia Female College opened its doors to ninety young ladies in 1838.

The college was provided, needless to say, with an all-male board of trustees. The president, George F. Pierce, was a bright young man of twenty-eight, full of ideas. In those days examinations were a public occasion, to which parents and friends came. In 1839 Pierce took the opportunity of Examination Day to give a long speech in which he developed his ideas on female education. He saw the school's very existence as reflecting the liberal and enlightened policy of those concerned with the intellectual elevation of the state. Women, he argued, had influence "powerful and immense . . . too mighty to be surrendered to chance, too valuable not to be summoned to the promotion of knowledge, patriotism, and religion." He held a spacious view of intellectual education: "the discipline and the furniture of the mind, the enlargement of its powers, and the storing it with knowledge." He recognized that this was not an easy thing to accomplish and was anxious that students should work hard and above all that they should learn to think for themselves.

He was sternly critical of what he called "the popular mode of Female Education" with its emphasis upon manners and music, demanding much less than women were capable of, and he decried what he saw as a tendency to train memory at the expense of reason. Women, he said, should be confident of their own capacity to think for themselves.

One reads the speech with mounting enthusiasm, thinking Georgia had indeed raised up an educational reformer much in advance of his time, when, suddenly, the educational statesman gives way to the southern gentleman. For how are these thoroughly educated, independent thinkers he proposes to graduate from this college to exert their influence for the "intellectual elevation of the state?"

Summon Woman's magic power to the aid of Literature, and you will refine the taste, ennoble sentiment, awaken emulation and diminish temptations to vice by multiplying the sources of rational enjoyment. Enlarge her attainments, enrich her mind . . . robe her character with the light of genius, people her bosom with noble thoughts, bid her walk amid the glorious mysteries of nature in the freedom of all her faculties, mingle the emanations of her mind with the pure affection of heart, and you invest her beauty with a brighter charm . . . make her home a vision of loveliness . . . luminious with virtue's purest light and redolent of blessing.[8]

Just this ambiguity, of which Pierce's speech is an excellent example, ran through the thinking of many, perhaps most, of the leaders who worked so hard to expand women's educational opportunity: no sooner did they develop plans for a liberating education than they were adding that, of course, women would use their trained minds to influence husbands and sons, rather than directly to achieve on their own. Lest you think it unfair of me to choose my text from the earliest days, listen to a Wesleyan trustee speaking to the students of the college nearly a century later:

You young women are soon to enter into the sphere of life's activities. No doubt all of you have thought of and discussed among yourselves the question of a *career*. In this modern work-a-day world of ours, women are more and more entering into every form of gainful occupation. Some are becoming doctors, others lawyers. . . .
    This new dream is not without its dangers, for it is diverting the mind and thoughts of the young women from the greatest of all careers— Motherhood. . . .
    This world-filling talk of the emancipation of woman and the equality of the sexes has brought our whole social structure into a crisis. This mixing on a basis of equality of the terms, lawyer, doctor, business executive, and engineer with those of wife and mother is little short of being monstrous . . . the supercareer of earth is that of wife and mother. Men know this Society rests upon it. History proclaims it. For God designed it so.[9]

I think the worried trustee was a little overanxious as far as Wesleyan was concerned, for four years earlier someone compiled the record of alumnae for the first ninety years—there were 3,000 of them—among whom there had been two physicians, two lawyers, ten librarians, ten journalists, forty missionaries, 329 teachers and 2,250 "homebuilders," in short, out of the 3,000 only sixty-four had gone beyond woman's traditional careers of homemaking or teaching.[10]

Nor was Wesleyan different from most other women's colleges. Let me quote John Goucher, the first president and heroic supporter of the Woman's College of Baltimore, later to be named for him: "To help woman become an aid to man, the Woman's College of Baltimore was founded. The Woman's College comes before the public to elevate womankind and make the weaker sex a helpmate for the stronger."[11]

Both Wesleyan and Goucher were women's colleges being run by men. Goucher's first faculty included only one woman full professor, and she was in the field of hygiene. Actions tell more than words: women's intellectual abilities were not to take them into the top level of the faculty. Wesleyan's first faculty included also one woman who taught painting, drawing, embroidery, and French. Neither college had a woman trustee.

In a brilliant master's essay a young woman from Carrollton, Georgia, has demonstrated that from the very beginning the Woman's College of Duke University suffered from what the author of the essay calls "feminist confusion"—a commitment to the best education so long as there was no threat to the southern ideal of womanhood which the author suggests was "an illfitting cloak for an educated being." She argues that while on the surface Duke made no intellectual distinction between the sexes, in many ways the treatment of women students was shaped by a conviction that they were to become southern ladies.[12]

It is no wonder, given the evidence, that Mabel Newcomer writing in 1958 on the history of a century of higher education for American women concluded:

> The fact that homemaking is woman's most important role has never been seriously questioned either by those arguing in favor of college education for women or by those opposing it. Those opposing higher education for women have usually expressed the fear that it will encourage them to pursue independent careers, foregoing marriage; or if they marry, that it will make them dissatisfied with the homemaker's lot. Those promoting higher education have, on the contrary, insisted that college women make better wives and mothers than their less educated sisters.[13]

Again we must ask, what kinds of ambivalence was created in the minds of women students who were getting these contradictory messages? Is it any wonder that freshmen sometimes showed higher aspirations than seniors? Or that a leading psychologist could build a scholarly reputation upon a few experiments in which she demonstrated what she called the "will to fail" on the part of bright women? For what could be more discouraging than to be told that you *are* bright, but that many of the places where intelligence and talent can be fully used are off-limits? Colleges diligently engaged in walking a tightrope, trying to educate women without spoiling them as wives, may have succeeded in simply exacerbating conflict in their women students.

But you will say, *was* there any other line of argument? The third outlook I identified was also present, and it too goes back a long way. Plato in the fifth book of *The Republic* argued that for a community to thrive it must make use of all the talent available, including that which happened to come in female packages. In his utopia, therefore, able women were to be educated in the same way as men so that they might contribute to the government of the state. We find similar views in the writings of Erasmus and Sir Thomas More, and John Stuart Mill, who wrote that the benefit of giving women what he called "the free use of their faculties by leaving them the free choice of their employments, and by opening to them the same field of occupation and the same prizes and encouragements as to other human beings, would be that of doubling the mass of mental faculties available for the higher services of humanity."[14]

If we retrace the debate over the higher education of women in the United States after 1820, occasionally, though they are not nearly so visible as representatives of the first two lines of thought, it is possible to find spokesmen for what we might call the J. S. Mill point of view: that women's talents deserve the fullest educational development so that they will be available for use in any aspect of the life of the community. Perhaps the first American spokesman in this tradition was Margaret Fuller, that extraordinary transcendentalist, friend of Emerson, Thoreau, and Horace Greeley and author of *Woman in the Nineteenth Century*. "We would have every path laid open to Woman as freely as to Man," she wrote. "Were this done and a slight temporary fermentation allowed to subside, we should see crystallizations more pure and of more various beauty. We believe the divine energy would pervade nature to a degree unknown in the history of former ages."[15]

Margaret Fuller, however, was born too early, and no college offered her the chair she would have filled so well. Nothing daunted, she organized what she called her "Conversations" to which Boston women paid admission. Inventive and adventurous though she was, Fuller suffered a good deal in her own life from the cultural expectations whose crippling effects she understood and described.

The outstanding American proponent of the J. S. Mill point of view applied to women's higher education was Martha Carey Thomas, the woman who became dean of Bryn Mawr College when she was twenty-eight, and president when she was thirty-seven, a post she then held for three decades. She was to that college what George F. Pierce was to Wesleyan—the person who set the framework and guided its early development. Carey Thomas was not troubled by conflicts about woman's proper role, nor did she believe that God had intended all women to be wives and mothers. It may not be true, as sometimes alleged, that she once told a group of Bryn Mawr girls: "Only our failures marry," but it is true that she believed firmly in the most rigorous education followed by entire freedom for women to use whatever talents and skills they possessed. "It seems self-evident," she said in 1908, "that practically all women, like practically all men, must look forward after leaving college to some form of public service, whether paid, as it will be for the great majority of both men and women, or unpaid does not matter. Why should not women, like liberally educated men, fit themselves after college for their special work?"[16]

Though President Thomas was perhaps the most visible and articulate spokesman of this forthright view that all possibilities should be open to educated women, there were other places where the same spirit was evident. Vassar during a large part of its history certainly conveyed this message—both by the quality of its women faculty and by the spirit of its administration. As early as 1890 it was reported of Vassar's first 1,000 alumnae that twenty-five had become medical doctors; forty-seven were writers of some significance; twelve were important scientific investigators; and 118 had gone on to advanced degrees. At Mount Holyoke under the presidency of Mary E. Woolley and at Barnard when Virginia Gildersleeve was dean, women were encouraged to take a broad view of their own potential. In 1952 the percentage of Mount Holyoke alumnae going into scientific careers exceeded that of many men's colleges. I suspect that a careful comparative study of alumnae of these institutions and a number of others would reveal a differential effect of education upon women students which would reflect the degree of unambiguous support for independence the college provided. Such a study has yet to be made, but when it is, we may understand better the relationship between the ideas prevalent in a college and the subsequent lives of its alumnae.

To recapitulate:

I began by asking why it is that American women have made enormous progress in achieving equality of opportunity in higher education without commensurate progress in their record of achievement outside their homes.

I have suggested that while educational opportunity increased another factor worked at cross purposes with educational goals—a factor which grows out of the social role defined for women in this society by men. The idea that women no matter how well educated were to wind up as wives and mothers confined to domestic responsibilities has shaped the atmosphere of expectation which women have experienced in many, perhaps in most, institutions of higher education.

I have identified and described what I take to be three sets of attitudes which have co-existed in American higher education and noted that each of these outlooks implies a "proper" role for women in American society.

I have argued that these attitudes have affected women's actual achievement. The second set of assumptions has been dominant for most of the time that women have been going to college. The message women got was: you are intelligent and capable and worthy of the best education BUT the proper place for you to exercise your educated mind lies in the home. This ambiguous expectation, with the conflict it can create in the individual, has had a great influence on women's failure to achieve. Women have not felt free to develop their talents fully, since to do so was to threaten their prospects for marriage and since they would, in any case, find it difficult to operate against the social mores and in opposition to the expectations of the significant men in their lives.

This is, I believe, an accurate analysis of what has happened to many, perhaps most, women college graduates in the past.

What about the future?

I have also described a minority outlook, which has been around for as long as the majority view, one brilliantly described by John Stuart Mill in 1869 in his essay which is still the best on the subject in English. The minority view may now be on the way to becoming the majority view, and its tenets are being written into legislation and into the policies of more and more organizations. It is being accepted by an increasing number of men.

One reason that view is increasingly accepted, I suspect, is that in a time when economic growth is becoming suspect and the need to limit population is becoming clear, a good many people dimly sense that it no longer makes sense to urge all women to be concerned with only marriage and family life.

Because their role is no longer being defined so narrowly, women's education is increasingly seen as preparation for achievement and vital social contribution. If my thesis is sound, we should expect to see performance change as expectations change. It is a sign of the times, for example, that in 1974 hundreds of women ran for public office in political jurisdictions all across the country, and that many were elected, including the governor of an important state. It is a sign of the times that in North Carolina a woman who studied economics at Vassar is the leading consumer advocate in the state and that Smith College for the first time since its founding has appointed a woman president. Hundreds of women are enrolled in law and medical schools, and many others are in posts which not so long ago were labelled "for men only."

Given a change in the kinds of expectations to which college women are exposed, it is possible to imagine a situation in which half of all our scientists, writers, scholars, government officials, doctors, and lawyers will be women. It is possible to envision a society in which housekeeping is cooperative, and men as well as women take time from their careers to raise children. It is possible to envision, as Margaret Fuller and John Stuart Mill did, a society much invigorated by the contributions of women's talents and energies.

NOTES

1. J. J. Rousseau, *Emile* (London, 1948), p. 328.

2. *Ibid.*, p. 333.

3. Fletcher Green, "Higher Education of Women in the South," in *Democracy in the Old South and Other Essays*, ed. J. Isaac Copeland (Nashville, 1969), p. 126.

4. Edward W. Johnson, head of the Bedford, Virginia, Female Academy, quoted in *ibid.*, p. 205.

5. Dorothy McGuigan, *The Dangerous Experiment* (Ann Arbor, 1970), ch. 3.

6. G. S. Hall, *Adolescence* (New York, 1904), 2:636-40.

7. Lynn White, *Educating Our Daughters* (New York, 1950).

8. George F. Pierce, *An Address on Female Education* delivered in the chapel of the Georgia Female College, on Thursday, the Last Day of the Examination (Macon, 1829).

9. William F. Quillian, *A New Day for Historic Wesleyan, 1836-1924* (Nashville, 1928), pp. 33-34.

10. *Ibid.*

11. The Baltimore *Sun*, Nov. 14, 1888. In an unpublished paper on the history of Goucher, Mindy Gae Farber has documented the shift in emphasis from the purposes of the women who initiated the Woman's College of Baltimore to those of the male culture and the extraordinary emphasis upon the training of proper ladies which came to pervade the college under the leadership of male trustees and administrators.

12. Dara DeHaven, "On Educating Women—The Coordinate Ideal at Trinity and Duke University" (M.A. thesis, Duke University, 1974).

13. Mabel Newcomer, *A Century of Higher Education for American Women* (New York, 1958), p. 210.

14. J. S. Mill, *The Subjection of Women* (Chicago, 1970), pp. 220-21.

15. Margaret Fuller, *American Romantic*, ed. Perry Miller (Ithaca, 1970), pp. 149-50.

16. M. Carey Thomas, "Present Tendencies in Women's College and University Education," reprinted in Barbara Cross, *The Educated Woman in America* (New York, 1956), p. 166.

Getting to Be a
Notable Georgia Woman

In this second foray into American women's history I want to illustrate a method which historians call "collective biography" and, in the process, to raise once again some questions about the effect of cultural expectations upon women's achievement.

Collective biography can mean several different kinds of analysis. For one, it can be used to study a large group of women when only a few things are known about any given individual. For example, suppose a social historian began to suspect that a large number of households in Georgia in the decade after the Civil War were headed by women and began to wonder what effect this fact (if it was fact) had upon the way society and even the economy were operating. Using the manuscript census returns for 1870, we could identify each woman who headed a household and could note her age, the number of her children, her occupation, marital status, how much land she owned, how much property she claimed to pay taxes on. This material could be coded and fed into a computer, and we could then find out (1) how many such women there were; (2) what percentage they were of the total number of heads of household; (3) what their median or modal age was; (4) what their typical marital status was; (5) how many children they had on the average; (6) how much property they owned, and so on.

With this material in hand the historian could then make at least an informed guess about the importance of women heads-of-household in the economy and the society of post–Civil War Georgia. That is one way historians use collective biography.

A second kind of collective biography is the study of a smaller number of women about whom a good deal is known. While the first kind of study is useful to increase our understanding about large masses of people whose lives are not well documented, the second is useful when we are interested in elite groups. Indeed the method was originally developed by political historians anxious to understand the origins and typical characteristics of governing groups, and the relations between the members of such groups.[1]

What I propose to offer here is an example of the second kind of collective biography. The women I have chosen to study are all those women born in Georgia (and one born in Virginia, but whose career was in Georgia, and whose tombstone reads "Georgia's Greatest Woman"), who appear in the biographical dictionary *Notable American Women*.[2]

That dictionary, published in three volumes in 1971, contains biographies of 1,359 American women, who lived and died between 1607 and 1950, selected by the editors from a long list of candidates as the most significant women in American history; women, as they put it, of "more than local importance."

It seemed to me it would be interesting to examine the Georgia women in this group to find out what activity led to their identification as "notable," what social classes they came from, what their educational experience had been, whether it would be possible to say that they had anything or many things in common, and in what ways they differed from what might be called "typical" Georgia women, as well as how they might differ from other women in the dictionary who came from other regions.

Of course, this is a very small number of people, twenty-three in all, and generalizations based on such a sample are bound to be very tentative. Nevertheless the sketches of these women provide material for analysis, and a close look at their lives gives rise to some interesting questions about the relationship between culture and achievement. Wherever possible I have gone beyond the biographical sketch in *Notable American Women* to find additional information about the woman in question. Sometimes there has been a good deal, sometimes not much.

Suppose some female spirit waiting to be born in Georgia anytime after 1699 had said to herself: what must I do so that long after I die my life will be recorded in a volume devoted to *Notable American Women?* What advice could we give that aspiring spirit?

The first suggestion would be: to improve your chances, by all means get yourself born between 1840 and 1870 (since sixteen of the twenty-three were born in those years), and even better, arrange to be born in the decade of the 1860s. It may only be random chance, but the largest number of our sample were born in that Civil War decade.

The next advice for this ambitious spirit would be: pick a lawyer for your father. One-third of our sample were lawyer's daughters. If she couldn't manage a lawyer, her next best bet would be a cotton planter. On down the line she could pick a storekeeper, cotton broker, teacher, and minister. Three fathers of the group had been slaves, and two were slave masters—fathers of mulatto children.

Your chances are somewhat better if you are born white, but five of our notables were black. It would be better not to choose to be born an Indian, for only one Indian woman made the grade.

Now, having chosen a father wisely, what should she do about a mother? The best suggestion would be to look around for someone who can be described by her friends as "strong-minded," "strong-willed," "something of a feminist," a person of "great vitality," given to encouraging her daughters. In short, be sure to find a mother who has visible strength of character, and who, if called upon to take over the responsibility for the family, will do so very effectively.

As to *where* our spirit should choose to be born, her chances are better in a town than in the country; Athens, Augusta, Savannah, Atlanta, and Columbus each provided two notable women. It also helps to choose a family with some money and position in the community and to find highly educated parents, preferably community leaders. If you are born black, it makes a great deal of difference if your parents have white friends who are likely to be interested in your education.

Let us suppose that our aspiring spirit has taken all this advice and chosen the right family, in the right place, with the right friends. She is born, begins life with considerable advantages, and is encouraged by both parents to make something of herself. One thing she must do is to get some education. A wide variety of institutions will serve: ranging from the Rome Female College or the Lucy Cobb Institute, on one hand, to Mt. Holyoke, Smith, or Atlanta University, on the other. In one case the girl was taught primarily by her mother. But the best thing she can do is to enroll here at Wesleyan, the only college at which more than one of our group studied.

Having gone to college and graduated, usually with honors, what must she do then to improve her chances of achieving that long-sought goal of being identified as a notable woman? The best choice is to avoid matrimony altogether, as nine of our twenty-three did. Or if she must marry, she should arrange to be divorced or widowed (as happened in eight more cases) or failing that, to marry a much older man who will provide the money and will not try too hard to control his wife. Only four of the twenty-three filled the traditional wife-and-mother role through most of their adult lives. Of the twelve who ever married, only seven had children of their own. Thus more than half of the total group were childless. In all this, of course, they were swimming very much against the current of nineteenth-century society, in which the role of wife and mother was the only one for which women were considered to be well suited.

Having made all the other necessary steps there still remains the crucial question: what field should she choose for a career? In Georgia the best road to notability was to be a writer—seven of the twenty-three made their mark thus. The next most likely career was to be found in some aspect of education, whether as founder of schools, or administrator, or teacher. Whatever else they did, many of these women were also teachers at some time in their lives. Next in order was work in social welfare. Politics, journalism, foreign missions, and the Girl Scouts provided roads to fame for others, while one was an early exponent of the blues in jazz, and one achieved notability by marrying a man who became president.

On the whole, notable women live a long time. Five, to be sure, died before fifty and one more before sixty, but all the rest lived beyond sixty, nine beyond seventy, five beyond eighty, and two died in their nineties. For these figures to tell us anything we would need comparisons with the population at large, but my impression is that their longevity was much better than the average for women born before 1900. Certainly their educational accomplishment was far beyond that of the population at large, when you realize that as late as 1900 only 6 percent of all Americans had graduated from high school. Their marital experience was certainly atypical, and by undertaking careers in their own right they were very much out of step with the general expectations of women in their time.

A closer look at some of the individuals who make up the group confirms the impression that they were in many ways mavericks: unusual, able, and complex human beings.

To begin alphabetically, we might look for a moment at Eliza Frances Andrews, born in Washington, Georgia, in 1840 and growing up in the family of a distinguished judge. She went to LaGrange Female College and decided when she was in her early twenties not to marry but to follow "the career I have marked out for myself." Such a decision was exceedingly rare among southern women in the 1860s. The family resources were wiped out by the Civil War, and Judge Andrews died soon after. Fanny, as she was known, was suddenly called upon to be self-supporting, which she managed by teaching, writing articles, and novels, and editing a country newspaper. A man was officially listed as editor. He paid her half his salary to do all the work. When he moved away, she applied for the job in her own right and was told that no woman could possibly edit a newspaper. She taught French for a good many years here at Wesleyan and at the same time educated herself so well in botany that she was able to write what became a standard text, one that was translated and used in France as well as in many parts of the United States. In her sixties, having become a socialist, she published her Civil War diary with an introduction in which she applied Marxian analysis to the history of slavery and the Civil War. She was an ardent feminist and, as seems often the case with ardent feminists, she lived to a ripe old age, dying at ninety and willing the royalties from her botany text to the town of Rome to buy and maintain a public woodland in which children could look at trees and "veterans of life's struggles," as she put it, could find peace and rest. She was, in the vernacular, quite a gal.

But then, so was the next woman on the list. Janie Porter, the child of former slaves, was raised and educated in a white famly here in Macon. Her white benefactor planned to send her north to school so that she could "pass" into the white community. Janie's mother, however, didn't like that idea at all and insisted that her daughter enroll instead at Hampton Institute in order to find out about life among her own people. Inspired by a novel which had a social worker for a heroine, this well-brought-up black woman began teaching among sharecropping families in Georgia, then married a member of the Hampton staff, and turned her home into a settlement house for her poorer neighbors in the vicinity of the college. She had four children and was fully occupied with them, her settlement work, and her work in the Virginia Federation of Colored Women's Clubs when her husband died. Virginia Negro women had been pushing for the establishment of a school for delinquent girls, and when Janie Porter Barrett was widowed they prevailed upon her to take charge of the newly founded Virginia Industrial School. She found for the first time a challenge which called on all her talents — under her leadership it became an outstanding institution, one of the best in the nation. Like

Eliza Frances Andrews, hard work and a demanding job must have kept her young: she died at eighty-three.

It would be interesting to discuss every woman on the list, but in the interest of brevity I must skip a few, passing over Martha Berry, founder of the Berry Schools, Alice Birney who organized the prototype of the Parent-Teacher Association, Anne Virginia Cole, who among many other philanthropies, financed the very significant Southern Sociological Congresses, and Ellen Craft, abolitionist, to pause a while with Mary Clare DeGraffenreid, who began her career by graduating from Wesleyan at age sixteen with highest honors, and immediately brought on a crisis with a commencement address—the year 1865—which was a scathing attack on the federal forces then occupying Macon. The commanding officer threatened to close the school in retaliation—I don't know exactly how the powers-that-be talked him out of it. After a few years of teaching in a proper female seminary, Clare DeGraffenreid applied for a job in the newly founded Bureau of Labor in Washington. This was in 1886 and, identified by the director of the bureau as a bright young woman, she was trained as a special investigator to study the wages, hours, and working conditions of women and children workers. She thus became one of the first labor investigators in this country. She published twenty-seven articles on various subjects having to do with the labor movement, a number of which were translated into various European languages. In 1889 she won the American Economic Association Prize for the best essay on child labor, and two years later another prize for an essay on "The Condition of Wage Earning Women." In 1891 in a brouhaha reminiscent of her commencement address, she stirred up a great deal of antagonism in the South with an article on "The Georgia Cracker in the Cotton Mill," in which she tried to tell the truth as she saw it about the miserable conditions of life for many southern cotton mill workers. A forthright woman, she argued against trying to impose middle-class values on poor people and emphasized the need of all people for self-respect. "So long as Christian workers keep up the hollow mockery of the 'Lady' succoring working women, so long will working women resent or hold aloof from such beneficence," she wrote. A colorful and independent minded person, vigorous opponent of child labor, student of educational theory, and early housing reformer who campaigned for slum clearance before the words had been coined, she also presided over a salon in Washington to which leading political figures were fond of going. She was an outspoken feminist.

Choices are hard, but I shall skip over the doughty Rebecca Latimer

Felton, a political power in Georgia for forty years, and the first woman to sit in the U.S. Senate, as well as Corra Harriss, an interesting and somewhat puzzling author whose novel *The Circuit Rider's Wife* is a valuable piece of social history, to pause with Laura Haygood, who also graduated from Wesleyan after only two years of residence, thanks to the excellent college preparation she had received from her mother. She started a private school for girls in Atlanta which was so successful that when the city opened its first public high school for girls in 1872 she was promptly made its head—as well as teacher of Latin, English literature, moral science, and mental philosophy! In her spare time she organized and pushed Home Missions among Methodist women, thus initiating what came to be a seminal social movement. She seems to have had all the talents, which, in the person of her brother Atticus Green Haygood, helped him to become a bishop. At thirty-nine she gave up her successful career in Atlanta to go to China as a missionary where she, among many other things, founded a school for young women of the same quality as the highly respected Anglo-Chinese college for men.

In 1884, writing on the relation of female education to mission work, she thanked God "that there is no longer a question as to women's having a part in the world's work . . . She (woman) must understand . . . that the world is less good than God meant it to be if *she* fails to meet the measure of responsibility which He has placed upon her."[3] A fine scholar, a gifted organizer, a person of great magnetism, there can be no doubt of Laura Haygood's qualifications for being listed as a notable American woman.

Lucy Laney, born nine years after Laura Haygood, had a good deal in common with her. Lucy Laney's parents were slaves. Her mother had been given an education by the Macon family to whom she belonged. Lucy Laney, herself, had the extraordinary opportunity for a young black woman of being a member of the first class to be graduated from Atlanta University. She taught school for awhile before undertaking to organize a private school for Negro children in Augusta. The school was sponsored by the Presbyterian Board of Missions for Freedmen which, though full of good will, provided little money. If the school was to begin, Lucy Laney had to raise money herself, which she did, largely by appealing to wealthy women in the North. The Haines Normal and Industrial Institute prepared black children for college at a time when there were no public high schools in the state open to them. In addition Lucy Laney established the first kindergarten in Augusta and a nurses' training school, which eventually became part of the Georgia Medical School. A tough-minded, outspoken woman she lived to be eighty and died still working for the improvement of the school. I have seen no evidence that she and Laura Haygood ever met, but they would have understood each other.

I will pass over Octavia Le Vert, a writer of dubious distinction, and pause for a moment with Juliette Low because her biography illustrates dramatically what can happen when a woman of ability and talent who seems destined to spend her life doing nothing much but go to parties and spend money is suddenly thrown upon her own resources—in this case when her wealthy husband divorced her to marry his mistress. At the age of fifty-one Juliette Low met Sir Robert Baden-Powell, the founder of the Boy Scouts, and was seized with the vision of a similar organization for girls. Transformed from social butterfly to energetic organizer, she spent the rest of her life organizing and running, first individual Girl Scout troops, and then the Girl Scouts of America. It was an extraordinary transformation, though one that occurs more often than we realize. "Suddenly in middle age," says her biographer, "[she] threw all her capabilities, driving power and a large part of her financial resources into an effort completely foreign to anything she had ever done before, showing a tenacity of purpose and an organizing and executive genius that those who knew her best had not dreamed she possessed."[4]

The rest of my list includes Maria McIntosh, writer; Victoria Matthews, who founded a pioneering association to help Negro women moving to the cities get training and find jobs; Margaret Mitchell, who wrote *Gone with the Wind*; Mary Musgrove, a Creek Indian, who was one of the most important figures in Georgia's colonial history; Frances Newman, novelist; Celestia Parrish, who brought John Dewey's educational ideas to Georgia and who spent the final seven years of her life as supervisor of rural schools for north Georgia, traveling around the back roads by buggy and wagon to work with 2,400 rural schools and their teachers; Mildred Lewis Rutherford, for forty-six years the principal of Lucy Cobb Institute in Athens; Gertrude Rainey, who helped develop the blues as a musical form; Augusta Evans Wilson, yet another best-selling novelist; and Ellen Axson Wilson, who made it into this volume by marrying Woodrow Wilson, but who, I suspect, might have gotten there on her own if she had never married.

Here they are, then, twenty-three women out of the millions who were born in Georgia between 1700 and 1900; what can we say about them in retrospect?

For the most part, we must ask questions.

What would we learn by comparing the careers of these southern women with a representative sample from other parts of the country? It is striking that in this list there are so many writers, teachers, and social workers, as well as founders of significant institutions, but no doctor, no lawyer, no great scholar. Does this say something about the culture in which southern women grew up before the middle of the twentieth century?

I do not know whether the number of Georgia women is small in proportion to population—but Virginia, to take a nearby example, is represented by forty-four women in these same volumes. North Carolina, on the other hand, has only eleven. Some state-by-state counts might be useful.

I should like to see a study made of all the southern women in these volumes, including a comparison of their characteristics and careers with those of women from other regions. Such a comparative study might suggest some insights into southern culture, things which we need to know to understand it even now.

I would like to know how many other women there are, lost to history and never turned up by the diligence of editors working in Cambridge, Massachusetts, who ought to have been included? I think for example of Alice Culler Cobb, who was a moving spirit of this institution for many years, who should indeed have been made president when the post fell vacant in the 1890s had not the Board of Trustees foresightedly voted that only a minister of the Methodist Church could be chosen— a test which automatically ruled out even the best-qualified woman. I think of Nellie Peters Black, whose work in Atlanta in the 1890s was also of great significance, or Rebecca Felton's sister Mary Latimer McLendon, a pioneer suffragist, and on and on. These women's lives and accomplishments are or should be a vital part of the cultural heritage of a state which prides itself on preserving the significant parts of our past. Yet hardly anyone knows of their existence. Why, indeed, must we wait for historians working in Massachusetts to give us back even these few? Why do we not have a volume of *Notable Georgia Women?*

Very few of the women in *Notable American Women* or those who ought to be there have yet been the subject of serious, full-length biographies, yet many of them led extremely interesting lives. It has sometimes been suggested that we in the South enjoy talking so much that we are slow to get down to the harder business of writing—yet here is a gold mine waiting to be tapped by industrious students of women's history.

Finally, of course, I would like to know how these women viewed their own lives and how they assessed the costs and benefits of swimming against the stream, of demanding the right to be people rather than—as was so often the case in the nineteenth century—female appendages, known only as "the wife of. . . ." As well as I can tell from the biographical information available nearly all of them would have said that the benefits far outran the costs and would have agreed with Laura Haygood that the world is less good than God meant it to be if women do not take their responsibilities.

NOTES

1. See Lawrence Stone, "Prosopography," *Daedalus*, 100 (Winter 1971), 46-49, for an extended discussion of the potential and pitfalls of this method of historical research.

2. Edward T. James, Janet James, and Paul S. Boyer, eds., *Notable American Women, 1607-1950*, 3 vols. (Cambridge, Mass., 1971).

3. Oswald Eugene Brown and Anna Muse Brown, *Life and Letters of Laura Askew Haygood* (Nashville, 1904), p. 89.

4. Gladys Denny Shultz and Daisy Gordon Lawrence, *Lady from Savannah: The Life of Juliette Low* (Philadelphia, 1958), p. 17.

Old Wives' Tales

Good friends expressed considerable skepticism when I undertook to spend the summer of 1972 reading the first three volumes of Notable American Women. *You will only get information overload, they said, and you won't remember one from another. Wait till you need the material, then read it.*

They were wrong. Reading straight through, one after another, those 1,359 biographies changed and expanded my view of nineteenth-century women. The essays also provided me with the building blocks for several arguments. In the case of this lecture, my charge was very broad: to say something provocative about women and aging. A very large audience of people, mostly over the age of fifty, seemed to find this historical excursion interesting. By now an "old wife" myself, I found it down right inspiring.

Is there anything left to be said about aging? Everywhere one looks it seems to be topic A—or at least running a close second to death and dying—for the attention of newspapers, columnists, television, publishers, the government, and the universities. At least three college alumni magazines have devoted attention to the subject recently—winding up, of course, with lots of handy advice on estate planning! If one boils down all the statistics, digests all the viewings-with-alarm, the exhortations to be up and jogging, and all the rest, three basic and intractable facts emerge which set the stage for my own examination of the topic.

First, whether we like it or not, our population is getting older. When George Washington was inaugurated, half the people in this country were under sixteen, and only a tiny handful were over sixty-five. Being

Reprinted with permission from Priscilla W. Johnston, ed., *Perspectives on Aging: Exploding the Myths* (Cambridge, Mass.: Ballinger Publishing Co., 1981), pp. 71-84.

president must have been something like being head of Boys' Town. Now thirty is the halfway point, and 10 percent of the population is past age sixty-five—and being president is not so much fun anymore. Furthermore, this trend is bound to continue, and unless someone slips up with a nuclear weapon, or lets loose some anthrax germs, or dumps one more lethal chemical in the Mississippi, the population will continue to grow older. This, we might say, is society's problem.

Second, looking at the same set of facts from the perspective of the individual, more and more of us will live a long time. Of every 100 persons born the year Washington took office, only twenty reached the age of seventy. Of every 100 children born this year (again, failing some man-made disaster), eighty will live past their seventieth birthdays. There are more Americans over age sixty-five alive at this moment than the total of all the people who reached that age in all the years that have gone before. So lots of people are going to have to learn to live as elder persons, and this we might define as the individual's problem.

Third, in each age group past forty-five there are more women than men, and by the time one reaches seventy-five, there are 156 women for every 100 men. I am not certain whose problem that is, but I am pretty sure it is one reason for considering the subject of women in a series on aging.

Aging is not solely a biological process. People live in particular historical circumstances, and the interaction between individuals and the society in which they happen to be born and grow up determines the special characteristics of their experience. Let us begin, then, by examining the broad social changes that have taken place in the way American women have lived and worked since the seventeenth century, asking how those changes have affected the process of aging and the experience of being an old woman. It has been nearly four centuries since the first women arrived in Jamestown, in response to the heartfelt cry of the men who were already there that they had nobody to do their washing. What can we learn from the experience of all the women who have preceded us that bears on the three problems I outlined in the beginning?

Those early Jamestown settlers and their successors for the next 200 years became partners in a domestic economy. That is to say, men, women, and children all worked together to make the family living—and *make* is indeed the correct verb, since the family created with its own hands most of what it consumed. There was always a clear sexual division of labor. Men chopped down trees, plowed and planted, built cabins, and harvested crops. Women kept gardens, took care of poultry, milked cows, churned butter, made cheese, spun, wove, and sewed cloth, preserved and prepared the family food, took care of sick people, and, if they were literate themselves, taught the children their ABCs. Artisans' wives learned their husbands' craft in order to carry on if he became ill or died.

Healthy women were pregnant on the average of every two years until menopause, and, though many children died in infancy or early childhood, enough survived to bring about very rapid population growth. Some families were large. We hear a great deal about colonial women dying in childbirth, and many did. However, so many men died of smallpox, yellow fever, pneumonia, tuberculosis, and other ailments that even in the eighteenth century there were times and places where widows outnumbered widowers.[1]

Old age was an experience confined to a small proportion of all those born in the eighteenth and nineteenth centuries, but of the 20 percent who lived to age seventy, many lived into their eighties, nineties, and beyond. The *American Register*, a sort of early version of *Time*, regularly carried a list of people in various parts of the country who had passed the 100 mark, with as much detail as could be gathered about their lives. For these truly aged folks social security lay almost entirely in the family, with the town government and the poorhouse as the last resort.

Colonial men were careful to provide support for surviving wives in their wills. Leaving the family house and land to a son, the father spelled out his widow's entitlements: "the parlor end of the house . . . with the cellar that hath lock and key to it," "free liberty to bake, brew and wash etc. in the kitchen," plenty of wood for her stove "ready cut and at her door," such furniture as she might need: "bedstead . . . bedding . . . the best green rug . . . the best low chair . . . and a good cushion." She might also be provided a cow or chickens and some help in taking care of them: the cow, for example, "to be brought into the yard daily" for her to milk. Sometimes she was to have a fixed share of apples and pears and a gentle horse to ride to church. Sometimes she was to have regular payments in wheat and corn, or books from her husband's library. The one I like best is the provision that she shall have "beer, as she hath now."[2] For a long time I worried about the lack of faith in filial responsibility which these wills seem to reflect, until it dawned on me that the suspicion probably rested less on the sons than upon the daughters-in-law.[3]

A woman who bore her last child at the age of forty-five did not have to worry much about an empty nest. Indeed, one eighteenth-century woman doubtless spoke for many when she wrote in her journal: "I have often thought . . . that women who live to get over the time of Childbareing if other things are favourable to them, experience more comfort and satisfaction than at any other period of their lives."[4]

Such was the mortality of the age, however, that orphaned grand-children or great-grandchildren were not uncommon. Benjamin Franklin's favorite sister, for example, in her seventies found herself taking care of three very young great-grandchildren whose mother had died in bearing her fourth child in four years. Franklin's sister wrote him that the children probably needed "some person more lively and Patient to watch over them continually," but since no such person volunteered, she did it anyway, and without complaint. When the children were finally off her hands, she retired to a little house in Boston with a favorite granddaughter for a companion and wrote her brother a complete description of her life. She spoke thankfully of having a warm house, a good bed, plenty to eat, neighbors to visit, the companionship of her grandchild, and then she added: "When I look around me on all my acquaintance I do not see won I have reason to think happier than I am and would not change my neighbour with my Self where will you find one in a more comfortable State as I see Every won has their Trobles and I sopose them to be such as fitts them best & shakeing off them might be only changing for the wors."[5]

This was a woman who had borne twelve children and watched eleven of them die, who had been driven from her home during the Revolution, and who had often in her long life had to work very hard to provide food and clothing for her children, grandchildren, and great-grandchildren. The fervor of her appreciation for food, heat, and kind company suggest that such amenities could not be taken for granted by elder persons, especially women, in her day. Indeed some poor widows among her contemporaries were being told to leave certain New England towns and villages because the town fathers did not want them to be a burden on the taxpayers. It is hard to imagine where such women went or how they survived.

If we turn from our very meager information about the realities of women's lives in those early days to the question of how women were defined by the society, we can find a few clues. The law provides one index of social attitudes, and a woman who was married had no independent legal existence. Common law viewed husband and wife as one, and that one the man. Women's property as well as their persons belonged to their husbands. Women could neither vote nor serve on juries, nor determine the guardianship of their children.

Another index of status is the availability of education. At the most basic level there were far more illiterate women than illiterate men, and at the highest level, none of the nine colonial colleges admitted women to study. Indeed, one colonial governor had told his friends that a certain woman in his town had gone mad from reading books and doing other things he considered unbecoming a female. Ministers and other self-appointed advisors counseled women to defer to their husbands in all things and warned them that a public difference of opinion with a husband was a calamity to be avoided at all cost.

It is no wonder that some lively and strong-minded women chose to remain single. For example, Susanna Wright, a Quaker woman living in western Pennsylvania, was well known as a kind of home-grown lawyer, medical advisor, and general counselor to the community. She was also a champion of the rights of Indians. Considering that she was born in 1697, I was rather intrigued to find that though one Samuel Blunston had repeatedly asked her to marry him, she preferred simply to live as his closest friend and to manage his affairs. Evidently "meaningful relationships" were not invented in the twentieth century. Upon his death he left her all his possessions.[6]

When we come to ask specifically how aged women were viewed, we have less information. From what one can surmise, a great deal depended on social class. A woman who had property to dispose of could count on more respect than a poor widow who might become dependent on the town or her children for support. Not all widows were as realistic as one in South Carolina who noted in a letter to her son: "The death of . . . Parents who leave property is considered more a gain than a loss."[7] Respect also appears to have been a function of usefulness. A grandmother able to spin, weave, churn, and mind the children was more likely to be a valued member of the family than one who sat in the chimney corner complaining about the cold and the younger generation.[8]

If we turn to linguistic evidence, I regret to say that I have found no female equivalent for the word "sage," but there are an unsettling number of times when one finds old women being called hag, crone, or witch. And indeed in Salem old women were actually accused of being witches and hanged. One must conclude that poor women, especially those who were servants or slaves, had a very hard time of it if they outlived their capacity for useful work.

In summary, woman's life in what we nowadays call the preindustrial society was not an easy one. Whether she was an ordinary farmer's wife working from daylight to dark, or married to a wealthy planter with responsibility for the clothing and feeding and medical care of many slaves, whether she was the wife of a small craftsman who helped in the shop and learned his trade, or whether she was one of those who set out for the backwoods and helped her husband clear a field and build a cabin, she had little time to worry about her condition. Without women's labor the economy could not have been built as rapidly as it was, and certainly America would not have been so rapidly populated that by 1776 it was ready to cast off from the main ship and become independent. As for aging women, two in ten made it to age seventy, and for those two the quality of life depended on the economic situation of the whole family connection, on the personalities of their children, and on the woman's own energy and disposition.

From this glimpse of what we do and do not know about our preindustrial forbears, let us take a large leap into the late nineteenth century when the country was in the throes of transformation from a rural to an urban-industrial society. Let us ask: What did that great change mean for women? Until 1920 half our population continued to live on farms, and for farm wives the situation was much as it had been earlier, for they continued to perform essential manual labor and to thrive or wilt depending on the family's total economic situation and their own health and disposition.

For the growing number of women who lived in towns and cities, however, the structure of daily life was changing in fundamental ways. It is important to note that the majority of urban dwellers were wage earners, who often lived on the margin of subsistence. Many were immigrants. It was usually necessary for married women in this segment of the population to contribute to the family income, either by working for wages outside their homes or by taking in what was called "home work"—stitching shoes or clothing or making hats in their own houses. Failing all else, wives of working men took extra people into the family. The estimate is that one in five of all working-class families in the latter part of the nineteenth century took in boarders in the effort to make ends meet.

For obvious reasons these women were less likely than their more prosperous contemporaries to be long lived, but for both men and women in this group the fear of a dependent old age was an ever-present fact of life. There was then no social security, no private pensions. Jane Addams has written about an Italian immigrant weeping bitterly at the death of his fourteen-year-old daughter, and when she tried to comfort him he turned to her and said, "But now who will take care of me when I can no longer work?" The industrialist who told a congressional committee that when his machines wore out he threw them out, and his workers likewise, was probably an extreme case, but it was some variation on that view which made possible the rapid industrial development of this country. I think that for workers the horrors of old age were about equal for men and women.

While the process of industrialization kept the majority of urban wage earners constantly on the edge of unemployment and disaster, for the luckier minority who shared in the newly created wealth, industrialization meant prosperity and upward social mobility. Women in such families experienced something quite new in history: time for something other than working with their hands and bearing and raising children. The demographers tell us that the birthrate began to drop in the year 1800 and that it went down steadily for the rest of the century. The combination of rising family incomes, cheap immigrant or black servants, fewer children, and the early forms of household conveniences created a new social class of women. Some turned to dress and social gatherings, big houses and fine carriages, and developed ever more refined ways of wasting time and money. Such women, in the nature of things, leave very little evidence that they have lived, and so the historian is hard put to find out much about the inner nature of their lives. If it is true, as one of my friends once remarked, that whatever you are like when you are young you will be more so when you get older—then women like these just became steadily more useless as time went by.

But there were other women who, presented with the unprecedented gift of time, began to look beyond their homes to the community, to the social problems of the industrial society, and began to organize reform groups, participate in church work, seek education, and think about their own place in the world. As early as 1797 a group of such women in New York formed a Society for the Care of Poor Widows with Young Children, setting an example that would be followed in hundreds of old and new communities for the rest of the century, of women taking responsibility through voluntary associations for what we would nowadays call welfare work. In new towns on the frontier women joined together to found churches and schools and temperance groups. In the Northeast they began to agitate for the freedom of the slaves and for better educational opportunities for themselves. By 1848 three women, veterans of the abolition movement, sent out a call to all who might be interested to meet in Seneca Falls, New York, to discuss the rights of women — and with only a few days' notice 300 people came. Once there they adopted a ringing statement, based on the Declaration of Independence, calling for an end to legal discrimination, for educational opportunity, for the right to enter the professions, and — most controversial of all — for the right to vote. American feminism was not born at Seneca Falls. It had existed here and there for a very long time, but in 1848 it came out in the open, and the Declaration of Sentiments, as it was called, provided an agenda for a women's rights movement that was to bring about some of the most pervasive social changes in the ensuing century of revolutionary social change.

Feminism was sometimes overt, as in the organized women's rights movement, but more often it was covert, as women built organizations of all sorts and created community institutions to carry out things they wanted to accomplish. Shut out, as they usually were, from traditional social structures — the bench, the bar, the medical profession, the ministry, and higher education — women created their own social organizations that they themselves could run. Women doctors, denied access to male-run hospitals, built their own. A woman lawyer, refused admission to the bar in Illinois and told by the Supreme Court of the United States that God did not intend her to be a lawyer, created a legal newsletter to report things lawyers need to know; it was so thoroughly well done that it soon became indispensable to male lawyers in the Middle West. Women denied admission to Harvard and Yale organized and ran Radcliffe and Bryn Mawr. Women denied the right to vote organized a political movement that after seventy years of unremitting effort wrested the suffrage from all-male Congress and all-male legislatures. Denied the right to preach, they organized the Woman's Christian Temperance Union and developed their skills in the ministry though its multiple programs. Seeing social needs, women invented solutions: kindergartens, juvenile protective associations, consumers' leagues, the Indian Rights Association, the Women's Trade Union League, the Woman's Peace party, not to mention hundreds of local clubs with civic reform as their purpose. The voluntary association was their principal tool, and with it they changed and shaped nineteenth-century America and in the process changed and emancipated themselves.

As a fringe benefit of all this effort—none of it, I might say, easy— many women seem to have enjoyed extraordinary longevity and, what is even more important, to have remained active and effective into very old age. Evidence for this interesting fact may be found in the three-volume biographical dictionary called *Notable American Women*, which contains biographies of 1,359 women, mostly nineteenth-century women, and many of the kind I have just been describing. Out of that number (nearly all were born before 1900 at a time when life expectancy was much lower than it is now), 40 percent lived to be seventy-five, and nearly 30 percent lived to be anywhere from eighty to ninety-nine.

What is even more impressive than sheer longevity—though that is impressive enough—is that so many were active and effective in their chosen fields until very late in life. It would take too long to tell about each of the 364 who lived past eighty, but here are some random examples: Elizabeth Agassiz, the founder of Radcliffe, was still its president at seventy-seven; Amelia Barr, a novelist, wrote her last novel when she was eighty-seven; Lenora Barry, who organized women for the Knights of Labor, was still making public speeches at seventy-eight; Clara Barton, the founder of the Red Cross, was at her desk when she was ninety and was said to be still "vigorous and of youthful appearance." Alva Belmont, suffragist, at seventy-seven appeared before an international gathering to urge the removal of legal disabilities against women. Joanna Bethune, daughter of the woman who founded that first Society for the Care of Poor Widows with Young Children, was still active in the affairs of an orphan asylum at ninety. Elizabeth Blackwell, one of the first woman doctors, practiced medicine until she was seventy-four and continued active for ten years after that. Her sister-in-law Antoinette Brown Blackwell, suffragist and minister, gave her last public lecture at the age of ninety.

In other words, feminism—which I think of as women standing on their own feet and acting in any sphere of life where there is important work to be done—is one of the few effective antidotes to aging we have yet discovered. Being an independent woman with a purpose in life does not provide immortality, of course, but it certainly seems to promote longevity and, what is more important, seems to be the best way to experience a useful and interesting old age.

I suppose there are some statisticians and demographers who are ready to take issue with my evidence and to offer other possible explanations for the longevity represented in this particular group of women, but the more one studies the biographies themselves, the more the explanation seems valid. There is, I would argue, a strong relationship between the willingness of these women to commit themselves to serious tasks and hard work and the nature of their aging.

In the course of writing a biography for a forthcoming supplement to *Notable American Women*, I stumbled on what might almost be called a laboratory experiment bearing on this question. Probably no state in the union was less open to the idea of woman suffrage in the 1880s than the state of Mississippi, but a woman living in Greenville, a leader in her church and in the Woman's Christian Temperance Union, thought women should vote, and so she organized, in spite of considerable social disapproval, the Mississippi Suffrage Association. She was a born politician. Even though she could not vote, she became one of the two leaders of the Democratic party in her county, and when the nineteenth amendment passed, she, at age sixty-one, was the first woman elected to the Mississippi legislature. There she developed an outstanding record; among other things, a committee she chaired reorganized the administration of welfare institutions in the state. In 1924, in her mid-sixties, she represented Mississippi at the Democratic convention and attracted considerable national attention for the leadership she exerted there.

Her life went on in this vein until, at seventy-three, she began to develop cataracts, and in her usual way of taking life head-on, she left Greenville, which had always been her home, and built a little house next door to her son who lived in another town. In a few months her children were startled to see their mother begin to grow old, to lose interest in life. Fortunately, one daughter diagnosed the problem at once and urged her mother to return to Greenville where—as she herself had put it— she could always stir something up by just walking down the street. Sure enough, back in the milieu of her active political life, she shed her aging ways. She found a doctor who cured the cataracts without an operation. Sixteen years later she was still teaching a popular Sunday school class, making public addresses, writing interesting letters, and managing her own money so skillfully that though she had had only a modest inheritance she was able, when she died at eighty-nine, to leave her children a substantial legacy. The only regrettable part of this story is that in 1948 with her usual skill Mrs. Somerville supported Strom Thurmond's States'

Rights party, and of course with that kind of skill at his disposal, he carried the state.

One could go on and on, but it is time to turn to the final point: Are there lessons in all this history that bear upon our own problems, those which I set forth at the beginning? Let me take them up in reverse order.

First, when women outnumber men in large numbers, the importance of being an independent woman is obvious. If one must expect to live for some significant part of life as a widow, it is important to have one's own identity and one's own work. If a woman has always been defined as somebody's wife or somebody's mother, she is not in very good shape at age sixty-five to become a person in her own right. Furthermore, if one is likely to live till eighty or ninety, it is exceedingly important to have a great deal of unfinished work on hand to make it worth getting up in the morning. While some few of us are designed for the contemplative life, many more are most alive when most involved with real problems beyond their own daily existence.

Perhaps therefore it is fortunate that the growing size of the aging population provides just such a set of social needs as historically have called forth the best in women. We are inundated with statistics about the problems of older people and by demands that the government or the foundations or somebody do something about them. Without denying the importance of things the government should and must do, perhaps we should begin to look in a different direction. Just as a substantial number of Americans have turned their backs on the seemingly endless debates in Congress over an energy policy, and have begun to put on sweaters, build greenhouses, polish up their bicycles, create car pools, invest in new kinds of woodstoves, and turn out the lights, just so I would suggest that it is time for those of us who are passing those magic deadlines of sixty or seventy—or 100 for that matter —to turn our attention to what we ourselves can do for the aging population to which we belong. At most the government can make sure that old people have enough to eat and adequate medical care, but beyond that it cannot in the very nature of things meet all the thousand-and-one other needs which older people share. On the other hand, the list of do-it-yourself possibilities is long. We have hardly scratched the surface in community cooperation, for example. No individual can solve the problem of rising energy costs, but communal experiments may help. Some of our children have demonstrated how much can be done to cut loose from the money economy and yet live a good life. I wonder how many of us have the courage to follow their example?

Because in this society women are healthier and live longer than men, and also because their whole history shows that they have been exceedingly good at forming voluntary associations to meet social needs, it seems obvious to me that the next step is for older women themselves to take the lead in organizing to meet some of these well-identified needs. I think it was a woman who coined the slogan, "Don't agonize, organize."

Discrimination against the aged is a complex phenomenon, part of which rests on age-old stereotypes and prejudices, but some of it is a reflection of fear, fear that the increasing numbers of older people will become an intolerable burden on the young. The eighteenth century has something to tell us on this score: useful people are respected no matter how old they are. There are so many things to be done in this society that there is no need for anyone to become old from simple lack of useful work to do. If more people believed this and acted on it, I think the problem of discrimination against the aged would diminish considerably.

Furthermore, there is the great incentive, the fringe benefit of what serious undertakings outside one's own personal life can do for the person. Our nineteenth-century forbears are witness to this: when the society seemed forbidding, saying, "Because you are a woman, you can't do that," they took their own initiatives, created their own groups, and in the process found themselves developing into healthy, long-lived, and interesting people. Just so, I would argue, when someone says, "You're too old to do that," the response must be: "Who says so?"

Such attitudes have been held by women for a long time. For several years two quotations have hung over my desk. One comes from a letter written by that extraordinary suffragist Elizabeth Cady Stanton to her close friend and collaborator Susan B. Anthony. Stanton had just given birth to her sixth child, and Anthony, who was single, had complained about the way numerous babies were delaying their mother's work for suffrage. "Courage, Susan," Stanton wrote, "We shall not reach our prime before fifty and then we shall have twenty good years at least." Her expectation, as it turned out, was too modest; they lived to be eighty-two and eighty-three, respectively, each working to the last day of her life.

The other quotation is from a letter written to Julia Ward Howe (an all-purpose activist through her ninety-three years) by an older aunt when

Howe herself was approaching middle age. "Julia!" the aunt wrote with appropriate exclamation marks, "Never grow old. Whenever you think you cannot do something, get up and do it."

Both these women understood what I have been restating here: the process of aging is to a large extent a self-fulfilling prophecy. If one expects to grow feeble and dull and to be scorned by the young, it is very likely to happen. If one is, like the women I have been describing, too busy even to think much about aging, the process in some mysterious way seems to slow down and to be less debilitating than among people whose minds are on themselves.

I have been talking mainly about women, but clearly the underlying thesis is not tied to sex. All of us, like Tennyson's Ulysses, know in our hearts that it's dull to "pause, to make an end,/To rust unburnished, not to shine in use!/As though to breathe were life!" And so Ulysses called his friends, his shipmates, to a cooperative endeavor: "'Tis not too late to seek a newer world/Push off, and sitting well in order smite/The sounding furrows."

If we too can push off, even in new directions, perhaps some historian of the future will be writing that in the last decades of the twentieth century, the United States of America developed a new élan, not in spite of, but because of, its aging population.

NOTES

1. Alexander Keyssar, "Widowhood in Eighteenth Century Massachusetts: A Problem in the History of the Family," *Perspectives*, 7 (1974), 83-119.

2. John Demos, "Old Age in Early New England," in John Demos and S. S. Bocock, eds., *Turning Points* (Chicago, 1978).

3. Mary E. Wilkins Freeman, *In Colonial Times* (Boston, 1899), contains some insightful short stories that illuminate this subject.

4. Elizabeth Drinker, Journal for 1797, Historical Society of Pennsylvania, Philadelphia.

5. Carl Van Doren, ed., *The Letters of Benjamin Franklin and Jane Mecom* (Princeton, 1950).

6. Gertrude Bosler Biddle and Sarah Dickinson Lowrie, *Notable Women of Pennsylvania* (Philadelphia, 1942).

7. Ray Mathis, ed., *John Horry Dent: South Carolina Aristocrat on the Alabama Frontier* (University, Ala., 1979).

8. Edward James, Janet James, and Paul S. Boyer, eds., *Notable American Women, 1607-1950*, 3 vols. (Cambridge, Mass., 1971).

Are We the Women
Our Grandmothers Were?

This lecture was composed for a collaborative venture between Spelman College and various other Atlanta groups interested in the history of women. The audience was diverse and much engaged in the topic. Many of the ideas will have become familiar to the reader who has made it this far, but perhaps more clearly than any other essay in this volume this one reflects my firm belief that activists of the late twentieth century will find inspiration in their history of the forebears.

It is not difficult to make a case for the fact that the human race is in a bad way. Whether we look at the whole globe, observing its depleted resources, enlarging deserts, polluted oceans, and violent weather; or at the people on that globe, half of them hungry all the time; many, even in the rich countries, living at the margin of existence; others engaged in political struggles which constantly threaten to turn violent; or at our own country, seemingly unable to deal with its own economic problems much less those of the rest of the world—there are more than enough causes for despair.

The virtue—if it is one—of being a historian at a time like this is that one knows, if nothing else, that troubles are not new, that the human race has, most of the time, been in a bad way. It is instructive to remember the Irish monk, writing the history of his own time in 1350 while the Black Death raged across Europe: "I leave parchment to continue this work, if perchance any man survive and any of the race of Adam escape this pestilence and carry on the work I have begun."

Reprinted with permission from the *Atlanta Historical Journal*, 25 (Fall 1981), 5-18.

Or the chronicler 150 years later, leaving a few blank pages in the unlikely event that something else *might* happen before the Day of Judgment, which he was sure must be at hand since everything he could see was in a state of decay. The year was 1492.

At particularly black moments I like to remember the story of the Connecticut Assembly meeting one day in the seventeenth century when an eclipse of the sun occurred—there had been no such event in the memory of those then living, and a good many people argued that it signified the end of the world. The Assembly solemnly debated whether, in that case, it should adjourn. Then the speaker took hold of the situation. "Let the candles be brought," he said. "For if this is indeed the end of the world, let the Almighty find us doing our duty."

I am assuming that whatever Fate has in store for southern women, we want to be found doing our duty.

Southerners, whether historians or not, have more reasons than most Americans to know that life can be very difficult and that happy endings are not inevitable. We were, until 1972, the only Americans who had ever known military defeat, the only Americans who ever thought they might be doomed to permanent poverty. For perspective on our present troubles, let me drop back for a few minutes to Georgia as it was a century ago, in the year 1880.

In that year the entire state contained fewer people than there are today in the five-county metropolitan district surrounding Atlanta— about 1.5 million in all, half of whom were black and a majority of whom had been born in slavery. One hundred twenty thousand white people over the age of ten were illiterate, as were 400,000 black people.

In spite of the fact that half of all the deaths in the state each year were children under five, the population was very young. The median age was twenty-one, and a third of the whole population was of school age.[1]

In 1880 Georgia had had a public school system on the books for ten years, but two-thirds of the children were not in school, and the legislature had shown the greatest reluctance to appropriate money for education.[2]

There was, of course, a university at Athens—criticized by the farmers as being hopelessly aristocratic and by church people as being hopelessly godless—but it hardly made much difference since it enrolled only 200 students each year and spent only $45,000 of the state's funds. For black students there was Atlanta University, chartered in 1867 by the

American Missionary Society and the Freedmen's Bureau and dependent for its existence on northern philanthropy.[3]

In 1880 the Civil War was only fifteen years behind, and the state had just been "redeemed," as the politicians liked to put it, from Reconstruction government. In politics contending groups agreed on the importance of maintaining white supremacy but argued about almost everything else. An overwhelming majority of the people depended on agriculture for a living, and farmers—black or white, poor or not-so-poor—suffered from the consequences of war, neglect, soil depletion, low fertility, and a complex system of borrowing money. The whole state —as the historian of Georgia populism once said—was run like a giant pawn shop.[4]

People who had been planters before the war, most of them at any rate, wanted to establish a labor system as close to slavery as they could come without bringing down the wrath of the federal government. Meanwhile, of course, the freedmen were quickly learning the very limited nature of "freedom" when they had neither land nor money.

While the agricultural majority, about equally divided between black and white, struggled with different degrees of poverty, an all-white urban minority was caught up in the glorious idea of a "New South," which would develop industry, business, and commerce and grow rich. A small group of lawyers, businessmen, industrialists, and politicians combined to build railroads, textile mills, banks, and modern enterprises of various sorts. The state government—which these men effectively controlled— helped them along by such means as the convict-lease system, an arrangement which permitted private citizens to rent convicts for as little as 7¢ a day and use their labor in any way they wished. There were, of course, no laws to prevent women from working long hours for meager pay; children did have the protection that they could only work from sunup to sundown.

One argument for overthrowing the Reconstruction government had been its corruption, but in the new native-born administration of Governor Alfred Colquitt both the state treasurer and the controller were impeached on charges of corruption. Disgraceful scandals surrounded the convict-lease system, though one would have thought its mere existence was scandal enough.[5]

Atlanta was the ideological center of this New South doctrine and was, in comparison with the rest of the state, a boom town. Fulton County, which had only 3 percent of the state's people, controlled 10 percent of its wealth. The city itself had 37,400 people, three miles of paved streets, 10½ miles of tracks for horsedrawn streetcars (you could ride anywhere for a nickel!). Two-thirds of the houses had no indoor plumbing, and a pest house just outside the city limits accommodated the victims of smallpox.[6] Culture with a capital "C" was represented by an opera house, but the young Woodrow Wilson, who spent some time here in the 1880s waiting for a law practice that never materialized, wrote that "the studious man is suspected as a visionary; hereabouts culture is very little esteemed; not indeed, at all because it is a drug on the market, but because there is so little of it that its good qualities are not appreciated."[7]

While enthusiasts talked about the prosperity economic development and industry would bring, the darker side of southern life was very dark indeed. Poverty, illiteracy, night riders, lynchings, people suffering from what would eventually be diagnosed as hookworm and pellagra, despair alleviated by strong drink and religious revivals, and the profound oppression of the freed blacks—all these were part of the social reality.

Among the handful of intellectuals the gravest problem was the narrow limits upon free speech. One of the best of the chancellors of the university said that "every man who thought above a whisper did so at the peril of his reputation" and added that it was a wonder that any leader emerged in light of what he called "a deadly paralysis of the intellect caused by the enforced unanimity . . . the illiberality that is ready to inflict injury or rebuke or ostracism as a penalty for difference of opinion."[8]

In view of all these problems it is not surprising that one of the chief exports of the South was talent, or that it was often the strong and ambitious who left.

For the South as a whole from 1865 to 1905, 2½ million white people left and less than half that number came in. Many national leaders had been born in the South but had had to go elsewhere to use their talents. In the 63rd Congress, for example, the Senate contained six native-born Kentuckians, six Mississippians, four Tennesseans, four North Carolinians, and four Virginians. In all, thirty-six of the ninety-six members were southern born, although only twenty-two represented southern states.[9]

I have spoken chiefly of Georgia, but the rest of the Old South was much the same. Some places were poorer; some had richer land and did a little better; but for the rest of the nineteenth century and well into the twentieth all shared the characteristics described by one worried Alabama man in 1904: "The vast stretches of rural territory (more than seventeen millions of human beings living in places of less than a thousand inhabitants), the prevailing isolation, the few railways, the poor roads, the absence of strong centres of social organization, the remaining poverty, the comparative lack of diversity in industrial life, the schools — and last but not least the two races dividing the land, dividing the churches, dividing the schools — here, indeed, is a task for stout hearts."[10] Yet it was precisely at this dismal time that a few southern women, literally or figuratively the grandmothers of those of us here, began slowly and tentatively to emerge from the confines of what had for so long been defined as "woman's sphere" — that is, the home and the church — into the public arena where these nearly overwhelming social and economic problems would have to be met.

I'm sure I do not have to remind you that in the 1880s all southern women, white or black, old or young, were part of a profoundly patriarchal system. Men of all kinds — planters and politicians, lawyers and businessmen, ministers and plain farmers — took it for granted that they were born to be the decision-makers. Women could be admired, praised, told that they were by nature better than man, exploited, relied upon for various kinds of hard work; they could, of course, bear and raise children; but that they should have opinions about public policy, much less that they should attempt to translate these opinions into political action, was perceived as a dangerous and radical idea, if not indeed a Yankee plot.

Women raised and socialized in this system were given to speaking of themselves as "timid," "shrinking," or "retiring" and to avoiding a great many activities which the society told them were unladylike. Their labor was essential to the survival of the community, but hardly anyone thought that gave them a right to hold public opinions about the way that community functioned.

The change, when it began to come, was the work of a small minority. Of the millions of women alive in the South in 1880, the vast majority, black and white, were fully engaged in simply keeping themselves and their families fed and clothed and in bearing and raising children. Many of them could not read or write and knew little about anything beyond the boundaries of their immediate experience.

There were a few, however, who for various complex reasons were beginning to take a wider view. Identifying those reasons is a challenge to the student of social change, and to do so fully would require more time than I have today. Certainly the experiences of war and Reconstruction, with all the new responsibilities both brought to women, were part of it. Part was the infiltration of outside ideas and most especially the inspiration of certain women from outside: Julia Ward Howe, Susan B. Anthony, and Frances Willard all traveled widely in the South, and we have repeated testimony to the energizing effect their visits had upon women who heard them speak.

One quotation must stand for many: a Mississippi woman who had heard Julia Ward Howe recorded the effect upon herself: "For many years an earnest desire had possessed me to behold a genuinely strong-minded woman—one of the truly advanced type. Beautiful to realize she stood before me, and in a position the very acme of independence—upon a platform delivering a speech."[11] Before long the woman who wrote these words was herself standing on many platforms giving many speeches— and in 1924 she would become the first woman member of the Mississippi Senate—but that gets ahead of my story.

The chief instruments for change were women's voluntary associations.

First to appear were numerous church groups usually called missionary societies. These had existed before the war, but in all the evangelical denominations, black and white, they grew rapidly in the 1870s and 1880s.

Then, following Frances Willard's visits, local units of the Woman's Christian Temperance Union rapidly appeared all over the South.

Next, in the 1880s, secular woman's clubs began to take shape. Their purposes were various—some were principally literary; some were, from the beginning, interested in what they called "civic betterment"; some evolved from one thing to another. For many, women's clubs offered a chance for the education they never had; for others, they were a chance for sociability and exchange of ideas; for still others, they provided a chance to exercise talents for which the organized institutions of the society seemed to have no use. In a few communities black women were beginning to organize their own, all-black, women's clubs with many of the same purposes.

Out of all these in one way or another came, finally, women's suffrage organizations.

Although these four kinds of groups appeared in succession, they continued to exist side by side and with a great deal of overlapping membership. Each was a little more radical than the one which had preceded it, and somewhere among them women of many different temperaments could find compatible associates. The dynamics of all these groups were similar, and the leaders had a good deal in common. They came from highly respectable and reasonably well-to-do families. In the case of black women, they were the wives of ministers and teachers or single women who were themselves teachers. They had, usually, some formal education, but in any case were people who liked to read and write and were nearly always devout church members who believed that women were the moral guardians of society. Many harbored a profound sense of grievance about the ever-present paradox that women, always described by men as superior beings, were constantly treated as inferior ones.

One thing led to another in a fascinating progression. In church societies, for example, women first met together to pray for their salvation. It occurred to someone that since there were so many children who were getting no schooling at all, it might be their Christian duty to organize Sunday schools. When the children came and some showed themselves eager to learn, the women began asking why there were no public schools for them. From such small beginnings came the women's part of the so-called "educational revival" which swept over the South after 1880, encompassing many legislators, the so-called educational governors, northern philanthropists, as well as hundreds of women's groups. Always at the grass roots one finds the women, working away to build school houses, encourage appropriations, and find teachers.

Tracing this development further, we come at once to another track —if there were to be schools, who were to be the teachers? There were not enough qualified men available to fill the need. But if woman were to teach, they must first be taught—and so we find the movement for state-supported teachers colleges spreading across the South, first in Mississippi, then in places like Milledgeville, Georgia, or Greensboro, North Carolina. Some of the women who enrolled to earn a teaching certificate found higher education very much to their liking and began to look for further opportunities. Two case histories—much abbreviated— will illustrate the point: Celestia Parrish, born in Virginia in 1853, orphaned by the war, began teaching to support herself at the age of sixteen. Dissatisfied with her own performanace, she managed to enroll in a local female institute and then in a six-weeks teachers' institute at the University of Virginia. Both these experiences reinforced her ambition to become a truly educated woman, but she had no money and, of course, the University of Virginia was closed to women. There was, however, a normal school open to women at Farmville where she enrolled and did so well that she was put on the faculty. In the course of this experience, she conceived a burning ambition to attend a real university, and in 1891 she spent some time as a student at the University of Michigan. Back in Virginia, she was hired for the faculty of the new Randolph-Macon Woman's College, and by studying summers at Cornell she finally—at age forty-two—completed the work for a college diploma. Enrolled one summer at the University of Chicago, she met John Dewey who was in the midst of his crusade to improve elementary education, and in 1902 she came to Georgia to teach in the state normal school at Athens. There she organized the first elementary school in the South based on Dewey's ideas and began training teachers according to her own standards. Eight years later she was made state supervisor of rural schools in north Georgia, where she had responsibility for 2,400 rural schools and 3,800 teachers in those mountain counties, all of whom she managed to visit once a year. She drove her horse and buggy in and out and over mountains seeking to improve teaching and convince communities that they must support the schools. There is literally no way to measure the effect the work of this one woman had for the children of Georgia, nor of the significance for her of the fact that a normal school was available when she was fired by the ambition to become a teacher.[12]

The second example is Lucy Laney, born in slavery in 1854 and raised by a white family which had owned her mother before emancipation. She went to high school in Macon and then entered the first class in the new Atlanta University. She graduated in 1873 and for the next twelve years taught in public schools. In 1885 she persuaded the Presbyterian Board of Missions for Freedmen to help her open a school for black children in Augusta, which eventually became the Haines Normal and Industrial Institute. Despite financial problems, a typhoid epidemic, a fire, and a flood, the school survived and by the time of World War I had 900 pupils. It was at that school that Mary McLeod Bethune began her teaching career.

Like Parrish, Laney aimed to train good teachers for the public schools. She also established the very first kindergarten in Augusta and a nurses' training school, which eventually became the nursing school of the University of Georgia Medical College. She lived to be eighty, a splendid illustration of the value of Atlanta University to the state.[13]

There are many stories of individual women who were beginning to reshape the fundamental institutions of the South, but time is short so let me say a little about the evolution of associations which began in a small way and developed in unexpected directions.

The Woman's Christian Temperance Union (WCTU) came into being because of concern women felt about the social consequences of alcohol, and in the beginning it simply tried to reform drunkards. But as the members visited men in prison or tried to help families impoverished by the alcoholism of the breadwinner, it was not long before they began to think that social conditions might be at the root of the problem. Whereas once they had been sure that people were poor because they drank, it began to occur to them that some, at least, drank because they were poor—and because they could see no hope for improvement. A few brave—or were they naive?—souls began to wonder aloud whether if wages were better so that families could live decently, the saloon might lose some of its charm.

One such question led to another, and I have no hesitation in saying that by the turn of the century the WCTU was not only one of the most significant social forces in the South (in terms of the kinds of questions it was asking and the kinds of women it was attracting), but also that it was in some ways one of the most radical. It is not surprising to find that when Rebecca Latimer Felton, next to Tom Watson the most crusading reformer to come out of postwar Georgia, decided that the women ought to tackle the notorious convict-lease system, she rallied the WCTU to help her. It took a long time, but they finally got rid of it.

The convict-lease fight—which was carried on in one southern state after another by women's groups—is also a good example of how these self-styled conservative women moved step by step toward demanding the right to vote. As they began to ask questions about the existing order, it soon became apparent that many of the changes they wanted to bring about would require legislation. So they began to appear, in their flowered hats and white gloves, before legislative committees. They were received with a maximum of chivalry and a minimum of serious attention. It did not take them long to realize that elected officials were far more sensitive to the demands of voters than to those of the disfranchised. Thus it was that the WCTU became a nursery for suffragists.

If we were to write the history of southern women's voluntary associations over the half century that followed their small beginnings in the 1880s, we would be struck by the ability of the active minority to sustain effort in the face of opposition, apathy, and sometimes outright efforts to shut them up. We could list their goals under at least two major headings: first, they wanted to create institutions which would enrich the life of the community—schools, libraries, parks, kindergartens, and the like. These things, though they required sustained work, did not require unusual courage. The principal problem was persuading enough people to be willing to tax themselves for community improvement.

The Atlanta Neighborhood Union is a good example. It was founded in 1908 by the faculty wives and women in the neighborhood of Spelman and Morehouse colleges and began with a playground for black youngsters. Women ran it, and as they met together they began to talk about other neighborhood problems that needed attention. In time they came to describe their purpose as the "moral, economic, and social advancement of Negroes in Atlanta." They undertook a wide range of social services, including summer schools for children and clubs for mothers. After a time they were ready to engage in systematic lobbying as well as coop- eration with white religious leaders and white women. Probably the key person in this particular organization was Lugenia Hope, wife of the president of Atlanta University.[14]

There was another important category of women's work. As time went by and women looked with more and more discernment upon the society in which they were living and raising their children, they began to question certain institutions and practices which were a source of profit to some of their fellow citizens. The convict-lease system was one such institution, and in Georgia it took twenty years of hard work to bring it to an end. Child labor and the low wages and bad working conditions in the textile mills were another. When middle-class women began to take a deeper interest in such matters, they suddenly found chivalry going out the window. Angry textile magnates told them they were unladylike, unfeminine monsters in petticoats and that they should not talk about things that their female minds were incapable of under- standing, such as the relationship between low wages and high profits. But it did not stop there. Husbands of such women, if their businesses happened to be vulnerable, were told—as, for example, happened in North Carolina—keep your wife out of this or lose our business. The YWCA was told that there would be no further contributions from the business community if it persisted in seeking to investigate working conditions in the mills. The effort to put an end to child labor was characterized as the work of outside agitators. And so on.[15]

Of all issues the most sensitive was that of race relations. Yet, as early as 1900, some southern white women were beginning to express their uneasiness about the conflict between Christian doctrine and the structure of race relations as they experienced it. The first open discussion of this subject, as far as I can determine, took place in Methodist missionary societies, and it was one of them which took the first initiative to set up settlement houses in black neighborhoods. It was Methodist women, I think, who first began to ask in their meetings, what does Christian doctrine demand of us in respect to justice for black people?

Lily H. Hammond, a Methodist woman whose husband was president of Paine College in Augusta, published a book in 1914 called *In Black and White*, which, though it certainly did not call for social equality, developed in detail the need for justice.

Black women, of course, had no doubt that the system of race relations in the South—indeed in the nation—was evil. For reasons that are obvious, many black women leaders were in the North—though I suspect there were also many in southern communities whose work has gone unrecognized.

To take just one example, let us pause one moment with Ida Wells, born in Mississippi of slave parents in 1862, freed along with them at the end of the war. She went to a freedman's high school and an industrial school in Holly Springs, Mississippi, and then when her parents died in the yellow fever epidemic she began—at age fourteen—teaching school. By the 1880s she was teaching in Memphis and going to summer school at Fisk University. While traveling on the Chesapeake and Ohio Railroad, she refused to move to the car designated for black people, and when she was forced to do so, sued the railroad. She won her case in the circuit court but lost on appeal.

She wrote articles for a local paper and in time became half-owner of a Memphis paper called *Free Speech*. When she began to write about the inadequate schools for black children, she was fired from her school job and thus became a full-time journalist. In 1892 she denounced the lynching of three Memphis black men, charging that their only fault had been competing successfully with white storekeepers. Finally, her paper was mobbed and burned, and she had to leave the South. From New York she launched a one-women antilynching campaign. Though she married and had four children, she continued her career as a social reformer and by the time of her death in 1931 was one of Chicago's leading citizens. Her autobiography has been published by the University of Chicago Press.[16]

Even now, twenty-five years since I first began to discover evidence of this early activity, it still amazes me to find these so-called shy, retiring, southern white women and their oppressed counterparts in the black community coming to the fore in what would soon be called interracial work. The resistance was tremendous, and through the eyes of black women what the white woman did was the merest beginning. But compared to what the society as a whole was willing to think about between 1900 and 1914, this little group of church women must be seen as radical pioneers. A recent book, Jacquelyn Hall's *Revolt against Chivalry*, details the work of Jessie Daniel Ames and the Association of Southern Women for the Prevention of Lynching and tells about the 40,000 church women in small towns and cities across the South pledging to use their influence to prevent lynching in their own communities and insisting that their honor was in no way protected by brutality.[17]

While the most active women were consciously trying to bring about changes in the society, they were also—perhaps less consciously—changing themselves, revising their own self-images. In the long run, they would help bring about a profound change in the status of women in southern society.

Probably many people here could write this part of the story by analogy with their own experience. These self-styled shy, retiring, timid women who came together from a variety of motives organized themselves according to parliamentary procedures and set about their projects of self-education, civic improvement, and social exchange. In order for this to happen, it was necessary for some of them to preside over meetings, to collect and account for money, and—in due time—to speak in public to men, even legislators and governors.

I am not going to try to tell you that the result of these experiences was the same for every woman—and if I did you would not believe me. Nor do I mean to suggest that every woman who joined a missionary society or a woman's club became overnight a skillful and sensitive critic of society prepared to work for its improvement. You and I know too many people in this supposedly enlightened age for whom voluntary associations are a place to wear a new dress, or to exchange gossip, or just to get out of the house, to attribute any such general virtue to our grandmothers.

But for the few, for those who felt themselves growing in skill and effectiveness and liked the feeling, for those who found they could think about public issues and have new ideas, for those who enjoyed the public eye, women's groups provided an almost unique opportunity, and women made the most of it.

In their letters to each other, in speeches to all-women groups, feminist sentiments abound. The concrete manifestation of the growth of feminism cannot be wholly measured by the minority of southern women who openly espoused suffrage. There were all degrees of latent discontent, and the close reader of letters, diaries, even of stories and poems written by women during these years will pick up a great deal of evidence for it.

In 1920, no thanks to southern legislatures, the nineteenth amendment was ratified, and white women everywhere had the right to vote. For black women, though the legal right existed, it was four decades before the Civil Rights Act of 1964 made the right a reality. Among white women the story of what happened next in the South is as interesting as what went before. It was as if a considerable accumulation of energy had been somehow blocked and was suddenly released. The women who had worked so hard for suffrage began at once to try to use that newly acquired right to bring about some of the changes which they had so long envisioned. They worked tirelessly to inform women of their rights and to teach them what they needed to know about registration and voting and about political action. Groups ranging from the United Daughters of the Confederacy and the Daughters of the American Revolution on the conservative side to the YWCA and the League of Women Voters on the more liberal end of the spectrum joined in legislative action committees in every state capital. Male politicians were astounded, and on the whole not much pleased, by the outburst of energy and the women's talk about cleaning up politics.

The progressive movement, which historians have solemnly declared died in World War I, turns out to have been alive and well in many southern states in the 1920s. No one has yet made a careful, systematic study of what these women's legislative campaigns were or made up a won-lost statement of the causes they supported. Certainly the political game turned out to be more difficult than many of them had allowed for, and they were often out of step with the mood of the decade. In spite of all this, I think when that careful study is made we will find that a good many things were accomplished, some of which are still making life a little easier for lots of people today.[18]

When an opportunity comes to tell stories about these amazing women — our grandmothers — I find self-restraint difficult; the temptation is to go on and on. But time presses, so let me stop and make the major point. What these women were doing, by action more than by theory, was to change the pevailing social values of the South in their day and generation.

It was a time of trouble; it was a time when many people thought that the most pressing need was for economic growth and development. I have no doubt that many women thought so, too, and that they welcomed any improvement in the wealth of the community and enjoyed it when it came to them personally.

But they stood firmly on the principle that people were more important than profits. They were constantly asking—to use the modern phrase which has become a cliché—about the quality of life. They were in the habit of using the Bible as a source of inspiration, and they referred often to the question: What profiteth a man to gain the whole world and lose his soul?

Looking backward, it is easy to call them naive; nothing in their education or their experience prepared them to make a fundamental analysis of the relationship of economics to politics. But they had been raised to believe that women were the moral guardians of the society, and they saw things which they did not believe were right: poor schools, injustice to black people, subsistence wages, exploitation of those who could not protect themselves. They realized that the prosperity of individuals did not automatically lead to improvement in the community.

And so they began to ask questions, began to work to achieve the things they thought ought to be done. No one could claim that they succeeded in changing all of the fundamental values of the society, but they did bring about significant modifications. This is nowhere clearer than in the area of race relations. We have still a very long way to go; but that way would be longer still if our grandmothers had not begun the enormous task of bringing about essential change in attitudes. Schools were built; the convict-lease system was abandoned; wages were somewhat improved and protective legislation for women laid the groundwork for protective legislation for all workers; parks and libraries and even trees improved the quality of life in hundreds of communities. Opportunities were created for women themselves which have made possible the lives you and I have been able to live in the twentieth century. At first glance my title probably seemed to you ridiculous. Are we the women our grandmothers were? The answer is so clearly NO. We, with our equal access to education, our freedom to marry or not marry, to determine the number of children, to hold any job, to sit in legislative bodies, even to become mayors and senators—are we not unrecognizably different? And, of course, at one level we are. Here in Georgia women have been prodigiously important in nearly every significant change of the past thirty-five years.

But—again because of their tendency to read the Bible—our grand-mothers were fond of saying something to the effect that as our needs are, so our strength shall be. I hope it is true.

Because, as they did, we confront society in which troubles appear on every hand and in which—to oversimplify dramatically—the issue is wealth versus people, and the issue of the true cost of economic growth is just beginning to be clear. The 220 million Americans of 1980 are richer by far than the 50 million in 1880; whether they are wiser, happier, or more likely to survive is an open question.

And underlying the complex, interdependent problems that we see everywhere, there are, for Americans, once again issues of fundamental social values.

What do we, as a community of people, think really matters? If we think that driving cars, owning houses, eating and drinking and dressing well are the most important things in life—no matter what the cost to the environment, to the limited resources of the globe, to our relations with the poorer peoples of the globe, or indeed to the poorer people in our own communities—then we shall in the end certainly lose those things.

The question for southern women in the 1880s came to be, What really matters? So it is for us. We do not have much time to decide. The meaning of my title is really this: are we, in relation to our greater means, our greater freedom, as committed to the overall good of the community as our grandmothers were? From those to whom much has been given, much can be expected. Perhaps thinking about the women I have here labeled our grandmothers will be some help as we try to find our way.

NOTES

1. J. T. Henderson, *The Commonwealth of Georgia* (Athens, 1974). See also *Compendium of the Tenth Census* (Washington, D.C., 1885).

2. Alex M. Arnett, *The Populist Movement in Georgia* (New York, 1922), p. 64.

3. *Atlanta University, 1865-1965*, pamphlet in the collection at Duke University, Durham, N.C.

4. C. Vann Woodward, *Origins of the New South* (Baton Rouge, 1951).

5. *Compendium of the Tenth Census.*

6. Ray Stannard Baker, *Life and Letters of Woodrow Wilson* (Garden City, N.Y., 1927), 1:169.

7. Walter Hill, writing in *The Nation*, Jan. 1906, p. 6.

8. *Congressional Directory* 63rd Cong., 1st sess., 1913.

9. Edgar Gardener Murphy, *Problems of the Present South* (New York, 1904), p. 284.

10. Belle Kearney, *A Slaveholder's Daughter* (New York, 1900), p. 108.

11. Edward James, Janet James, and Paul S. Boyer, eds., *Notable American Women* (Cambridge, Mass., 1971), 3:18-20.

12. *Ibid.*, 2:365-466.

13. Gerda Lerner, "Community Work of Black Club Women," in her *The Majority Finds Its Past* (New York, 1979).

14. Anne Firor Scott, *The Southern Lady: From Pedestal to Politics, 1830-1930* (Chicago, 1970), pp. 134-61. See also Mary O. Cowper Papers, Department of Manuscripts, Duke University.

15. Alfreda M. Duster, ed., *Crusade for Justice* (Chicago, 1970).

16. *Crusade for Justice: The Autobiography of Ida B. Wells* (Chicago, 1970).

17. Jacquelyn Hall, *Revolt against Chivalry* (New York, 1979).

18. Scott, *Southern Lady*, pp. 185-211; Marion Roydhouse, "The Universal Sisterhood of Women: Women and Labor Reform in North Carolina, 1900-1932" (Ph.D. diss., Duke University, 1980).

Education and the
Contemporary Woman

In January 1966 Wayne Booth, who was then dean of the College at the University of Chicago, organized a conference on the subject of "the knowledge most worth having" and asked me to talk about women's higher education in that context. Since the invitation came rather late, the paper was composed in some haste, and until page proofs arrived I had not suspected that it would become part of a book. Its somewhat telegraphic style and the number of inadequately developed ideas make me wince a bit, but I am reprinting it here because it represents an early effort to formulate the idea which came to be called "women's studies." Earlier feminists had understood the importance of providing young women with the history of their own sex, and the nineteenth century saw the production of many fat volumes devoted to the biographies of great women in the past. Early suffragists were acutely conscious of preserving their records, and in the 1920s Goucher College had offered a college course in women's history. By the mid-1960s all that had disappeared, and no college was then offering a course in any of the fields we now call women's studies. It seemed to me that women in colleges and universities would respond to some academic attention to the history of their sex, though I had no vision of the explosion of courses which would take place in the following decade.

I can think few more risky ways of spending an academic hour than discussing the education of women. Many gallons of ink, much breath,

Reprinted with permission from Wayne Booth, ed., *The Knowledge Most Worth Having* (Chicago: University of Chicago Press, 1967), pp. 141-50.

and maybe even a little blood are spent on this subject every year—
without in the least promoting general agreement.

Yet it is a subject that I find impossible to avoid, as I examine the
inadequacies of my own education, the hopes I have for a fifteen-year-
old daughter, and the daily concerns of young women in my classes. In
the process of examining this subject over the years, I have acquired a
vast grab bag of ideas, bons mots, obiter dicta, and the like, picked up
from all kinds of people (mostly men) who write on the subject. What
your invitation has forced me to do is to ask myself, Can I make any
sense of all this talk? What do I myself really believe?

One means of making sense of any subject is to try to put it in some
kind of order, and so my first step is to sort out the grab bag into three
boxes: (1) How did we get here? In short, what do I know about the
history of women's education? (2) What are the problems confronting
women who seek to become educated today? (3) What are some of the
elements I would like to include in the education of young college women
of this generation?

Women in any society or culture are always educated by the culture
itself as to what the female role is. This is true in civilized societies as
well as in primitive ones, but civilized societies are also concerned about
whether women need formal education, and if so what its nature should
be. Plato in the Fifth Book of *The Republic* finally decided that his female
guardians would need the same education as the male guardians, even
though he had some emotional doubts about this. Regardless of Plato's
theory, however, we do not find any women taking part in the Socratic
dialogue, which was the higher education of Plato's day.

Down the road a few kilometers from Athens, the Spartans had also
given thought to the education of women and prescribed a very vigorous
program, aimed at excellent physical development. This was primarily so
that the women would have strong, healthy children—and if you follow
the arguments about educating women through the ages you will frequently
find that the central question is not, Does the woman need to be educated
for her own benefit? but, Will it be good for the children?

In the Middle Ages most women were too hard at work even to
learn to read, but a few great ladies were excellently taught; you may
have heard of the *professoressa* at the University of Bologna who was so
beautiful she had to wear a veil in order not to distract her students who
were, presumably, mostly male. You have heard that Queen Elizabeth read
Latin for pleasure (she said it was pleasure, anyway), and you may also

know the remark in one of Daniel Defoe's essays: "A woman well bred and well taught is a creature without comparison. . . . She is all softness, and sweetness, peace, love, wit and delight. . . . Rob her of the benefits of education and . . . she degenerates to be turbulent, clamorous, noisy, nasty and the devil."

I am not sure that Defoe's opinion was shared in seventeenth-century Massachusetts, where Mistress Anne Hutchinson used her formidable learning in theology to threaten the theocracy, or by Napoleon in the nineteenth century when he was so intimidated by intellectual prowess of Madame de Staël that he ordered her not to come within forty miles of Paris. Madame de Staël's younger American contemporary, Margaret Fuller, calmly remarked: "I now know all the people worth knowing in America and I find no intellect comparable to my own." Which, as Perry Miller has commented, may have been the simple truth.

Few of these women, of course, had been to school. And they stand out because they are exceptional. Their experience tells us very little about the educational experience of everywoman. For that, let us rely for the moment only on American history.

In order to understand the history of education in this country, it is necessary to realize — and here I lean heavily on Bernard Bailyn's wonderful little book, *Education in the Forming of American Society* (Chapel Hill, 1960) — what happened to the educational process when it was transferred to North America by the colonists. Bailyn cogently argues that it was in the American colonies that the process of separating education from the family — a process now far advanced in many parts of the world — began. Education became the preeminent means of adjusting to a rapidly changing world. It became the basis for social mobility and the road to power. Look at the Constitutional Convention, for example, with its high proportion of college graduates.

Now what about women in all this? As long as education was a process of growing up in an extended family, in which fathers taught sons what they needed to know and mothers taught daughters, the women were as well educated for their role in life as the men. But in the colonies, with their wealth of free land, the extended family did not long survive. Parents' experience was no longer adequate to the needs of the new world: indeed, the children, being more malleable, might adjust better. And when schools outside the home flourished and colleges (such as Harvard, William and Mary, Kings, and Princeton) were founded for men only, what then?

The status of women had improved in America compared to England at the same time, but on this point able women had reason to feel aggrieved, and so they did. Read Abigail Adams's letters to John, deploring her lack of learning. Or note the wide sale of Mary Wollstonecraft's book in America.

If you add to the great importance that education assumed in the making of American society, the vast changes brought about by the Industrial Revolution, which gradually removed from the home many of the duties which had constituted woman's significant contribution to the economy and well-being of the family—in due course you get enough discontent to power the engine of change.

By the third decade of the nineteenth century, in conjunction with some men whose observation had convinced them that women cut off from what was becoming the mainstream of life did not make very good wives, a handful of women began to found colleges (as Mary Lyon at Mount Holyoke) or to attend colleges newly opened to women (as Lucy Stone at Oberlin). This was the beginning of a great revolution in the status of women in America.

Lest you think that it came easy, go back and read some of the bitter arguments of the time. Woman's physical structure could not stand the strain of study, it was said. They would get brain fever. And anyway their brains were too small. Above all, it was unladylike. Marion Talbot, who was the first dean of women at the University of Chicago, said that when she decided to go to college certain of her mother's friends never afterward spoke her name, and added that only in Washington "women were kind to me for they did not know I was a college graduate."

And lest we grow too smug about how much was accomplished, it may be worth remembering that as late as the 1940 census only 3.7 percent of the women over twenty-five in this country had had four years of college. Even today only 15 percent of the young women in this country go to college.

Social change works in mysterious ways. The first generation of women college graduates were, intellectually speaking, "all dressed up and no place to go." They were educated (and had not died of brain fever), but the world did not welcome them as doctors, lawyers, college teachers, or in any of the hundreds of jobs in the business and professional world. One result was that many of them invented jobs for themselves —the most spectacular case in point taking place not many miles from here, on the corner of Polk and Halsted, where Jane Addams, who had gone to Rockford, and Julia Lathrop, who had been to Smith, Florence Kelley, a Cornell graduate, and Alice Hamilton, an early woman medical doctor, created at Hull-House one of the most vital centers of social thought and action in America, and incidentally invented the profession of social work.

These and others like them created an alternative image for young American women.

Forty years earlier a girl had two possible destinies: if she was poor she might leave the farm and work in a factory where, with luck, she died young. If she stayed on the farm or if she was a member of the comfortable middle class, she grew up and got married, and if she failed in that goal she would be an old maid and live out her days as an unpaid servant in the house of some relative, the kind maiden aunt in all the stories, whom everybody imposed on because failures get imposed on.

By 1900 — thanks to the bold pioneers — there was another alternative. You could grow up and go to college (if your father could be persuaded) and learn how to earn your own living, and then if the right man never came along you could stand on your own feet and even, if you had talent, carve out for yourself a significant place in the world. It is almost impossible for us today to comprehend what this meant to women who were not certain that the right man *would* come along, and who knew from firsthand experience how many miserable women there were, married to men they did not like or respect, and trapped with children they did not want (not in such numbers, anyway), because marriage was woman's only proper estate.

The first generation or two of women for whom education was available reveled in their freedom, to work, to travel, not to marry unless it suited them. But generations turn over quickly, and as college education for women became more common, the pioneering spirit began to dim. Girls found they might earn an A.B. and yet be married (Martha Carey Thomas, the formidable president of Bryn Mawr, had once remarked — "Only our failures marry" — but that was in the early days when women's colleges were working so hard to be as intellectual as Harvard or Yale that they overshot the mark and became more intellectual than Harvard or Yale ever thought of being).

Then another generation or two went by, and for reasons much discussed but by no means clear, there seems to have been a vast falling off in ambition. Girls still flock to college (all 15 percent of them, that is), but among able high school graduates fewer women than men go to college. Of those who do, some drop out before finishing, and it seems to be a problem if not a disgrace if one arrives at graduation without an engagement ring (a paradoxical inversion of Thomas's celebrated comment). Of women lawyers, the proportion remains about the same today as in 1910. Of women doctors the number remains small, and in the colleges and universities female professors are a small minority, becoming smaller. The women physicists in this country can hold a meeting in a hotel room, and the women economists do not require much more space. When President Lyndon Johnson said in all sincerity (having counted the voters and find women outnumbering men) that he wanted to appoint fifty women to high federal office not half that number could be found.

For nearly a decade discussion has swirled about this phenomenon, and, though many theories have been advanced, no one has come up with a comprehensive explanation of the tides of fashion in women's role. Without knowing precisely why things are as they are, we can still ask what questions may be raised about women's education by this curious pattern of a revolution in reverse.

1. You will hear it said that some women are as capable as some men of doing any job, but that in this culture the subtle expectations of women's roles are such that girls grow up believing they are not capable of comprehending the really hard subjects or of doing the really hard jobs. This problem of expectation is to be identified all the way from kindergarten to graduate school, in overt and covert forms. Science and mathematics are the favorite examples of subjects that in some cultures girls flock to, but, which in ours are shunned. In the Moscow High School for example, 80 percent of the college-bound women are said to be science majors.

2. You will hear it said that men are afraid of competition from women, and therefore—having got there first—bar the door. If this is a major problem, we should not waste our time worrying about the education of women but should forthwith embark upon the re-education of men. (This is not a joke, but may indeed be the heart of the matter.)

3. You will hear it said that society, since it really does not believe in achieving women, makes it as difficult as possible for women to marry and do something else in addition. Day care is only for the poor, household help is hard to get and inefficient. Children must be car-pooled where public transport is insufficient, and in any case they need, or seem to need, large amounts of maternal supervision.

This is a perfectly enormous problem that cannot be tossed off lightly even in its relation to women's education. But it is a problem of the larger society.

If we come back to special questions of women in college, the arguments about curriculum and program planning for women students usually turn out to be based on one of three assumptions: (1) we should plan women's education according to their needs (usually unspecified, and rightly so, since no one knows for sure what they are); (2) we should plan women's education according to their capacities (which may or may not be the same as those of men, even if they are just as large); or (3) we should plan women's education according to the lives they are going to lead.

The trick would be to figure out a plan that would be based on all three of these assumptions. Is it possible?

1. As to needs, beyond food, shelter, and sex, I am not certain that any two psychologists have ever agreed on an inherent human need, much less one specific to women. Nevertheless, without being dogmatic perhaps one can say that most sensitive people feel a need to figure out what life is all about. Part of what they want from college is help in making sense of their experience, in order to answer the questions: What is it to be a man? What is it to be a woman? To male students we offer, as part of a liberal education, what men have thought on this question, from Plato to David Riesman.

To the extent that the question is a human question, a girl can learn a great deal by reading Aristotle or Locke or Rousseau. But in my ideal curriculum for women we will have also a seminar for freshman girls that will be based on reading what *women* have thought and felt about life, men, children, art, and religion—from Sappho to Margaret Mead. We would read the diaries and memoirs and letters and poems of women who were trying to make sense of their experience.

Beyond this, my ideal curriculum for women (as well as for men) would take each student in depth into at least one major area of knowledge so that by graduation the student would have a sense of mastery, of competence, which is the basis for self-respect. Such competence can have a subtle effect upon a woman's whole image of herself and a very pervasive influence upon her future life.

2. As to capacities, here I think the difference between men and women is insignificant. In each sex there are the truly remarkable, the very able, and the run-of-the-mill. All I ask for women is that the truly remarkable not find themselves rejected when they aspire, and that the

very able and run-of-the-mill have a chance to find out what options life holds beyond those they have experienced in their own families. This is as much a matter of faculty concern and attitudes as it is of curriculum.

3. As to educating women for the life they are going to lead, this is where some hard thinking needs to be done. It is clear that a woman's life pattern, even if she elects to remain single, is going to be different from that of her contemporary men friends. If she marries, and if she has children, it will be very different.

I suspect the colleges should face up to this. I suspect that instead of commenting on all the difficulties and drawbacks that biology presents, we should ask ourselves how many of these could be turned into assets for women and for society. So, as I would offer the freshman girls a seminar on women through the ages, I would offer senior girls a seminar called "Where do you go from here?" I would encourage them to think, analyze, and shape their future plans to a program of on-going self-education. Much of women's daily life is concerned with direct experience, without the mediation of books, but this experience can be turned to account for educational purposes.

Most young women will leave the world of school and the world of work while their children are small. Does this mean stagnation, mental and physical? Not necessarily, but it does mean that planning and foresight are of the essence.

Obviously the ramifications of all these ideas are complex and would require the most careful thought. They are not parts of a tidy program, but an effort to reach out a bit from where we are and take hold of some visible problems.

Woman's Place Is in the History Books

I can no longer remember where or when I first gave this lecture, but had I had the foresight to keep copies of its successive versions I would have now a reasonable outline of the development of the field over the past ten years. In this particular form it became the opening lecture for a summer seminar for college teachers of American history sponsored by the Woodrow Wilson Fellowship Foundation and the National Endowment for the Humanities in 1979. The seminar was one of the most successful of many efforts to address the question: How do the findings of historians of women change our view of the American past?

The anticipation with which many people regard the opening of a new decade is an example of the way artificial structures, in this case the Gregorian calendar, can take on a life and symbolic power beyond their original purpose. Even rational historians are not immune to the sense that somehow the 1980s will be different from the 1970s—and I suppose the more we think so, the more it is likely to be so.

It may be only coincidence that we are in a new decade, but I am reasonably sure that we are witnessing a new phase in the development of what we have been calling women's history. The existence of this institute, and a number of similar ones, reinforces that conviction. But before we talk about where we are going it might be useful to look at where we have been—to examine briefly the history of women's history.

For more than 100 years an occasional, perceptive observer commented upon the fact that written history usually overlooked half the human race. Many of these observers were well-educated feminists rather than professional historians. A number of them compiled or wrote books about women, past or contemporary, in an effort to fill this gap. But the "real" historians—and that is to say the men—took little notice. Their books, articles, and collections of documents continued, as they always had, to center on the male past.

The reasons for the persistence of this one-sided vision are too complex to be completely unraveled in a single lecture. Speaking broadly, however, we can say that historians of the United States in the eighteenth and nineteenth centuries were preoccupied with politics and diplomacy, two areas of life for which voluminous archival sources were readily available, and two areas in which, coincidentally, nearly all the actors were male. Even when history was broadened to include attention to institutions, economics, or ideas men were still the focus.

Now written history always reflects the particular historian's conception of the past, whether or not he has articulated it or is even aware of his assumptions.

Listen, for example, to Jack Hexter, a distinguished historian of early modern Britain, writing more than thirty years ago in a review of Mary Beard's book, *Woman as a Force in History*. After condescending to Beard by suggesting that she was not saying much that was new, Hexter added that, of course, women had always been part of society, but since they had never had the power to bring about significant change, the historians were quite right to ignore them. Such power, he went on, resided in the councils of princes, the magistracies of towns, the great leagues of traders, and the faculties of the universities. He wound up with this bit of verbal pyrotechnics: "Through no conspiracy on the part of the historians, the College of Cardinals, the Consistory at Geneva, the Parliament of England, the Faculty of the Sorbonne, the Directors of the Bank of England, and the expeditions of Columbus, Vasco da Gama, and Drake have been pretty much stag affairs." (He overlooked, of course, Isabella and Elizabeth, without whom Columbus and Drake might never have sailed.) But—in any case—so much for Beard. Hexter's view of what really mattered in the past was clear.

Though an occasional maverick asked different sorts of questions of the historical record—one thinks, for example, of Frederick Jackson Turner, Arthur Schlesinger, Sr., Dixon Ryan Fox, and Edward Eggleston—the overwhelming preponderance of American historical writing at least until the 1920s was based on assumptions quite similar to those Hexter revealed in the statement I have just read. Politics, diplomacy, and great men "made" history.

In 1940 Caroline Ware, introducing a volume of essays called *The Cultural Approach to History*, presented a very different view and fore-shadowed some important changes that were soon to come: "The concept of culture implies that any given society is an integral—though not necessarily a completely integrated—whole, in which basic processes of living and characteristic social relationships constitute a pattern of social behavior. The pattern of culture conditions individuals, providing their basic assumptions and their tools of observation and thought, and setting the frame for their living. It determines the forms of institutions, the types of personality which will be developed, and the types of conduct which will be sanctioned" (pp. 10-11). She went on to argue that to reconstruct fully the social reality of the past, historians needed to study the *whole* culture, not just one or two of its manifestations. By the end of World War II a good many scholars here and in Europe began to move in that direction.

In the 1950s and 1960s a growing number of American scholars thought of themselves as social or cultural historians and had come to that definition of what they were doing by a variety of routes. Some had been influenced by mentors like Schlesinger, Sr., or Oscar Handlin; some had been inspired by E. P. Thompson or the Cambridge Group in England; some were influenced by the *Annales* school in France; some were self-made. But disparate as they were, they had in common an interest in social institutions and cultural values, and the belief that in the long run the more visible and easily described diplomatic or political events were an expression of these institutions and values. Thus they were inevitably interested not just in leaders, but in all the people who made up the society.

In order to pursue such lines of analysis they were forced to experiment with new methods and to put new questions to old data. We have seen a good deal of painstaking work in demography, in family reconstitution, and in various kinds of cultural values. Such studies are egalitarian: of necessity they deal with all kinds of people and both sexes.

As these new intellectual currents were taking shape in the discipline, an important force came from another direction. In the early 1960s American feminism, which had been somewhat dormant for two decades, suddenly came to life with great vigor, and on every hand women were once again asking questions about their place in the world and their role in society and once again protesting the constraints upon their chance to develop. Among the questions they were raising was the old one: Why are women historically invisible? Some among them took things into their own hands and began to train themselves as historians of women. Thus the convergence of an intellectual development and a social movement gave rise to a new field in American history. Once in existence, it grew with what I think was unprecedented speed.

In 1958 all the historians of women in the United States could have met in the tiny hotel room, which was all any one of the three could afford at historical meetings. Twenty years later conferences on women's history attracted 2,000 people and overran whole college campuses.

I know of no phenomenon like it in the whole history of American intellectual life. Indeed, it presents itself as an interesting subject for analysis by some student interested in the sociology of knowledge. Not only the speed with which the field developed, but also the immense energy and commitment which it called forth are worth some study. From undergraduates writing term papers to old scholars engaged in summing up their life work, the history of women commands a level of involvement with the source material which makes for sustained excitement. I have not been alone in observing that undergraduates in a course in women's history will work much harder than those same people would be likely to do in another course.

In addition to commitment, community has characterized this group of scholars. Nowhere else in the discipline as far as I can judge has there been so much sharing of resources, so much helping along of other people in the sometimes rocky paths of academic scholarship. In a profession where competition is the norm and where occasionally it is possible to witness the war of all against all, historians of women are a notable exception. I hope that this is not just a phenomenon of the early, beleaguered stage of development, but that it will continue now that we are a bit more established.

The output from all these scholars has been widely various. There has been an intense interest in the social dynamics of women's education and women's voluntary associations. Women's work has been examined in many ways. The plantation, the frontier, and various wars have been reexamined to ask: What were women doing? Family life, sexuality, birth control, and prostitution have found their historians. The nature of female friendships and the structure of women's networks have been studied. Comparative studies are beginning to be made. Numbers of impressive individuals have been discovered or rediscovered, and biographical studies are proliferating.

In addition to the articles and monographs that are filling in so many gaps in our written history, two significant works of reference have had a vastly stimulating effect. First, in 1971 came the three-volume *Notable American Women*, a compilation of 1,359 biographies which, taken together, show what a vital role women have always played in the development of American culture and provide the basis for a more complete understanding of American feminism than had previously been possible. One of the major insights which came to any person brave enough to read through all the volumes had to do with the importance of women as creators of institutions. There was a great deal of evidence about women's part in creating the nation's educational system; there was documentation for what some of us had long suspected: that women had provided many of the ideas and much of the energy for the Progressive movement. Women's movement into the professions, women inventing their own careers, women working out new adjustments to the life cycle —all this and much more presented itself for reflection and further study. In 1980 the first supplement to *Notable American Women* was published, containing biographies of women who died between 1950 and 1975. The total pool of names from which 400 had to be painfully chosen was nearly as large for those twenty-five years as had been the total pool for the first three volumes covering three centuries—evidence again of the dramatic change in women's opportunities in the late nineteenth century.

The second great event has been the publication of the *Women's History Sources Survey*, the result of an eight-year effort to identify and describe manuscript collections with significant material about women. More than 18,000 collections are described in this volume. Reading through—the way some people enjoy sitting down to read a dictionary —I am torn between high excitement at all the possibilities these collections offer and despair that there will never be enough historians to do the work.

As scholarship has developed, so has pedagogy. High school as well as college and university courses have been organized, and Ph.D. candidates in many places are now able to specialize in the history of women. Regular positions exist in a good many history departments; the Berkshire Conference is well established. If we date the new women's history roughly from the publication of Eleanor Flexner's *Century of Struggle* in 1958, we can say that the first twenty-two years have been years of high achievement. We must now ask, what next?

The next great need is the one which this institute is designed to address. If you ask what have the new discoveries, the new concepts of women's history contributed to historical scholarship generally, the answer must be, not much. The same answer comes if we ask how has women's history changed textbooks and introductory history courses?

It is my impression that few historians in other fields are yet reading women's history and asking, "What are the implications of this study for my own work?" Community studies still appear in which men are the only characters; family history is still occasionally written as if the definition of family was a man and his sons; economic historians overlook the important role of women in the early stages of industrialization; educational historians seem blithely unaware that Horace Mann did not invent teacher-training or that women, in many communities, were the prime force behind the beginning of public schools.

Textbook publishers, to be sure, are sensitive to what they perceive as trends, and they dutifully make sure that a woman's name appears every fifty pages or so, along with a suitable illustration. However, if you *read* these trendy inserts, you can only be horrified by how little they owe to any recent research.

Add to this list of woes the fact that very distinguished male historians still refer to women's history as a fad that will pass; one such person announced that things had "gone too far" because a historian of women had been elected president of a historical association.

Add the fact that courses in women's history seem still to attract mostly female students . . . and you can see that the hard work is still ahead.

What you are setting out to do here in the next four weeks is to remedy some of these ills not by some superficial plugging in of a bit of women's history here and a bit there but by a fundamental rethinking of what it is we teach students. Rethinking is not a matter of filling in this or that gap, or tacking on bits and pieces of information. It is not solely a matter of bringing to life notable women who have slipped out of our collective memory. It is not a matter of issuing a coin bearing Susan B. Anthony's portrait, though women have not missed the irony that the Anthony dollar is so small and light it is easily mistaken for a quarter — and that it has now become almost totally invisible.

No, I am talking about a fundamental reexamination of American social history to take into account events, movements, and institutions which, because they were primarily the work of women, have been ignored. And because they have been ignored, our history is incomplete and one-sided. Examples come readily to mind.

For instance, in survey courses it is customary to dwell with enthusiasm upon the rapid economic development after 1815, and the startling fact that except for England this recently independent nation moved more rapidly to "modernize" than any other. The reasons usually given are abundant natural resources, stable government, an educated labor force, and outside capital. Only recently are we realizing that one indispensable element in this picture was the availability of a large group of underemployed, literate women who, since social constraint forbade most other occupations, were available to work in the early mills.

If we continue to focus our attention upon women in the Age of Jackson, we can find further ramifications. At least one of the reasons that Emma Willard, Catharine Beecher, and Mary Lyon were so intent upon improving opportunities for women's education was to offer teaching as an alternative to mill work. By training women to teach they helped to inaugurate the public-school movement, which has traditionally been analyzed largely in terms of the work of men like Horace Mann and Henry Barnard. Not only our economic history but our educational history is woefully partial.

Without leaving the Age of Jackson we can go on to reexamine the ferment of reform which Ralph Waldo Emerson so eloquently described in his essay "New England Reformers." In every one of these movements, temperance, health, education, or abolition, women were a driving force and in each case challenged men within the movement as well as the society they were trying to change.

Ah, I can hear someone saying, even if all you say is true, what difference does it make? We are interested in what happened, not whether men or women, or both, were the agents of its happening.

To which I must respond that I think it does matter because the more we examine women's experience, women's behavior, and women's cultural values, the clearer it becomes that they are often different from those of men. I do not know whether the difference should be attributed to nature or to nurture—and am content to leave that question to the sociobiologists—but I do know that sex is one of the basic determinants of life experience and therefore of behavior and even of values. From the moment of birth to the moment of death women experience life differently from men, they think about it differently, they deal with it differently—and since this is true, it follows that their influence in families, communities, and ultimately in the whole society is different from the influence of men, and both must be understood if we are adequately to describe the social dynamics of any particular situation.

I am coming to believe that through most of our history, institution-building has rested upon a sexual division of labor. We are all brought up on the picture of the men on the Mayflower signing a compact to set up a local government or of the men in London establishing the Virginia Company to found a colony and carry out trade. Government and business, were, for a long time, men's work. Other institutions were far from the exclusive work of men. A family requires two sexes for its creation and for its maintenance (think of those colonial widowers who married within a week because family life required the female presence). Churches on the frontier were often the creation of women, though they sought men to be ministers. Even more often, schools were the work of women, even though they often found men to be teachers.

In a way we have always known that an all-male community (the mining camp, the logging camp, Jamestown in the first year) had very different characteristics from a community made up of women and men. The folklore in this area is extensive. Yet somehow historians never made the leap from that reasonably self-evident fact to the question: How did the women in communities shape the values and behavior of its members? All the sentimental nineteenth-century talk about women as a "civilizing" group turns out to represent something that really happened, which contemporaries understood, but which we have not understood partly because of the sentimentality of their descriptions.

Emma Willard and Catharine Beecher and Mary Lyon sending the young women out to carry republican culture to unruly frontiers of the community were building on an already established tradition.

Women's institution-building did not stop with the frontier stage of community life. As towns grew, and along with them churches and schools, and as urban problems—the inevitable problems of the dependent poor, the orphaned child, the alcoholic, and the juvenile delinquent—arose, women broadened their responsibilities into what we would now call social services. Thus what we have called our progressive movement is a prime target for reinterpretation, and the materials are so voluminous and so varied that it will take time. The standard interpretations of progres-sivism have already been battered a good bit by quantifiers, skeptics, psychohistorians, and others, so I suppose in one sense there is no single agreed upon conventional interpretation. This may make the task of formulating one which includes women easier. The cast of characters is intriguing, to say the least. Here there is only time to suggest a few of the lines along which investigation might go.

A person taking up this challenge would want to stir around in the early 1880s in search of the early formulations of moral concern about industrial society to find out how much that concern was first stimulated by observation of the lives of working-class women. One would read carefully books like Helen Stuart Campbell's *Problem of the Poor*, published in 1882, and her articles in the New York *Herald Tribune*. One would go over the documentary material from the first fifteen years of Hull-House, and others of the early settlements. One would look at what was going on in the industrialized states among women reformers and suf-fragists. One would dig out legislative programs of the Woman's Christian Temperance Union and the General Federation of Women's Clubs and would study the manuscripts of the National Child Labor Committee . . . and so on. What I would expect such an inquiry to find would be that a number of the basic assumptions of progressivism in its social justice aspect and much of the serious investigation upon which legislation was based was the work of women. It is somehow symbolic that all the preparatory work for the famous Brandeis brief in *Muller vs. Oregon*, for example, was done by Brandeis's sister-in-law, Josephine Goldmark, who had gotten her training in socioeconomic research from Florence Kelley.

A systematic study of women and the progressive movement will require years of patient work, which I hope someone is about ready to undertake. At the end, a more comprehensive understanding than we have yet had will be possible.

One further idea, and then I will stop and ask you to raise questions. It is not only that a careful effort to look at various parts of our past with attention to women as well as to men will force us to rewrite history, it is not only that such rewritten history will come closer to what Ranke said history should be — "what really happened" — but it is also true that such a line of inquiry may direct our attention to hitherto neglected institutions and processes which are essential parts of American social development.

One example will have to serve. Historians frequently quote Toc-queville on the importance of voluntary associations in the United States and all of us know in a vague sort of way that such associations have been part of the warp and woof of American society from early times. Interestingly enough, however, there is almost no serious historical study of the voluntary association as an institution, and precious little even of specific organizations. The pathbreaking book on women's clubs, for example, was only finished two or three years ago; no study of the WCTU, so far as I know, has yet been completed; the history of the League of Women Voters, though complete, has not been published. Community studies touch lightly on voluntary associations—Don Harrison Doyle's *Social Order of a Frontier Community* does the best job of those I have seen in this area. But all in all, the subject has been badly neglected by historians and only slightly less so by political scientists. Only the sociologists have given it its due, and in most cases they are not much interested in the past.

Yet, it seems to me beyond doubt that historians of women can hardly go much further until they know how women have used voluntary associations not only to gain control over some areas of community life but also to make a place for themselves in public life. If we set out to study this matter thoroughly, we must also, inevitably, develop some data and probably some theories about the voluntary association, whether made up of women or men or both, as a major institution in the shaping of American society as a whole.

This is yet another kind of example of the way in which taking women's history seriously will cause us to reexamine our present interpretations of the American past.

Once you begin thinking in these terms, there is no end in sight.

This, I take it, is what you are here for, and I think you may justly look upon yourselves as an historic group—in more ways than one.

Epilogue

"But where is your conclusion?" I find myself saying over and over to students who go to a great deal of work and trouble to produce a fine paper and then, in the end, just stop writing. "What have you learned? What does it all mean?"

At the conclusion of this collection of essays should I be able to answer those questions? What, indeed, *have* I learned? What *does* it all mean?

As a partial answer I offer certain convictions, none original, which have grown upon me over the years since the day I asked Oscar Handlin what I should read if I wanted to become a real historian and he replied in his usual Delphic style: "Gibbon's *Autobiography*." I dutifully did read it, wondering what on earth he had in mind.

The convictions, as well as I can formulate them, do not form a logical whole, but they run like this:

1. It is worth trying to understand the past because in the process of doing so one learns so much about the possibilities and mysteries of human existence at the same time that one is learning how partial and incomplete is even the most careful reconstruction of lives, events, and social movements. Sometimes I am willing to say, with Leonard Woolf, The Journey Not the Arrival Matters.

2. If the historian truly understands what he or she wishes to say, it can be made accessible to any literate, reasonably intelligent, interested person. The last point is vital, for if people don't care, there is no way to be heard. Marc Bloc thought the ideal was to speak in the same tone to the savant and the school boy . . . few of us can quite do that, but it is a reasonable goal. For some historians writing only for one's peers is satisfying, and much indispensable work has been based on that view. For myself, the imagined audience must always go beyond other historians.

3. Life is always more complicated than the historian's categories. Hence a certain tentativeness in conclusions is always in order.

Beyond these convictions lie unanswered questions. Perhaps the overriding one for me is what *is* the link between the individual experience, the individual decision or action, on the one hand, and the larger social movements we identify and describe retrospectively, on the other? How can the historian or the social analyst identify and describe the modes of aggregation by which what is happening to or is done by millions of individuals comes together to shape what we have traditionally called "history"?

One could pick up a number of threads in this book as examples. Women's education, for example: first, there had to be a handful of women who very much wanted formal education; then there had to be social needs that made it worth spending scarce resources to that end; then those who had a chance for education became different from their sisters and had different effects on family, community, and a different definition of women's role. Once it reached a certain point, women's education became self-perpetuating, an established part of the social order. But the links in the chain are virtually invisible and difficult to demonstrate.

Another recurrent question grows out of the work collected here: How do ideas travel, and what happens to them in the process? This question presented itself forcefully as I worked through the Emma Willard materials and realized how swiftly Pestalozzian notions spread through this country, brought initially by a handful of people yet in a very short time constituting the conventional wisdom of schoolteachers in remote frontier villages. There was no radio, no telegraph—only some mysterious grapevine—and the effects were clearly widespread. This would be a study in intellectual history which as far as I know no one has attempted.

The sudden efflorescence of women's benevolent societies in the first three decades of the nineteenth century is another example. What modes of communication led to the remarkable similarity of ideas and concerns, even words and phrases, from one end of the country to another? It could not have been simply similar conditions bringing forth similar responses when women in a tiny New Hampshire village sounded so much like those in a slaveholding southern city. How can we get hold of the transmission of cultural inventions?

I wonder, too, about leaders and followers: the age-old question is what difference do great men make? For me the question becomes what difference do great women make? Much as I have learned from studying social structures in which ordinary people live and move, I cannot persuade myself that history would have been the same if Emma Willard had died of infant diarrhea or Jane Addams of tuberculosis, as so many of their contemporaries did. But how does one get hold of the issue?

Finally, there is the largest question, which doubtless we all ponder —who is going to put the pieces together? How are we to aggregate the thousands of books and articles in which individual historians try to push back the boundaries of our ignorance? Or is the very notion of "American history," "world history," "modern history" an ideal construct while the reality will always be a patchwork of bits and pieces?

It is no particular comfort to realize that our colleagues in every field —whether physics or philosophy, biology or literature—face the same question. Can we hold on to the somewhat improbable belief that we are all building toward something better than we can envision?

As I come to the end of this project I remember Oscar Handlin's sixtieth birthday party, at which many of his seventy-two Ph.D. students extolled his work, his influence, and his accomplishments of all sorts. Finally, in some desperation Handlin himself took the floor: "Look, friends," he said, "it's not all over yet!" He was right, of course, and as I come to the end of this project I share his feeling—and hope that there will indeed be more to come.

Index

A Note on the Author

ANNE FIROR SCOTT is W. K. Boyd Professor of History at Duke University, Durham, North Carolina, where she has been a member of the department since 1961. Prior to that time, she was a history lecturer at Haverford College, Philadelphia, and the University of North Carolina, Chapel Hill. In 1984 she is Distinguished Visiting Scholar at Radcliffe College and Visiting Professor of History at Harvard. Her books include: *The Southern Lady: From Pedestal to Politics, 1830-1930; One Half the People: The Fight for Women's Suffrage* (with Andrew M. Scott); and *American Woman: Who Was She?* (editor).